# US Government and Politics

## Books in the Politics Study Guides series

# US Government and Politics

## Second edition

**William Storey**

Edinburgh University Press

**For my wife, Juliana Sackle Storey**

© William Storey, 2010

First edition published 2007

Edinburgh University Press Ltd
22 George Square, Edinburgh
www.euppublishing.com

Typeset in 11/13pt Monotype Baskerville by
Servis Filmsetting Ltd, Stockport, Cheshire, and
printed and bound in Great Britain by
Polestar Wheatons, Exeter

A CIP record for this book is available from the British Library

ISBN  978 0 7486 3880 2 (paperback)

# Contents

# Boxes

# Tables

# A Beacon on the Hill?

In 1787, leading figures from the thirteen states that had freed themselves from British rule gathered to salvage a radical, bold political experiment that was failing. They had rejected the system of government used in Europe, based on rule by an unaccountable and unconstrained monarch whose position was due to an accident of birth. They had also rejected the strict controls which meant that most Europeans had extremely limited opportunities for personal advancement and even faced restrictions on what they could say and believe.

The USA was to be a meritocracy in which success or failure would be based only on talent, hard work, determination and, perhaps, luck. No one would be held back on the basis of social class or beliefs. And the key to establishing, and maintaining, a meritocracy would be a political system that would make it difficult, even impossible, for a European-style elite to emerge and run society for its own benefit. Americans expected such a system would be so clearly superior to other forms of government that it would become the standard that all other people around the world would want to see introduced into their countries. The US system of government would become a 'beacon on a hill', for all others to see and respond to.

Is it possible, however, to set up a system of government that ensures that the positive values of freedom and opportunity are entrenched and that makes it almost impossible for power to become concentrated in a few hands? After the War of Independence, American leaders had tried to produce such a system and the results had been, at best, mixed. Their second attempt produced the Constitution, and political system, that remains in place to this day. At the heart of this book is one simple question: to what extent does the US political system live up to the high aspirations of those who established it?

As with all substantial political questions, this one has produced spirited, even passionate, debate and continues to do so. This book provides a guide through those debates, together with an understanding of how the US political system works – providing the reader with the opportunity to participate in the debate and reach an informed conclusion.

*Part 1* covers the framework of the US political system. Chapter 1 examines the Constitution, its aims, structure and development, and discusses rival views on how well it has met its original aims. For a substantial proportion of Americans, the most important constitutional feature is Federalism, designed to ensure that power would remain fragmented, thereby preventing any group of people from becoming politically dominant and using their power oppressively. Chapter 2 explores this feature of the US political system in depth, explaining why there are sharply divergent views on whether it has worked as intended. Chapter 3 examines the US Constitution, and the political system that it produced, from another angle. Does the experience of racial and ethnic minorities demonstrate that the USA has produced the appearance, but not the reality, of a meritocracy? It outlines the fierce debate over whether the government has a moral and constitutional responsibility to ensure that there is genuine equality of opportunity.

*Part 2* covers the mechanisms that the Founding Fathers expected to ensure that power would remain fragmented, preventing any group of people from becoming politically dominant and using their power oppressively. Chapter 4 examines whether the sheer number and frequency of elections ensures that the powerful are held effectively to account or whether the cost of elections, together with their frequency, ensures that representatives are more concerned with the interests of their financial donors than the interests of the humble voter. Chapters 5 and 6 evaluate whether the organisations which represent the interests of all sections of society, political parties and pressure groups, are effective vehicles for ensuring that the concerns of all groups are properly considered when policies are being developed or whether they promote the interests of a wealthy, influential minority.

Having considered the purpose of the political system and the methods used to achieve its aims, *Part 3* examines the three branches of the Federal government and asks whether the limitations on their power have worked as intended. Chapter 7 examines the role of the Supreme Court in enforcing the provisions of the Constitution, its role in ensuring that the Constitution lives up to its ideals and the political debate that has developed over the way that the Court has used its position as the guardians of the Constitution's aims and values. Chapter 8 explains the constitutional responsibilities of the two houses of Congress and analyses how effectively it fulfils them. Chapters 9 and 10 explore the development of the President's powers in domestic and foreign affairs and evaluate how this institution's powers have developed since the Constitution came into operation in 1789.

Does the US political system provide its 300 million diverse citizens with the liberty and equality of opportunity that the Founding Fathers aimed to guarantee? This book outlines the arguments and offers the evidence to help its readers decide.

# PART I
# THE FRAMEWORK OF US POLITICS

# CHAPTER 1

# The Constitution of the United States of America

## Contents

### Overview

*Freedom and equality of opportunity for all?*
On 20 January 2009, Barack Obama became President of the USA and immediately announced, in his inauguration address, his intention to reverse his predecessor's security policies. 'We reject as false,' he proclaimed, 'the choice between our safety and our ideals.' In the same speech, he also made it clear that he had a very different view to President George W. Bush of the role of government in promoting opportunity for Americans. 'The question we ask today is not whether our government is too big or too small, but whether it works – whether it helps families find jobs at a decent wage, care they can afford, retirement that is dignified.'

When, on 25 May 1787, 55 men gathered in Philadelphia for a convention which would produce the Constitution of the United States of America, they were equally divided on similar issues. What was the best way to protect their country, while promoting the ideals of freedom and liberty? What was the appropriate role of government in the day-to-day lives of the citizens?

This chapter examines the conflicts between the Founding Fathers as they wrestled with these issues, how they crafted the Constitution and the continuing debates in the twenty-first century on how to achieve the best balance between government activities that are seen as positive and those that are seen as negative or dangerous.

### Key issues to be covered in this chapter

- The origins of the Constitution
- How the Constitution was written
- The debate on the Constitution's advantages and disadvantages while it was being ratified
- The key features of the Constitution
- The extent to which the Constitution has lived up to its ideals

Thus, the first two questions, how these emerging societies should be governed and the extent of religious freedom, were dealt with at an early stage. The third, whether a commitment to freedom could ever be compatible with slavery, was not resolved until the Civil War in the 1860s.

### Conflict between the New World and the Old World

In contrast to representative forms of government in North America, in the UK the monarch could issue Royal Proclamations and the British parliament could pass laws, without consultation, which each colony had to obey. After the Seven Years War (1756–63) Britain gained land in North America from France and Spain which seemed to provide new opportunities for expansion by the thirteen colonies. However, Parliament expected the colonies to contribute towards the cost of the war, which meant higher taxes, and the King issued a proclamation reserving the new territories for Native Americans. These two steps, as well as simmering discontent with other decisions taken in London, led to demands for self-government for America.

### Political theory

Additionally, well-educated Americans were familiar with the political thinkers of their era and, in some cases, heavily influenced by them. The ideas of the English theorist John Locke, in particular, were well-received in the American colonies. He argued that all people, simply by virtue of being human beings, possessed natural rights that no one – not even the government – was entitled to take away. He believed that it is these rights that distinguish people from animals and that their loss amounted to the loss of humanity and reduced people to something less than fully human, making them little better than beasts.

### The Declaration of Independence

Ultimately, Americans were prepared to fight for their freedoms. The War of Independence, which lasted for five years, began with the Declaration of Independence, issued on 4 July 1776. This document made it clear that armed rebellion was not just an outburst of violence, driven by frustration or rage, but a fully justified political response to tyranny.

It did this by outlining the rights that all people are entitled to and explaining the ways in which these had not been respected by the British:

- The first part of the Declaration of Independence asserted that:

  > We hold these truths to be self-evident, that all men are created equal, and that they are endowed by their Creator with certain inalienable Rights, that among these are Life, Liberty and the pursuit of Happiness. That to secure these rights, Governments are instituted among Men, deriving their just powers from the consent of the governed. That whenever any Form of Government becomes destructive of these ends, it is the Right of the People to alter or to abolish it, and to institute new Government . . .

- The second part listed twenty-seven examples of the British government, especially the King, abusing its power, which, in turn, justified the revolution, including:
  - He has made Judges dependent on his Will alone
  - He has kept among us, in times of peace, Standing armies without the Consent of our legislatures
  - He has affected to render the Military independent of and superior to the Civil power
  - Imposing taxes on us without our consent
  - Suspending our own Legislatures.

**The War of Independence**
The American Revolutionary War, that led to the thirteen states becoming independent from Britain, lasted from 1775 to 1783. During the war, the nation's political leaders designed a new system of government based on the central principle that their country would not replace one tyrannical government (in London) with another (in the USA). Consequently, they set up a weak central government, mainly to conduct foreign affairs. It had no executive branch to propose and co-ordinate policies and no **judicial branch** to enforce laws.

**Had the pendulum swung too far?**
The Articles of Confederation certainly ensured that the government could not interfere in the affairs of the thirteen states, or oppress the

citizens, but they also ensured that the government could do little to resolve problems facing the country.

A border dispute between Maryland and Virginia in 1785 illustrated the need for greater co-ordination between the States. The dispute was resolved by a successful convention held at Annapolis, in Maryland. However, to ensure that there was a more effective mechanism for dealing with such disputes, it was decided to review the system of government at a Constitutional Convention, to be held in Philadelphia.

## The Constitutional Convention

The Constitutional Convention began with 'the sole and express purpose of revising the Articles of Confederation'. The delegates elected George Washington as Chairman of the Convention and agreed a simple set of rules:

- Delegates from at least seven of the thirteen states had to be present for each meeting
- Discussions would be secret, to enable the delegates to speak freely without coming under pressure from their state
- Each state had one vote
- A simple majority was required for all decisions
- When the process was complete, all thirteen states would be bound by the outcome once nine of them had ratified it

They started work on 25 May 1787.

### Bitter disputes

Despite their shared political culture, there were two main areas of disagreement between the delegates that caused intense and bitter debate:

- *Big states v. small states* At the start of the Convention, the largest state, Virginia, proposed a strong central government based on three principles:
  - A two-chamber legislature, elected by the people, with wide-ranging powers
  - A strong executive, chosen by the legislature
  - A national judiciary, appointed by the legislature

Because such a legislature, making all the important decisions, would be dominated by representatives of the states with the largest populations, this plan was unacceptable to states with smaller populations. One of them, New Jersey, put forward a counter-plan, also based on three principles:

- A single-chamber legislature, with one vote for each State and strictly limited powers
- A weak executive, consisting of more than one person, chosen by the legislature
- A limited national judiciary, appointed by the executive

Debate on these plans resulted in deadlock for much of the summer of 1787.

- *Slavery* At the time of the Convention, almost one-third of the people of the Southern states were enslaved Africans. Three Northern states – Connecticut, Pennsylvania and Rhode Island – had put an end to slavery. Two others – Massachusetts and Delaware – had ended the importation of slaves. Delegates from these and other Northern states wanted all slaves to be counted for taxation purposes, effectively increasing the cost of slavery, but not for representation in the legislature. Delegates from the Southern states, whose prosperity depended on slavery, wanted the opposite, fearing that slavery would not last unless they were well-represented. In addition, they wanted to ensure that no law could be passed interfering with the slave trade, which provided additional slaves from overseas. They made it clear that they were not prepared to accept a constitution that restricted slavery.

## Compromises

- The deadlock between supporters of the Virginia Plan and the New Jersey Plan was resolved by the Connecticut Compromise. This adopted features from both plans for each branch of government but the key element was an agreement that the legislative branch would consist of two chambers, the lower based on population and the upper having two members from each state.
- The deadlock on slavery was resolved by the three-fifths compromise which gave the Southern states most of what they wanted. Slaves were counted as three-fifths of a person for the purposes of

both taxation and representation. Although the word 'slave' does not occur in the Constitution, a clause was also included which protected the slave trade until at least 1808.

### The 'miracle of Philadelphia'

It was comparatively straightforward to recognise that, under the Articles of Confederation, the pendulum had swung too far in the direction of protecting the people from tyrannical government. It was far more difficult, potentially even impossible, for people with conflicting interests to agree on how far it should swing in the opposite direction.

The compromises reached meant that when the Convention ended, on 17 September 1787, it had been able to find a balance between effective government and personal freedom that a majority could accept. None of the delegates found the outcome ideal but, as the imperial European nations were growing in strength and territorial ambition, all recognised that the only way for their newly independent nation to survive was to find a way to work together. As Benjamin Franklin said at the start of the War of Independence, 'we must all hang together or, most assuredly, we shall all hang separately'.

## Ratifying the Constitution

### A ferment of ideas

The arguments on the best balance between liberty and effective government did not end when the Constitutional Convention completed its work. Before the Constitution could become law, nine of the thirteen states had to ratify it and this provided an opportunity for renewed debate on its advantages and disadvantages. With the general population to persuade, supporters and opponents of the Constitution launched a massive propaganda campaign in newspapers and pamphlets in every state.

The debate was dominated by the divide between one view, that the Constitution gave the national government too much power and provided inadequate safeguards, and the contrary view that the country needed a strong national government and that the safeguards against abuse of power were sufficient. The first group became known as the anti-Federalists, while the second group became known as the Federalists.

### The anti-Federalist argument

Although this group was not very unified, they shared a fear that the national government had been given too much power and would, ultimately, become oppressive. Their main criticisms of the Constitution were:

- A strong executive, even with **checks and balances**, could develop into a tyrant, like the king they had fought against.
- A strong legislature, with the power to raise an army and impose taxes, was being given the tools of oppression that the British had used.
- **Separation of powers** were not strict enough. In particular, the Senate's role in ratifying the President's appointments might make it reluctant to fulfil its role of closely scrutinising the people it had helped appoint.
- Representation could only be effective if the government was close to the people and understood the people. This would be difficult in a country as large and diverse as the United States, and especially for the President, who represented the entire country.
- States' rights would erode over time as a strong national government would inevitably accumulate power at the expense of the states.

At the very least, therefore, they argued that the Constitution should be strengthened to protect liberty in the following ways:

- Representatives should have shorter terms of office, a limit to the number of terms they could serve and there should be a system for recalling (sacking) representatives failing to meet the wishes of their constituents.
- A Bill of Rights should be added to the Constitution to reinforce the checks and balances already included to protect individuals' freedoms.

### The Federalist argument

The argument of the Federalists was simple: the greatest threat to the fledgling nation, in their view, was not the emergence of a local tyrant but the powerful imperial European countries, led by monarchs with no interest whatsoever in liberty, who would seize on the weakness of the USA to recapture lost land in North America and extend their empires. The events leading up to the Constitutional Convention had demonstrated that the USA was divided and lacking clear leadership. An effective national government with substantial powers was seen by this faction as essential to the country's survival: the Confederate system had clearly demonstrated that it was not possible to govern through powerlessness.

Many Federalists opposed the addition of a Bill of Rights because, as one put it, 'if we list a set of rights, some fools in the future are going to claim that people are entitled only to those rights enumerated, and no others'.

### The Madison Compromise

James Madison, who is credited with drafting much of the Constitution, initially sided with the Federalists in the public debate that raged across the nation after the Convention ended. However, he came to accept that the Constitution would only be ratified if a Bill of Rights was added. Having changed his view, he not only campaigned in favour of accepting this concession to the anti-Federalists, but also wrote the amendments to the Constitution himself.

## Key features of the Constitution

### The purpose of the Constitution

The aims of the Constitution are clearly laid out in its preamble. Its goal is to:

- Form a closer union between the states
- Establish justice
- Provide effective defence
- Ensure liberty

### The powers of government

In order to ensure that the goals laid out in the preamble could be met, the national government was given far more power than its predecessor under the Articles of Confederation.

Congress (the legislature) was expected to be the most important branch of government and was given eighteen specific powers, known as enumerated powers. Five of them relate to the economy (such as imposing taxes, borrowing money and regulating commerce); seven relate to the armed forces (including the power to declare war), with the remainder covering a range of other issues such as responsibility for communication systems (which, in the eighteenth century, meant post offices but today includes telephones, television, radio, the internet and so on).

The final enumerated power has proved to be the most significant. It gives Congress the right to make all laws 'necessary and proper' to carry out its responsibilities. This has become known as the 'elastic clause', as it has enabled Congress to 'stretch' beyond its enumerated powers to additional implied powers – enabling it to address issues that could not be foreseen when the Constitution was written.

The presidency (the executive branch of government) was established under the Constitution primarily to conduct foreign policy and to implement laws passed by Congress. Most of the specific presidential responsibilities outlined in the Constitution relate to foreign policy, as this was the area where Presidents would be playing a leading role. However, in the age of sailing ships and with over 3,000 miles of ocean between the USA and its potential enemies, it was not expected that this would be a significant role.

In domestic affairs the Constitution only specifically mentions the President having the power to pardon and to suggest legislative priorities to Congress in the annual State of the Union Address. Otherwise, there seemed to be an expectation that the President would play the secondary role (as symbolised by the presidency being covered in the second article of the Constitution) of serving Congress, ensuring that the legislature's will was carried out. As a result, the President was given the vague power to 'faithfully execute' national laws which, like the 'elastic clause', has been the basis for substantial increases in power over time.

The Supreme Court (the judicial branch) was set up to rule on disputes that stemmed from national laws, any cases involving disputes between the states and the rare cases in which a foreign diplomat was put on trial.

Its powers were outlined in Article III of the Constitution, implying that the judiciary was of lesser importance than the other two branches of the national government. Also, it did not address the issue of who would be responsible for deciding whether or not the Constitution had been properly respected – a role that would require careful examination of the text coupled with mature judgment and would seem, logically, to be suited to the nation's highest court. When, fourteen years after the Constitution was adopted, the Supreme Court took on the role of constitutional interpretation, the judiciary became very significant and, arguably, the most powerful of the three branches of the national government.

### Safeguards on government power

The Founding Fathers (especially the anti-Federalists) were alert to the possibility that, over time, the additional roles and responsibilities given to the national government could be used as a platform to extend its powers. This could result from the best of intentions, with frustrated politicians sincerely believing that they could do more for the people they serve if they had more power. For the Founding Fathers, however, the inevitable consequence of an overly powerful national government would be minor abuses of power, leading to more significant misuse of power and, ultimately, tyranny. Much of the Constitution, therefore, is devoted to preventing this from happening by:

- Limiting the amount of power available to the national government.
- Dividing that power into smaller fragments by dividing the national government into separate branches and providing each with distinct, limited roles.
- Stopping the branches of the national government from working together to weaken the effectiveness on these safeguards against excessive power.
- Holding politicians to account for the use they made of powers available to them.

*Federalism:* This serves to limit the amount of power available to the national government. The Constitution aims to restrict the national government to decisions which affect the whole country, outlining which powers are needed to do this. All other powers belong to the states. These are called reserved powers. The importance of these powers to the Founding Fathers was demonstrated by the 10th Amendment, that reinforces the principle that any powers not explicitly given to the national government by the Constitution belong to the states or the people.

Federalism has never been a purely theoretical device for limiting power. It has always had importance on a practical level in a country where the national government has been distant and remote to a great majority of the population. Even when the US consisted of just thirteen states on the Eastern coast of the continent, the capital city was many days of difficult travelling for most people. Today, despite the development of modern transport systems, with Washington DC separated from the West coast of the country by over 2,000 miles, that sense of remoteness remains.

The national government has also often been seen as culturally, as well as geographically, remote. The population of the USA has been diverse from its earliest days, with pious religious refugees having little in common with the economic refugees who had crossed the Atlantic to make their fortune – apart from their fear and hatred of tyranny. Consequently, all national policies that are applied in a uniform way across the country have always been quite likely to be seen as inappropriate or unsuitable by significant sections of the population. National policies made by distant policy-makers who have no direct experience or understanding of the impact of their decisions on particular groups or communities have, therefore, always had the potential to replicate the relationship the USA had once had with the King of England.

Thus, both theoretically and practically, Federalism has been directly associated with the types of freedoms that Americans fought for when they broke away from the United Kingdom and is regarded by many as the most important feature of the Constitution. Such is its significance that the next chapter is devoted to examining how it has developed over the past two centuries and its place at the heart of US political debates today.

*Enumerating powers:* By listing the specific powers of Congress (which was intended to be the most important branch) the Founding Fathers aimed to reinforce Federalism, as the list would serve to limit the government's ability to extend its role into any policy area that had not been specified. Furthermore, Article I of the Constitution lists eight restrictions on Congress, known as denied powers.

*Separation of powers:* Anticipating the possibility that the three branches of the national government might work together to expand their powers, the Founding Fathers drew up arrangements that would ensure that the three main roles of the central government (passing laws, carrying out laws and ruling on the application of laws) would be carried out by different groups of people. Thus, the Constitution prohibits anyone from working in more than one branch of government at the same time, thereby creating strict separation of personnel. For example, in 2009, President Obama appointed several members of Congress to his administration: they all had to resign from the legislature before taking up their posts in the executive branch.

*Checks and balances:* For separation of powers to be effective, the Founding Fathers sought to create a situation in which each branch of government would treat the others as rivals. As the author of the Constitution, James Madison, put it, limits on the national government would be effective as a result of 'ambition counter-acting ambition'. If ambitious members of any of the three branches attempted to expand their powers, they would inevitably take power from one of the others – but the equally ambitious members of the other branches could be relied upon to vigorously resist losing the limited powers they had. In this way, each branch would serve as a check on each other. Thus, the Constitution sets out ways in which each branch constrains the others, with a particular emphasis on limiting the powers of the President to prevent the emergence of a national leader who could act as a dictator. To complement the checks, the Founding Fathers aimed to ensure that there was an appropriate balance of power between the three branches as they would not be able to effectively protect themselves from intrusion if one of the branches was much more powerful than the other two.

*Elections:* It was possible that voters could be persuaded to elect one political group to both the legislature and the executive branches of government (who would then appoint their supporters to the judiciary) which would undermine the system of checks and balances. To prevent this, they organised:

- *Indirect elections* The upper chamber would consist of Senators appointed by state legislatures. The President would be elected by the people, but their views would be filtered through an electoral college.

- *Staggered elections* There would never be a time when everyone in the national government would be elected simultaneously. Members of the lower chamber would be elected every two years. The President would be elected every four years. Senators would hold office for six years but only one-third of them would be appointed at each election cycle.
- *Defined election dates* To ensure that those in power could not use a crisis, or create a crisis, to extend their time in office, elections would be held on set dates regardless of circumstances.

*Amending the Constitution:* To ensure that politicians would not be able to evade or dilute these restrictions, the Founding Fathers made the Constitution extremely difficult to amend.

There are two mechanisms for changing the Constitution, outlined in Article V of the document. Both are slow, complicated processes and require the support not of a slim majority of the people but a 'super-majority'.

- The first method requires a two-thirds majority in both houses of Congress to propose an amendment and at least three-quarters of the states to agree to the amendment for it to become law.
- The second method requires at least two-thirds of the states to call a national convention, similar to the Convention at Philadelphia that wrote the Constitution, to propose and agree to an amendment. This method has never been used.

Over 5,000 amendments have been proposed but only twenty-seven have ever been passed, of which the first ten are generally considered to be a part of the original constitution (see Bill of Rights, below).

The Equal Rights Amendment (ERA) illustrates the difficulty in amending the constitution. Providing a constitutional guarantee of equal rights for women, this amendment was passed by Congress in March 1972 with a seven-year deadline for it to be ratified by three-quarters of the states. Twenty-two of the necessary thirty-eight state **ratifications** were achieved in the first year but the pace slowed as opposition began to organise. There were only eight ratifications in 1973, three in 1974, one in 1975 and none in 1976. In 1977, Indiana became the thirty-fifth and last state to ratify the ERA. A demonstration of 100,000 supporters of the amendment in Washington DC led to Congress granting an extension until 30 June 1982, but with no further support from the states the deadline passed, leaving it three short of the required threshold.

Even clearing the first hurdle is a considerable achievement. Recent examples of proposed amendments that opinion polls demonstrated had considerable popular support but failed to gain the necessary two-thirds support from Congress include:

- **Balanced budget amendment**
- Flag desecration amendment
- School prayer amendment
- Tax limitation amendment
- Defence of marriage amendment

Persistence may pay off, however. The 19th Amendment (granting the vote to women) which was introduced in Congress 118 times before its passage and the 27th Amendment (restricting the ability of members of Congress to give themselves pay rises) was not passed until over 200 years after it was originally introduced.

### The Bill of Rights

During the Constitutional Convention and the ratification process, the Federalist faction resisted adding a Bill of Rights to the document on the grounds that it would be unnecessary or even possibly damaging. If the other safeguards designed to limit the power of government proved effective, they argued, then the government would simply be unable to infringe the liberties of the people. Conversely, if aggressively ambitious politicians managed to break through the constitutional safeguards then they would be unlikely to respect a charter of rights. Hence their view that a Bill of Rights was, at best, pointless. The only practical impact of a Bill of Rights, they concluded, would be to impose a limit on rights, as some people would use it as a reason to refuse to recognise rights that were not specified.

Using the Bill of Rights as a justification for denying rights that are not specified has become a significant issue in US politics, as will be demonstrated in the chapter on the Supreme Court. However, the other argument advanced by the Federalists, that a Bill of Rights would add little to the Constitution, have proved groundless. Indeed, the Bill of Rights has clearly added an important dimension to the Constitution by making it difficult for politicians to take away the rights of sections of the population that are disliked or feared by the democratic majority who elected them.

For centuries, groups excluded from the mainstream of society have been persecuted – often with the enthusiastic support of the rest of the population. Most of the constitutional safeguards offer no defence against this type of oppression – the **tyranny of the majority**. Separation of powers and checks and balances do not protect marginalised groups if each branch of government is controlled by people who have no sympathy for the fringe group. Similarly, elections often serve to empower politicians to be oppressive when one community's priorities are driven by hatred for another community. Moreover, Federalism can be used as an excuse for local tyrants to resist interference from the national government when they are mistreating or discriminating against sections of the local population. However, because the Bill of Rights applies to everyone, including minority and marginalised groups, it serves to protect everyone or, at the very least, provide justification for arguing for equal treatment. Thus the Bill of Rights has a distinctive **counter-majoritarian** character, guarding those who may be adversely affected by decisions taken by the majority, and has served as a platform for excluded groups to campaign for full inclusion in the mainstream of society.

The first ten amendments of the Constitution, which make up the Bill of Rights, came into force on 15 December 1791. There is a distinct pattern to these amendments:

- Amendments I and II protect individual freedoms from the government, including freedom of religion, freedom of speech and freedom of assembly. Freedom of the press is also guaranteed.
- Amendments III and IV protect private property from government intrusion.
- Amendments V, VI, VII and VIII ensure proper treatment of people who have been arrested through custody, trial and sentencing.
- Amendment IX guarantees rights not covered in the previous eight.
- Amendment X reinforces the principle of Federalism.

It is notable that of the ten amendments, four relate to the rights of people who may be criminals. The fact that the Bill of Rights explicitly protects this group of people, detested by most through the ages, emphasises its counter-majoritarian character.

### Amendments to the Constitution

As with the Bill of Rights, there is a distinct pattern to these amendments:

- The 11th, 12th, 16th, 17th, 20th, 22nd, 25th and 27th Amendments all clarify or revise the work of the three branches of government, for example:
  - Senators have been elected since the 17th Amendment was passed in 1913.
  - The 22nd Amendment, passed in 1951, limited the number of terms a President can serve to two.
  - If the President is temporarily unable to serve, the 25th Amendment, passed in 1967, sets out the procedure for replacing him.
- The 13th, 14th and 15th Amendments are generally known as the Civil Rights Amendments. After the Civil War, the three Amendments abolished slavery (1865), extended the protections of the Bill of Rights to African Americans (1868) and gave African Americans the right to vote (1870). By the 1960s these rights still did not apply to African Americans and the poll tax, one of the methods to stop them from voting, was abolished by the 24th Amendment, passed in 1964.
- The 19th, 23rd and 26th Amendments expanded the range of people entitled to vote. Women gained the right to vote in 1920, people living in Washington DC gained the right to vote in presidential elections in 1961 (but are still not represented in Congress) and the voting age was lowered from twenty-one to eighteen in 1971.
- The 18th Amendment, passed in 1919, prohibiting alcoholic beverages, proved to be a disastrous failure and had to be repealed, by the 21st Amendment, passed in 1933.

Prohibition is the only example to date of a constitutional amendment being passed which defined how Americans should lead their lives. The remaining successful amendments have served to 'tidy up' the political process, or to extend rights previously denied.

## Perspectives on the Constitution

The Founding Fathers, like the their ancestors from England who had originally colonised North America, aimed to create a 'Beacon on the Hill', a nation based on a set of ideals – political and legal equality and individual freedom – which would serve Americans and be a model for the rest of the world. Have they succeeded?

The answer, even at the time that the Constitution was being written, depended on the political viewpoint of the person being asked the question. Whether the best possible balance had been struck between liberty and effective government was a matter of fierce disagreement during the Constitutional Convention and remains so today, not least because Americans have different views on what is meant by 'freedom' and 'opportunity'.

### The Constitution from the perspective of fiscal conservatives

In the twenty-first century, a significant proportion of the population of the USA shares the deep distrust of government that was expressed by the anti-Federalists of the eighteenth century. Referred to as 'small government conservatives' or 'fiscal conservatives', people with these views believe that there should be no government interference in their lives unless it is absolutely necessary.

Their views are underpinned by a belief that the word 'freedom' means an absence of interference. People should be allowed to pursue whatever goals they see fit, as long as it does not cause harm to others. Virtually all government action, other than enforcing law and order and national defence, is seen as incompatible with the form of **negative freedom** advocated by this strand of conservatism. The only exceptions to this general rule are policies made by local politicians responding to the particular needs and wishes of their communities.

Fiscal conservatives argue that limited government has, demonstrably, maximised freedom and created opportunity. If people can be certain that they will not be subject to government interference, for example regulations or excessive taxation, they will use their skills and talents to fulfil their potential. They point to the pioneer spirit of the early settlers and of those who led the expansion of the USA towards the West coast as evidence of this relationship. They believe that people with ambition, determination and creativity have, throughout the history of the USA, produced and implemented new ideas to improve the quality of life for themselves, their families and the wider community. However, they may be less willing to implement their ideas if there is a risk that government intervention – especially the prospect of the fruits of their labour being heavily taxed – means that they may not enjoy the benefits they expected. Alternatively, people may simply be unable to implement their ideas in the ways they choose because of 'red tape' (government rules and regulations). According to this view, to this day the greatest opportunities and the most creativity are seen in areas of life not regulated by government. For example, Microsoft emerged when personal computers were in their infancy and Google's dramatic rise happened in the largely unregulated world of the internet.

Furthermore, if government imposes high taxes and uses those taxes to provide benefits for the poor, people will have two reasons not to make the most of their potential: the limited gains from helping themselves and the benefits they may receive from government if they do nothing to help themselves. Thus, for fiscal conservatives, the Constitution works best when its provisions limit government intervention and is at its most ineffective where it permits government interference. They would wholeheartedly agree with the sentiments of one of the Founding Fathers, Thomas Jefferson, who said, 'That government is best that governs least'.

From their viewpoint, the fact that the Constitution has not proved an effective barrier to the expansion of central government over the past 200 years is evidence of its ineffectiveness. Initially consisting of just three departments, the Federal government now consists of fifteen departments, with an annual budget of $1.7 trillion. Additionally, the Federal government plays a major role in policy areas that the Founding Fathers intended to be reserved to the states (as explained in greater detail in Chapter 2). It was precisely developments such as these that the anti-Federalists warned of at the Constitutional Convention, if the Constitution did not place very strict limits on the powers of the national government. Fiscal conservatives believe that the anti-Federalists have been proved right by history and criticise the constitutional safeguards on the Federal government as being inadequate and, as a consequence, of limited effectiveness in protecting liberty.

Compounding these failings, in the eyes of these critics, the Federal government has not fulfilled its important legitimate role: the protection of law-abiding citizens. Instead, they argue, the Constitution has been misused to give undeserved rights to criminals. Since the 1960s the Constitution has been interpreted by the Supreme Court to mean that no one can be convicted of a crime if the investigation and/or trial has not been conducted properly. For example, under the 4th Amendment, a person or property can only be searched if there is 'reasonable cause' to believe that something is amiss. If it can be shown that there was no reasonable cause for the search (for example, the police raiding the wrong house by mistake) then any evidence found cannot be used in a trial. The Supreme Court has ruled that a confession cannot be used in a trial if the suspect has not been told of the constitutional right to remain silent (5th Amendment). It has also ruled that, during a trial, a defendant must have adequate legal representation (6th Amendment) and that the state must provide a lawyer if the defendant cannot afford one. All of these developments are seen as providing loopholes for criminals, making it easier for them to escape justice and more difficult for the government to protect the law-abiding.

There are aspects of the Constitution, however, that meet with the approval of 'small government' conservatives. They tend to be fierce defenders of the 2nd Amendment, which is seen as the ultimate defence against the national government continuing to grow in strength at the expense of local government, and becoming tyrannical. One consequence of the constitutional system of checks and balances can be **gridlock** in Washington DC (when disagreements between the President and Congress lead to little being accomplished). While other Americans may find this frustrating, fiscal conservatives see this aspect of the constitution as positive, as they prefer fewer (interfering) initiatives from the national government.

Moreover, for years, fiscal conservatives have argued that the Constitution could be improved with the passage of a constitutional amendment that would lead to a permanent reduction of government activity in Washington DC. They would like to see a balanced budget amendment. This would mean that the government would not be able to borrow money to fund programmes. It would either have to raise taxes, which would be unpopular, or reduce spending. Given this choice, fiscal conservatives believe that spending would be cut, leading to:

- Reduced activity by the national government.
- Less interference in local and personal affairs.
- Fewer welfare programmes.
- Greater freedom, and incentive, for communities and individuals to be creative in developing themselves.

In combination, these developments would promote greater freedom and opportunity.

Overall, therefore, 'small government' conservatives believe that the Constitution has failed to restrain the size and scope of the Federal government, as many of the Founding Fathers wished, and that the Constitution has failed to ensure that the Federal government fulfils one of its most important roles – protecting the law-abiding. However, it has positive features that should be defended and there is scope for improving it by adding a key amendment that would force the government to respect their conception of opportunity achieved through the negative freedom that comes with minimal interference.

### The Constitution from the perspective of social conservatives

Other conservatives take a slightly different view of how well the Constitution has worked. Social conservatives agree that the government should not interfere in the daily lives of citizens unless necessary. However, they are more likely than fiscal conservatives to support certain types of government intervention. This is because they believe that people need to be guided as to the best way to use their freedoms. The Declaration of Independence had claimed that the 'pursuit of happiness' was one of the 'inalienable rights' to which everyone is entitled. Social conservatives believe that the pursuit of happiness should not include activities or methods that are immoral or harmful and that the Constitution should guide government to set high standards in personal behaviour.

It is this type of thinking that led to the 18th Amendment, prohibiting the sale and transportation of alcohol, in 1919. It is also this approach that has led to social conservatives campaigning for constitutional amendments, such as:

- Banning abortion
- Banning deliberate damage to the flag of the USA
- Protecting the right of schools to begin the day with a prayer
- Banning gay marriage

In summary, social conservatives share the view of fiscal conservatives that the Constitution should have limited the size and scope of the Federal government – and that it interferes unnecessarily in the daily lives of citizens (for example, in providing welfare benefits). They also agree with fiscal conservatives that the Constitution has failed to ensure that the Federal government fulfils one of its most important roles – protecting the law-abiding. However, while they would like to see the government restricted in some ways they would also like to see an increase of government activity when it comes to promoting moral behaviour. It is in this respect that they part company with fiscal conservatives who argue that people should be able to do as they wish (for example, view pornography) provided that they are not harming anyone else.

## The Constitution from the perspective of 'liberal' (left-wing) Americans

At the other end of the political spectrum, liberals take a completely different view of what is meant by 'freedom' and 'opportunity'. They believe that it is an 'inalienable right' (despite not being identified in the Declaration of Independence) for all people to develop their individual talents, skills and abilities. Thus, 'freedom' means each person being able to fulfil their potential. This is known as **positive freedom**.

For people to attain freedom, they need the means to develop their potential (through education, for example) and for any obstacles to developing their potential to be removed (such as protection from discrimination). Liberals therefore reject the form of negative freedom

advocated by conservatives (especially fiscal conservatives) and argue
that simply being left alone by the government, or not interfered
with, does not necessarily lead to freedom. If being left alone by the
government means leaving people struggling simply to survive, then
those people lose some of their humanity and are not 'free' in the
positive sense of the word. Moreover, the wider community loses
the benefits of their abilities.

Not only do liberals forcefully disagree with conservatives about
the definition of freedom, they also contest the conservative version
of history that is the basis of the claim that opportunity flows from
non-interference from government. Much of North America's early
economic development – especially the cotton and tobacco industries
– depended on slave labour. Both slavery and the slave trade were
regulated and protected by the government. The development of the
West depended heavily on the purchase of land by the Federal government, or on wars conducted by the government to gain control
of land, as well as a system for distributing it and recording ownership under the **Homestead Act**. The development of large-scale
farming (prairies) and industry depended heavily on the growth of
the railway system which, in turn, depended heavily on the Federal
government providing land to the railway companies free of charge,
giving the companies the right to make compulsory purchases of
private land and providing direct subsidies to pay for the construction
of the system. Even today, major manufacturers such as the Boeing
aircraft corporation receive vast sums from the Federal government
for the development of any technology that may be of use to the
armed forces of the USA. Thus, liberals argue, many of the developments that fiscal conservatives associate with freedom *from* government interference were, in reality, only possible *because* of the help of
government.

Thus, liberals approve of those aspects of the Constitution that
allow, or even encourage, politicians to take steps to promote positive freedom and are frustrated by those aspects which limit their
ability to achieve this goal. Like the Federalists at the Constitutional
Convention, liberals see a strong central government (with appropriate safeguards) as a means to achieve freedom rather than as a
threat.

Consequently, liberals have been willing to test the boundaries of constitutional limits on the Federal government. Although liberals accept that most matters relating to the well-being of citizens are the responsibility of the states (such as providing educational facilities, libraries and so on) they argue that there are some social and economic challenges that are simply too big and challenging for state governments to resolve. Under these circumstances, in contrast to conservatives, they welcome the intervention of the Federal government even if this means exceeding the size and scope of the government envisaged by the Founding Fathers.

This applied to the **New Deal** in the 1930s, when President F. D. Roosevelt's policies to combat the economic depression led to the Federal government taking responsibility for matters that traditionally belonged to the states. In doing so, it redefined the relationship between state governments and the Federal government and, in the eyes of conservatives, breached the constitutional safeguard of Federalism that was supposed to protect freedom by limiting the amount of power that the central government could wield. Conservatives fiercely resisted Roosevelt's initiatives, but for liberals these developments were fully justified as they protected millions of Americans from languishing in poverty, their potential wasted.

Later, in the 1960s, liberals were willing to further test the limitations of the Constitution in enabling people to fulfil their potential, even though there was no national crisis to justify their policies. The **Great Society** programme was an attempt by President Johnson to eliminate poverty in America – seen by liberals as the greatest obstacle to personal development. This programme again redefined the relationship between the states and the Federal government, as state governments that were perceived not to be doing enough to help their most needy residents were bypassed and impoverished communities were provided with direct government support from Washington DC. (The full implications of the New Deal and Great Society for Federalism are covered in Chapter 2.)

In addition to trying to ensure the conditions for people to make the most of their potential, liberals have also sought to ensure that the Constitution makes it impossible for artificial barriers to be put in the way of achievement – especially in the form of discrimination. Liberals have been active supporters of campaigns to promote equality. They were a driving force behind the passage of the 23rd and 24th

Amendments to the Constitution (passed in 1961 and 1964 respectively). The 23rd Amendment granted people living in Washington DC, a large majority of whom were African American, the right to vote in presidential elections. The 24th Amendment made it unconstitutional to impose a poll tax (in effect a fee) on people registering to vote. The poll tax had long been used in Southern states as a way of preventing African Americans, a high proportion of whom were very poor, from voting.

Liberals were also the driving force behind the Equal Rights Amendment, an unsuccessful attempt to pass an amendment that would have made it unconstitutional to discriminate against women. The amendment passed Congress but was only ratified by thirty-five states. (It needs the ratification of thirty-eight states for a constitutional amendment to pass.)

The fact that the Constitution has proved sufficiently flexible to accommodate greater government intervention at times of crisis, such as during the New Deal, and that it has been possible to amend the Constitution to outlaw some forms of discrimination, demonstrate to liberals the strength of the system. Thus, like their conservative opponents, while they have been critical of the Constitution at times, overall they see it as a political framework that can be used to advance their goals.

In summary, liberals believe in positive freedom. They believe that the Federal government should create the conditions for everyone across the country to fulfil their potential and that the Federal government should be responsible for ensuring that discrimination – the main obstacle to people fulfilling their potential – is challenged and eliminated. Liberals have seen the Constitution as a means to meet these goals. Often, however, they have found the constraints of the Constitution, especially Federalism, frustrating. In contrast to conservatives, therefore, the main criticism that liberals have of the Constitution is that the Federal government is not strong enough. They do not want to see a Federal government without constraints, but they do want that government to be able to promote their vision of freedom.

### The Constitution from the perspective of centrists

While conservatives believe that the Constitution places too few constraints on the Federal government, putting personal liberty at risk, and liberals feel that the Federal government has difficulty creating the conditions for people to fulfil their potential due to constitutional restrictions, many Americans believe that the Founding Fathers struck the best possible constitutional balance between governing and protection from abuse of power, thereby promoting liberty and opportunity.

According to this view, the constitutional protections of freedom are so well known, so well understood and so treasured by Americans that liberty has become part of the culture and identity of the USA. Many of the most famous symbols of the nation are associated with liberty, such as the Statue of Liberty in New York City. Ordinary Americans, without in-depth political knowledge, know that the 1st Amendment protects freedom of speech, freedom of religion and the right to protest. They know that the 2nd Amendment protects the right to 'bear arms' – that there is much dispute about what exactly 'bear arms' means but that no government could ever completely ban the ownership of guns. The expression 'take the fifth', meaning the constitutional right to remain silent when accused of a crime, is even used by children who have misbehaved. On virtually every crime drama on TV, Americans are reminded that suspects are constitutionally entitled to a lawyer and that if they cannot afford one the state is constitutionally required to provide one. The USA has even produced a distinctive type of pressure group, not found in other parts of the world, that exists solely to monitor the extent to which the American political system is faithful to the core values of the Declaration of Independence and the Constitution, and to campaign for reform if the political processes are not effectively serving these values. One of them, Common Cause, with a nationwide membership of over 400,000, describes itself as 'a watchdog against corruption and abuse of power' and seeks to ensure that government officials will be 'held accountable for working within the rule of law and under high standards of ethical conduct' as well as protecting the 'civil rights and civil liberties of all Americans'. Centrists believe that, under these circumstances, no government could ever permanently take away fundamental liberties.

Centrists, like their political rivals, point to the evidence of American history to support their view that the constitutional protections of liberty are effective. The Founding Fathers believed that politicians *will* abuse their power, and have been proved correct throughout the history of the Republic, but the system of constitutional protections has always proved robust enough to ensure that liberty, in the long term, has been preserved.

For example, during the American Civil War, President Lincoln suspended the right of **habeas corpus**. This right is widely regarded as the most important guarantee of liberty. It requires arrested persons to be produced before a court to be informed of any charges against them so that they can defend themselves and thus ensures that they cannot mysteriously disappear in the manner associated with oppressive governments. This suspension was supported by Congress at the time but rejected by the Chief Justice of the Supreme Court in the case of *ex parte Merryman* (1861). The President simply ignored this ruling. However, habeas corpus was restored in 1866 after another Supreme Court ruling, *ex parte Milligan*, following the end of the Civil War.

A similar pattern was seen during World War II. Japanese Americans lost their freedom and were **interned** in 'War Relocation Camps' despite scant evidence of any spying. This policy, resulting from an **executive order** issued by the President, was upheld by the Supreme Court in the case of *Korematsu* v. *United States* (1944). Although it took many years, the government officially apologised for this infringement of liberty in 1988 and $1.6 billion was paid as reparations to those interned or their descendents.

More recently, the status of **enemy combatants**, detained in the **War on Terror** since 2001, has illustrated how government use of power can be restricted on the basis of constitutional protection of liberty. President George W. Bush declared a 'war on terror' following the attacks on the USA on 11 September 2001. The 'war' has included action taken by the armed forces and intelligence services abroad and by the police within the USA. Anyone detained as a result of evidence linking them with the groups that were behind the attacks of 9/11, or groups planning similar strikes, could be declared an illegal enemy combatant by the President and denied a trial in a civilian court. These measures were justified on the grounds that American freedoms could only be protected if strong measures were taken against enemies and potential enemies who do not value personal liberty. However, groups such as the American Civil Liberties

Union (ACLU), that are dedicated to ensuring that constitutional freedoms are not eroded, argued that the President was:

• Breaching the constitutional principle of separation of powers by taking over judicial responsibilities in relation to enemy combatants.
• Breaching the 5th Amendment's constitutional protection that the evidence against a suspect be independently reviewed to ensure that it is sufficient to justify a trial.
• Breaching the 6th Amendment's constitutional protection that suspects be shown the evidence against them, so that they can present their defence and be given a fair and speedy trial.

The argument between the President and civil liberties groups went before the Supreme Court in a series of cases:

• *Rasul* v. *Bush* (2004)
• *Hamdi* v. *Rumsfeld* (2004)
• *Hamdan* v. *Rumsfeld* (2006)
• *Boumediene* v. *Bush* (2008)

In each case, the Supreme Court ruled that the detainees were entitled to constitutional protections. In rejecting the arguments of the President, in the case of *Hamdan* v. *Rumsfeld*, the Court's judgment declared, 'a state of war is not a blank cheque for the president' and 'if this nation is to remain true to its ideals, it must not wield the tools of tyrants even to resist an assault by the forces of tyranny'. In the case of *Boumediene* v. *Bush*, the Court returned to this theme, quoting from the Founding Fathers that 'the practice of arbitrary imprisonments, have been, in all ages, the favourite and most formidable instruments of tyranny'. The Court concluded, 'the laws and Constitution are designed to survive, and remain in force, in extraordinary times'.

Centrists do not argue that the constitutional system is perfect. They acknowledge some flaws. A consequence of separation of powers is that when different branches of government do not co-operate with each other it can result in gridlock – the political process grinding to a halt. Ironically, centrists are also concerned that sometimes the different branches of government work too well together, usually when the same political party controls the executive and both houses of the legislature. When this happens, it can undermine constitutional freedoms and it can take some time for those freedoms to be restored.

In summary, therefore, when it comes to the fundamental issue of whether the Constitution strikes the right balance between governing and protection of liberties, centrists believe that the Founding Fathers got it right. The 'miracle of Philadelphia' is that the Founding Fathers found the best possible path between the demands of the most ardent anti-Federalists who wanted the government to have too few powers and those Federalists who wanted the government to have too many powers – and that balance has proved durable over two centuries of American history.

### The Constitution as a fundamentally flawed document

Each of the viewpoints considered so far criticises the Constitution to a greater or lesser extent but, on balance, sees it as providing a political framework that it can accept – perhaps with some amendments. There is another viewpoint, however, that challenges the Founding Fathers' design as deeply flawed.

The Constitution explicitly excluded Native Americans from its provisions (Article I, Section 2, Point 3). Also, as Frederick Douglass (a freed slave who became a leader of the **Emancipation** movement) declared, 'liberty and slavery – opposite as heaven and hell – are both in the Constitution'. After the abolition of slavery, laws that served to promote white racial supremacy were deemed to be consistent with the terms of the Constitution.

Far from commanding the respect shown by conservatives, liberals and centrists, the Constitution stands condemned for the denial of freedom and opportunity, on grounds of race, despite professing to 'establish Justice . . . and secure the Blessings of Liberty'. The reality, from this point of view, is that the Founding Fathers produced a framework to protect their interests, at the expense of racial minorities. Consequently, over the following two centuries, freedom and opportunity were systematically denied to the excluded groups, resulting in the USA developing as a country characterised by stark racial inequality.

This challenge to the very core of the US political system is so fundamental that Chapter 3 is devoted to analysing it, the policy implications of addressing its flaws and the highly charged political debate that has been ignited by demands to redress the failings of the system.

## Conclusion

When the Founding Fathers wrote the Constitution of the USA, they aimed to ensure that it would be extremely difficult for people in power to infringe personal freedoms and limit opportunity. Two centuries later, with that Constitution having been only slightly amended, the USA is associated with freedom by a substantial proportion of the world's population and is a magnet for ambitious people who believe that their own countries stifle opportunity. In this sense, the Constitution can be seen as extremely successful.

Yet, at home, there are a range of views on how successful it has been. Americans disagree with each other not only on the extent to which their Constitution has secured freedom (and, consequently, opportunity) but also on what they mean by freedom. These contrasting views have run so deep that they have led a civil war and a Civil Rights movement, both of which have transformed the political landscape.

Understanding how this political framework operates, the thinking behind it and why there are such sharp divisions on how well it works provides a foundation for understanding every aspect of the government and politics of the USA.

• • • • • • • • • • • • • • • • • • • • • • • • • • • • • • • • • • • • • • • •

## ✓ What you should have learnt from reading this chapter

- The Founding Fathers, determined to secure liberty for future generations regardless of how the country (and the wider world) might change, designed a Constitution to ensure that no individual or faction could accumulate sufficient power to become tyrannical.

- By creating a national government which would have specified powers (with the rest being held at local level) *and* those powers being distributed between the executive, legislative and judicial branches *and* keeping people from holding office in more than one branch at the same time *and* giving each branch responsibility for ensuring that their (potentially power-hungry) rivals in the other branches did not breach their designated boundaries *and* making people in power accountable to the general public in staggered elections, the delegates at the Constitutional Convention were satisfied that they had found the right formula for effective government while protecting the 'unalienable Rights' of 'Life, Liberty and the pursuit of Happiness'.

- Citizens with a political voice, however, were sceptical. During the public debate that accompanied the ratification process, it became clear the Constitution would only be adopted if a Bill of Rights was added to provide an additional layer of protection for citizens against their own government, in case the Founding Fathers' formula failed.

- In the two centuries since the Constitution was adopted, it has been subject to intense scrutiny and debate, focusing on one central question: has it met the terms of its remit of ensuring liberty and opportunity while providing the Federal government with enough power to be effective?

- There has been from the outset, and continues to be, substantial disagreement on how to judge whether the American people enjoy liberty and opportunity and the Founding Fathers struck the right balance.

- On the right, conservatives use the concept of negative freedom as a benchmark for judging the effectiveness of the Constitution and, with the growth of government over the past two centuries, argue that it has been of limited effectiveness in protecting liberty. However, with some amendments, these deficiencies could be rectified.

- On the left, liberals use the concept of positive freedom as a benchmark for judging the effectiveness of the Constitution and, with the constraints imposed on government (especially Federalism), also argue that it has been of limited effectiveness in protecting liberty – albeit for different reasons. However, past constitutional amendments have improved it and further amendments could improve it further.

- Centrists accept that the Constitution is not perfect but argue that the Founding Fathers found the best possible balance between the incompatible demands of effective government and maximising liberty.

- For those who did not have a voice when the Constitution was being written, the main concern has been the contrast between the high ideals of the Founding Fathers and the reality for groups on the margins of US society. In practice, the system protected the rights of white, male, able-bodied heterosexuals and enabled them to aggressively dominate anyone who did not display these characteristics. As one of the leaders of the movement to abolish slavery put it, 'liberty and slavery – opposite as heaven and hell – are both in the Constitution'. For African Americans, explicitly excluded from the protections of the Constitution, and for others implicitly excluded, the greatest challenge of US politics has been to ensure that society meets the high ideals of genuine freedom and equality for all.

# Glossary of key terms

**Balanced budget amendment** A constitutional amendment to guarantee that the government does not operate a budget deficit – enabling it to spend more than it raises in taxes (seen by some as leading to irresponsible and reckless policies).

**Checks and balances** A system of providing each branch of government with the means of limiting the powers of the other branches, so that none of them exceed the powers assigned to them in the Constitution.

**Counter-majoritarian** The principle that the democratic will of the majority may not always be wise or fair and, therefore, precautions need to be taken to protect those who may be adversely affected by decisions taken by the majority.

**Emancipation** Freedom from slavery.

**Enemy combatants** A term used by the administration of President George W. Bush to describe people accused of planning violent acts against the USA, or its citizens, but not treated as prisoners of war.

**Executive branch (of government)** The arm of government with constitutional responsibility for ensuring that the laws are of the land are implemented (as set out in Article II).

**Executive order** A directive from the President to the staff of the executive departments that are responsible for implementing the laws of the nation.

**Great Society** A package of policies that aimed to eliminate poverty in the USA.

**Gridlock** The inability to pass laws because the executive and legislative branches are unable to co-operate or compromise.

**Habeas corpus** The principle that no one can be imprisoned without a properly conducted trial.

**Homestead Act** A law, passed in 1862, that provided land for a small fee to any farmer who occupied it. Officially defined as 'unoccupied', this gave farmers the legal right to land that had belonged to Native Americans.

**Intern** To hold a section of the population in detention because they are seen as a threat to the state, even though they have not been properly tried and convicted.

**Judicial branch (of government)** The arm of government with constitutional responsibility for interpreting the laws of the land (as set out in Article III) and, later, for interpreting the constitution.

**Legislative branch (of government)** The arm of government with constitutional responsibility for passing laws and for close scrutiny of the executive branch to ensure that it does not develop into an institution resembling a monarchy (as set out in Article I).

**Negative freedom** The idea that people should be allowed to live as they please, without interference from government, provided they do not cause harm to others.

**New Deal** A package of policies to boost the economy and provide support to people most affected by the economic situation during the depression of the 1930s.

**Positive freedom** The idea that people are only truly 'free' if they are able to make the most of their talents or potential.

**Ratification** The process by which the Constitution, after it had been written, was debated and agreed by the thirteen original states, enabling it to come into force in 1789.

**Separation of powers** The distribution of power between the three branches of government to ensure that no single person, or group, is able to make, enforce, interpret and enforce the law.

**Tyranny of the majority** The idea that the democratically expressed will of the majority of the people will not always have a positive or constructive outcome: numerical advantage may be used to oppress the minority (or minorities).

**War on Terror** A term adopted by the administration of President George W. Bush, following the attacks on the USA on 11 September 2001, covering all actions taken by the armed forces and intelligence services abroad and by the police within the USA against those who mounted the attacks or were planning similar attacks.

## ? Likely examination questions

Issues examiners may expect students to be able to effectively analyse include:

- Whether the checks and balances written into the Constitution still work today

- How well freedoms are protected by the Constitution

- Whether the Constitution is an aid or obstacle to effective government in the twenty-first century

- Perspectives on the effectiveness of the Constitution

Thus, examples of the kind of questions which could be asked include:

Explain why conservatives are critical of the Constitution.

'The US system of checks and balances is ineffective.' Discuss

##  Helpful websites

www.constitutionalcenter.org – the museum in Philadelphia (where the Constitutional Convention took place) dedicated to the Constitution and related issues. Detailed, in-depth but very accessible.

www.justicelearning.org – accessible material on the constitutional implications of the main political issues today, produced by two highly respected news organisations, National Public Radio and the *New York Times*.

www.billofrightsinstitute.org – site dedicated to 'educate young people about the words and ideas of America's founders'. Particularly useful to teachers/lecturers.

## Suggestions for further reading

For a more in-depth understanding of the passionate debates surrounding the writing and ratifying of the Constitution, read all or parts of *The Federalist Papers* by Alexander Hamilton, James Madison and John Jay. Their articles not only capture the flavour of their time but raise questions that continue to be debated today.

A modern version of writings which attempt to capture the spirit of the Constitution is *A Patriot's Handbook* by Caroline Kennedy. A collection of songs, poems, stories and speeches, it offers a perspective on America from a wide variety of angles expressed in a diverse range of voices.

# Federalism

## Contents

## Overview

### States' Rights?

On 20 March 2009, during a deep economic downturn, Governor Mark Sanford of South Carolina announced that he was rejecting $700 million in aid from the Federal government. He argued that strict rules on how the money could be used 'cuts against the notion of federalism and the idea of each state having the flexibility to act in a manner that best suits its needs'. He was expressing the frustration felt by sections of society at what they see as the remorseless growth of the Federal government. After all, the War of Independence was sparked by fury at decisions made by a remote government that had no understanding of, or concern for, the people affected by them.

Other Americans argue that state and local authorities cannot, or will not, provide the support that their communities need. Additionally, it is argued by some that there have been many local leaders who, far from being guardians of freedom, have been tyrants who have actively oppressed one section of their community to curry favour with another and that it has often taken the Federal government to protect freedoms.

This tension between those who distrust their national government and those who believe that government has played a crucial role in defending the interests of the most vulnerable Americans has been one of the most significant issues in US politics. This chapter examines the development of Federalism and considers the current balance between the states and the government in Washington DC.

## Key issues to be covered in this chapter

- The states at independence from Britain
- Federalism in the Constitution
- The evolution of Federalism
- Federalism in the twenty-first century
- The extent to which an appropriate balance has been struck between the powers of the states and the powers of the central government

# The states at independence from Britain

### Dominance over the national government

When the thirteen colonies broke away from Britain in 1776, they had already been developing their own traditions and identities for up to a hundred and fifty years. Initially, these states set up a **confederate** system of government in which the national government had very limited resources and were dependent on the states for money, soldiers and to enforce the law. It consisted of a legislature (Congress), with no executive (President) or courts, and nine of the states had to give their agreement before any action could be taken. In this arrangement most policy decisions affecting ordinary Americans were taken by the political authorities of each state, with the national government being restricted to international relations, national defence and inter-state disputes.

### The disadvantages of a confederate system

The weaknesses of this system quickly became evident:

- Congress could not raise its own revenue and states could not be relied on to provide adequate funds.
- Congress could not regulate trade. Economic disputes broke out between a number of states and Congress could not play a role in resolving them.
- Congress found it difficult to make decisions. Often only nine or ten state delegates were present at meetings and nine votes were required for a law to be passed.
- When Congress was able to make decisions, without an executive branch or court system, they had no means of enforcing them.
- This lack of effective co-ordination meant that the country was vulnerable to invasion by the powerful European imperial countries.

Thus, the national government was unable to effectively carry out even the limited responsibilities that it had been given and pressure grew for it to be given increased powers.

However, the states valued the main advantage of the system: they retained almost complete **sovereignty**, or control over their affairs. Also, in an era when local decision-making was associated with freedom (and laws that had been passed by the distant King of England were associated with tyranny) proposals for a strong national government were met with deep suspicion.

### Redefining the relationship between the states and the national government

A recognition of the need for a more effective national government led to the Constitutional Convention of 1787 (see Chapter 1 for more details). One of the Convention's main challenges was to ensure that the states would be able to retain as much sovereignty as possible. Consequently, they devised a system in which:

- The Constitution gave some power to the states. These were sovereign powers, which belonged to the states. Their powers had come from the Constitution, not the national government, and could not be taken away from them.
- The Constitution gave some power to the national government. These were sovereign powers, which belonged to the national government. Their powers had come from the Constitution, not the states, and could not be taken away from them.
- Neither the states nor the national government would have excessive power, meaning that the Federal system helped to protect the people from oppression and to guarantee their liberty.

### Powers given to the states

Article I, Section 9 of the Constitution listed powers that could be exercised by the states but not Congress. These included, at the time, the right to trade in slaves and the right to raise an income tax. Both of these limitations were later removed but others, such as not allowing Congress to tax goods that move from one state to another, remain.

Article IV provided for 'full faith and credit', meaning that any law, government action or court decision in one state would be recognised in all of the other states. Therefore, no one would be able to evade the law in one state by escaping to another with different laws. On the other hand, it would be possible to go to another state to take advantage of their laws without punishment at home. For example, the marriage laws vary from state to state.

Article V gave the states a role in deciding whether the Constitution should be amended. No amendment is possible without the agreement of three-quarters of the states (thirty-eight of the fifty states).

The 10th Amendment gave the states power over all matters which were not given specifically to the Federal government. These are known as **reserved powers**.

### Powers given to the national government

Article I, Section 8 of the Constitution listed seventeen powers that only Congress could exercise. Crucially, the eighteenth clause gave Congress the right to pass any laws required to fulfil their powers. Known as the 'elastic clause', it has been used by Congress, controversially, to intervene in matters traditionally thought of as the responsibility of the states. Section 10 listed the areas the states cannot interfere with, for example, foreign affairs.

Article II outlined the powers and duties of the President.

Article III outlined the powers and duties of the Supreme Court. At that time, the powers did not include judicial review which, like the 'elastic clause', was to become controversial.

Article VI, Section 2 was the 'Supremacy Clause', which established that when state and Federal governments were in conflict, the Federal government was supreme.

Some of the powers given to the Federal government were clearly written into the Constitution. These are known as **expressed powers** or **enumerated powers**. In order to use their powers, the Federal government also has **inherent powers**, such as the power to set up a diplomatic service to manage foreign relations. The Federal government may also have to take less obvious steps to use their powers, by making use of **implied powers**, such as the controversial 'elastic clause'.

### Powers shared between the states and the national government

Both the Federal and state legislatures have always had the right to pass laws that define crimes and appropriate punishments. Since the 16th Amendment was passed in 1913, allowing the Federal government to impose income taxes, both Federal and state governments

| Table 2.1  Division of powers | | |
| --- | --- | --- |
| **National Government** | **Shared Powers** | **State Governments** |
| Foreign affairs | Raise taxes | Regulate trade within the state |
| Defence of the nation | Borrow money | Administer elections |
| Resolving disputes between states | Spend money for the welfare of the population | Protect the public's health, welfare and morals |
| Regulating trade between the states | Pass and enforce laws | |
| Managing the economy | | |

have had the right to tax individuals. These shared powers are known as **concurrent powers**.

The consequent division of powers was as above:

## The Constitutional Convention: debating Federalism

### An unsatisfactory compromise?

Before the Constitution could become law, nine of the thirteen states had to ratify it. Federalism, like so much of the Constitution, represented a compromise, and across the country there was fierce debate as to whether the right balance had been struck between the powers given to the national government and the states.

### The States' Rights position

Those who feared that the Constitution gave the national government too much power, and could become a threat to liberty, argued that:

- The original thirteen states had existed before independence and had come together to create a Constitution that placed strict limitations on the Federal government.
- Any doubts about where power belonged, perhaps caused by disagreement over an issue not directly covered by the Constitution, should therefore *always* be resolved in favour of the states.
- This approach was justified by experience, that decisions are best

taken by people closest to those affected by them, and by the Constitution itself, which, in the 10th Amendment, reserved to the states any powers not specifically given to the Federal government.

The most extreme supporters of this view developed the theories of nullification and interposition: that if the Federal government passed laws or took actions that increased its own powers, then the states should overrule them.

### The Nationalist position

Those who feared that the country, and its liberties, would not survive unless the Constitution provided the national government with enough power to effectively co-ordinate affairs, argued that:

- The Constitution was created to serve the people and gave both the Federal and state governments the powers they needed to do so.
- Therefore, any doubts about where power belonged should be resolved according to the needs of the people, not automatically in favour of the states, and should take account of the fact that the Federal government has responsibility for all the people while each state has responsibility for only some of the people.
- Furthermore, the Constitution created a Federal government strong enough to protect the nation from external aggression and internal disputes, and had given the government the right to use 'necessary and proper' means (the 'elastic clause') to carry out its duties.

### The continuing debate

The Constitutional Convention did not provide a final resolution to the debate on how powers should, in practice, be allocated between the national government and the states. It erupts each time that circumstances, or political priorities, cause questions to be asked about whether the existing balance is satisfactory.

## The development of Federalism

### The Marshall Era and the Civil War

Within two decades of the Constitution being adopted, rulings by the Supreme Court under Chief Justice John Marshall altered the balance in favour of the national government.

- *Fletcher* v. *Peck* (1810) This case ruled that a law passed by the Georgia state legislature had violated the United States Constitution and was therefore invalid. Before this decision, it was generally understood that the legitimacy of state laws was determined by state constitutions and state Supreme Courts.
- *McCulloch* v. *Maryland* (1819) This case ruled that Maryland was not allowed to impose a tax on the national bank, set up by Congress, and that in a conflict between the national government and a state the national government was supreme.
- *Dartmouth College* v. *Woodward* (1819) This case ruled that the State of New Hampshire acted unconstitutionally when it attempted to take over a college by removing its trustees.
- *Gibbons* v. *Ogden* (1824) This case ruled that Congress had the right to regulate inter-state commerce. Before this decision, it was generally understood that the Constitution allowed states to close their borders to trade if they chose.

The Court's attitude to Federalism was summed up by Chief Justice Marshall's observation in *McCulloch* v. *Maryland* (1819) that to allow states to exercise power over a Federal institution would 'render the government of the Union incompetent . . . and place all powers under the control of the State legislatures'.

Also, in this period, the slave trade was banned. The Constitution contained a clause, in Article I, Section 9, which prohibited the abolition of the slave trade until 1808. As soon as it was allowed to do so, however, Congress outlawed the slave trade, with the inevitable effect on the states that depended on slavery for their prosperity.

Later in the century, the Civil War (1861–5) established that no state had the right to leave the Union and that if they refused to abide by the Constitution the Federal government had the right to impose its will on the states. Between the end of the war in 1865 and 1877, the Southern states which had tried to break away were ruled by military governors who took their orders from Washington DC.

The 13th, 14th and 15th Amendments to the Constitution, known as the **Civil Rights Amendments**, were passed after the Civil War to ensure that the newly freed slaves would be given the same rights as other American citizens. For the leaders of the Southern states, who believed in white racial superiority, this was seen, like the end of the slave trade (1808) and slavery (1863), as the North deciding how their communities should be organised and imposing their values on the South.

## Dual Federalism

Apart from the brief period when the Marshall Court asserted the supremacy of the national government, and the exceptional circumstances surrounding the Civil War, for much of the nineteenth century and the first two decades of the twentieth century, there was a widespread acceptance that the national government would confine itself to taking responsibility for foreign and inter-state affairs while the state governments took responsibility for all other matters. This approach has become known as **Dual Federalism** – also sometimes referred to as **layer cake Federalism** (using the image of one cake resting on top of another, completely separate, cake). Indeed, after the end of the military occupation of the South in the aftermath of the Civil War, there was a period of over fifty years when the Supreme Court routinely ruled against interference in state affairs:

* In *Plessy* v. *Ferguson* (1896), the Court upheld a Louisiana law that provided for 'equal but separate [train] accommodations for the white and colored races'. The Court ruled that such laws 'do not necessarily imply the inferiority of either race to the other'. This ruling gave Federal permission to states to pass segregation laws (collectively referred to as Jim Crow laws) if they wished.
* The Supreme Court, in this period, repeatedly struck down laws passed by Congress to regulate business and working conditions, arguing that unless it could be clearly shown that the laws affected only inter-state commerce then Congress was trespassing on state matters. As one ruling put it, unless the courts kept Congress in check in this way, 'the power of the States over local matters may be eliminated, and thus our system of government be practically destroyed'.

## Co-operative Federalism

The uneasy balance between the states and the Federal government in Washington DC was decisively altered by the prolonged economic depression that struck the USA after the Wall Street Crash in 1929.

The proposals of the President to end the economic crisis, which meant interfering in matters that were traditionally the responsibility of the states, met with fierce resistance.

During the depression of the 1930s, state governments proved unable to rise to the challenge of mass unemployment and homelessness because:

- Conservative politicians, running some states, believed that the economy would correct itself and the problems they faced would be solved by market forces.
- Liberal politicians, running other states, were limited by the requirement of all state constitutions (except Vermont's) to balance their budget, meaning they could not borrow money to provide help in difficult times.

The Federal government faced no such restrictions, and when Franklin D. Roosevelt was elected in 1932, he put forward a plan, known as the **New Deal**, to provide financial help for the unemployed in the short term and to provide employment programmes to get people back to work in the long term. The work programmes were expected to have two benefits:

- The income for people on the programmes would be spent on produce, which would create new jobs which, in turn, would create demand for more produce – the 'multiplier effect'.
- The programmes would produce new roads, bridges, hospitals and schools, which would benefit everyone in society.

For the Federal government to take responsibility for unemployment benefit, work programmes and providing local schools was a major departure from traditional Federalism and altered the balance between the national government and the states. With both having a role in local affairs, the image of two cakes, one sitting on top of the other, was no longer accurate. The new relationship, **Co-operative Federalism**, was more like two different mixtures contributing to the same cake, or **marble cake Federalism**.

The New Deal was seen as destroying Federalism and was fiercely opposed by conservatives. However Roosevelt's Democratic Party controlled both the White House and Congress. Conservative resistance was therefore led by the Supreme Court, where they were in the majority. Between 1933, when Roosevelt gained power, and 1937, the Supreme Court ruled key elements of the New Deal unconstitutional:

- The National Industrial Recovery Act provided employment through the building of bridges, schools and hospitals, and introduced a forty-hour week for workers. In *Schechter Poultry Corporation v. United States* (1935), the Court ruled the Act unconstitutional on the grounds that it regulated all companies, including those that traded only locally, which was the responsibility of the states.
- The Agricultural Adjustment Act helped farmers, at a time of falling prices for their crops, by providing them with subsidies in return for reducing production. In *United States v. Butler* (1936), the Court ruled the Act unconstitutional on the grounds that it interfered with the responsibilities of the states.

In response, in 1937, President Roosevelt proposed his 'Court-packing' plan. Congress has the power to change the number of judges on the Supreme Court. In 1937 President Roosevelt, frustrated that he was unable to implement his New Deal, offered to 'help' all judges over the age of seventy with their workload by appointing another judge to assist them. This would have added six new judges to the Court. The proposal was rejected by Congress but, thereafter, the Court did not reject any of the President's New Deal projects and the new balance in Federalism became firmly established.

Indeed, it could be said that the Supreme Court went to the opposite extreme, accepting Congressional claims to interfere in state matters on the flimsiest of arguments. In the case of *Wickard v. Filburn* (1942), the Court upheld a law allowing Congress to regulate farm produce that would be consumed locally on the grounds that agricultural trade between the states could theoretically be affected by produce that was kept back for local use.

Although the effects of the depression ended when America entered the Second World War in 1941, Co-operative Federalism continued because:

- During the war, the government needed to control much of the economy to ensure that the armed forces had the equipment they needed.

- When the Second World War was over, the government played a major role in providing support to those who had risked their lives for their country, in the form of financial and medical help for the wounded and educational opportunities for all former soldiers. This meant that the Federal government became a major provider of healthcare and education.
- As soon as the Second World War was over, the Cold War with the Soviet Union began and the government invested heavily in new weapon systems to ensure that the USA kept a technological lead over its enemy. This meant that the government became a major source of employment.
- The Cold War, at times, erupted into a hot war, although not directly with the Soviet Union: in the 1950s the Korean War broke out and in the 1960s America was drawn into the civil war in Vietnam. This meant that conscription was, for the first time in American history, used when the country was not officially at war.

For those who feared that the constitutional safeguards against the concentration of power at the national level were inadequate, Co-operative Federalism was a troubling development. Of particular concern was the inability of the Supreme Court, as defenders of the Constitution, to resist the pressure from the President to redefine the relationship between the states and the Federal government. To this day, staunch States' Rights advocates argue that the New Deal permanently damaged the fabric of US society as crafted by the Founding Fathers. Referring to Co-operative Federalism, Justice Janice Rogers Brown, who sits on the Court of Appeals for the District of Columbia Circuit (widely regarded as the second most powerful court in the country), has argued that 'Where government moves in, community retreats, civil society disintegrates, and our ability to control our own destiny atrophies. The result is: families under siege; war in the streets; unapologetic expropriation of property; the precipitous decline of the rule of law; the rapid rise of corruption; the loss of civility and the triumph of deceit. The result is a debased, debauched culture which finds moral depravity entertaining and virtue contemptible.'

**Table 2.2  Comparison between Kennedy and Johnson**

| Kennedy | Johnson |
|---|---|
| From 'liberal' Massachusetts | From 'conservative' Texas |
| Youthful and glamorous | Extremely experienced in both the House of Representatives and the Senate |
| Relatively inexperienced | |
| Catholic | Protestant |

## Creative Federalism

The next significant change in the relationship between the national government and the states occurred not as a result of a change of circumstances, but because of the political priorities of Lyndon Johnson when he became President after the assassination of President Kennedy.

Lyndon Johnson had been chosen as John F. Kennedy's running mate in the 1960 presidential election to 'balance the ticket'. His role had been to attract voters to whom Kennedy did not appeal.

These differences worked well in the election campaign, but less well once the presidency had been won. President Kennedy's closest advisors distrusted Lyndon Johnson and he played a minor role as Vice President. When he became President, he was determined to demonstrate that he was committed to the policies they had campaigned for in the election and that, with his experience, he could deliver more than his young predecessor. Four months after he became President, he announced the **Great Society** programme, with the liberal (some would even say socialist) objective of eliminating poverty.

Poverty in America tends to be concentrated in specific groups. President Johnson believed that if there were an intense effort to improve the quality of life for these groups, poverty would become a thing of the past. However, he believed that such an effort would have to come from the Federal government because:

- Only the Federal government could have the resources for a massive anti-poverty programme.

- Only the Federal government could co-ordinate such a large programme.
- Only the Federal government could be relied on to have sufficient commitment to make the programme work: poverty in some areas was the result of neglect or active discrimination by state governments.

The groups to be targeted were:

- The elderly, many of whom could not afford healthcare and had many medical needs.
- Inner cities, where unemployment and crime was high and the quality of housing, education, leisure facilities and public transport was low.

There were three methods used to deliver the programme:

- Direct Federal aid/support for targeted groups. This was the first time that aid of this kind had been offered when there was no national crisis – which was a change in the nature of Federalism.
- Providing financial support for local government, bypassing the state government. Since many of the areas of concentrated poverty were in the cities, it was logical to work closely with the local authorities in those areas. However, local government is, constitutionally, accountable to the state government and for the Federal government to intervene in this relationship amounted to a change in the nature of Federalism.
- Providing **categorical grants** instead of **block grants**. Previously, grants from the Federal government had been in the form of block grants, which could be used in whichever way the state chose. Categorical grants were given by the Federal government for a specific purpose, and the state could not put the money to any other use, regardless of local priorities. For the Federal government to dictate how states spent money also amounted to a change in the nature of Federalism.

In relation to the healthcare needs of the elderly, in 1965 the government introduced:

- Medicare, to provide help with the cost of medical treatment and medicines.

- The Older Americans Act, to ensure that communities provided effective planning and services to the elderly, especially the most frail.

In relation to the inner cities, the government introduced:

- The Equal Opportunity Act (1964), to address employment discrimination that meant that many inner-city residents, African Americans and other racial minorities, either could not get jobs or were denied promotion.
- The Mass Transit Act (1964), which provided funds to subsidise bus, subway and rail systems so that if inner-city residents were offered jobs, they were able to get to work.
- The Higher Education Act and Head Start Act (1965), which improved funding and new approaches to education in inner-city areas, to provide the basic skills needed to qualify for employment at a time when the number of unskilled manufacturing jobs was declining.
- The Demonstration Cities and Metropolitan Act (1966), which aimed to improve the quality of life in inner cities by funding parks and leisure facilities.
- The Housing and Urban Development Act (1968), to clear slums and provide decent, affordable housing in inner cities.

The effect of the Great Society programme was that the amount of money spent by the Federal government on the welfare of citizens, traditionally the responsibility of the states, rose dramatically. For the first time, the amount of money spent by the Federal government on welfare programmes was greater than spending on defence. Welfare spending increased from $10.6 billion when President Johnson came to power in 1963 to $259 billion by the time he left the White House in 1969.

During this period, the Supreme Court also played an important role in defending the interests of vulnerable groups, particularly suspected criminals, from the actions of their state governments. In *Gideon* v. *Wainwright* (1963), the Court ruled that defendants in criminal cases who could not afford a lawyer were entitled to one provided by the state in order to ensure a fair trial, as required by the 6th Amendment of the Constitution. In *Miranda* v. *Arizona* (1966), the

Court ruled that a suspect must be told of the right, guaranteed by the 5th Amendment, not to incriminate themselves and to remain silent during police questioning.

### New Federalism

For conservatives, who had opposed Co-operative Federalism but learned to live with it, the Great Society programme was a step too far. They had three main objections:

- Many believed that the programme undermined the core principles of American society. They believed that prosperity had been built on rugged individualism in which people had to rely on their own hard work, determination and creativity. Taking away the incentive to use these qualities was, in the view of the programme's opponents, damaging to society as a whole and to the poor in particular, who would never learn how to compete or tap their own inner resources.
- Many believed that the programme undermined Federalism and the states' ability to decide which issues were a priority and what the best ways were to deal with them. The New Deal, in the 1930s, had eroded Federalism and President Johnson's 'War on Poverty' had virtually destroyed it.
- Above all, for the Federal government to be making decisions on what happened in housing estates and parks in cities as far away as 3,000 miles from Washington DC, where the decisions were being made, appeared to undermine the core principle of Federalism, which was designed to ensure that such decisions were taken as close as possible to the people affected, and to ensure that there were limitations to the power that could be accumulated by the national government.

These attacks, coupled with the unpopularity of his other flagship policy, the war in Vietnam, were the principal reasons that President Johnson did not run for re-election in 1968. The winner of the election, Republican Party candidate Richard Nixon, came to power having campaigned for the support of conservatives who wanted to move back towards the traditional model of Federalism.

**President Nixon and New Federalism**

To reverse the policies of the Great Society, which involved social policies being developed in Washington DC rather than in the states, President Nixon reduced the total amount available for anti-poverty projects. At the same time, the President introduced a policy of **General Revenue Sharing**, in which many categorical grants, given to cities for specific purposes, were replaced by block grants that could be spent as each state saw fit.

However, it took time for the general political climate to change and while the President was attempting to pass power to the states, the Supreme Court continued to insist on Federal standards being applied to state laws and actions. In 1972, in *Roe* v. *Wade* (1973), the Court struck down a Texas law that severely restricted abortion, ruling that the 9th Amendment, which protects rights other than those mentioned in the Constitution, provided a right of privacy and that any state law which made abortion illegal was an 'unjustifiable intrusion by the Government upon the privacy of the individual'.

**President Carter and New Federalism**

By the time President Carter came to power in 1976, it appeared that a pattern had developed of the Democratic Party centralising control in Washington DC, undermining Federalism and the importance of the states, and the Republican Party defending the interests of the states and loosening the grip of the Federal government. However, President Carter, although a Democrat, was formerly the Governor of Georgia and believed that governors should have as much freedom as possible to decide what was in the best interests of their states.

President Carter did not alter the system of General Revenue Sharing. Also, there was growing public concern about the size of the Federal deficit and one way in which the President reduced expenditure was to reduce financial aid to the states. This required them to depend to a greater extent on their own resources.

**President Reagan and New Federalism**

During his election campaign, one of the slogans of President Reagan (Republican) was 'Government is not the solution to our problem, government is the problem.' He was a firm believer in the conservative view that Federal government support undermined

each with the shared aim of reversing the steady centralisation of power that had taken place as a result of the New Deal and Great Society Programmes. The policies that fall under the banner of New Federalism often had little in common, apart from their shared objective. President Nixon's General Revenue Sharing, for example, was cautious and made limited impact and the developments under President Clinton were, in part, the by-product of wider economic policies that boosted the income of the states, while President Reagan's initiatives were a bold, determined effort to re-empower the states. Their overall effect, however, was to infuse the states with increasing self-confidence and make them increasingly self-reliant.

## Federalism in the twenty-first century

### The tide turns again

Events, and the political inclinations of the two twenty-first-century Presidents, have led to power once again flowing from the states to the national government.

President George W. Bush, who was a former governor and ideologically committed to giving the states as much freedom as possible, believed that the national government should play a less intrusive role in the lives of ordinary Americans. When he took office, he was committed to a fiscal conservative agenda, believing that if taxes were cut the national government would be forced to do less and people would increasingly rely on their personal resources and local government, which understood their needs. This approach, which its supporters call 'starving the beast', would encourage personal responsibility and further strengthen state governments. However, during his two terms in the White House, the scale and scope of the national government expanded dramatically because of:

- *Bursting the 'dot-com' bubble* Much of the boom in the 1990s had been based on new, high-technology companies exploiting the opportunities offered by the internet and the soaring prices of their shares on the stock market, even though many of them had yet to make a profit. The surge in income of many states was based on taxing these shares. When the bubble burst, so did the value of the shares and the income of the states. In 2000, state governments had built up financial surpluses of $47 billion but by 2003, thirty-one states were cutting spending while eighteen were increasing taxes. As with previous crises, the states looked to the Federal government for solutions. Reluctantly, President George W. Bush gave $7.7 billion in aid to the states in 2003, with the promise of more the following year.

- *9/11* With business already struggling to cope with the collapse of the stock market, the attack on the financial district of New York and the destruction of the World Trade Center tipped the country into an economic recession. The states found themselves facing the effects of failing businesses, resulting in reduced taxation and a reduction in tourism revenue. More significantly, there was a sharp shift in public opinion, which looked to the national government, in particular the President as Commander-in-Chief, to improve protection from further attacks and take the fight to the leaders of Al-Qaeda and its supporters around the world. Far from 'starving the beast', the national government has been fed with billions of dollars of additional funds to spend on reconstruction in New York City, military interventions in Afghanistan and Iraq and the development of new weapons to fight a different kind of conflict in which the enemy is not a conventional army. Instead of the government becoming less intrusive, a new government department for Homeland Security has been set up, which can direct state and city governments to provide protection against potential terrorist attacks. For example, in the city of Seattle, with two sports stadiums and a busy seaport to protect, the Federal government provided $11 million in 2003 to pay for civil defence equipment and training. However, the Federal government was not prepared to pay for staff salaries of the police trained to use the equipment which, they insisted, was the responsibility of the city.

- *Interventionist instincts* Despite his background as a state governor and his ideological commitment to smaller government, George W. Bush's administration committed itself to a range of expensive spending commitments in his first term, including:
    - In May 2002, the Farm Act was signed into law, providing financial support to the agricultural sector at the cost of an estimated $83 billion over ten years.

- The Medicare Act, signed into law in December 2003, to improve medical care for the elderly, was estimated at the time to cost $400 billion over ten years. By September 2004, the cost estimate from the White House had risen to $534 billion.
- Less than a month after making the immense financial commitment to Medicare, in January 2004 the President announced a plan to send astronauts to the Moon and Mars, at an initial cost of $12 billion over five years. Commentators estimated the full cost of a manned Moon programme at $15 billion, with the cost of the Mars programme at ten times that amount.
- In August 2005, the President signed into law two more expensive pieces of legislation. The Energy Act, which provides funding for projects intended to guarantee that the country has sufficient energy to meet its needs, cost $12.6 billion over four years. The Highways Act, which funds the upkeep and improvements in the country's transport systems, cost $286 billion over five years. Among the projects included in the latter Act (later scrapped because of the public outcry) was the $223 million 'Bridge to Nowhere', which linked a small Alaskan town with its local airport, replacing a seven-minute ferry ride.
- Perhaps the most significant measure of President George W. Bush's first term, in respect of Federalism, was the passage of the No Child Left Behind Act, which not only increased spending by the national government but extended control over an area of policy that was traditionally the responsibility of the states. The Federal government's contribution to the cost of education in schools rose from $28 billion in 2000 (out of a total of $400 billion) to $42.5 billion by 2004. In return for this money, it required the states to introduce a Federal system of accountability which meant that unless schools met specified targets in reading, maths and science, students would be allowed to transfer to other schools which were meeting the targets.
- *Hurricane Katrina* The serious damage inflicted on the city of New Orleans raised questions as to whether the city should be rebuilt

in its vulnerable location (below sea level and surrounded by water on three sides). However, the President committed himself to 'whatever it takes' to rebuild the city and made an initial request of $105 billion for damage and restoration work.

- *Economic slump* Shortly before the end of the President's second term, the USA was hit by a banking crisis that led to a wider economic depression. The Bush administration spent billions of dollars on rescuing financial institutions deemed too big to fail, such as AIG, and persuaded Congress to fund a $700 billion bailout of the financial sector.

President Barack Obama, in his first year in office, demonstrated a similar combination of being willing to provide whatever funds are necessary to address a crisis and of promoting initiatives that have the effect of further increasing the scope of the Federal government:

- *Stimulus package* Less than a month after he became President, Barack Obama signed into law a package of measures designed to revive the slumping economy, worth $787 billion.
- *Healthcare reform* The centrepiece of President Obama's domestic policy in his first year in office was ensuring that all the 40 million Americans without health insurance would have access to health-care. Historically, however, the welfare of citizens was seen as the responsibility of the states in the Federal system of the USA.

## Conclusion

### Not a one-way street

The controversies surrounding the substantial shift of power from the states to the national government since the Federal Constitution was adopted in 1789 can serve to obscure just how important the states remain in the daily lives of Americans. For example:

- For young people growing up, where they go to school, what they learn and the resources available to their teachers are mainly determined in their one community.
- The age at which people can learn to drive or get married, and what entertainment is available to them are decided at state or local level.

- Most policies on law and order, what is deemed to be legal or criminal, what penalties are imposed, even whether someone can be sentenced to death, are determined at state level.
- It is up to state and local authorities to set the level and quality of public services as well as the level and type of taxes that people have to pay for them.

Moreover, even at times that the national government is playing a dominant role, as it has in the current millennium, the states are willing to assert themselves if they see the opportunity or need. Thus, when President George W. Bush refused to sign international agreements on measures to tackle climate change, eleven states seized the initiative to introduce air quality regulations which are much more strict than the Federal government's.

### Conservative perspectives on Federalism

For conservatives, who pride themselves on their commitment to States' Rights, the Federal model designed by the Founding Fathers is hard to recognise in the modern USA. The government in Washington DC has far more power than was ever envisaged and intervenes in local affairs in ways that the Founding Fathers intended to prevent. From this point of view, the watershed was the New Deal, in which the President was able effectively to bully the Supreme Court into accepting a fundamental change in the relationship between the states and the Federal government. This demonstrated the validity of the concerns long voiced by advocates of States' Rights: that the Constitutional safeguards against the concentration of power at the national level were inadequate.

Furthermore, developments since the introduction of New Federalism have indicated that even politicians who support States' Rights, such as Ronald Reagan, are unable to do more than slow the drift of power to the centre and, in the case of George W. Bush, a Republican former governor, even supporters of this position are unable to resist the temptation to use a national crisis to increase the powers at their disposal.

Conservatives believe, however, that they do not have to accept a situation that they see as so unsatisfactory. The main reason that the national government is able to tackle situations that the states are unable to address is that the national government can borrow money while all of the states (except Vermont) are required by their own constitutions to balance their budgets each year. If, however, the national government were also constitutionally bound to balance its budget, the resources available to it would be proportionate to those available to the states and they would no longer be able to turn to Washington DC to solve their problems. Therefore, conservatives advocate the strengthening of Federalism through the passage of a **balanced budget amendment** that would severely curtail the ability of the national government to fund measures with borrowed money. They believe that this is an achievable goal as, in 1995, a proposed balanced budget amendment won more than the required number of votes in the House of Representatives and fell just one vote short of the required number in the Senate (and opinion poll data indicated that it would have had enough support in state legislatures to become a constitutional amendment if it had got through the Senate).

### Liberal perspectives on Federalism

In many states, for much of America's history, far from being a protection from a tyrannical national government, local rule has itself been oppressive to minority groups. In the Southern states, political leaders have turned the slogan 'States' Rights' into a doctrine of the denial of rights for anyone not like themselves. Insofar as it has taken the intervention of the government in Washington DC to ensure that the aims of the Constitution, as outlined in its preamble, to 'establish justice' and promote the general Welfare and secure the Blessings of Liberty to ourselves and our Posterity' are met, the evolution of Federalism has been welcomed by liberals.

Many liberals believe that local politicians are, too often, unable or unwilling to effectively address the needs of their communities. This is sometimes taken as a sign that liberals are hostile to Federalism and that they would prefer a unitary system with all power being transferred to the national government. This, however, is not the case. Liberals have welcomed progressive policy initiatives that have emerged from the states, such as the climate change measure outlined above and the extension of the right of marriage to gay couples which has been adopted by a number of states, starting with Massachusetts in 2004.

Thus, for liberals, Federalism represents both threats and opportunities. They want the Federal government to monitor developments in the states closely and to be willing to intervene if local power is being used in ways that disadvantage sections of the community. However, they also see favour the use of state power to pioneer progressive policies that can then be extended to the rest of the country.

### Centrist perspectives on Federalism

Centrists tend to be less concerned than conservatives about the erosion of Federalism since the Constitution was adopted, not least because of the prominent role that state authorities continue to play in the daily lives of Americans (see the section 'Not a one-way street', above). Moreover, centrists believe that Americans have absorbed the values embodied in the Constitution, including the principle of power being exercised as close to the people as possible, and that they would not accept the national government having more power than is necessary.

Thus they have been able to accept increased intervention by the national government at times of crisis, confident that the states will reassert themselves when the circumstances permit, as they did in the 1990s. Indeed, they point out that politicians at the national level may learn from their counterparts at state level (not only in respect of 'progressive' policies), as with the Wisconsin school vouchers policy which was adopted by George W. Bush for his presidential election campaign in 2000.

Overall, therefore, for centrists, Federalism has proved to be flexible enough to meet the changing needs of the country while remaining true to the aims and objectives of the Founding Fathers.

. . . . . . . . . . . . . . . . . . . . . . . . . . . . . . . . . . . . . . . . . .

### ✔ What you should have learnt from reading this chapter

- To restrict the power that Federal politicians could wield, the Founding Fathers relied on a system of Federalism that would place strict limits on the amount of power at the disposal of the national government. The balance between state and national government power was one of the sources of disagreement during the Constitutional Convention and has remained so ever since, especially when power has been centralised.

- The power of the national government has grown dramatically. From the original 'Dual Federalism' model, in which the states and the national government would each have their own spheres of responsibility, the system has evolved, through 'Co-operative Federalism' and '**Creative Federalism**', in ways which have served to increase the influence of Washington DC at the expense of the states.

- During the final three decades of the twentieth century a variety of strategies were adopted to redress the balance and re-empower the states.

- In the twenty-first century the trend has once again been for power to flow from the states to the national government.

- The growth of the national government, overall, has greatly alarmed conservatives who associate the centralisation of power with tyranny. They would like to see a balanced budget amendment added to the Constitution to limit the power of the national government in future.

- Liberals have been less concerned by the growth of the national government, not least because it has often stepped in to help vulnerable sections of society that state and local authorities have not provided with support. However, they have also welcomed progressive policies pioneered by states.

- Centrists tend to believe that the system of Federalism has served the USA well, providing the flexibility for the national government to intervene when necessary while allowing the states to be the most important influence on the daily lives of most Americans.

## Glossary of key terms

**Block grants**  Financial aid from the national government to state authorities that can be used in ways that the state authorities find most appropriate to their needs.

**Categorical grants**  Financial aid from the national government to state authorities which must be used in ways specified by the national government.

**Civil Rights Amendments**  The 13th, 14th and 15th Amendments to the Constitution that were passed after the Civil War to ensure that the newly freed slaves would be given the same rights as other American citizens.

**Concurrent powers**  Powers possessed by both the national and state governments, such as the power of taxation and passing laws.

**Confederate**  A system of government in which regional (or state) governments have more power than the national government.

**Co-operative (marble cake) Federalism**  Name given to the new relationship between the national government and the states resulting from the measures to cope with the economic depression of the 1930s.

**Creative Federalism** Name given to the new relationship between the national government and the states resulting from the measures taken in the attempt to eliminate poverty in the USA in the 1960s.

**Dual (layer cake) Federalism** Name given to the relationship between the national government and the states in the early decades of the history of the USA.

**Enumerated (or expressed) powers** Those powers belonging to the national government that are specifically mentioned in the Constitution.

**General Revenue Sharing** A policy introduced by President Nixon to replace categorical grants (see above), given to cities for specific purposes, with block grants (see above), that could be spent as each state saw fit.

**Great Society** Massive welfare programme, introduced by President Johnson in 1964, that aimed to eliminate poverty in the USA

**Implied (or inherent) powers** Those powers belonging to the national government which are not specifically mentioned in the Constitution, but are obviously needed for the government to meet its constitutional responsibilities.

**Layer cake Federalism** Informal term for Dual Federalism (see above).

**Marble cake Federalism** Informal term for Co-operative Federalism (see above).

**New Deal** Massive welfare programme, introduced by President F. D. Roosevelt in 1933, which aimed to reduce the impact of the economic depression and stimulate the economy.

**New Federalism** Name given to the strategies adopted, since the 1960s, in response to concerns that the national government had acquired too much power. Each strategy was designed to empower the states and reverse the tendency of power flowing from the states to Washington DC.

**Propositions** A form of direct democracy in which the electorate decides whether to adopt a new law.

**Reserved powers** Those powers belonging to the states because, as stated in the 10th Amendment, the Constitution did not award them to the national government.

**Sovereignty** Control over an area or territory, free from external interference.

**Unfunded Mandates Act (1994)** A law restricting the Federal government from imposing regulations on the states, such as environmental standards, unless the Federal government was prepared to pay for the cost of enforcing them.

**Welfare Reform Act (1996)** A law transferring the responsibility for welfare from the Federal government to the states.

# ? Likely examination questions

Issues examiners may expect students to be able to effectively analyse include:

* The constitutional role of Federalism in diffusing power

* The power that local communities have over their own affairs

* The development of the relationship between the national government and the states

* The effectiveness of Federalism during the open-ended 'war on terror'

* Perspectives on Federalism

Thus, examples of the kind of questions which could be asked include:

Outline how and why Federalism has changed since the 1960s

How Federal is the USA in reality?

# Helpful websites

www.nga.org, www.ncsl.org and www.usmayors.org – the official websites of the National Governors Association, the National Conference of State Legislatures and the US Conference of Mayors, which all have sections on state and Federal issues.

www.stateline.org – a website which has news from all fifty states.

# Suggestions for further reading

For a more in-depth study of this subject, the best book is *Federalism in America: An Encyclopaedia* by Troy Smith, Joseph Marbach and Ellis Katz. Over two volumes, this work provides a comprehensive reference explaining the major concepts, institutions, court cases, epochs, personalities and policies that have shaped, or been shaped by, American Federalism.

For an entertaining description of the diversity of the USA, read any of the books by Bill Bryson on his travels around the country. Born and raised in the USA, but having lived for extended periods in the UK, he offers an affectionate outsider's view of the American landscape and its inhabitants. *The Lost Continent*, a witty account of his travels through thirty-eight of the fifty states, is particularly recommended.

CHAPTER 3

# Race and Ethnicity in US Politics

## Contents

## Overview

*'We the people . . .?'*

On 26 January 2009, in a special commemorative edition, *Time* magazine carried an article by the veteran civil rights campaigner, Andrew Young, who wrote of Barack Obama that, 'we are proud of him, but the fact is that [with a white mother and Kenyan father] he has not had the experiences of deprivation, humiliation and racism that I had to grow up with . . . he has the label of African American but without the scars'.

The 'scars' he was referring to was the history of exclusion from the American mainstream that was written into the Constitution and had been reinforced by political authorities at national and local level for generations thereafter. Civil rights leaders, such as Andrew Young, insist that despite the historic election of 2008, the nation's 'scars' have yet to fully heal and that it remains the great challenge of US politics to ensure that society meets the constitutional ideals of genuine freedom and equality for all, regardless of race or ethnicity.

This perspective is strongly opposed by many other political leaders. Acknowledging that not all people have been treated equally, they argue that the inclusive language of the Constitution has provided openings for previously excluded groups and that it is now possible for all to play a full role in the mainstream of society. This chapter examines debate between these contrasting points of view.

## Key issues to be covered in this chapter

- The Constitution and race
- The extent of racial inequality
- Factors contributing to racial inequality
- The emergence of Affirmative Action as a response to racial inequality
- The extent to which racial equality has been achieved in the USA

# The Constitution and race

The Constitution is widely credited among Americans for creating the conditions for a society in which people can live where they want, travelling freely to whichever part of the country holds out the greatest prospects for personal advancement; where people can take advantage of educational opportunities that, at their best, are unrivalled anywhere in the world; where people can enjoy the fruits of their labour, with lower taxation and fewer government regulations than comparable countries; and where people can speak freely, challenging anyone who may threaten their freedoms. In short, the Constitution is widely associated with providing the solid foundations in which it is considered 'normal' for hard-working, resourceful people to build on the achievements of previous generations and improve their circumstances.

However, two racial groups, Native Americans and African Americans, were explicitly exempted from the Constitution's protections. In Article I, Section 2, Clause 3 of the Constitution, that determines how the people of the USA should be represented in Congress and thereby hold those in power to account, calculations were to be made 'excluding Indians' and defining 'all other persons' (meaning black slaves) as 'three-fifths' of a person. In addition, the slave trade, that permitted the treatment of people as nothing more than commodities, was guaranteed by the Constitution until at least 1808 (the first twenty years of the Constitution) in Article I, Section 9, Clause 1. And, at a time when not all of the thirteen states practised slavery, Article IV, Section 2, Clause 3 required the return of any slave who escaped and managed to reach a free state.

For these groups, 'normal' has described a very different type of America. For both African Americans, confined to plantations as slaves, and Native Americans, increasingly confined to isolated patches of the continent's least productive land, there was no freedom of movement, no education, few or no fruits of their labour to enjoy, and challenges to those who enforced limitations were likely to result in death. This continued to be the case for African Americans even after the end of slavery, as a system of brutally imposed racial segregation meant that freedom brought few benefits. Meanwhile, Native Americans, often confined to reservations with poor resources and services, were not even recognised until 1924 as citizens of the land they had lived in for centuries. And both groups, as well as some Hispanics (especially those of Mexican origin), argue that contemporary political and economic policies continue to erect obstacles to their progress, either because of a presumption that people from these racial minorities will be unsuited to certain roles (because their lack of progress is blamed on racial characteristics) or because of a failure to recognise the adverse impact of policies on communities whose history and circumstances are different to those in the mainstream. In short, the Constitution and US political system that are credited with having created opportunity for the majority of Americans are also responsible for the lack of progress of these three racial minorities. Moreover, having fostered advancement for those in the mainstream while hindering advancement of racial groups actively excluded from the mainstream, US political processes are responsible for the consequent racial inequality.

These two versions of normality, and how the political system contributed to them, are the focus of the claim that the Constitution is deeply flawed – having always fallen far short of its aims to translate universal values into political reality for all – and that US society will be blighted by racial division and conflict until the consequences of these flaws are effectively addressed.

This chapter considers this perspective on the Constitution by adopting the format of a court case:

- First, it presents 'the case for the prosecution', that deep racial inequality is a major feature of US society, and outlines the causes of this inequality as seen from the perspective of those who blame the US political system for having created it.
- Second, it presents the prosecution's case for addressing racial inequality, **Affirmative Action**, together with an account of how this remedy has operated in practice.
- Third, it presents the argument that, in the face of continuing racial inequality as well as continuing racism, Affirmative Action programmes are still needed and that there may be a case for going further and paying **reparations** to those affected by centuries of systematic discrimination.

- Fourth, it presents 'the case for the defence', which argues that inequalities between groups may owe more to the characteristics of the groups than the political system which, if true, would make Affirmative Action unnecessary, unfair and possibly counter-productive. It also argues that even if one were to accept that there have been flaws in the political system in the past, they have now been dealt with and there is no longer any need for programmes to correct these faults.
- Finally, having summarised the challenges made by each side of the key points, this chapter invites you, the reader, to act as the jury – detaching yourself as far as possible from these highly emotive issues – to reach a conclusion as to which case is the more persuasive.

## The extent of racial inequality in the twenty-first century

There are about 4.5 million Native Americans, including those of mixed race. This makes up around 1.5 per cent of the population of the USA. The Native American population is split between cities and federal reservations. The reservations possess the right to form their own government, to enforce laws (both civil and criminal), to tax, to establish requirements for membership, to license and regulate activities, to zone and to exclude persons from tribal territories.

Native Americans living away from the reservations are spread across the country but large clusters can be found in Alaska, New York City, Los Angeles and San Diego. With most other Americans only rarely encountering Native Americans, their circumstances have not tended to be the focus of national politics or widespread public concern. This is despite the fact that the indicators of well-being indicate a wide gulf between Native Americans and white Americans. Although urban Native Americans are less impoverished than those living on reservations, there is a general pattern of:

- High unemployment
- Elevated high-school drop-out rates
- Suicide
- Alcoholism

- Poor health
- High crime rates

Specific statistics mirror those of African Americans, set out below.

African Americans comprise around 13 per cent of the population of the USA, living mainly in and around large cities or the countryside of Southern states. With a large proportion of the rest of the American population either encountering, or taking deliberate steps to avoid encountering, black Americans, their circumstances have been the focus of political and public attention to a far greater extent than those of Native Americans. Many have enjoyed great success and prominence, becoming role models for all Americans:

- African Americans have made substantial contributions to literature, from Richard Wright to James Baldwin, Alice Walker, Toni Morrison and Alex Hailey, whose novel *Roots* opened the eyes of many people to the African American experience when it was turned into a TV mini-series.
- In the field of entertainment, Will Smith, Denzel Washington, Morgan Freeman and Halle Berry have been some of the most successful Hollywood actors, while Oprah Winfrey's talk show has proved hugely influential, as illustrated by the Book Club she started in 1996 to encourage more people to read and which led to the sales of featured novels increasing by as much as a million copies.
- In the field of sports, African Americans have become not only stars but the symbol of their particular sport, such as Michael Jordan. Famously, according to an advertisement that appeared to strike a chord with the American people, everyone wanted to 'be like Mike'.
- In the field of politics, both the Secretaries of State during the administration of President George W. Bush (Colin Powell and Condoleezza Rice) were African American and, of course, Barack Obama was elected President of the USA in 2008.

Outside the world of the arts, sports and politics, evidence of African American success is more patchy. For example, only seven African Americans have risen to lead one of the 500 largest American companies. And, more representative of the broader African American population, statistics indicate that there continues to be a gulf between black and white Americans. The statistics in Table 3.1 (below), published in the summer of 2008, were compiled by one of the world's largest data analysis companies for an American **Civil Rights** organisation, the National Urban League. (The accompanying comments, in the *Explanation* column, were added by the author.) They may be seen as telling the story of:

- The contrast between white Americans, who have been able to take advantage of opportunities to build up wealth over many generations, and African Americans, who have not had similar opportunities.
- The advantages that white Americans continue to enjoy, on average, in terms of income and educational opportunities (which is often the basis of getting a well-paid job).
- The impact, in terms of quality of life, of economic disadvantage.

Words and figures do not, by themselves, adequately convey the practical realities for those who live in communities affected by the statistical indicators in the table, and their uneven impact.

A significant proportion of the African American community has seen substantial, sometimes dramatic, progress in the past half-century (although it has often been insecure progress, not backed by inherited wealth or assets to provide a cushion in times of trouble). However, for those left behind, deprivation is far more intense than the statistics suggest and for people growing up in poor, overwhelmingly black, districts life is often shaped by the severely limited range of opportunities:

- The quality of services, especially education, in majority-black districts is often extremely poor, leading to low levels of literacy and numeracy and high drop-out rates from school – thereby making many young people effectively unemployable.
- Even for those who acquire basic qualifications, finding a job may be difficult because of employers being unwilling to take a chance on applicants with zipcodes from the rougher areas.
- With few well-paid legitimate jobs, the local role models for 'success' may be those demonstrating the determination and

resourcefulness to become leaders in illegal activities such as the drug trade.

- Under the pressures to find a way to cope with the demands of a consumerist society, when there are so few opportunities, the likelihood of succumbing to some form of addiction, either drugs or alcohol, is high. This, in turn, raises the likelihood of acquiring a criminal record and a further reduction of opportunity.
- The same pressures reduce the likelihood of stable relationships and boost the number of single-parent households.
- Thus, the next generation is born into a cycle of deprivation from which escape is unlikely.

The highly acclaimed television series *The Wire* won praise for successfully depicting life in a black ghetto and the ways in which everyone, regardless of their personal qualities and abilities, had their futures largely determined by the conditions in which they lived. (Warning: the series contains graphic violence and sex, and almost incessant swearing.)

### Table 3.1  Gulf between black and white Americans

|  | Black Americans | White Americans | Explanation |
|---|---|---|---|
| **Economic Indicators:** |  |  |  |
| Home ownership | 47.9% | 75.8% | *Property is a key asset that can be used as collateral, eliminates a major cost when the mortgage is paid off and can be passed on to later generations, providing them with a foundation that they can build on.* |

## Table 3.1  (continued)

| | Black Americans | White Americans | Explanation |
|---|---|---|---|
| Average value of homes | $80,600 | $123,400 | *While three-quarters of white Americans enjoy this form of wealth, just under half of African Americans own their homes, and their average value is over $40,000 less than the average.* |
| 'Sub-prime' mortgages | 53.4% | 17.5% | *The rate of interest being paid by black homeowners is much higher than that paid by their white counterparts. Sub-prime mortgages charge at least 3 per cent above the standard rate. Also, this is the category of homeowner most likely to lose their homes to repossession.* |
| Unemployment | 8.3% | 4.1% | *Black unemployment runs at roughly twice the rate of white unemployment and in the past the gap has tended to widen during economic downturns.* |
| Car ownership | 70.2% | 89.2% | *For many Americans, a car is a necessity. Getting to work by public transport may not be a practical option. Thus car ownership may be linked to employment rates.* |

| Table 3.1 (continued) | | |
|---|---|---|
| | **Black Americans** | **White Americans** | **Explanation** |
| Living in poverty | 31% | 11% | *A third of all African Americans live in poverty, compared to about a tenth of white Americans (although, because whites make up a much larger share of the total population, the total number of whites living in poverty is higher than the number of blacks).* |
| Average annual household income | $31,969 | $52,423 | *Overall, the categories above show African Americans tend to have less inherited wealth, fewer assets and higher average costs. This category indicates that any attempt to bridge these gaps has to be done with a lower average income.* |
| **Education:** | | | |
| Expenditure per student in areas with high levels of poverty | $5,937 | $7,244 | *This category is significant as students in these districts do not have the option of leaving the state-funded sector and attending private schools.* |
| Household with a computer (and access to broadband) | 46% (37%) | 66% (45%) | *Clearly, access to the more educational sites on the internet increases the likelihood of educational success.* |

## Table 3.1  (continued)

| | Black Americans | White Americans | Explanation |
|---|---|---|---|
| Percentage of the community with university degrees | 19% | 28% | *Poorer schools and facilities tend to lead to fewer people reaching, and being properly prepared for, university.* |
| **Health and Life Expectancy:** | | | |
| Percentage of the community who are overweight or obese | 71.8% | 61% | *There is a well-established link between wealth and weight. Poorer people tend to eat less healthy food. Given the economic indicators above, it is not surprising that a higher proportion of black Americans are overweight than white Americans.* |
| Deaths from diabetes (per 100,000 of the population) | 48 | 21.5 | *This statistic is the consequence of a variety of factors coming together. People with African or South Asian heritage are genetically more disposed to diabetes. However, this is compounded by being overweight, lack of education and lack of access to healthcare.* |
| Healthcare insurance | 39.5% | 59.4% | *Without healthcare insurance, it is highly unlikely that any preventative medical advice or care will be* |

| Table 3.1 (continued) | | |
| --- | --- | --- |
| **Black Americans** | **White Americans** | **Explanation** |
| | | provided, treatment for medical conditions may be inadequate and any economic gains may be swiftly wiped out by medical bills. |
| Life expectancy | 73.1 years | 78.3 years | |

## Racial inequality: the 'back-story'

Critics of the US political system argue that racial inequality (outlined above) can be attributed to deliberate, sustained political policies. This section explains why they have reached this conclusion.

### Slavery

When the Founding Fathers permitted slavery to continue after the adoption of the Constitution, they were authorising a system that had far-reaching implications for the way that society is organised. In order to force an entire section of the population to undertake gruelling labour with miserable living conditions and no prospect of ever improving their circumstances, it was essential that those people were seen as being unworthy of anything better. Especially in a society that proclaims that all people have a God-given right to liberty, this means denying the humanity of those enslaved and actively working to convince everyone in that society (including the slaves) that they are less than fully human. This message was conveyed in both words and treatment:

- The language used to describe slaves mirrored that used for animals: men were 'bucks' that had to be 'broken' to be productive.
- Slaves were denied any sense of having come from a civilisation with its own culture and identity – not being allowed to use African languages, religious practices, music or even their own African names.

- They were denied families, a nurturing, bonding environment: slaveowners chose which of their slaves should 'breed' together to produce the biggest, strongest field hands.
- They were denied an education: it was illegal for slaves to be taught to read and write, giving them access to ideas beyond those their owners thought suitable for them.
- Slaveowners and overseers regularly used female slaves for their own sexual pleasure, making rape a routine part of slavery. Again, the message sent to all slaves was that their inevitable destiny was to do whatever their owner needed them to do. (The mixed-race children who resulted also became slaves.)

While these measures were intended to make black people accepting of their situation, there were also brutal punishments for anyone who did not, including:

- Slaves who demonstrated any signs of independence of mind (expressions or tone of voice), or who did not work hard enough would be severely punished in front of other slaves to teach all the consequences of such behaviour.
- Attempted escape received greater punishment, including amputation of a foot, castration or death, depending on the number of escape attempts.

Thus, in the 'land of the free', one of the key roles of all of the institutions that shape society, whether it be law enforcement, education services or the church, was to actively deny liberty and opportunity to people on the basis of their race and, in doing so, to deprive them of the skills and support systems that they would need if they should attain freedom.

### Reconstruction

For a period of time, after the Civil War and the abolition of slavery, it appeared as if the Federal government would actively work to provide African Americans with the skills and resources needed to be able to make the most of the opportunities offered by society – thus creating the conditions for genuine equality of opportunity across all races. In the period from 1865 to 1877, known as the **Reconstruction**, the following steps were taken:

- The abolition of slavery was incorporated into the Constitution, in the 13th Amendment.
- The 14th Amendment was passed, intended to extend the protections of the Bill of Rights to black Americans.
- The 15th Amendment was passed, intended to guarantee the right to vote to black Americans.
- The Southern states were kept under military occupation for twelve years after the end of the Civil War and, during that time, new voter registration lists were compiled that included black citizens and excluded many whites who had fought in the Confederate army. As a result, African Americans were able to win elective office at local level (as sheriffs, judges and city councillors) as well as at national level, as members of the House of Representatives and the Senate.
- The **Freedmen's Bureau** was set up by the Federal government in 1865, and funded schools for ex-slaves in the South as well as helping to set up a number of black universities.
- In 1865, General Sherman of the Union army issued **Special Field Order No. 15** that provided freed slaves with forty acres of land and a mule with which to farm it.

However, these limited, and short-lived, efforts to provide a viable economic and legal basis for meaningful freedom for the former slaves were undermined by a series of decisions taken by each of the three branches of the Federal government.

- Congress closed down the Freedmen's Bureau in 1872, after just seven years, and passed control of education to the authorities of the Southern states still crippled by the war.
- President Andrew Johnson (who had taken over after the assassination of President Lincoln) reversed Special Field Order No. 15 and took away the land that had been given to freed slaves.
- The President and Congress withdrew Union troops from the South in 1877, opening the door to white Southerners regaining full political control of the region.
- The Supreme Court made a series of rulings that effectively made the 14th Amendment meaningless:
  - In the *Slaughterhouse Cases* (1873), it was ruled that the 14th Amendment only applied to laws and actions of the Federal government, not state governments.

- In the *Civil Rights Cases* (1883), it was ruled that a Civil Rights law, extending the 14th Amendment to the state governments, was unconstitutional.
- In *Plessy v. Ferguson* (1896), it was ruled that separate facilities were constitutional provided that they did not infringe the equality clause of the constitution (ignoring the self-evident reality that separate facilities were intended to reinforce unequal treatment of races).

The combined effect of these political measures was summed up by a black leader of the time, Frederick Douglass, who wrote, 'When the Russian serfs had their chains broken and given their liberty, the government of Russia gave to those poor emancipated serfs a few acres of land on which they could live and earn their bread. But when you turned us loose, you turned us loose to the sky, to the storm, to the whirlwind, and worst of all, you turned us loose to our infuriated masters.' Thus, although **emancipated** from slavery, once the Federal government effectively washed its hands of the South, the local authorities established economic, political and social systems that ensured that African Americans would continue to be denied the kind of freedoms and opportunities enjoyed by white Americans.

### 'Jim Crow'

Once white control of the South, where most African Americans lived, had been fully regained, the pattern of political and social institutions actively working to deny the 'blessings of liberty' to people on the basis of race was re-established.

In the post-slavery era, the system for asserting white supremacy became known as **Jim Crow**. It consisted of economic, political and social measures to restrict black opportunity and freedom.

In economic terms, slavery was replaced by sharecropping. After the decision not to provide former slaves with land and equipment, the majority of them had no choice but to work on the same plantations on which they had been held as slaves, farming on white-owned land which they leased and paid for by turning over a proportion of their harvest equal to the value of their annual rent. They had to buy their seed and equipment from the landowner, at prices set by that landowner, and the calculation of how much their harvest was worth (and therefore how much had to be turned over) was also made by the landowner. With prices being set, and calculations made, by the landowner, African Americans, who had been denied an education as slaves, were often in no position to challenge decisions even if they strongly suspected that they were being cheated. Unsurprisingly, under these circumstances, it was rare for a sharecropper to make a profit and be able to improve their own, or their family's, circumstances. Moreover, any black families that managed, despite this system, to build up the resources to buy land frequently encountered a practice known as **whitecapping** – being terrorised until they sold up and moved away because they were living demonstrations of black achievement and potential inspiration for other African Americans.

These barriers to economic advancement were complemented by the political and judicial system that the South was allowed to construct, designed to make African Americans second-class citizens. Any facility which offered an opportunity for the races to mingle was strictly segregated by law, from schools, hospitals and libraries to public transport, restaurants, hotels and swimming pools. The law-makers of the South were particularly concerned about inter-racial intimacy, with dating, sex and marriage between the races made illegal. African Americans were not allowed to serve on juries, meaning that any challenge to a white landowner or someone involved in whitecapping would be judged by an all-white jury and highly unlikely to succeed. Schools and hospitals were segregated, resulting in vastly inferior provision of these vital services for African Americans. For example, by the 1930s, the medical provision offered was:

- In the South, for whites, one doctor per 1,200 people in the states with the best services (Virginia and Louisiana) down to one doctor per 1,800 people in the state with the worst services (Mississippi).
- In the South, for black residents, the best medical provision was in Georgia with one doctor per 7,100 people and Louisiana with one doctor per 8,600 people, while in the worst state, Mississippi, there was only one doctor for every 18,000 African Americans.

And, to ensure that African Americans could not use political strategies to change these laws and improve their opportunities in life, they were denied the vote. Despite the passage of the 15th Amendment, which protected the right to vote for people of all races, the Supreme Court refused to do anything about voting qualifications that had the effect of excluding mainly African Americans. Typically, these did not mention race (such as literacy tests and property qualifications) but, as a result of the deprivations of both slavery and segregation, they made it impossible for most black citizens to register to vote.

The economic and political features of Jim Crow were reinforced by a brutally enforced social code that served as a daily reminder, whenever there was contact between people from the black and white communities, of the message of white supremacy. The following three examples serve to illustrate the vast array of ways in which African Americans were routinely belittled and humiliated:

• African American men were invariably called 'boy', regardless of age and social standing.
• If two people, one white and one black, could not pass each other on the pavement without the risk of bumping into each other, the black pedestrian had to step into the road to allow the other to pass.
• Whenever black people went to buy a hat (worn, until recent times, at all formal occasions) they had to line the inside with tissues before trying it on.

Any African American campaigning against these restrictions on their rights, or in any other way challenging the established order, risked being lynched. A range of white supremacy organisations emerged after the Civil War, the most famous being the Ku Klux Klan, to ensure that black people were kept 'in their place'. These organisations used **lynching** as a public demonstration that white people (including 'respectable' members of the community) all considered the use of extreme violence acceptable against any black person who defied strict racial separation. They all knew that there was virtually no risk of arrest or punishment – meaning that African Americans were denied the protection of the law. People would even pose for pictures in front of their victims.

The effectiveness of lynching as an instrument of terror was such that the mere threat of a possible lynching – a burning cross – could intimidate an entire black community for weeks. And periodically, the scale of attacks escalated and entire black districts were destroyed, such as the 1921 burning of the Greenwood Section of Tulsa, in Oklahoma, when dozens of businesses were destroyed.

The logical response to Jim Crow was to leave the South and move to the Northern or Western states. When there was demand for labour, such as when car plants were being established in the Detroit area, African Americans took full advantage of the opportunity to escape the restrictions and improve their circumstances. At other times, however, fearing such an influx, many Northern states required a cash security-bond before an African American was allowed to become a resident – with the rate set at a level that few would be able to afford. Also, while less visible than in the South, discrimination was a problem in the North in a variety of ways:

- Accommodation was almost impossible to obtain outside established black areas, such as Harlem.
- Wage rates were lower for black workers than whites doing the same job and access to skilled work was denied by both employers and trade unions.
- African Americans were barred from jury service in many large cities.

In sum, in the South, segregation reinforced existing disadvantages and reinforced the message of the slave era that being black meant being racially inferior. Meanwhile, the rest of the country either turned a blind eye to lack of freedom and opportunity or, in subtler ways, contributed to the relegation of African Americans to second-class status.

### Race-laden legislation

Even some of the government initiatives of the mid-twentieth century that are associated with improving the circumstances of poor and marginalised Americans served to widen the racial gap because of the way in which they were implemented.

In contrast to the openly racial character of legislation passed by state and local authorities in the South, these Federal initiatives made no explicit reference to race but nonetheless served to divide people along racial lines – a tactic known as **race-laden legislation**.

*The New Deal:* In the 1930s, as the USA was going through the Great Depression, the Federal government introduced the New

## Box 3.1 Congressional seniority

The legislative process is covered in detail in Chapter 8. For the purposes of this chapter, it is sufficient to know that, for the legislation to pass through Congress, it has to gain the support of the chairmen of key committees. Committee chairmanships have traditionally been determined by **seniority** – the person on the committee who has served the longest – and for much of the twentieth century the majority of chairmen were Southerners. This was because after the Civil War, white Southerners refused to vote Republican, the party of Abraham Lincoln who had inflicted the military defeat on them (a situation that only began to change in the 1970s) and, with most African Americans being unable to vote, this meant that the South was effectively a one-party state. Thus, Southerners who won Congressional seats generally kept them for as long as they wished. This, in turn, meant that they gained seniority and therefore dominated committee chairmanships which gave them the power to block legislation that they opposed.

Deal, to reduce unemployment and poverty. However, Southern representatives in Congress were in a position to block the passage of the New Deal legislation (see box) and they demanded the inclusion of clauses that would have the effect of excluding African Americans from the New Deal's provisions.

As a condition for passing the New Deal legislation, Southern members of Congress insisted on a clause that excluded farm workers and domestic workers from Federal help. The effect of this clause was that over 65 per cent of all African Americans fell outside the provisions of the New Deal 'safety net' to protect the most vulnerable in society from destitution and, in the South, where most African Americans lived, over 80 per cent were affected by this clause. Later, these exclusions were extended to include 'any practice incident to farming', meaning anyone who had made a living from preparing, packing, storing or transporting farm produce. This meant that virtually everyone in segregated black rural communities who had lost their livelihood because of the recession was barred from receiving state aid.

In addition, the legislation gave responsibility for distributing

## Box 3.2 Ethnic Europeans

Jews and European Catholics, mainly from Ireland, Italy and Poland, had arrived in large numbers in the nineteenth century and had tended to live in their own communities engaged in a limited number of manual trades. They faced considerable hostility and discrimination, finding it difficult to find work, gain promotion or mix socially with white Anglo-Saxon Protestants. In these ways, their opportunities were limited for many decades although, with the power of the vote, they were able to protect their interest through the political process, with the Irish in particular establishing a strong presence in public services such as the police and fire services. The war provided an opportunity for them to more fully integrate with other white Americans as equals, breaking down stereotypes and weakening barriers, and to benefit from training opportunities provided by the armed services. Then, after the war, they were able to take advantage of government help for ex-soldiers that enabled many of them to move out of their ethnic enclaves and integrate into mainstream America.

funds, made available under the New Deal, to state and local officials. They had the power to provide aid to very poor families with children. This power was used in many Southern states to help white families affected by the exclusion of farm workers and domestics from other forms of state aid.

*The Second World War:* Although the USA was fighting two countries that based their policies on the principle of racial superiority, the American armed forces maintained rigid racial segregation – with black units under the leadership of white officers. The war required far more people to develop new skills than had previously been the case, thus opening the door to new opportunities. This was especially beneficial to some ethnic communities who had previously lived on the fringes of the American mainstream (see box).

However, a very limited number of African Americans benefited from these opportunities because:

• Very poor educational facilities in the South meant that a high proportion of African American men failed to qualify for any kind of military service.

- In a segregated military, if there were no suitable facilities to provide accommodation and meals on a segregated basis, black soldiers were not allowed to join training courses.

*The GI Bill:* In the 1950s, the Federal government introduced a massive programme to help those who had served in the armed services to build a new post-war future. Known as the GI Bill, it provided funds for ex-soldiers to:

- Go to university
- Attend training courses to develop new skills
- Start new business ventures
- Buy homes

The GI Bill is credited with opening the door to new opportunities for millions of Americans, providing them with a chance to get an education and a firm foundation for their family lives. However, because of the number of African Americans who had not qualified for military service in the Second World War, a lower proportion of African Americans were eligible for the GI Bill than their white counterparts. Moreover, because university education was racially segregated across the USA, not only in the South, any black veteran wanting to take advantage of a Federally funded degree course had to do so in a black college. These had a limited number of places. For example, in Mississippi, more than half of the state's population was black, but just seven of its thirty-five higher education institutions were black. Therefore, many black veterans failed to take up the educational opportunities to which they were entitled (over 20,000 refused places in 1947 alone, with up to 50,000 not applying because of the shortage of places).

Similarly, any black veteran wanting to take up a job-training place encountered obstacles not faced by white veterans. An employer had to commit to taking on an applicant before he could enrol in the training course. Unsurprisingly, in the South, where most African Americans lived, white employers refused to make such offers and there were far fewer black-owned businesses to take on new trainees. In the first two years of this programme, across the South, 102,000 veterans participated in the training programme, of whom just 7,700 were black.

The GI Bill also helped veterans find jobs. In the South, local agencies administering the programme placed white veterans in 86 per cent of the skilled or semi-skilled positions available, while African Americans were placed in 92 per cent of less well-paid unskilled jobs.

Most significant was the lack of opportunity for African Americans to access the loans available under the GI Bill. A mortgage for a home represents:

- An asset that is likely to increase in value over time
- Wealth that can be passed on to the next generation
- A financial cushion in difficult economic times

A business loan represents (potential) financial independence that, for African Americans, could mean a certain level of insulation from racial discrimination. However, the Federal government did not make direct loans to veterans. Instead, it provided guarantees for loans made to veterans by local banks. Across the USA, in the post-war period, banks routinely practised **redlining**, refusing mortgages to African Americans attempting to buy property in white areas. Black veterans were denied loans for new businesses on the ground that they were 'high risk' – even though a loan secured (i.e. guaranteed) by the government represents no risk to the bank.

As usual, the most extreme examples of this practice were found in the South. In 1947, of the 3,229 secured business loans in Mississippi, precisely 2 went to African Americans. However, the experience in New York City and its surrounding areas, including Northern New Jersey, demonstrates the widespread nature of these practices. Of the 67,000 secured mortgages issued in this region, fewer than 100 went to non-white families.

### The Civil Rights movement and 'Massive Resistance'

The Federal government's first clear, demonstrable commitment to the cause of racial equality since Reconstruction came in 1948 when President Truman signed an Executive Order declaring that it was 'the policy of the President that there should be equality of treatment and opportunity for all persons in the armed services without regard to race, color, religion or national origin'. Then, in 1954, in the case of *Brown* v. *Board of Education*, the Supreme Court ruled that 'separate but equal' educational facilities were 'inherently unequal', stripping away the constitutional justification for segregation (although the Court broke with tradition by ordering not the immediate enforcement of the rights it had pronounced but that non-discriminatory admissions to schools should be achieved 'with all deliberate speed' – suggesting that it could be done quite slowly, which the Southern states took as a signal that they could delay racial integration, possibly indefinitely). The ambivalence of the Court, together with President Eisenhower's well-known reluctance to enforce the *Brown* decision, further emboldened the die-hard segregationists who used any tactic, legal or illegal, to resist the dismantling of Jim Crow. It thus took eleven years of campaigning to highlight the denial of constitutional rights, before the Federal government acted decisively to bring an end to segregation (see box).

In 1964, the administration of President Johnson pushed the Civil Rights Act through Congress. This was not the first legislation to ban racial discrimination but, crucially, it was the first to use the power of the Federal government to enforce the law. Under the Act, the Department of Justice could initiate legal action against a state, city or town to ensure equal treatment or, alternatively, the government could withhold Federal funds on which many communities depended. In the face of these threats, Southern leaders began to end segregation without local campaigns being necessary.

The following year, in 1965, the Voting Rights Act was passed. To guarantee the right to vote, this law did the following:

- It abolished the devices used to deny the vote to African Americans such as literacy tests.
- It required states to get clearance from the Federal government before they introduced any new electoral regulations to make sure that new devices did not replace the old ones.
- Finally, it gave the Department of Justice the power to send Federal voter registrars to any area to ensure that no one was being denied the right to register for the vote.

Thus, as summarised in Table 3.2, a dominant feature of US history has been for political choices to be made that have served to create, then widen, a gulf between African Americans and the rest of society as well as resist efforts (both after the Civil War and during the Civil Rights campaign) to create a legal basis for equal citizenship.

## Box 3.3 The Civil Rights movement

What has become known as the Civil Rights movement was a series of separate campaigns, following the *Brown* decision, to bring public attention to the South's defiance of the Supreme Court's ruling that racial segregation was unconstitutional and highlight the failure of the presidency to enforce the Constitution. Its most famous campaigns included:

- The Montgomery Bus Boycott in 1955, sparked by the refusal of Rosa Parks to give up her seat in the black section of the bus. Led by Martin Luther King, the boycott took over a year to force the bus company to end segregation.
- The desegregation of Little Rock High School (Arkansas) in 1957. It took troops to get nine students into the school and protect them while they studied.
- Sit-ins. The campaign, led by African American students, to be served at lunch counters in stores in the South in 1960.
- Freedom Rides. In 1961, campaigners for the integration of interstate buses were met with extreme violence but succeeded in forcing the Federal government to order desegregation.
- In 1963, Martin Luther King delivered his famous 'I have a dream' speech to the March on Washington for Jobs and Freedom. It is not always remembered that by this stage of the Civil Rights movement, the campaign was widening its focus from winning rights to the practical means to make the most of those rights and that Dr King was actively involved in this, more radical, phase of the campaign.
- The campaign for African Americans to be allowed to register to vote in Selma, Alabama, in which campaigners were attacked by police in 1965.

The end of legalised segregation, however, did not do anything to address the racial inequality that had been established by slavery, widened by the segregation laws and widened still further by Federal legislation during the New Deal, the Second World War and the GI Bill. With politicians at local and Federal level having responsibility for creating this situation, all permitted by a Constitution that proclaims that it stands for liberty and opportunity, what responsibility did those same political institutions have for redressing racial inequality?

| Table 3.2 Timeline of slavery and segregation | |
| --- | --- |
| **Dates** | **Main Historical Features** |
| 1789–1865 | Slavery already existed when the Constitution was written. By allowing it to continue, the Founding Fathers legitimised practices that promoted racial inequality. |
| 1865–77 | Reconstruction. Over a period of twelve years, following the emancipation of slaves, the Federal government introduced a series of measures to ensure that African Americans would be able to make the most of their freedom. |
| 1877–1965 | Jim Crow. All branches of the Federal government allowed the reassertion of white supremacy in the South, with racial segregations enforced by law – wiping out the gains of the Reconstruction and, by restricting black opportunity while other communities were able to advance, widening racial inequalities. |
| 1933 to the 1950s | The New Deal/The Second World War/The GI Bill. In addition to the continuing practice of legalised racial segregation, Federal programmes to help all Americans were implemented in ways that had contrasting effects on different races, thus serving to reinforce Jim Crow and further widen racial inequality. |
| 1954–65 | The Civil Rights movement. The process, requiring eleven years of campaigning in the face of violent resistance, led to the end of legalised segregation. |

The next section examines the view that the USA cannot meaningfully claim to stand for liberty and opportunity unless, and until, it has addressed racial inequality.

## The rise of Affirmative Action

The speech by President Lyndon Johnson that launched the set of programmes that are collectively known as Affirmative Action

## Box 3.4  Justification for Affirmative Action

In June 1965, the President delivered a speech to the students of Howard University (one of the black universities set up during Reconstruction) in Washington DC, entitled 'To fulfil these rights'. Earlier that month, the Voting Rights Act had been passed which, together with the Civil Rights Act a year earlier, effectively ended all remaining forms of legalised racial discrimination. Quoting Winston Churchill, he said that the dismantling of legal barriers for black people 'is not the end. It is not even the beginning of the end. But it is, perhaps, the end of the beginning.' He asserted that it would take much more for African Americans to 'be treated in every part of our national life as a person equal in dignity and promise to all others'. Achieving this goal was 'the next and the more profound stage of the battle for civil rights'.

His speech laid out the challenges still to be faced, with some policy proposals for overcoming them. The President acknowledged that some African Americans, even in the 1960s, had made significant progress. However, for the majority, 'the poor, the unemployed, the uprooted and the dispossessed – there is a much grimmer story . . . They are still, as we meet here tonight, another nation.' This, he pointed out, was because African American poverty had a particular character, stemming from 'the devastating heritage of long years of slavery; and a century of oppression, hatred and injustice'. In that sense, black poverty 'is not white poverty. Many of its causes and many of its cures are the same. But there are differences – deep, corrosive, obstinate differences – radiating painful roots in the community, the family, and the nature of the individual.' He made a point of emphasising that this distinction between African Americans and their white counterparts applied to those ethnic groups, principally the Irish, Italian and Jewish communities that had faced considerable prejudice and lived in poverty for many years. Even these groups 'did not have the heritage of centuries to overcome, and they did not have a cultural tradition which had been twisted and battered by endless years of hatred, nor were they excluded because of race or color – a feeling whose dark intensity is matched by no other prejudice'.

Against this background, he insisted that 'freedom [from discriminatory laws] is not enough. You do not wipe away the scars of centuries by saying: Now you are free to go where you want, and do as you desire, and choose the leaders you please. You do not take a person who, for years, has been hobbled by chains and liberate him, bring him to the starting line of a race and then say, "You are free to compete with all the others," and still justly believe that you have been completely fair. Fairness, President Johnson argued, required that the government introduce a range of policies that would help African Americans make up for the racial inequalities that were the result of laws and policies that had been sanctioned under the Constitution over the previous two centuries. He did not claim to have all the answers to the issues he had raised, but promised to 'dedicate the expanding efforts of the Johnson administration' to promoting genuinely equal citizenship.

remains one of the best explanations of the thinking behind the policy.

During President Johnson's presidency, the following Affirmative Action policies were introduced:

*   *Education* In 1966, the Department for Housing, Education and Welfare (HEW) tightened the regulations for integrating schools, which in many areas remained segregated despite the Supreme Court's *Brown* v. *Board* ruling of 1955. Also, using powers given to it by the 1964 Civil Rights Act, HEW threatened to withhold funds from school districts that had failed to desegregate.
*   *Housing* The Housing and Urban Development Act was passed in 1968, providing both funds for increased construction of public housing and subsidies for the private construction of homes for low-income and middle-income families in cities. Also, the Fair Housing Act was passed in 1968, which prohibited racial discrimination in the sale or rental of housing and required the Department of Housing and Urban Development (HUD) 'affirmatively to further the purposes' of fair housing.

President Johnson's successor, Richard Nixon, had a complicated relationship with Affirmative Action (see box). Although he was a Republican, whose victory in the 1968 presidential election owed much to white resentment at policies directed at improving circumstances for African Americans, some of the most far-reaching affirmative policies were introduced by his administration.

The Equal Employment Opportunity Commission (EEOC), a government agency, wanted the power to be able to force a change in hiring practices, through the courts if necessary, if an industry demonstrated a clear pattern of racial discrimination. In 1969, President Nixon agreed and the **Philadelphia Plan** was launched. This enabled the EEOC to monitor all contractors doing business with the Federal government and, if there was clear evidence of discriminatory employment practices, require them to establish 'goals and timetables' for the hiring of minorities and to draw up plans to demonstrate that they were taking active steps to meet their targets. The policy began with the construction industry in the racially mixed Philadelphia area, which was dominated by whites-only unions, and led to the employment of more African Americans. The plan has been seen by many as the single greatest development of Affirmative Action, as it not only directly improved job prospects for African Americans in the construction industry but led to improved black employment prospects in other businesses that introduced Affirmative Action plans, using the 'Philadelphia' model, to avoid similar pressure from the government.

In the 1970s, Affirmative Action also developed as a result of decisions taken by the Supreme Court. School desegregation was making only slow progress in some parts of the country. In the case of *Swann* v. *Charlotte-Mecklenburg* (1971) the Supreme Court not only demanded a rapid end to segregated schooling but specified the means of achieving it – the bussing of white and black children to each other's schools. In 1974, another Federal judge, Arthur Garrity, ordered the same remedy for the schools of Boston, Massachusetts.

In 1976, the Supreme Court ruled in *Beer* v. *United States* that any plan to redraw district boundaries should not leave ethnic minorities worse off in terms of political representation. In response, some states created race-conscious districts in which voters of the same race were grouped together.

In summary, the 1960s and early 1970s saw concerted efforts from all three branches of the Federal government to improve the circumstances of African Americans in relation to:

- Education
- Housing
- Employment
- Political Representation

## Box 3.5  President Nixon and Affirmative Action

Richard Nixon had a complex, and often contradictory, record on race. In the 1950s he was a member of the Civil Rights organisation, the NAACP, had proposed the first Civil Rights bill for over eighty years and generally enjoyed good relations with African American leaders. Yet, as an ambitious right-wing politician wary of alienating conservative voters, his public statements appeared unsympathetic to racial minorities. Thus, when Nixon ran unsuccessfully for the presidency in 1960 he was silent when Martin Luther King was arrested during a Civil Rights demonstration and his campaign made less of an effort to court black voters than the Kennedy campaign.

The same mixture of personal commitment to Civil Rights and political strategies to attract right-wing voters was evident during his presidency. The 1968 presidential election result was heavily influenced by the **white backlash** against policies seen to benefit racial minorities. Richard Nixon's victory owed much to disgruntled white voters defecting from the Democratic Party. In addition, Governor Wallace of Alabama, a staunch defender of white supremacy, had run as an independent and won 13.5 per cent of the national vote, capturing the electoral college votes of the states of Alabama, Arkansas, Georgia, Louisiana and Mississippi. As President, Richard Nixon saw the potential for the Republican Party to make further electoral gains in the future by attracting Wallace's supporters. To this end, he implemented his **Southern strategy**, taking every opportunity to be seen to be on the side of white Southerners who saw themselves as the victims of 'regional discrimination'. He nominated two Southern judges with records of opposition to racial integration to the Supreme Court, both of whom were rejected by the Senate; his administration opposed the extension of the Voting Rights Act and it supported the State of Mississippi's reluctance to desegregate its schools.

Yet, at the same time, Nixon was committed to 'giving those who haven't had their chance, who've had it denied for a hundred years, that little extra start that they need so that it is in truth an equal chance'. It was this thinking that led to the Philadelphia Plan, opening new work opportunities for racial minorities. His administration also established the Office of Minority Business Enterprise, which was intended to promote what Nixon described as 'black capitalism', and he also proposed the 'Family Assistance Plan' (rejected by Congress) that would have established a minimum annual income for the poor.

As *Time* magazine put it, on race the Nixon administration seemed 'to be suffering from a mild case of schizophrenia'.

## Limitations on Affirmative Action

As indicated above, there was almost instant reaction against Affirmative Action when it was introduced in the mid-1960s. Just three years after President Johnson made his speech outlining the purpose and justification for Affirmative Action, the Republican Party won the presidency on a campaign that owed much to opposition to the policy.

Then, in the early 1970s, other groups that had long felt marginalised began campaigning for Affirmative Action to be extended to them:

- In 1970, the women's rights movement adopted new tactics – a direct action campaign, the Women's Strike for Equality, was combined with lawsuits against 350 universities for sex discrimination with, in 1971, pressure on Congress to pass an Equal Rights Amendment to the Constitution.
- Hispanic Americans began a national campaign for equality in 1971.
- Also in 1971, a gay-rights campaign was launched.

For many Americans, Affirmative Action became associated with ever-escalating demands on government for special treatment at the expense of 'ordinary' hard-working people. On their televisions, they saw anger and resentment against Affirmative Action erupt in Boston in 1975 when court-ordered bussing in Boston, to ensure the integration of schools, was met with violent resistance. Buses taking black students to schools in white areas were stoned, leading to them being escorted by police. Black people who strayed into white areas were attacked.

Some of the most highly respected newspapers and magazines in the USA carried articles that questioned the validity, and especially the fairness, of Affirmative Action, such as:

- 'Is Equal Opportunity turning into a witch-hunt?' *Forbes* magazine
- 'Anti-discrimination run amok' *Time* magazine
- 'Reverse discrimination – Has it gone too far?' *US News*
- 'Affirmative Action: How much is enough?' *Washington Post*

In this political atmosphere, policy-makers began to place limits on Affirmative Action – especially the Supreme Court that had previously played an important role in extending Affirmative Action.

The first significant Supreme Court ruling, restricting Affirmative Action, came in 1974 in *Milken* v. *Bradley*. A bussing plan, to integrate the mainly black schools of the city of Detroit with the mainly white schools of the surrounding suburbs, was ruled illegal. The grounds for the decision was that the suburbs, which fell into different education districts, were not responsible for creating all-black schools in the city and therefore were not responsible for remedying the situation. The effect of the *Milken* case was to ensure that schools in and around Detroit remained, in practice, segregated.

The most important case by far in limiting Affirmative Action was *Regents of the University of California* v. *Bakke* (1978). The ruling rejected the use of Affirmative Action as a remedy for past discrimination. Affirmative Action would only be allowed if it was used to achieve 'wide exposure to the ideas and mores of students as diverse as this Nation' – meaning that it could only be used to achieve racial and ethnic diversity in education. Even then, to achieve diversity, a range of characteristics could be taken into account, of which race was an important one but not of overriding importance. This ruling undermined the central justification of Affirmative Action – to correct the racial imbalances that had occurred in the past, with the permission of the political authorities, including the Courts.

Following this decision, the Supreme Court narrowed the scope of Affirmative Action programmes in other aspects of society. In *City of Richmond* v. *J. A. Croson Co.* (1989), a policy that guaranteed a minimum of 30 per cent of the value of city contracts went to minority-owned firms was challenged. In line with the *Bakke* decision, the Supreme Court ruled against the city council on the grounds that Affirmative Action could not be used to remedy past discrimination in general.

Cases were also brought before the Supreme Court that challenged attempts to increase ethnic-minority political representation through the creation of race-conscious districts in which voters of the same race were grouped together. In the cases of *Shaw* v. *Reno* (1993) and *Miller* v. *Johnson* (1995), the court rejected redistricting plans in which race was the 'predominant factor'.

Opponents of Affirmative Action have also used direct democracy at state level to limit Affirmative Action. In 1996, Proposition 209 was passed in California that banned the use of Affirmative Action in the state. Other states, including Washington, Florida and Michigan, have since passed similar initiatives, although other states (such as Colorado) have rejected such proposals.

Thus, by the mid-1990s, Affirmative Action continued to be used in many areas of American life, but only to a limited extent. This was a situation that left both its supporters and opponents dissatisfied and provided the basis for the current debate on the extent to which there is an obligation on political authorities to continue to play an active role in ensuring that all Americans are able to play a full role in society regardless of their race.

## The debate on Affirmative Action

### Arguments in support of Affirmative Action

For supporters of Affirmative Action, the policy has two distinct dimensions. It tends to be seen both as a set of specific strategies that can have a direct, tangible impact on the opportunities of individuals and as a more general indicator of the level of commitment of the Federal government and American people to making racial equality a political priority.

Thus, the limitations placed on the use of Affirmative Action as a result of the *Bakke* decision, just thirteen years after the first programmes were announced, caused considerable alarm. It was a development that appeared to be a troubling echo of the Reconstruction era following the Civil War when:

- Measures to ensure meaningful opportunity for black Americans were reversed after just twelve years.
- When Reconstruction ended, the American public in general, and Federal government in particular, paid little attention to racial inequality – feeling no pressure to address this issue.
- In this atmosphere of disinterest, segregation had emerged.
- Almost all Americans were aware of legalised racism in the South but had turned a blind eye to it for over sixty years.

Was history about to repeat itself – with a brief response to the injustices of racism, followed by a national loss of interest? Surely, they argued, no one could honestly claim that the consequences of many generations of African Americans being subjected to racially discriminatory laws had been seriously addressed by Affirmative Action programmes between 1965 and the constitutional restrictions placed on them by the *Bakke* case in 1978.

Moreover, in recent years, there have been signs of race-laden measures replacing those eliminated as a result of the Civil Rights movement, for example:

- ***Racial profiling*** In a practice mockingly referred to as 'driving while black', the police use traffic enforcement as a justification to investigate African Americans and other minorities in numbers far out of proportion to their presence on the road. Examples include:
  - Maryland, where the state police admitted in 1992 that on Interstate 95, approximately 17 per cent of drivers were African American while 77 per cent of those stopped and searched were African American.
  - Studies revealed similar patterns in areas as diverse as Ohio, North Carolina and Texas.
  - In 1999, the Governor of New Jersey admitted that the state police had practised racial profiling for many years and promised to take action against it.
- ***Disenfranchisement*** Thirteen states take away the vote, for life, of people who have committed a felony (serious crime such as selling drugs). When combined with racial profiling these restrictions mean that an estimated 13 per cent of all African American men have lost the right to vote.

The limitations on Affirmative Action, and the increasingly high-profile campaigns to have Affirmative Action banned altogether, have been seen as evidence of Americans returning to their old habit of allowing minorities to languish on the margins of society and ignoring racism and its consequences (especially as the most vocal opponents of Affirmative Action have often come from sections of society that were silent when race policy was disadvantaging minorities).

However, supporters of Affirmative Action have been divided on the best strategy to defend, or extend, Affirmative Action programmes. Supporters of Affirmative Action can be divided into two groups:

- Some are categorised as moderate/pragmatic (meaning practical or realistic).
- Others are categorised as radical (meaning favouring dramatic or thorough change).

Moderate supporters of Affirmative Action: They tend to draw on a political tradition dating back to the early twentieth century when the first Civil Rights organisation to promote a multi-racial society, the National Association for the Advancement of Colored People (NAACP), was set up. Following the thinking of the NAACP's founder, W. E. B. DuBois, who believed that racial harmony would only be achieved through the building of a multi-racial coalition (often referred to, in modern times, as a **rainbow coalition**) that could demonstrate the practical benefits to all Americans of a more integrated society. In recent years, pragmatists have sought to promote this goal though Affirmative Action, while recognising that public support for this policy has never been very great (especially among white men) and has been declining for many years. The thrust of their arguments, therefore, is to persuade the public that Affirmative Action has been beneficial to American society and that it can bring further benefits.

They emphasise the extent to which Affirmative Action has made the USA a fairer, more integrated society, in a range of different ways, including:

- *Employment* In 1960 only 15 per cent of African Americans worked in white-collar jobs such as clerical or sales positions, compared to 44 per cent of whites. Black workers were virtually excluded from apprenticeships for skilled trades such as plumbers and electricians. By 2002, the proportion of African Americans in white-collar jobs had risen to almost 70 per cent.
- *Housing* Until the 1960s the small proportion of African Americans who had been able to build up some wealth were unable to buy or rent property outside of black districts because of housing discrimination. Since the passing of the Fair Housing Act (1968), there has been a steady flow of African Americans out

of the cities and into the suburbs they were previously excluded from.

- *Politics* In 1970, there were ten African American representatives in Congress. After the 2008 elections, there were forty-two, all Democrats, although there was only one black Senator (only the sixth in US history).
- *Education* The percentage of African Americans completing high school rose from 39 per cent in 1960 to 86.8 per cent in 2000. The number of African Americans with a university degree was 15.5 per cent, an increase of 43 per cent since the 1970s.

However, they argue that the task of overcoming the legacy of racial injustice is incomplete and that some of the greatest challenges have yet to be addressed. Indeed, it is argued that the success of some sections of the black population has exposed the extent to which middle-class African Americans, in the past, tended to dilute the worst effects of racial segregation by providing positive role models and political leadership, and boosting the overall income of the community. Their exodus has served to leave the poorest black communities with all of the long-term consequences of decades of discriminatory political policies but without the resources to tackle them. Concerted government action, therefore, is needed to both reinforce and build upon the progress made since the 1960s, and to address the concentrated deprivation that has emerged, particularly in the following policy areas:

- *Housing* The movement of African Americans to the suburbs has, in some respects, produced more segregation rather than less. In the past, the black middle class were forced by housing discrimination to share the same schools, churches and shops as the less successful. Their departure, together with the local taxes they pay, has led to ghettoes becoming even poorer than before, indeed becoming islands of deep poverty, with minimal health provision, appalling schools, the growth of substance abuse and increased violence. Advocates of Affirmative Action, mindful of the widespread view that these problems should be addressed by the communities affected by them, stress the importance of individuals making responsible life choices and of the wider community working together to improve their collective circumstances.

But they also stress that the deep-seated social problems that have arisen as a result of policy decisions made outside the black community cannot be resolved by local initiatives alone. For example, when it comes to healthcare, individuals can take responsibility to manage their diet, take exercise and recognise the symptoms of common ailments, and communities can organise campaigns to draw attention to problems that are specific to their districts (such as the presence of hazardous waste sites). However, as long as the healthcare system is based on private commercial providers the best care will tend always to be drawn to the wealthiest districts, leaving the poorest who cannot afford health insurance with substandard provision, and this issue can only be addressed by the government.

- *Employment* The advances made by African Americans are precarious and, compared to the rest of the population, limited. When African Americans lose their jobs, they often suffer a dramatic decline in their standard of living, as one of the legacies of slavery and Jim Crow is that the black community was not allowed to build up capital such as land and homes, which can serve as a cushion in difficult times. And for those outside the mainstream economy, prospects have deteriorated in recent decades. As the manufacturing industry has declined in the USA, there have been fewer secure jobs paying an adequate wage for all unskilled Americans, regardless of race. People in this category have had to find work in the growing service sector (for example, fast-food outlets) which often employs people only on a part-time basis and provides minimal employment benefits such as health insurance and pension contributions. Thus, poor unqualified Americans often have to juggle several jobs while barely providing an adequate income for their families. For African Americans, Native Americans and some Hispanics, this problem has been compounded by employment discrimination. Some employers simply do not consider applicants living in certain districts, including those with appropriate skills and qualifications. As a result, unemployment in the poorest black areas can be twice as high as that in comparable white areas, with as many as 50 per cent of people in parts of New York and Chicago (two of the USA's wealthiest cities) not having a job. This means that people living in some black districts may have no contact whatsoever with the mainstream America seen by tourists and portrayed on TV. It also means that the next generation, growing up in these areas, may simply not equate qualifications with opportunity, which has a knock-on effect on the education system. Affirmative Action advocates campaign for government intervention to help people who may be struggling to survive financially while working hard, through such measures as increasing the minimum wage in line with rises in the cost of living (there was no Federal minimum wage increase from 1994 to 2006) and boosting tax credits for poorly paid workers. They also want to see anti-discrimination legislation strengthened. Such measures would benefit all poor Americans, but would disproportionately help racial minorities who have experienced the most concentrated poverty.

- *Education* While the educational achievement of African Americans has improved overall, and there is more scope than in other policy areas to make a real difference through local initiatives to raise standards, black campaigners continue to argue for improved funding and facilities for schools and colleges in deprived areas. Since the nineteenth century, African Americans have developed ideas and projects to promote education and make it relevant to the circumstances and experience of the community. For example, the Harlem Children's Zone in New York City operates on the basis that children living below the poverty line will only succeed academically, and play a full part in mainstream society, if a range of family needs are addressed – so it provides guidance for young mothers, relationship counselling to nurture stable families, and after-school and summer activities as well as conventional school classes. However, advocates of Affirmative Action argue that political authorities have a responsibility to provide sufficient resources in deprived districts for local schools to be able to deliver a high-quality, rounded curriculum. Classes of over forty students are not uncommon in poorer areas and non-core subjects such as arts and sport are cut whenever there is a funding crisis.
- *Criminal justice* The concentrated deprivation in the poorest black districts has been accompanied by a rise in drug use and the drug trade in these areas. At the same time, penalties for drug-related crime have become increasingly harsh. The combination of these

two developments has resulted in sky-rocketing imprisonment of African Americans to the point that one in every three black males and one in every eighteen black females are jailed at some point in their lifetime. This affects every other aspect of life in poor communities: family instability, increased difficulty in finding legitimate work and a lack of confidence in the future that makes qualifications seem irrelevant. There are programmes in every community to counter these trends, from extra-curricular activities for children to substance-abuse support groups for adults. However, activists have been pressing for policy changes that will give non-violent offenders a second chance: the greater use of drug courts, used in some states, which offer the option of supervised treatment for addicts instead of prison; the amendment of the 'three strike' law (which imposes a life sentence for a third conviction) so that it only applies to violent and sexual crimes and not to minor offences; rehabilitation programmes in prisons that address deficiencies in education and skills and effective reintegration and the continuation of these programmes in the community after release to limit the likelihood of re-offending. They point out that the existing system is clearly not working, as drug use in poor communities has not been falling and imprisonment is hugely expensive.

## Radical advocates of government intervention

While moderates do their best to convince a sceptical public of the achievements of Affirmative Action, and the case for maintaining Affirmative Action, more radical voices claim that this is not enough. This strand of opinion builds on a long tradition of policy proposals, designed to create the conditions for black economic self-sufficiency, that puts African Americans in a position to insulate themselves from white racism. This approach to black advancement dates back to Booker T. Washington, who was a contemporary and rival to W. E. B. DuBois and set up schools and colleges to provide vocational educational courses to African Americans, to Marcus Garvey, who tried to establish a black economic network that linked African American communities to each other and to the West Indies and Africa, to Malcolm X, the Black Panthers and the Black Power movement of the 1960s that prioritised the empowerment of African Americans over integration.

The radical view is that Affirmative Action needs to be not just protected but extended. Radicals assert that the aims of Affirmative Action, as outlined by President Johnson in 'To Fulfil These Rights', have never been met. White public opinion has never accepted a concerted effort to attack black poverty and disadvantage. Radicals insist that this is because the public debate on Affirmative Action has focused on a form of 'fairness' that ignores the deep-seated racial unfairness that has developed over the past two centuries. Moderates, from this point of view, have failed to challenge this focus and have been on the defensive as a result. Radicals aim to regain the initiative, moving the debate to the specific form of fairness that puts contemporary policy in its historical context, **corrective justice**. This is the idea that genuine fairness can only be achieved when a deprived group has been compensated for losses, and for gains unfairly achieved by others, as a result of governmental action. Since they contend that this goal has not been achieved through Affirmative Action programmes, and there is no prospect of this being achieved as long as the Supreme Court upholds the *Bakke* verdict, radicals propose another approach. They argue that the Federal government should pay reparations to the African American community for the accumulated affects of over 200 years of lost liberty and opportunity. This would, they believe, change the balance of power between the races in the USA, with African Americans having the resources to implement solutions to problems that are unique to their communities, making them less reliant on the (limited) goodwill of the white majority for social and economic advancement and much less vulnerable to racism.

Their argument is as follows:

* Reparations for human rights abuses, often made to the descendents of the victims, is firmly rooted in international law (supported by the USA).
* Affirmative Action can be likened to taking a mild painkiller to treat a serious illness: just enough to take the patient's mind off the pain and make everyone feel that something is being done.
* There needs to be recognition of the scale of the *Maafa* (meaning disaster) which befell African Americans, and the damage done to the fabric of black communities.

- This means recognising that slavery, and to a lesser extent Jim Crow, had such a devastating impact and enduring effect that they fully merit being classified as crimes against humanity. It thus becomes appropriate for the government, on behalf of society, to acknowledge the impact of these policies and to provide compensation for the damage done. This is no different to the response to other crimes against humanity.

- In the past fifty years, apologies and financial compensation have been given to a wide range of groups. This includes both survivors of the Jewish holocaust and descendents of the victims, Japanese Americans who were imprisoned during the Second World War as suspected enemy sympathisers, and Native Americans who had had their land illegally seized, all of whom have received reparations from the government of the USA. The Canadian government has similarly compensated indigenous people deprived of their land and resources.

- African Americans have been demanding compensation for slavery since the end of the American Civil War. Immediately after the abolition of slavery, the demand was for forty acres and a mule to ensure they would not be dependent on their former slave-owners. Then, between 1890 and 1917, there was a movement to lobby the government for pensions to compensate for their unpaid labour under slavery. Since 1989, each year Congressman John Conyers Jnr (Michigan) has introduced a bill to study the case for reparations. Each of these initiatives has been largely ignored by the political establishment.

- Reparations would ensure full recognition of the scale of the *Maafa* (and, at the same time, undermine those who claim that there is no further need for Affirmative Action).

- Reparations would also compensate for slavery, provide psychological relief for black anger and white guilt resulting from centuries of racial oppression and, as a result, build a more united nation based on a common understanding of American history. It would also provide black communities with the resources to address their social problems without relying on the goodwill of the rest of society.

- To those who argue that it would be impossible to determine who should pay, how much should be paid and who should receive, supporters of reparations have a response. They argue that the principle should be established first and the details can be worked out later, with a range of suggestions having been put forward, including programmes that would benefit all African Americans, for example free healthcare and college education. However, a final decision should await the study proposed in Congressman Conyers' bill. Moreover, any suggestions that a reparations programme would simply be too expensive have been undermined by the events of 2008–9 when the government demonstrated the political will to find well over $1 trillion to bail out the banking sector: there ought to be an even greater political will to fund compensation for a crime against humanity.

These two sets of arguments in favour of substantial government intervention to create greater racial equality are not necessarily rivals. Some moderates support reparations as a long-term goal but are reluctant to invest time and effort in a set of ideas that have been mainly discussed by intellectuals in universities, and support has certainly grown as a result of Congressman Conyers' bill that introduced the idea of reparations to a wider audience. However, the moderate view has received far more attention in mainstream political debate.

## Arguments against Affirmative Action

Like their political rivals, opponents of Affirmative Action are divided on exactly what they hope to achieve and how best to achieve their goals. There are more resolute opponents who challenge the claim that there is racial inequality, caused by the political system, in the USA, which leads them to the conclusion that there has never been a legitimate justification for Affirmative Action and that the policy should be banned. There are also more moderate opponents of Affirmative Action, who accept that there are serious levels of inequality in the USA but believe that race-conscious policies are not the best way of addressing them.

Hard-line opponents of Affirmative Action want to see Affirmative Action abolished, and have worked to achieve this goal using a twin-track approach: they initiate propositions, in states that use direct democracy, to have Affirmative Action declared unlawful;

they also sponsor test cases that can be used to persuade the Supreme Court to declare Affirmative Action unconstitutional, thereby ending it at a stroke across the entire country.

They challenge the view of history outlined above, that emphasises the obstacles and denial of the opportunity faced by racial minorities. This group of opponents of Affirmative Action favour a view of history that stresses the extent to which all sections of American society have faced immense challenges on arrival in the USA, including discrimination, and have succeeded through determination, hard work and creativity with minimal government involvement. Obviously, in each community there are those who have not made progress but in a competitive capitalist system this is inevitable and every racial and ethnic group has its slums, deprived enclaves and ghettoes. However, from this point of view, the consequent inequality in society is not racial in character and is not necessarily a bad thing: it provides incentives for others to emulate the achievements of the most successful, thus spurring innovation and effort. And if there is a distinctive character to poverty in the poorest black and Native American communities, this may be explained by the distinctive lifestyle choices made in those communities (such as widespread drug or alcohol use).

This political viewpoint also argues that economic deprivation, and its associated social problems, tend to be aggravated rather than solved by government intervention. Attempts to help, through welfare programmes, may lead to a culture of dependency in which people passively wait for support rather than look to their own resources to solve their problems, and this adds to any other disadvantages they may have in a society as competitive as the USA.

Thus, Affirmative Action, which they characterise as a race-based form of welfare, both damages the economic and social model that has made the USA so successful and has a particularly harmful effect on those it is intended to benefit in the following ways:

- It may encourage them to be lazy. Why work hard if Affirmative Action programmes virtually guarantee progress?
- It may encourage them to have unrealistic expectations. For example, students who gain entry to elite colleges because of Affirmative Action may be ill-equipped to cope with the academic demands.

- Equally damaging is the message they send that the beneficiaries of Affirmative Action do not owe success to ability, determination and hard work but to 'preferential treatment'.

These arguments were given a boost in 2003 with the publication of *No Excuses* by Abigail and Stephen Thernstrom. This book, which is widely used by opponents of Affirmative Action, provides an in-depth study of the racial gap in educational achievement. The authors argue that people who have equal skills and knowledge will have roughly equal earnings, which suggests that racism is no longer a major barrier to equality of opportunity, and that inequality of races can be erased if unequal educational achievement can be addressed (a claim fiercely contested by many other academics). This, they claim, can be achieved by understanding the 'culture' of each race and, in the case of African Americans, changing their culture. Although they acknowledge that black academic underachievement has deep historical roots, they contend that contemporary factors, which can be changed, are responsible for an educational gap which has not closed since 1988. These factors include:

- African American children are far more likely to be born into a single-parent household, to a very young mother, which provides a poor basis for educational support.
- African American households, on average, contain relatively few books and children are allowed to watch far more television than children of other races, therefore having less educational stimulation around them.
- African American children, perhaps as a result of the two previous factors, are much more likely to be disruptive in class while being less likely than children of other races to be eager to learn new things or persist at tasks.
- In contrast, students from racial groups that are held up as **model minorities**, because of the speed with which they have integrated into US society despite substantial disadvantages such as not speaking English (notably Asian students from China and India), are likely to outperform their counterparts, including white students, because they follow parental orders to obey their teachers, even when they are from impoverished homes and study at inferior inner-city schools.

- The solution to racial inequality, they believe, is not Affirmative Action but cultural change in which all racial groups, whether newly arrived or long-term residents, conform more closely to American 'mainstream cultural norms'.

Moderate opponents of Affirmative Action are more willing to accept that there is racial inequality in the USA and that there is a case for some form of government intervention to address it. However, they criticise race-based Affirmative Action on two grounds – fairness and necessity. The first argument, fairness, is as follows:

- The central American values are fairness and equality for everyone. Policies which appear to favour one group over others are out of step with American values.
- It uses one form of discrimination to compensate for another. All discrimination causes fear and anxiety. African Americans continue to experience the fear of discrimination, and now Affirmative Action has extended that fear to white Americans, making the overall situation worse rather than better.
- Affirmative Action is a form of compensation by whites for slavery and Jim Crow. But why should today's white Americans pay for the sins of their forefathers, especially as their forefathers may have had nothing to do with slavery and Jim Crow?

The second argument is that Affirmative Action may have been necessary in the immediate aftermath of the Civil Rights campaigns of the 1950s and 1960s, but it is no longer justified and has proved ineffective. This argument makes the following points:

- A significant number of African Americans have prospered over the past thirty years yet they, and their families, can still benefit from Affirmative Action programmes, often at the expense of families of other races who are struggling to get by.
- Affirmative Action claims to help integrate society. However, over the past thirty years, as black families moved into established suburbs, white families which had, in previous generations, moved there to avoid having black neighbours moved on to other suburbs further away from the city. Affirmative Action may have done something to change the pattern of segregation, creating wealthy black suburbs, but little to affect the fact of segregation.

Despite all these criticisms of Affirmative Action, moderate opponents of the policy accept that there should be help offered to those for whom there seems to be no meaningful hope of a better life through their own efforts alone. However, they argue that these should be income-based programmes, to help all in poverty – not race-conscious programmes. Such programmes would not be perceived as racially discriminatory or of providing advantages to those who do not need them (such as the children of successful African Americans) but, because of the higher levels of deprivation in the racial groups that have benefited from Affirmative Action programmes in the past, key racial minorities would still get the help they need.

It has been argued that President Obama has endorsed this position by emphasising the importance of personal responsibility when addressing black audiences (especially that of black fathers to take care of their families) and by commenting that he would not expect his daughters to benefit from Affirmative Action as they grow up. However, he has also, in his book *The Audacity of Hope*, emphasised the distinctive nature of black poverty, shaped by American history, and the need for policies that are tailored to the consequent specific needs of black communities – something that income-based programmes, by their non-racial character, cannot address.

**Summary of the debate**
Most Americans claim to be committed to healing the deep racial divisions that have been a damaging feature of their society since independence in the eighteenth century (although there is still a significant minority openly committed to white racial supremacy). There is also widespread agreement that the principles of the constitution – especially opportunity for all – have to be the basis for a more harmonious society. In this sense, almost everyone believes in working towards fairness for all Americans. Beyond this point, however, the debate on race relations is characterised by deep disagreement, mutual suspicion and hostility.

Supporters of Affirmative Action strongly question the commitment to racial equality of their opponents. The strongest opposition to Affirmative Action comes from white Americans, especially conservatives. It was this section of the population that maintained, or turned a blind eye to, those practices, such as Jim Crow, that created America's stark racial inequalities. When such people campaign to reform Affirmative Action on grounds of 'fairness', therefore, their sincerity is questioned. Moreover, conservatives have a record of limiting, or seeking to eliminate, poverty reduction programmes. Thus, when such people propose to replace race-conscious Affirmative Action with income-based Affirmative Action, which would mean an extension of welfare programmes, their sincerity is again questioned.

Supporters of Affirmative Action reserve their fiercest criticisms for those who would abolish Affirmative Action altogether, whose arguments they see as deliberately misleading. Their arguments, given intellectual credibility by Abigail and Stephen Thernstrom in *No Excuses*, rely heavily on the claims that racism is no longer a major barrier to equality of opportunity, as equal skills and knowledge will lead to roughly equal earnings, and that the experience of 'model minorities' illustrates how progress can be made, even in the most challenging of circumstances, without the help of Affirmative Action. These claims are emphatically rejected by Affirmative Action advocates. There is ample evidence of racism continuing to be an obstacle to progress, especially for black Americans, as demonstrated by regular well-publicised events such as the 'Jena 6' incident in 2008 when a racial school fight in a school in Louisiana, provoked by white students, resulted in the white boys being reprimanded while the black students involved were charged with attempted murder. Above all, by using the experience of 'model minorities' to support their arguments, the Thernstroms downplay (dishonestly, in the opinion of supporters of Affirmative Action) the continuing effect of America's racial history. Supporters of Affirmative Action argue that President Johnson's statement of 1965 – when he said that no other group has had 'the heritage of centuries to overcome, and they did not have a cultural tradition which had been twisted and battered by endless years of hatred, nor were they excluded because of race or color – a feeling whose dark intensity is matched by no other prejudice' – is still valid.

Opponents of Affirmative Action are equally critical of the arguments advanced by the other side – that Affirmative Action leads to a fairer America. They point to the following weaknesses in the arguments put forward in defence of Affirmative Action:

- Ultimately, racial harmony can never be achieved through some groups receiving preferential treatment – which means that Affirmative Action can never achieve its stated goals.
- The focus that supporters of Affirmative Action place on the history of racial oppression, together with understating black progress over the past forty years, leads to a mentality of victimhood which, in turn, encourages an entitlement culture – one in which people expect others (particularly government) to meet their needs, rather than relying on themselves to make progress. This does not help the intended beneficiaries of Affirmative Action.
- Also, because others resent being taxed on their hard-earned income to support those who appear not to want to help themselves, it further damages already fragile race relations.
- If voting patterns are taken as a representative measure (over 90 per cent of African Americans support the more liberal, generally pro-Affirmative Action, Democratic Party) there are not many black opponents of Affirmative Action. However, the views of these opponents, such as the conservative Supreme Court judge Clarence Thomas, and Ward Connerly, who has led campaigns to have Affirmative Action outlawed at state level, have been actively promoted by opponents of the policy. They tend to stress the negative impact, as they see it, on the African Americans who are supposed to benefit from Affirmative Action, including:
    - The claim that measures to create a more level playing field through racial integration imply that anything predominantly black must be inferior. Justice Thomas, in particular, argues that black success does not, and should not, depend on a racially mixed setting.
    - The claim that Affirmative Action stigmatises all black success by creating the impression that it depends on help/assistance and not only merit.

## Conclusion

Overall, therefore, while almost all Americans accept that there continues to be substantial racial inequality in the twenty-first century, which is the basis for poor race relations in a highly diverse society, there is very little agreement on how to improve the situation.

Americans disagree on the cause of their race-relations problems. They disagree on solutions to these problems. They distrust the motivations of those they disagree with. Almost all believe that they are seeking justice – to make the constitutional values of freedom and opportunity meaningful. Yet almost all believe that their opponents are not looking out for justice – that they are looking out for 'just us'.

· · · · · · · · · · · · · · · · · · · · · · · · · · · · · · · · · · · · · · · · · ·

## ✓ What you should have learnt from reading this chapter

- One perspective on political developments since the Declaration of Independence and the drafting of the Constitution of the USA, is that they have restricted freedom and opportunity for specified racial groups – contrary to the claimed values and objectives of the political system.

- Each political policy designed to limit opportunity, from slavery to Jim Crow to race-laden legislation, has served to create and then widen racial inequality.

- Although some sections of the racial groups most affected by these policies have made significant progress in the past half-century, almost everyone continues to be affected by the lack of a financial cushion that other races have been able to establish over the past two centuries and, for those in ghettoes, the cycle of deprivation created by a legacy of discrimination has got worse in recent decades.

- When official racial segregation ended in the mid-1960s, President Johnson pioneered policies to redress the continuing effects of past racial discrimination. Collectively, these government measures are known as Affirmative Action.

- Some fifty years later, there is passionate debate about whether these measures continue to be needed.

- Some argue that Affirmative Action has made the constitutional aim of opportunity for all meaningful for millions of people for whom it was an empty promise, but that there are millions of others for whom the 'American Dream' remains out of reach and that Affirmative Action is therefore still needed – tailored to the realities of the twenty-first century.

- Further, they question the sincerity of those who would substantially reform, or end, Affirmative Action. This is because the most vocal criticisms come from groups whose commitment to 'fairness' is suspect (as they were able to justify, or were willing to turn a blind eye to, the discriminatory policies of the past) or who have never accepted the need to remedy the consequences of past policies.

- Others would go even further, advocating reparations that would reflect the scale and cumulative consequences of over two centuries of relentless, brutal racial discrimination.

- On the other side of the debate, some opponents of Affirmative Action argue that the policy is counter-productive, because it uses one form of discrimination to fight another, and unfair, because everyone from some races can benefit even if they have no need of government support, and that it does not advance the cause of racial harmony but creates resentment between races. They acknowledge that some poor communities continue to be adversely affected by past discriminatory policies but argue that the most appropriate response to this is to link Affirmative Action with income rather than race.

- Other opponents of Affirmative Action simply argue that substantial government intervention is never appropriate in America's competitive free-market society and that Affirmative Action is a particularly unacceptable form of intervention because it actually adds to the disadvantages that racial minorities may face by making them less able and willing to compete – as demonstrated by other 'model' racial groups, who have rapidly prospered without government help.

- With each side claiming that their argument is consistent with the core values of the Constitution, there is little prospect of this debate being resolved.

## Glossary of key terms

**Affirmative Action**  Programmes to remedy the effects of past discrimination, combat current discrimination and prevent future discrimination.

**Civil Rights**  The rights enjoyed, and protected, by people as a result of their citizenship of a country.

**Corrective justice**  The idea that genuine fairness can only be achieved when a deprived group has been compensated for losses and for gains unfairly achieved by others.

**Disenfranchisement**  Taking away the right to vote – often from people who having committed a felony (serious crime such as selling drugs).

**Emancipated**  Freed from slavery.

**Freedmen's Bureau** A government agency, set up by the Federal government in 1865, which funded schools for ex-slaves in the South and helped set up a number of black universities.

**Jim Crow** Term for laws requiring the segregation of races, primarily in Southern states.

**Lynching** Punishment by a group of citizens, not the legal authorities, usually involving a severe beating or death.

**Model minorities** Racial minorities who have become established as part of the mainstream of society with minimal tension or conflict.

**Philadelphia Plan** A policy of requiring contractors doing business with the Federal government to demonstrate that their employment practices are not discriminatory and, if necessary, to establish 'goals and timetables' for the hiring of minorities and to draw up plans to demonstrate that they were taking active steps to meet their targets.

**Race-laden legislation** Laws that make no explicit reference to race but serve to disadvantage people of some races compared to the rest of the population.

**Racial profiling** The practice, by law enforcement officials, of targeting racial minorities as being more likely to commit crimes than the rest of the population.

**Rainbow coalition** A multi-racial alliance to win power and achieve political gains for each group in the coalition.

**Reconstruction** Term applied to the period between the end of the Civil War in 1865 and the withdrawal of Union troops from the South in 1877, when most of the constitutional rights enjoyed by the white population were extended to African Americans.

**Redlining** The practice of financial institutions refusing mortgages to African Americans attempting to buy property in white areas and/or real-estate agents steering black clients away from properties in mainly white areas.

**Reparations** Compensation, making amends, to the victims of crimes against humanity, or their descendents.

**Seniority (Congressional)** The principle that the person on a Congressional committee who has served the longest will be awarded the chairmanship.

**Southern strategy** President Nixon's attempt to attract the support of white Southerners by being seen to share the view that they were victims of 'regional discrimination'.

**Special Field Order No. 15** An order, issued in 1865 by General Sherman of the Union army, that provided freed slaves with forty acres of land and a mule with which to farm it.

**White backlash** Opposition by white Americans to policies seen as benefiting racial minorities.

**Whitecapping** The practice of terrorising black home and landowners until they sold up and moved away because they were living demonstrations of black achievement and potential inspiration for other African Americans.

## Likely examination questions

Issues examiners may expect students to be able to effectively analyse include:

- The extent, nature and causes of racial inequality in the USA

- The arguments in favour of government intervention to redress racial inequality

- The arguments against government intervention

- Evidence of increasing/continuing/diminishing racial inequality that are used to support the above arguments

Thus, examples of the kind of questions which could be asked include:

Explain why conservatives are critical of Affirmative Action.

'The American Dream is a myth for most racial minorities in the USA.' Discuss.

## Helpful websites

- Issues of particular interest to African Americans are addressed on the websites of the two largest Civil Rights groups, the NAACP and the National Urban League. Their web addresses are: www.naacp.org and www.nul.org.

- Two more academic organisations sympathetic to Affirmative Action are the Joint Center for Political and Economic Studies, at www.jointcenter.org, and Harvard University's Civil Rights Project at www.civilrightsproject.harvard.edu.

- The best sources of articles and books that set out the case against Affirmative Action are the websites of the two leading conservative think-tanks in the USA, the Heritage Foundation and the Cato Institute. Their web addresses are: www.heritage.org and www.cato.org.

##  Suggestions for further reading

- To capture the flavour of the American South during the era of segregation, and the effect it had on both white and African Americans, read either of two classic novels that viewed segregation through the eyes of children, *To Kill a Mockingbird* by Harper Lee or *Roll of Thunder, Hear My Cry* by Mildred Taylor.

- The National Urban League publishes a magazine, *Opportunity*, which can be ordered through their website. They also publish an annual survey entitled *The State of Black America*.

- Two influential books, one on each side of the debate, are *No Excuses* by Abigail and Stephen Thernstrom and *The Covenant with Black America*, introduced by Travis Smiley.

# PART II

# THE LIMITS ON FEDERAL POWER – PLURALISM

CHAPTER 4

# Elections

## Contents

## Overview

### The Voice of the People?

On 8 June 2008, in the case of *Caperton* v. *Massy*, the Supreme Court acted against an elected official who they saw as misusing his power by favouring a key donor who had made most of the financial contributions used by the official in his successful election campaign. The official in question was an elected judge in the state of West Virginia who was accused of having decided a court case, worth $50 million in compensation, in favour of someone who had donated $3 million to his election campaign.

Five of the justices on the Supreme Court argued that there was 'a serious risk of actual bias – based on objective and reasonable perceptions'. The other four judges claimed that the ruling would have the effect of undermining all politicians even when there are no justified grounds for suspicion of bias. The case highlighted the long-standing concern that the electoral system in the USA does not always fulfil of its purposes of providing opportunities for the best possible candidate to be win office and to hold office-holders effectively to account.

This chapter examines how the electoral system works, explores in detail viewpoints on its weaknesses and presents rival perspectives on how it could be improved.

## Key issues to be covered in this chapter

- The Founding Fathers' dilemma: give 'the mob' the vote
- Extensions of democracy
- How the electoral system operates
- Concerns about electoral processes
- The extent to which the electoral system enables the people of the USA to shape policy and hold politicians to account

## Historical background

### The Founding Fathers' dilemma

The thirteen colonies that had broken away from Britain to establish the USA had proclaimed in the Declaration of Independence that all men were 'created equal' with certain 'inalienable rights' and that if a government becomes oppressive 'it is the Right of the People to alter or abolish it'. This clearly suggested that the government of the new United States of America would be a democracy, with the government held accountable by the people. Furthermore, representative legislatures had been in existence in the colonies since the Virginia Assembly was set up as long ago as 1619, elected by all men aged seventeen and over.

However, the colonial legislatures did not have the final say on laws and their decisions could be overruled by the representative of the English king.

When drawing up the Constitution, the Founding Fathers debated whether similar safeguards would be needed in their new nation as some of them doubted the voters could be entrusted with electing responsible representatives. George Washington himself referred to ordinary farmers as the 'grazing multitude', Alexander Hamilton described them as the 'unthinking populace' and John Adams termed them the 'common herd of mankind'. Should such people, presumably easily led and manipulated, be entrusted with holding law-makers to account?

### The debate at the Constitutional Convention

The debate between those who feared that democracy could under-mine freedom and those who believed that democracy was essential to protect freedom mirrored the wider constitutional debate between the **Federalists** and **anti-Federalists**, outlined in Chapter 1 of this book. While both sides agreed that the vote would be restricted to white men, they disagreed about how much power to put into the hands of the voters.

Anti-Federalists, highly suspicious of putting power in the hands of a strong national government, wanted an electoral system that:

* Made elected representatives directly elected by, and therefore accountable to, all citizens.

- Gave elected representatives short terms of office before being held to account at elections.
- Placed a limit on the number of terms they could serve.
- Provided a mechanism that would enable the people to recall from office any representative who was not serving them well.

In addition, they called for a Bill of Rights that would protect individuals from oppressive laws.

Federalists, committed to an effective national government, wanted an electoral system that:

- Provided elected representatives with enough power to ensure the nation's survival in a hostile world and to ensure that there was effective co-ordination between the states.
- Ensured that this power was wielded by responsible men. This would require some form of vetting of the choices made by ill-educated voters.

As with all issues debated at the Constitutional Convention, the outcome was a compromise between the two positions, with the Federalists somewhat more satisfied with the result than the anti-Federalists.

The anti-Federalists won short terms for people elected to the House of Representatives, which was considered to be the most important part of the national government, as it had the final say in raising and spending taxes. However, they lost the argument on term limits and **recall elections**. (The two-term limit on the President was not introduced until 1951, when the 22nd Amendment came into effect.) They also failed to persuade the Convention that all politicians in the national government should be directly elected: Senators were nominated by state legislatures until 1913, when the 17th Amendment came into effect, and the President is elected though an electoral college (see below) that was originally designed to ensure that the masses did not choose an unsuitable person to run the executive branch of government.

# The evolution of democracy

### Votes for African Americans

When the Constitution went into effect in 1789, African Americans made up about 10 per cent of the US population. Most were enslaved and denied the vote. Further, they were defined by the Constitution as less than fully human, as three-fifths of a person. Despite this, they were counted when calculating how many seats each state should have in the House of Representatives, helping to boost the representation of those who enslaved them. Even free African Americans were only allowed to vote in a few states.

This situation was supposed to be transformed, after slavery was abolished, with the passage of the 15th Amendment, passed in 1870, which stated that no citizen could be deprived of the right to vote 'on account of race, color, or previous condition of servitude'. However, each state has always been entitled to regulate who can vote and many states, especially those that had resisted the abolition of slavery, used regulations to limit and discourage the participation of African American voters.

The three most common devices were:

- *The Grandfather Clause* Incorporated into the Constitutions of most Southern states, only people whose grandfathers had voted before 1867 were eligible to vote. Although clearly contrary to the 15th Amendment, such clauses ruled out anyone whose forefathers had been slaves.
- *Literacy Test* Many states have required citizens to pass literacy tests before qualifying to vote, to ensure that they were able to read newspapers and election literature and, therefore, cast an informed vote. In those states that were determined to stop African Americans from voting, election officers used their discretion to declare literate any white voter who could write their own name while disqualifying any African American who failed to adequately explain the meaning of parts of the state or national constitutions. Even African Americans with advanced degrees in Political Science were known to fail the tests.
- *Poll Tax* This was a payment which had to be made before voting. As it had to be paid for all previous unpaid years, as well as the

current year, it made the cost of voting unmanageable for the poorest people. This affected people of all races but, because of slavery and subsequent forms of racial discrimination which impoverished black citizens, African Americans were dispropor-tionately affected by this device. The 24th Amendment, passed in 1964, outlawed this practice.

In practice, the vote only became available to most African Americans after the passage of the Voting Rights Act (1965). This gave Federal government officials the power to take over the regis-tration process in any district where less than 50 per cent of African Americans were on the electoral register, or where it appeared that local officials were discriminating against African Americans. It also required states to get clearance from the Federal government before they introduced any new electoral regulations, to make sure that new devices did not replace the old ones.

While these measures led to a significant increase in the number of African American voters, they did not at first lead to a significant increase in the number of African American representatives in the corridors of power. Then, in 1976, the Supreme Court ruled in *Beer* v. *United States* that any plan to redraw district boundaries should not leave ethnic minorities worse off in terms of political representation. In the spirit of increasing political representation for minorities, some states created race-conscious districts in which voters of the same race were grouped together. By 2008, there were forty-two African American representatives in the House of Representatives, up from ten in 1970, but only one Senator.

Clearly, a lot of progress had been made but there continues to be concerns about the ability of African Americans to exercise their right to vote. Despite the Voting Rights Act, suspicion remains that in some Southern states there are political leaders who are always looking for ways of disenfranchising African Americans. For example, in 2005, the State of Georgia passed a law requiring citi-zens to use government-issued ID when voting. With car ownership much lower among the African American population than white resi-dents and with no DMV office within nine miles of Atlanta, with its large African American population, the law appeared likely to reduce black participation at elections.

## Votes for women

Women had to fight for the vote for over seventy years, from the mid-1800s, before the 19th Amendment was passed in 1920, stating that the vote 'shall not be denied or abridged by the United States or by any state on account of sex'.

The campaign had been fought in each individual state, as well as in Washington DC. By 1914, women had won the right to vote in eleven states, all of them West of the Mississippi River. Before the successful passage of the 19th Amendment, however, it had to be introduced in Congress 118 times.

## Votes for Native Americans

Despite their presence on the continent for centuries before the arrival of European settlers, Native Americans were not recognised as US citizens until the Snyder Act of 1924. Even then, they were not entitled to vote in all states as there were provisions in many state constitutions restricting the voting rights of Native Americans. In 1948, the Arizona Supreme Court struck down a provision of its state constitution that kept Indians from voting. Other states eventually followed suit, concluding with New Mexico in 1962, the last state to enfranchise Native Americans. Even with the lawful right to vote in every state, Native Americans suffered from the same mechanisms and strategies, such as poll taxes, literacy tests, fraud and intimidation, that kept African Americans from exercising their voting rights, and they were beneficiaries of the Voting Rights Act (1965).

## Votes for eighteen-year-olds

Until the 1960s, the minimum voting age in most states was twenty-one. During the Vietnam War, however, the average age of the soldiers fighting in South East Asia was nineteen, and it was argued that if they were old enough to die for their country then they were old enough to vote in elections for/against the people who sent them to fight and funded the war.

The 26th Amendment, ratified in record time, was passed in 1971 and stated that the right of people 'who are eighteen years or older to vote shall not be denied or abridged by the United States or by any state on account of age'. The amendment expanded the electorate by over 10 million people.

# The electoral system at state and local level

## State and local elections

Citizens of the USA are entitled to vote for a wide range of local officials who make decisions which can affect the quality of life in a community. The pattern varies in different parts of the country, but this
may include the people in charge of the justice system, including the
most senior police officer (the Sheriff), the senior prosecuting officer
(the District Attorney) and the district judge responsible for sentencing anyone convicted. All across the USA, school boards responsible
for delivering a high quality of education are elected and in many
areas the commissioners of sanitation services, such as garbage collection and water supplies, are elected. In each case, the principle of
accountability applies: if the quality of education at the local school
is poor or the garbage is not collected, with the associated hygiene
risks, someone should be held responsible for the situation and for
improving it. All this is in addition to the elected local representatives
found in most countries, such as the mayor and town council.

Furthermore, in America's Federal system, there are also state
representatives to be elected. As at the national level, states are run
by a head of government, the governor, and a legislature which, in all
but one state, has a direct equivalent to the House of Representatives
and the Senate. The exception is Nebraska, which has a single-
chamber assembly. Unlike the national level, however, many of the
people who work under the head of government are not appointed
but directly elected, such as the Lieutenant Governor (equivalent,
at state level, to the Vice President). In addition, in many states the
senior judges are also elected.

As elections for state and local representatives are often scheduled
to take place at the same time as Federal elections, ballot papers can
become extremely long and, at times, confusing. Adding to the con-
fusion is the likelihood that voters will not be asked to vote only for
people but also on issues, such as amendments to the state constitution, initiatives, propositions or recall elections.

## Amendments to state constitutions

Each of the fifty states has its own constitution, separate from the
national Constitution covered in Chapter 1. While the national

Constitution is difficult to amend, state constitutions are amended frequently. In most cases, this requires the support of the electorate in that state and these decisions are added to the ballot papers at elections.

Often the issues covered are highly technical and of little interest to a majority of the voters. Thus, in Colorado in 2008, there were fourteen proposed amendments to the state constitution, ranging from banning Affirmative Action and abortion in the state to the introduction of new taxes on the oil and gas industries.

### Initiatives, propositions and referenda

In twenty-three states and Washington DC, voters may be asked to vote on issues that have not been addressed by the state legislature but which groups of ordinary voters feel strongly about. These are known as **initiatives** or **propositions**. If the required number of signatures can be obtained (ranging from 5 per cent to 15 per cent of the electorate depending on the state) the initiative will appear on the ballot paper at the next election for the voters to approve or reject. If the initiative is approved, it becomes law.

The most publicised initiatives in recent years have been in California. In 2008, following a ruling by the California Supreme Court recognising gay marriage, a proposition was put on the ballot paper to limit marriage to heterosexual partners. Known as Proposition 8, it passed by 52 per cent to 48 per cent (much to the surprise of outsiders who think of all Californians as social liberals).

**Referenda** are a similar process, but instead of proposed laws being put on the ballot by private citizens, the state legislature offers the voters an opportunity to express a view on a law they have drafted.

### Recall elections

Recall elections are the process (permitted in twenty-six states) of removing officials from public office before their term of office has expired. Before the vote is held, signatures of registered voters (usually equal to 25 per cent of votes cast in the previous election) have to be collected and verified; two votes are cast, one to decide whether the post-holder should be 'recalled' and another, if necessary, to choose the replacement. The winning candidate then serves the remainder of the term of office.

The recall election for the post of Governor of California in 2003, which led to the election of Arnold Schwarzenegger, brought this process to public attention around the world.

## Direct democracy

Recalls, amendments to state constitutions, initiatives, propositions and referenda are all modern forms of **direct democracy**. This form of democracy has a number of obvious advantages:

* It gives people a direct say in decisions that many of them feel strongly about and that may have a significant impact on everyone in the state.
* It strengthens popular control of government, ensuring that elected officials remain acutely aware of the views of the electorate.
* By providing a means of taking direct action on issues of great interest, it helps to maintain a high level of interest in the political system.
* Discussion of political issues, which surround direct-democracy campaigns, help educate the electorate.
* In the case of recall elections, the procedures allow voters to correct electoral errors, as long complicated ballot papers may allow incompetent officials to slip unnoticed into elected positions.

However, direct democracy also has a number of disadvantages:

* Many of the issues people are asked to vote on may be not be easy to understand and, in some cases, are deliberately made obscure. For example, the amendments to the Colorado state constitution in 2008 (see above) included one entitled 'Definition of a person'. As it defined 'person' to mean 'any human being from the moment of fertilization', it would have had the effect of making any abortion an act of ending a human life, that is, murder. However, the word abortion was not used in the proposed amendment, nor in the information booklet issued by the authorities to help people understand the significance of these ballot measures.
* When the majority of voters may have a poor grasp of the full implications of their vote, the public debate on the issues tends to be dominated by the most extreme supporters and opponents of the measure.

- Campaigns around single issues on a ballot paper will attract the support of groups that may be well-funded and able to be disproportionately influential.
- Direct democracy may undermine the effectiveness of elected representatives, as they will have to apply laws that they may find unhelpful. Additionally, elected representatives may be overly cautious when making proposals, concerned that they may trigger a recall campaign by any powerful group that opposes the proposal. Effectively, recall elections can be used as a form of political harassment.
- As direct democracy can be used by large or wealthy groups to advance their political agenda, it can work to the disadvantage of already vulnerable minority or poor groups unable to muster the number of votes or funds to defend their interests.
- In the case of recall elections, democratic principles may be undermined rather than reinforced by the process:
  - In all states which use recall elections, there are provisions to remove corrupt officials by impeachment and officials found guilty of crimes unrelated to their office are automatically barred from public service. Therefore, recall elections are used to remove people prematurely from office for inadequate reasons.
  - Recall elections give the losing party a second opportunity to win office.
  - The incumbent has to win over 50 per cent of the vote to stay in office; the replacement, especially in a crowded field, does not and could win with 20 per cent of the vote or less. (In the California recall, there were 135 candidates. Governor Gray Davies won 45 per cent of the first vote; Arnold Schwarzenegger won 48 per cent of the second vote.)

## The electoral system: Congressional elections

There are two types of elections to the national legislature: for politicians who represent specific districts (to the House of Representatives) and for politicians who represent a state (to the Senate).

In both of these elections, the **First Past the Post** electoral system is used, which has the virtue of simplicity (the candidate with the most votes being declared the winner) but also has the disadvantage of effectively denying political representation for people who have not voted for the winning candidate, in contrast to systems of proportional representation where parties are rewarded in proportion to the votes they have won.

Another feature of these elections is that they take place on fixed election dates. In many countries, the government decides when to call elections and, unsurprisingly, do so when they are popular or postpone elections because of a crisis (which they could have deliberately created). This can be seen as reducing the effectiveness of elections at holding those in power to account. In the USA, Federal elections take place on specific dates, and not at the discretion of those in power: on the first Tuesday in November, every two years, even in the most extreme circumstances such as wartime.

### The House of Representatives

The Constitution gave the House of Representatives primary responsibility for raising taxes and deciding how Federal funds should be spent. Determining taxation levels was seen as the most important power available to politicians at the time of the Constitutional Convention and, accordingly, elections to the House are designed to ensure that its members are held regularly to account. They face re-election every two years and, before each election, may be challenged by one or more persons for the right to represent the party in a public contest called a **primary** (see below).

Each member of the House of Representatives is elected to serve a district, with the number of districts in each state based on the size of its population. Initially, there was to be one district for every 30,000 people but as the population grew it was decided, in 1929, to limit the number of representatives in the House to 435. Since then, the number of seats allocated to each state has been adjusted to reflect shifts in population after each census, which takes place at the start of each decade. One consequence of this is that, as the population of the USA continues to grow rapidly, the average size of a Congressional district grows proportionately. Based on the census of 2000, the average population of a Congressional district is 646,952, an increase from the average size of 572,466 based on the 1990 census.

## The Senate

The Founding Fathers were concerned that the electoral arrangements for the House of Representatives clearly allowed for the possibility of 'mob politics'. Elections to the Senate, therefore, were designed to act as a counter-balance to this threat. Originally, selection was by indirect election, with the state legislatures choosing suitable representatives.

Senators serve six-year terms of office, enabling them to consider the long-term consequences of Congressional decisions. In addition, to ensure that the interests of their states were protected, all states were given an equal number of Senators (two) regardless of their size or population. The Senate developed rules that enabled a small minority (even just one Senator) to block measures that they strongly disagreed with.

The Constitution also set up a system whereby the terms of office of one-third of the Senators came to an end every two years. This meant that there would never be a time when everyone in the national government was replaced simultaneously. This is intended to ensure that even in the event of a tidal wave of opinion sweeping the country some of the elected representatives are insulated from it to some extent. As with members of the House of Representatives, members of the Senate may be challenged for the right to represent their party when an election is approaching, in a primary.

The 17th Amendment to the Constitution, passed in 1913, changed the method of election so that the Senate, like the House of Representatives, became directly elected. The Amendment also made arrangements for situations in which a Senate vacancy occurred (usually through death or resignation). The state governor nominates a replacement until a special election is held. In the event of a death, the governor often nominates a relative of the deceased. Thus, in 2000, when Mel Carnahan was killed in a plane crash, his widow, Jean, was nominated to represent Missouri in the Senate in his place. She faced a special election in 2002, which she lost by a margin of 1 per cent.

## Box 4.1 Mid-term elections

Elections to Congress take place at the same time as, and tend to be somewhat overshadowed by, presidential elections. However, they also take place between presidential elections. When this happens, they are referred to as **mid-term elections** (taking place halfway through a presidential term). Even though elections to Congress are the main political event in the mid-terms (with state elections also taking place), they attract less public attention and lower turnout than in presidential election years, creating a sense that they are of limited political significance. Yet they can have a substantial impact in a variety of ways, including the following:

- A change in the control in Congress can make the President's ability to work with the legislature much harder. This happened to President Clinton in 1994, when the Republican Party won a majority in both houses of Congress. It also happened to President George W. Bush in 2006 when it was the Democratic Party that seized control of both chambers in the legislature.
- If the result is seen as a verdict on the performance of the President, it may cause him to change his tone and policies. President Clinton was seen to adopt a much more centrist, moderate political position after the setback of the 1994 mid-terms.
- On rare occasions, the opposite happens, with the President's party making gains in the mid-terms, as happened in 2002, in the aftermath of 9/11 when the President was riding a wave of national popularity. This can make the President's job easier.
- The key themes of the mid-term campaign may set the tone for the next presidential election. For example, the 2006 mid-term election results demonstrated that the electorate was becoming increasingly disenchanted with the Republican Party that had been the dominant force in Congress since 1994 and the presidency since 2000. The theme of 'change' that proved so successful in the 2006 mid-terms was adopted by Barack Obama and swept him to the White House.

## The electoral process: the presidency

### Presidential terms of office

The President and Vice President are the only people elected by voters from across the country. Although the Founding Fathers went to great lengths to limit the scope of power they could wield, this fact alone gives them the status of representative of all the people. They were given four-year terms of office and, like the Senators, they were indirectly elected, through an **electoral college** (explained in detail below). Also, like members of Congress, they are elected on a fixed date.

Although the Constitution did not provide for term limits, after the first President, George Washington, stepped down from office after two terms it became the custom that all Presidents, however successful, limit themselves to two terms. Although both Ulysses S. Grant and Theodore Roosevelt sought third terms, this custom was not broken until Franklin D. Roosevelt was elected to a third term in 1940 and a fourth in 1944. In 1951, the 22nd Amendment to the Constitution was passed, which ensured that no one would again be elected to more than two terms.

### Types of presidential election

The fact that Presidents are not allowed to run again after serving two terms influences the nature of the election. When this happens, as in the 2000 and 2008 elections, a number of candidates from both parties compete to win their party's nomination. The field was particularly crowded in 2008 as (for the first time since 1952) neither the incumbent President nor the incumbent Vice President was running.

To some extent, candidates from the party that already controls the White House will be judged by the performance of the outgoing President, but there will be opportunities for all candidates to establish their own identities as the campaign unfolds.

When the President is running for re-election after one term, as in 2004, the election campaign becomes effectively a referendum on his performance. It is conventional political wisdom that an effective, or popular, President is highly unlikely to be defeated, even if facing a strong opponent, and therefore does not usually face a strong challenge as the most effective opposition politicians wait for a more promising time to stand for the nation's highest office.

### The start of the process: testing the waters

Halfway through a President's term of office, after the mid-terms, the political media starts focusing on who might be a candidate at the next presidential election. If the incumbent President is thought likely to run for re-election, the media will usually concentrate on the possible contenders from the opposition party (although, occasionally, a President may face a challenge from someone in his own party as was the case in 1980 when Senator Edward Kennedy ran against President Jimmy Carter).

Indications that politicians are seriously considering running for the presidency include:

• Visits to the states where the first primaries and **caucuses** will be held (New Hampshire, Iowa and South Carolina).
• Appearances on TV talk shows.
• In some cases, the publication of a book that outlines the politician's ideas or compelling life story.

The response of political commentators and colleagues to these activities may determine whether these potential candidates have the credibility for a full campaign. Those who attract positive feedback may take the next step and set up an **exploratory committee** that legally entitles them to raise a limited amount of money (maximum $5,000) that can be used to conduct opinion polls to see if the wider public shares the view that they are viable candidates. Sometimes, these polls can deliver harsh messages that contradict the rosy picture drawn by those close to the potential candidate. In late 2006, the former Governor of Virginia, Mark Warner, who had been seen as a promising candidate, abruptly announced that he would not run for the presidency in 2008.

At this early stage of the process, any potential candidates who are considered promising may find themselves having to declare their intentions (even if they are not testing the waters). By early 2005, Republicans Condoleezza Rice and Jeb Bush had been forced to publicly rule themselves out of the 2008 campaign.

**The invisible primary**
Once a candidate formally announces that he or she will run for office, that individual must file with the FEC a Statement of Candidacy and becomes bound by campaign finance rules. After a number of candidates have declared, the '**invisible primary**' begins. This is the term given to the period before the start of the

## Box 4.2  Presidential candidates in 2008

*Democrats:* Hillary Clinton and Barack Obama were the leading Democratic candidates in the early stages of the campaign. Hillary Clinton led in the opinion polls for most of the invisible primary in 2007 but Barack Obama was able to match her in fundraising. Two other candidates considered strong early contenders were John Edwards, former Senator and vice-presidential candidate in 2004, and New Mexico governor Bill Richardson, who had demonstrated that he could attract votes from independents and moderate Republicans. None of the remaining candidates was ever considered by political commentators to have a realistic chance of capturing the Democratic nomination. They were Joe Biden, Senator for Delaware, Christopher Dodd, Senator for Connecticut, Mike Gravel, a former Senator for Alaska, and Dennis Kucinich, a Congressman from Ohio.

*Republicans:* Despite their unpopularity, demonstrated in the midterm elections, a sizeable field of Republicans joined the race to succeed President George W. Bush. Early polls showed Rudy Giuliani, former Mayor of New York City, as the most popular Republican. Leading the Republican fundraising race, however, was Mitt Romney, former Governor of Massachusetts. John McCain struggled to raise funds during the invisible primary, not least because he had never been shy of voicing any disagreements with his own party and they responded by turning down his requests for donations. Fred Thompson, former Senator from Tennessee but best known as the conservative DA in the television series *Law & Order*, faded early as his public performances were disappointing, while Ron Paul, a little-known Congressman from Texas who had been one of the few Republicans to oppose the Iraq war, attracted something of a cult following on the internet. Towards the end of 2007, with the conservatives in the Republican Party finding none of the leading candidates to be especially appealing, Mike Huckabee, former Governor of Arkansas and a Baptist minister, emerged as a significant challenger. None of the remaining candidates was ever considered by political commentators to have a realistic chance of capturing the Republican nomination. They were Duncan Hunter, a Congressman from California, Tom Tamcredo, a Congressman from Colorado best known for his strident opposition to immigration, and Alan Keyes, an African American who had previously lost two Senate races and had twice previously attempted to win the Republican presidential nomination.

official process in which each party chooses its presidential candidate. All contenders have to become sufficiently well-known across the country and to have raised sufficient funds to be able to present themselves as a credible presidential candidate.

Throughout the invisible primary, the media closely track the fortunes of the candidates, rating their progress according to:

• The amount of money they raise in preparation for the nomination campaign: this has become increasingly important since the 1980s as the nominees for the two main parties have, in most cases, been selected early in the election year, which has meant that anyone trailing when the process begins has little chance of catching up.
• Their standing in the opinion polls: these indicate how well known each candidate is, their perceived strengths and weaknesses and their overall popularity.
• Their effectiveness as campaigners: the media follows each aspect of the candidates' campaign, from how well they relate to ordinary voters (this proved to be the Achilles heel in 2007–8 for the Republican frontrunner, multi-millionaire Mitt Romney, who appeared uncomfortable when meeting voters) to how well they perform in head-to-head debate, to their ability to keep up with a long, gruelling campaign lasting close to two years (which undermined the campaigns of Republicans Fred Thompson and Rudy Giuliani, who were both seen as lacking the determination and drive to win the presidency).

**Primaries**

Early in the twentieth century, concern by ordinary members that the party leaders were controlling who could stand for election, blocking anyone who did not agree with them, led to the introduction of primaries, which are elections allowing voters to express their views on who should represent the party at the next election.

After the First World War, use of primaries declined, with the main form of selection being a caucus. This is a series of meetings in which all those with sufficient commitment to attend can attempt to persuade each other to support their preferred candidate. Caucus meetings tend to be dominated by party activists who are sufficiently committed to the party's cause to take part in each stage. Supporters of the caucus system believe that it leads to the best candidate being selected. However, meetings are closed (that is, not opened up to anyone other than a party member) and historically they have been dominated by a small group of influential men selecting people with whom they were comfortable.

Primaries re-emerged after the 1968 presidential election campaign, after leaders of the Democratic Party chose a candidate without consultation with ordinary party members, and have become the dominant method for choosing candidates.

Presidential primaries take place across the country in election year starting in January (with the first caucus taking place in Iowa and the first primary taking place in New Hampshire a week later) and continuing until June. They usually take place on a Tuesday. In each contest, the candidates compete to win delegates to the **national convention** that takes place in the summer, where the party formally adopts its candidate. The number of delegates to be won in each primary is proportional to the population of the state where it is held, so that there are many more delegates at stake in the largest states such as California than in smaller states such as Rhode Island.

The two main parties have different systems for allocating delegates. The Democrats award delegates proportionately, so that all of the candidates win delegates in proportion to their share of the vote in each state. Further complicating matters, in order to ensure that the judgement and experience of the party's most important members is given some weight in the nomination process, senior Democrats (such as members of Congress, Democratic Governors, ex-Presidents etc) are given votes in the selection of a presidential nominee. These are known as **superdelegates**. The Republicans have a winner-takes-all system that means that the winning candidate in each state is awarded all of the delegates for the state. This makes it easier for a Republican to establish a decisive lead early in the contest which, if it happens, may cause the other candidates to withdraw from the race.

Primaries take two forms:

- *Closed primaries* Only voters who have declared their affiliation to a party can participate in this form of primary. In most states, people are asked to declare an affiliation when they register to vote and may, as a result, participate in any closed primary for the party they support. In some states, people are allowed to declare their affiliation at the polling station when they arrive to vote. Then they cast their vote for their preferred choice. Thirteen states use this form of primary, with another thirteen using a modified form of closed primary in which independents are allowed to vote in at least one party's primary.

The advantages of this type of primary are that people who vote in these contests have to have demonstrated some commitment to the party, they are likely to be better informed of the merits of the candidates than the wider electorate and the party is somewhat protected from '**raiding**' by supporters of the other party who cross over and vote for a weak candidate.

- *Open primaries* Anyone can vote in this form of primary, including people who have not declared a party affiliation. On arriving at the polling station, voters are given two ballot papers, one for each of the main parties. Voters have to decide which party's primary they wish to participate in and return the ballot paper they do not wish to use. Then they cast their vote for their preferred choice. Twenty states use this form of primary.

The advantages of this type of primary is that they enable wider participation in the nomination phase of an election than closed primaries, candidates who do well in these primaries are likely to reflect the views of the electorate as a whole rather than those of the party activists (often more extreme than average) and they open the nomination process to outsiders who have not built up a track record and strong relationship with the party activists.

In addition, four states used to use **blanket primaries**, in which voters could participate in the primary of both main parties, but this form of primary was declared unlawful by the Supreme Court in 2000, in the case of *California Democratic Party* v. *Jones*, as it allowed non-party members to decide who would represent the party in elections.

Overall, the use of primaries to choose candidates for high office has a number of advantages:

- They are more democratic than party leaders deciding on the candidates that voters can choose from at the election, with the possibility that the electorate will not like either of them.
- As a result of the influence of party leaders being diluted, candidates who would have had little chance of being selected by them may stand for election.
- The competing candidates usually offer a range of policies and election strategies, and the result of the primary will provide a strong indication of which approach has the most electoral appeal, especially if independents have been allowed to participate.
- In the case of open primaries, all voters have the opportunity to participate at this stage of the election process, which increases political participation by a wide cross-section of the adult population.

However, primaries also have a number of disadvantages:

- Experienced party leaders may make a more informed decision on suitable candidates for their party than the wider electorate.
- Some candidates may campaign on their personal qualities, rather than issues, serving to obscure rather than promote the party's message.
- The competition between candidates of the same party can become so intense, with mutual insults and accusations, that the party's public image is seriously damaged ahead of the election.
- In the case of open primaries, there is the opportunity for 'raiding' by supporters of one party who cross over and vote for a weak candidate of the opposing party.
- When (as in the Republican primaries of 2008) a victor emerges early in the process, the voters in all states that have not yet held their primaries do not have the opportunity to play a significant role in the process.

This swift conclusion was due, in large part, to the **front-loading** of primaries. In the 1980s, Southern states started to hold their primaries on the same day, always in early March, to increase their influence over the result. This day was dubbed '**Super Tuesday**' by political commentators and aimed to propel any of the candidates that did very well on that day, winning all or most of the South, towards their party's nomination. So successful was this tactic that other states started to move their primaries ahead of Super Tuesday, in February (hence the term 'front-loading') so that their voters could affect the outcome of the contest. In 2008, this game of leapfrog resulted in over twenty states holding their primaries on 5 February, dwarfing all previous Super Tuesdays.

Front-loading has been subject to criticism for several reasons, including:

- The importance of the 'invisible primaries' has grown. Candidates need to have raised substantial funds, established name recognition and gained endorsement from prominent party members to make an impact in the first, crucial, weeks of the primaries. Anyone who has failed to do so may find themselves effectively written off as a credible candidate before the primaries even begin.
- The importance of the first primary, in New Hampshire, and the first caucus, in Iowa, is also magnified, as carrying early momentum into Super Tuesday is essential.
- Candidates who perform unexpectedly well in the first primaries, such as John Edwards in 2004, have little time to build on their success through fundraising, building their campaign teams and buying additional campaign advertising.
- The primary season can develop the feel of a cross-country tour bus, where the candidates stop just long enough in each state to wave and move on to another contest.
- This, in turn, may mean that the public does not get to know the candidates well.
- Voters in states that do not hold their primaries early in the season may be effectively disenfranchised in the selection process.
- The process, overall, creates a sense that election campaigns start very early and last too long.

There are also advantages to front-loading, including:

- In some cases, front-loading has resulted in the nomination process being virtually over by the end of March. This has meant that any battles between members of the same party have been short, reducing the damage to the party ahead of the general election campaign and preserving resources for that phase.

## Box 4.3  The 2008 primary campaign

John McCain won the nomination of the Republican Party. Yet, in July 2007, one of America's most respected electoral commentators wrote, 'Mr McCain's campaign is over. The physicians have pulled up the sheet; the executors of the estate are taking over.' Seven months later, in February 2008, the same commentator proclaimed Senator McCain 'all but unstoppable'. The transformation said a great deal about his relationship with the party. Famously independent, John McCain had been more than willing to take a stand on policy issues that are unpopular with committed Republicans. The party's **social conservatives**, who favour policies underpinned by Christian values, have never really forgiven him for his attack on some of their leaders in 2000 when he branded them as 'agents of intolerance'. **Fiscal conservatives**, another influential force within the Republican Party, favour measures to reduce government intervention and have their own list of disagreements with the Senator. They were angered by his opposition to tax cuts proposed by President Bush in 2001 and 2003; they were hostile to his stance on climate change that would increase regulation on American business; they disliked his willingness to increase controls on gun purchases and they have challenged in court his legislation to regulate campaign finance, on the grounds that it limits free speech. In addition, in the first half of 2007, as the contenders were seeking to raise money for their presidential campaigns, Senator McCain supported legislation that would provide citizenship for most illegal immigrants, a policy fiercely opposed by most Republicans. He also gave his full support to increasing the number of troops in Iraq, thus tying himself to the most unpopular policy of an increasingly unpopular President Bush. It was not surprising, therefore, that he had great difficulty raising funds in 2007.

However, all of the other leading contenders demonstrated that their judgement and/or personal failings were greater than those of Senator McCain. By the autumn of 2007, Rudy Giuliani was leading the pack. He made the decision to use his national profile, based on his performance on 9/11, to deliver a knockout blow to the rest of the field on Super Tuesday when twenty-two states across the country would be holding their primaries. Calculating that none of the other candidates would be able to gain significant momentum by winning all of the early primaries, he expected to be able to sweep past them in early February. On one level he was right: the first three Republican primaries were won by three different candidates. However, he failed to recognise that spending the first month of the campaign on the sidelines would have the effect of making him appear marginal, even irrelevant, and by the time he started participating wholeheartedly it was too late to reverse that impression. The candidate who seemed to hold the greatest appeal to the conservatives in the party was Fred Thompson. An actor-turned-politician, he sought to follow in the footsteps of the modern hero of the Republican Party, Ronald Reagan, whose career had taken a similar path. However, Thompson's campaign was at times chaotic, with confused messages, and at times lacklustre, with far fewer public appearances than other candidates. Quite simply, he gave the impression of not wanting to win as much as the others. As Thompson's campaign fizzled, social conservatives turned to the Baptist preacher-turned-politician Mike Huckabee. He had a solid political record as the Governor of Arkansas, where he had been both pragmatic and effective. He also had an engaging personality that charmed audiences. However, despite his early success in winning the Iowa caucus, it was apparent that his appeal was limited to social conservatives (the 'religious right') and that he was only a viable candidate in states where this group made up a sizeable proportion of the electorate. That left only Mitt Romney, the former Governor of the very liberal state of Massachusetts. In preparation for his campaign, Romney distanced himself from his record as Governor and adopted more conservative positions. This attempt to court conservatives was probably futile both because Romney is a Mormon, part of a religious group much distrusted by the Christian evangelicals he sought to attract and because, at the same time, it created the impression that he was an opportunist who would say anything to get elected. (He even came out in opposition to the much praised healthcare plan he had introduced while Governor.) In addition, the tone of his campaign was highly negative as he attacked whoever appeared to be his main challenger at various stages of the contest. Finally, as an immensely wealthy man, who spent over $40 million on his own campaign, he seemed ill at ease with ordinary people.

Barack Obama won the nomination of the Democratic Party. However, he did not seal victory until June 2008, at the very end of the primary season, when his main rival, Hillary Clinton, withdrew her candidacy. Both of them entered the primary season having raised over $100 million. As the contest unfolded, each of them attracted distinct patterns of support from the groups that are the most reliable backers of the Democratic Party. Barack Obama enjoyed the loyal support of African Americans, younger people and highly educated voters while Hillary Clinton attracted the support of women, working-class white men and Hispanics. Neither coalition was strong enough for either candidate to establish a clear lead (partly because the party's system of proportional allocation of delegates meant that even victories in the most populous states such as California did not prove decisive), although Barack Obama was able to build a small majority with a string of consecutive wins in the spring. Ultimately, the nomination was decided by the superdelegates. Rather than bring their own experience and judgement to the process, however, most of them declared their support for the candidate who had won the most delegates in the primaries for fear that they would be seen to be undemocratic if they ignored the public vote. Thus, Barack Obama sealed the nomination with the support of the superdelegates.

- Backing from the most prominent leaders of the party is highly beneficial to candidates in a compressed primary calendar, giving the leaders an opportunity to influence the choice of candidate to represent them in the election.

## The national conventions

Each party holds a national convention in the summer of each presidential election year, with the Democrats usually holding their convention before the Republicans.

Historically, the convention served the following purposes:

- Selecting a presidential candidate, often in deals between powerful party figures in 'smoke-filled' rooms.
- A forum for party factions to debate which issues should be included in the party's platform (manifesto).
- Announcing the vice-presidential candidate.

In recent decades, the convention has arguably declined in importance, as it does not fulfil many of its traditional roles.

- With the growth of primaries, each party's presidential candidate is usually known well before the conventions. The last time there was brokered convention was in 1968 when the Democratic primaries failed to produce a decisive outcome and the party nominee was chosen on the convention floor amid rowdy scenes.
- Public debates at the convention create a sense of disunity and are largely discouraged. The last time a fierce debate was allowed was

at the 1996 Republican Party convention, when the focus was on abortion.

• Vice-presidential candidates are also usually selected well in advance of the conventions.

However, the conventions do play a number of significant informal roles in the electoral process:

• For one week, in election year, virtually all political attention is on the party holding its convention and it is a prime opportunity to convey a positive impression of the candidate and the party.
• It may help to build party unity, especially if the primary campaign has highlighted divisions.
• Occurring only once every four years, it provides the only opportunity for activists across the country to come together to build links and reinforce bonds between people who may have very different priorities.
• The convention may help provide a 'bounce' in the polls if it goes well.
• Perhaps of greatest importance, the convention serves to establish a 'narrative' for the election campaign. As the campaign is making a transition from the primaries (when candidates are mainly focusing on rivals from their own party) to the general election campaign (which is a head-to-head contest between the leaders of the two main parties), each nominee will attempt to define themselves, their opponent and the key issues in ways that give them an advantage ahead of the autumn.

**The general election campaign**
By tradition, the final part of a presidential campaign, when the two party candidates battle to be elected to the White House, begins after the Labor Day national holiday that falls on the first Monday in September. Periodically, the policies of a third-party candidate attract sufficient public attention for this phase of the election to become a three-way contest (see the section on minor parties).

As with the primary phase of the campaign, the candidates are effectively fighting not one campaign but fifty-one campaigns as they seek to win the support of each of the fifty states plus the District

## Box 4.4  The 2008 party conventions

The Democrats held their convention in Denver, Colorado, which signalled their determination to fight for the support of the Rocky Mountain states that had supported the Republicans in previous presidential elections. After a bruising primary campaign, the party's highest priority was demonstrating that it was uniting behind its nominee, which led to Hillary Clinton and her most leading supporters playing a prominent role in the convention to show that any bitterness had been put behind them. The secondary issue addressed by the convention was rebutting the Republican line that Barack Obama was too inexperienced and too left-wing to become the leader of the American people. Thus, his speech (and that of his wife) was designed to demonstrate that he was confident, assured, moderate and pragmatic. His choice of vice-presidential candidate, Joe Biden, one of the longest-serving Senators with expertise in foreign policy, served to reinforce this message. The convention succeeded in meeting these aims to the extent that the party enjoyed a 10 per cent 'bounce' in the polls.

The Republicans had a different set of challenges. John McCain needed to galvanise all of the conservatives in his party who had been lukewarm towards him since he announced his candidacy the previous year. His advisors had little doubt that conservatives would vote for him, but worried that they would not actively campaign for him. There was also a concern that the public saw him as too old: if elected he would be seventy-two years old when he took office. Finally, John McCain needed to distance himself from the deeply unpopular incumbent Republican President, George W. Bush. McCain's team took a huge gamble, to address all of these issues, by announcing, just before the convention, that the Governor of Alaska, Sarah Palin, would be his running mate. Young, glamorous, very conservative and with a record of fighting corruption in her state (even when the perpetrators were from her own party) she helped attract conservatives to the campaign, add youthful vigour and reinforce John McCain's message that his ticket sharply contrasted with the Bush administration as radical, maverick outsiders. Such was the success of this announcement that party enjoyed an even bigger bounce in the polls than the Democrats, giving John McCain a lead in the opinion polls in the early autumn.

## Box 4.5  The electoral college

The outcome of a presidential election is not determined by adding the national vote of the candidates. The Founding Fathers, concerned that the masses could be too easily tempted to support irresponsible politicians, created an electoral college to protect the nation from mob politics.

Established by Article II, Section 1 of the Constitution, the electoral college is created once every four years for the sole purpose of electing the President and Vice President. Each state is allocated a number of electors, determined by combining the number of Congressional representatives a state has (at minimum one) with its Senators (two). Thus, a state with a small population, such as Wyoming, is represented by just one person in the House of Representatives but, along with every other state, has two Senators. This means that it has three votes in the electoral college. By comparison, the state with the largest population, California, is represented by fifty-three people in the House of Representatives, which, with its two Senators, gives it fifty-five votes in the electoral college. In addition, Washington DC, which is not a part of any of the fifty states, has had three votes in the electoral college since the passage of the 23rd Amendment in 1961. (The people of Washington DC still do not have any representation in Congress.)

After each census, which takes place at the start of each decade, the number of seats allocated to each state in the House of Representatives is adjusted to reflect shifts in population; when this happens, the number of electoral college votes each state has is similarly adjusted. Thus, in the 2000 presidential elections Florida had twenty-five electoral college votes. By the 2004 election, as a result of the census that had taken place in 2000, Florida had been allocated two extra seats in the House of Representatives which was reflected in the electoral college, giving the state twenty-seven votes.

Although the distribution of votes changes every ten years, the total number of electoral college votes is fixed at 538, which means that a candidate requires a majority – 270 or more – to win.

The presidential candidate who wins a majority of votes in each state wins all of the electoral college votes for that state (with the exception of Maine and Nebraska, which allocate their electors on a proportional basis). This system means that presidential elections become fifty-one separate elections, with the candidates having to make informed decisions on which states they are almost certain to win, which ones they are likely to lose and which are likely to be closely contested, using their resources accordingly.

Once the votes of the electorate have been counted, respected political activists, chosen by their parties, act as electors and gather in the state capital to formally cast their votes, reflecting the views of the electorate. These votes are then conveyed to the US Senate, where the final result is announced.

Since the electoral college was set up to protect the nation from an irresponsible electorate, the electors may, in principle, ignore the result of the popular vote. Occasionally this actually happens and electors who vote this way are known as **faithless electors**. Since the founding of the electoral college, there have been 156 faithless electors. Seventy-one of these votes were changed because the original candidate died before the day on which the electoral college cast their votes. Three of the votes were not cast at all, as three electors chose to abstain from casting their electoral vote for any candidate. The other eighty-two electoral votes were changed on the personal initiative of the elector.

Sometimes electors change their votes in large groups, such as when twenty-three Virginia electors acted together in 1836. Many times, however, these electors stood alone in their decision. No faithless elector has ever changed the outcome of an election.

In the most recent act of elector abstention, Barbara Lett-Simmons, a Democratic elector from the District of Columbia, did not cast her vote for Al Gore in the 2000 presidential election, as expected. Her abstention was meant to protest the lack of Congressional representation for Washington DC.

As the actions of faithless electors demonstrates, the electoral college is an outdated institution. Despite this, it is still seen as having advantages, as follows:

- It requires candidates to concentrate on key groups of voters (men have a different pattern of voting to women; ethnic groups vote differently; old and young, rich and poor have different concerns) and to concentrate on all regions of the nation, with their distinct issues and needs.
- It ensures that the states with the smallest populations can have a significant impact on the outcome of the election. Thus, while it is important to win large states, such as California and Texas, in a close race it is important not to neglect the small states.

However, the presidential elections of 2000 and 2004 highlighted the electoral college's disadvantages, as follows:

- Some states are solidly Democrat (often referred to as **'blue' states**), others solidly Republican (referred to as **'red' states**). Neither candidate from the two main parties mounted serious campaigns in New York (whose thirty-one electoral college votes were almost certain to go to the Democratic candidate) or Texas (whose thirty-four electoral college votes were certain to go to George W. Bush in both elections). This meant that voters in those states were largely taken for granted and had very little influence over the final result.

- Consequently, other states have a disproportionate influence over the result.
    - Disproportionate influence may arise because all states must have at least three electoral college votes, making smaller states over-represented compared to larger ones. If California had electoral votes in precise proportion to the three given to Wyoming, it would have 180 instead of the 55 it had in 2004. In 2000, a high proportion of small states were solid supporters of George W. Bush, which is why he was able to win the electoral college despite polling 540,000 votes fewer than Al Gore.
    - Alternatively, disproportionate influence may arise, particularly in a close election, either because a state's voters are either fairly evenly split between the two main parties or because the state has a high proportion of voters without a strong party affiliation. In 2004, there were ten of these states, known as '**swing states**' or '**battleground states**', which were expected to be decisive in the outcome of the election. The swing state with the most electoral college votes was Florida, but the most significant was Ohio, which President Bush won by 120,000 votes. However, had just 70,000 people switched their vote in Ohio, John Kerry would have won the presidency despite losing the popular vote in the country as a whole by 3.5 million.
- Additionally, candidates representing minor parties have little likelihood of winning electoral college votes unless they have very high levels of support in a number of states. In 1992, a Texan oil billionaire, Ross Perot, stood as an independent for the presidency and attracted 19.2 million votes, but because he failed to come first in any state this failed to translate into any electoral college votes.

of Columbia in order to accumulate sufficient votes in the electoral college for victory.

To win the election, the candidates have to:

- Advertise extensively, using radio, newspapers and (especially) television in order to promote their own strengths, highlight the weaknesses of their opponents and respond to any damaging claims that the other campaign, or its allies, may make.

• Appear at campaign rallies that prove that the candidates can enthuse crowds, and also at 'town hall' events where they are expected to demonstrate that they can appeal to ordinary people and effectively address any questions that the voters may have.

• Participate in a series of debates in which they can challenge each other on policy issues. By tradition, there are three debates between the presidential candidates, over a period of about four weeks, each focusing on a different area of policy (such as the economy or foreign policy), and one debate between the vice-presidential candidates. The debates are organised by the Commission on Presidential Debates, set up in 1987 by the Democratic and Republican Parties. It allows a third-party candidate to participate in the debates if a range of opinion polls shows that the candidate is attracting the support of at least 15 per cent of the voters.

In these debates, the candidates need to:

– Demonstrate that they have a strong, effective grasp of policy issues (in 1992, the third-party candidate in the vice-presidential debate appeared to be completely out of his depth).

– Make the argument that their policies will be more beneficial for the country than those of their opponents.

– Show that they are articulate and able to cope well with the pressure of such an intense debate, watched by up to 50 million people.

– Ideally, deliver a knock-out line that leaves the other candidate grasping for a response or encapsulates the public's reservations about the other candidate. (In 1980, Ronald Reagan effectively dismissed lengthy, complex attacks by President Carter in the presidential debate with a simple, but cheerfully delivered, line: 'There you go again', making the President appear negative and out of touch with ordinary people.)

## Box 4.6  The 2008 general election campaign

Going into September, McCain held a slim lead in the opinion polls. However, on 4 November 2008, Barack Obama won decisively, with 365 electoral college votes (to 173 for McCain) and 53 per cent of the popular vote, which was the highest winning margin for twenty years.

The key factors that led to Barack Obama overtaking John McCain were:

- The 'Bush effect': the contest took place against the background of a deeply unpopular Republican President and the Democratic campaign relentlessly tied John McCain to the President's record over the previous eight years.
- The 'October Surprise': in the final two months of any presidential campaign, there is a high probability of an unexpected develop-ment that may affect the pattern of support for the candidates. When such a development occurs close to polling day, leaving little time for the candidates to react, it can prove decisive, which is why political commentators refer to it as the 'October surprise'. In the 2008 campaign, the October surprise arrived on 15 September, when the giant bank Lehman Brothers declared bankruptcy, triggering the near collapse of the financial sector. This crisis was widely blamed on the Republican preference for 'light touch' regulation, allowing banks to make dangerously risky investment decisions. John McCain lost his poll lead the day after the collapse of Lehman Brothers and never regained it.
- The temperament of the candidates: the response of the two candidates to the financial crisis, with Obama appearing more calm (and Presidential) under pressure than the more experi-enced McCain, added to the impact of the October surprise. John McCain initially suspended his campaign to return to Washington DC to address the crisis and called for the postponement of the first presidential debate. At a crisis meeting in Washington, however, he contributed nothing at all and then rescinded his call for the debate to be rescheduled. Barack Obama, meanwhile, attended the same crisis meeting while continuing his campaign and planning for the debate, observing that 'a President must be able to do more than one thing at a time'.
- The performance of the two candidates in the presidential debates: opinion polls conducted after each of the three debates indicated that a clear majority of viewers thought that Barack Obama won all of them.

- The Palin effect: after an initial positive public response to the choice of Sarah Palin as the Republican vice-presidential candidate, her impact on her party's campaign was largely negative. Her lack of experience meant that the McCain campaign was no longer in a position to question whether Barack Obama's limited time in high office (he had been a Senator for just four years) made him unsuitable for the presidency. As this had proved to be the most effective line of attack throughout the summer, it clearly weakened the campaign. In addition, her performance on TV interviews, especially the one conducted by Katie Couric, who had a very gentle style of questioning, proved disastrous, with Palin apparently unable to answer very straightforward questions, such as which newspapers she read and Supreme Court cases she found to be particularly significant. When combined with her staunch conservatism, these public appearances served to alienate independents and even moderate Republicans.
- The funding gap: Barack Obama had demonstrated a far greater capacity to raise funds than John McCain throughout the invisible primary and the primary season. In the summer of 2008, he made the risky decision not to accept public financing for the general election campaign. John McCain, in common with all previous presidential candidates, did accept public funds. This meant that once the party convention was over, he received $84 million for campaigning which he could top up with whatever leftover funds he had from the primaries, thought to total around $150 million. However, he was not allowed to raise any further campaign donations. Barack Obama received no public funds, which meant that his campaign would have to devote time and resources to meet, or exceed, the money available to his rival. Many commentators questioned the wisdom of his choice. However, he succeeded in raising record sums. He broke all previous records by raising $66 million in August, then shattered his own record by raising $150 million in September. This enabled him to outspend McCain in key states in the final weeks of the campaign and even make an 'infomercial', a half-hour programme that set out his views and policies, in the final week, that meant buying prime time on three of the four main networks (ABC refused to sell its time) and several cable channels.
- Internet-based campaigning: Barack Obama's campaign pioneered a new style of electioneering that combined traditional campaigning methods with innovative strategies that made use of opportunities provided by the internet. His website encouraged everyone who visited it to register for information on the campaign. Everyone who registered was sent regular emails to keep them up to date with developments and to encourage them to establish

links with other supporters, thereby creating a network of people who could identify with one another and help spread the campaign's messages. This network also became a key element in the campaign's successful fundraising. Of all the donations received by Barack Obama, more than a quarter were from people who had donated $200 or less and another quarter donated less than $1,000. In total, over 3 million Americans contributed to the Obama campaign, including many who had never previously become actively involved in campaigning. The network also provided the grass-roots volunteers that are crucial to a campaign's success. Thus, when the campaign began setting up its operation in Texas ahead of the primary, over 125,000 people had already signed up as volunteers. The enthusiasm, money and volunteers generated online were then funnelled into traditional campaigning. By the summer of 2008, the campaign had staff and offices in 21 states, 134 campaign offices open across the country and nearly 1,000 field staff on the ground who could co-ordinate the efforts of the volunteers. In addition, Barack Obama's online network provided him with a new way of responding to political attacks. Thus, when he made a speech on race in response to the controversy surrounding his pastor, Jeremiah Wright, his campaign sent an e-mail to all supporters with a link to the video of the thirty-seven-minute speech. It was viewed in its entirety on YouTube over 5.2 million times, offsetting the media's negative coverage of the issue.

- The negative tone of the Republican campaign: the official slogan of the McCain campaign was 'country first' which, tied to repeated suggestions that Barack Obama and his wife were not very patriotic and claims by Sarah Palin that only Republicans were truly committed to their country, struck a divisive note that alienated independents.

In combination, these factors resulted in Barack Obama winning all of the states that had supported the Democratic nominee four years earlier, plus nine that had voted for George W. Bush in the previous election.

## Concerns about the electoral system: campaign finance

With almost every US citizen able to vote, and so many opportunities to choose their political representatives and hold them to account, it would be reasonable to expect that the US electoral system would be highly valued at home and a model to be copied abroad. Instead, it is the subject of considerable debate and legislation, with the USA widely criticised in other countries, mainly for two reasons: the cost of elections and incumbency advantage.

## The cost of elections

The first stage of a US election campaign is the primary. With candidates competing with members of their own party, they have to use their own funds or campaign donations to promote their agenda. In the case of campaigns for the House of Representatives, this means addressing an electorate of over 600,000 people; for the Senate, this may mean an electorate of several million people (more than 26 million in California) over a vast territory (equivalent to the size of Britain and France combined in Texas); for the presidency, this means an electorate of well over 200 million, who have to be appealed to, state by state, across a geographically and culturally diverse continent.

Even after the primaries, when the political party they represent starts making financial contributions to the campaign, candidates continue to need substantial donations. Having gained the support of people affiliated to their party during the primaries, they have to reach out to the wider electorate through distributing leaflets, putting up posters, organising campaign rallies and co-ordinating volunteers who canvass voters in person or by phone. In a race for a Congressional district, this requires setting up a campaign office with full-time paid staff, and in a Senate race a number of offices will be required in the main towns/cities in the state. To judge the success of the campaign, and for guidance on any improvements which need to be made, the candidate will need to hire opinion pollsters and public-relations specialists. Above all, because neither the candidate nor the support team can expect to encounter a majority of the voters, the main method of conveying the campaign theme is TV and radio advertisements, which are expensive both to make and to broadcast. The pressure to raise so much money has two effects:

- People will only run for office in districts in which they have a reasonable chance of winning. There is little point in challenging

| Table 4.1  Summary of 2008 election campaign | | | |
|---|---|---|---|
| Election | No of positions being contested | No of candidates (including primary candidates) | Total amount raised |
| Presidency | 1 | 27 | $1.8 billion |
| Senate | 35 | 168 | $410.4 million |
| House of Representatives | 435 | 1,376 | $978.5 million |

a well-funded, popular incumbent. Consequently, there are a significant number of Congressional districts in which the incumbent may face no challenger for several elections. For example, in Georgia's 5th District, which covers the predominantly African American city of Atlanta, Congressman John Lewis – who was a Civil Rights leader alongside Martin Luther King Jnr – did not face a challenge in either a primary or an election in either 2002 or 2004. In 1998, the Republican Party, in an act of desperation, nominated a candidate also named John Lewis, in the hope that the people of Atlanta might vote out their Congressman by mistake.

- Where an effective challenge is mounted, the cost of an election is likely to be substantial, as illustrated by the 2008 election campaign.

The concerns that have emerged from such expensive contests are that:

- They make it impossible for people who do not have personal wealth, or connections to prosperous individuals or organisations, to run for office.
- Elected representatives, highly reliant on the individuals and organisations that fund their campaigns, may be more responsive to the needs/wishes of their donors than their voters.
- Donors, in turn, prefer to support candidates who have a proven record of electoral success and who have a record of supporting

their interests. This means that incumbents usually have a significant advantage in fundraising, reducing the likelihood of an effective electoral challenge.

The widespread suspicion that, once elected, representatives can remain in office for as long as they have the support of wealthy donors has raised questions of whether the electoral system fulfils its primary goals of holding representatives to account and limiting the amount of power they wield.

### The potential benefits of private financing of elections

It is possible for the reliance on private donors to fund election campaigns to be beneficial to US democracy. If the majority of donations were made by Americans from all walks of life, including those who can only afford to make very modest contributions, the overall level of political participation would rise because:

- Donors, by giving money to a campaign, are making a political statement or expressing an opinion.
- Donors tend to take an active interest in the campaign they support (and, as a consequence, rival campaigns), thus raising the overall level of political awareness.
- Donors, having participated in the campaign in one way, often participate in elections in other ways, such as volunteering, attending rallies and so on, thereby raising the overall level of participation.
- Donors are likely to share their views on the campaign with family, friends and associates, making them a source of political education.
- Donors are almost certain to vote, and to actively encourage others to vote, thereby boosting the turnout at elections.

### Finding the balance between the advantages and disadvantages of private donations to campaigns

Since the 1970s, when campaign finance rose to the top of the political agenda, policy-makers have been attempting to craft regulations that address the concerns associated with the private financing of election campaigns while promoting the active political participation associated with contributing to campaigns in this way.

## Watergate: political corruption and campaign finance regulation

It was the Senate investigations into the Watergate scandal in the early 1970s that brought concerns about campaign funding to the fore. After the discovery that senior advisers to President Richard Nixon had paid people, out of campaign donations, to break into the headquarters of the Democratic Party, to find out their election campaign strategy, further probing revealed a number of questionable relationships between the President and his donors. International Telephone and Telegraph contributed $400,000 at the same time as the Justice Department settled a lawsuit against the company and milk producers saw an increase in Federal subsidies after donating $600,000 to the President's re-election campaign.

The hearings demonstrated a clear need for campaign finance to be strictly monitored, and Congress passed a series of laws in the following years regulating how much could be donated and how the money could be used.

### The Federal Elections Campaign Acts (FECA)

The first of the acts was passed before the Watergate scandal broke. The **Federal Elections Campaign Act** of 1972 replaced all the legislation which had been passed since 1908 to address political corruption and was designed to reduce the influence of wealthy donors on elections.

These measures were greatly strengthened by the Federal Elections Campaign Act of 1974, passed in response to the Watergate revelations. It required all candidates to publicly declare the sources of their income, placed precise limits on campaign donations and set up a system of public financing of presidential elections to reduce the need for candidates to rely on wealthy private donors. It also set up the **Federal Elections Commission** (**FEC**) to enforce the rules.

Together, these Acts put in place a three-pronged strategy for managing the money in politics:

* *Disclosure* All campaign contributions must be declared and published so that anyone can see who has given money and judgements may be made as to whether the elected representative's actions appear to have been influenced by his/her donors.

- *Restrictions on the size of donations* To limit the dependence of candidates on a small number of extremely wealthy donors, the 1974 law placed strict limits on the donations they could accept. This would, it was expected, lead to such a wide range of donors for each campaign that it would be unrealistic for them all to expect some form of reward for their contributions. Individuals could donate up to $20,000 to a political party but were limited to contributions of $1,000 per candidate in a primary or election. Organisations were limited to contributing $5,000 per election through a **Political Action Committee (PAC)**. Again, to discourage too close a relationship between a candidate and a donor, the law stated that PACs had to receive contributions from a minimum of fifty donors and make contributions to a minimum of five candidates, thereby acting as a form of financial filter. Finally, to ensure that donors did not get around the regulations by making donations through many PACs, each citizen was restricted to making a maximum donation of $25,000 each year, including a donation to a political party.

- *Reducing election costs and reliance on private donations* The 1974 law dangled a carrot in front of all candidates running for the presidency. If they undertook to limit the total amount of funds raised through private donations, the Federal government would provide **matching funds**, boosting their campaign budget without the need to invest further time and resources in fundraising. The limit has increased over the years, linked to inflation, and in the 2004 presidential election was about $45 million. To qualify for the funds, candidates have to demonstrate that they have widespread voter appeal across the country by raising a minimum of $10,000 in small contributions of no more than $250 each. Additionally, they must demonstrate that the contributions came from at least twenty states, with small contributions of at least $5,000 from each of those states. In this way, it will be clear that the candidate is not reliant on wealthy contributors and has the active support of people beyond his/her home region.

It was apparent from the outset, however, that candidates would be reluctant to accept restrictions on their ability to raise private campaign funds when Congress decided not to apply the matching funds arrangements to campaigns for the House of Representatives or the Senate. Over the next thirty years, a variety of devices were used to limit the effectiveness of FECA.

### *Buckley* v. *Valeo*

In 1976, the Supreme Court upheld a challenge to the Federal Elections Campaign Act of 1974, which argued that it was unconstitutional to restrict how much a person could spend, of their own money, on an election campaign. This meant that personal wealth would be exempted from campaign finance regulations.

### Soft money

Then, in 1979, a number of technical amendments were announced by the FEC to campaign finance rules. These removed all restrictions on fundraising for campaigns to promote awareness of elections, the issues being debated and efforts made to ensure that people would be able to vote. This kind of fundraising became known as **soft money**.

Money donated directly to the election campaign, according to the FECA regulations, was known as **hard money**. These funds could be used to persuade voters to 'vote for', 'elect' or 'defeat' a candidate.

In the 1988 presidential election campaign, in order to bridge the funding gap with his opponent, the Democratic campaign began using soft money to 'explain' the issues in ways that clearly encouraged people to vote for their candidate. By carefully avoiding the use of the words which fell under the FECA regulations, the campaign was able to use soft money for purposes for which it was not intended. Once this device had been used successfully, all subsequent campaigns used it, undermining the effectiveness of FECA.

### The 'Failure to Enforce Commission'

For critics of these developments, the ineffectiveness of the Federal Elections Commission has also been a cause of concern. The commission is composed of six members, three Republicans and three Democrats, who are often deadlocked when deciding whether election laws have been broken. The result is that no action is taken. Critics, who have called the FEC the 'Failure to Enforce Commission', would like to see it replaced by an organisation with independent members and strong powers to severely punish anyone who breaks the rules.

## The McCain presidential campaign (2000)

With the money being raised for campaigning continuing to grow, by the 2000 presidential election there was a strong sense that FECA had been ineffective and needed to be replaced.

Running for the Republican nomination, Senator John McCain made campaign finance reform a centrepiece of his campaign and took pride in his reliance on many small donors, rather than wealthy contributors. Although he lost the nomination to George W. Bush (who went on to spend $187 million), his stand on this issue gave momentum to the drive for reform.

## The Bi-partisan Campaign Reform Act (BCRA)

In 2002, Congress passed a new Campaign Reform Act, sponsored by John McCain and Russell Feingold in the Senate and by Christopher Shays and Martin Meehan in the House of Representatives. The terms of the new law were:

- Hard-money contributions by individuals were increased to $2,000 per year. If a candidate faced a wealthy opponent, self-financing a campaign, the hard-money ceiling would be raised, depending on how much money the opponent was spending.
- Contributions from PACs remained limited to $5,000 per campaign.
- Total contributions that an individual could make to individual campaigns, PACs and political parties was raised to $95,000 every two years.
- Soft-money donations to candidates and political parties were banned.
- Pressure groups were banned from airing TV or radio electioneering advertisements one month before a primary election and two months before a general election.

The intention of the law was to reduce the total amount of money being spent in Federal elections and to make candidates more dependent on a large number of donors making hard-money contributions, rather than on a small number of donors making immense soft-money contributions. Like FECA, however, it immediately encountered efforts to evade its regulations.

## 527s

Having specified that candidates and political parties were banned from raising soft money, political activists were quick to spot that the rule did not apply to non-party organisations. Ahead of the 2004 presidential election, a group of trade union leaders set up organisations, under Section 527 of the tax code, for the specific purpose of raising soft money to spend on anti-Bush advertisements and to mobilise voters likely to vote against him.

In the election, 527s spent around $400 million. Of this, $146 million was donated by just twenty-five people. How influential they were, however, is questionable. As they were not allowed to co-ordinate with the political parties, it may be that they duplicated their work rather than complemented it and they were far less visible in the 2006 mid-term elections and the 2008 presidential elections.

### *Citizens United* v. *Federal Elections Commission* (2010)

On 21 January 2010, the Supreme Court struck down several campaign finance restrictions:

- Previously, only money that had been raised by companies and trade unions for the specific purpose of campaigning could be used to produce and air advertisements aimed at influencing the outcome of Congressional and Presidential elections. This ruling allowed them to use any funds available to them for this purpose, thus raising the prospect of wealthy groups being able to use unlimited resources to support their preferred candidate and attack candidates they oppose. Observers immediately highlighted the likelihood of a sharp increase of aggressive negative campaign adverts that would save associated candidates from being criticised for dirty campaign tactics.
- The ban on corporations and trade unions airing campaign adverts in the thirty days before a primary or sixty days before a general election was lifted.

However, restrictions on direct contributions to candidates and requirements on organisations to disclose election-related expenditure were kept in place.

## Box 4.7 Fundraising in the 2008 presidential election

The 2008 presidential election may prove to be a watershed in campaign finance in two ways, one positive and one negative.

The fundraising campaign of Barack Obama appeared to achieve the elusive balance that regulators have been attempting to find for over three decades: a mass movement contributing to the costs of the campaign that makes a candidate a formidable competitor without making him beholden to a small group of wealthy donors. He refused to take money from Political Action Committees or lobbyists, in order to limit the influence they may claim to have over him and assure the wider electorate of his political independence. More than 3 million people made financial contributions. Of all the money raised, half of it came from people who could afford less than $1,000 and, of this amount, half came from people who could afford less than $200. More than 2 million of these contributors became involved in his campaign in other ways, such as volunteering. It is quite possible that in future any candidates who are unable to build a mass movement to drive their financing and volunteering (probably linked by the internet) will lack credibility.

However, by refusing public funds for his general election campaign, he may have effectively destroyed the system of financial support that was designed to ensure that candidates with limited resources, but with a contribution to make to public life, can run for office. No leading candidate for the presidency has accepted public funds for the primaries since 1990, with the result that taking public funds has come to be seen as evidence of a candidate's weakness. In future, accepting public funds for the general election campaign is likely to be seen in the same way. This clearly has the potential to strengthen the position of those who are wealthy, or have connections to wealthy donors, and weaken anyone who lacks such links and is unable to compensate with the charisma or public persona of Barack Obama.

## The rising cost of elections

Campaign finance reformers face the challenge of trying to reduce the supply of money while demand rises. Factors that drive up the cost of elections include:

- *The length of elections* In early 2004, badges were on sale promoting Hillary Clinton for the presidency in 2008, months before the 2004 election had taken place.
- *Campaigning has become more professional* Highly-paid campaign managers are often credited with doing more than the candidate to win elections, such as George W. Bush's strategist, Karl Rove.
- *Campaign techniques have become more sophisticated* As well as television and radio advertisements designed to appeal to a range of specific groups of voters, candidates use opinion polls, focus groups and, in recent years, the internet to identify potential supporters, recruit volunteers and raise funds.

However, reformers have one major asset. It is clear that public confidence in the electoral system, and the politicians it produces, is being eroded by the perception that political decisions are unduly influenced by wealthy donors. Campaigns to 'strengthen public participation and faith in our institutions' and 'ensure that government and political processes serve the general interest, rather than special interests' strike a chord with many voters.

## Concerns about the electoral system: incumbency advantage

While concerns about the cost of elections centre on whether there is a level playing field for candidates, and whether contributions make successful candidates beholden to their donors, there are also concerns that the electoral system gives a substantial advantage to **incumbents** (people holding an official position), which may encourage them to become complacent and out of touch with the voters. In short, **incumbency advantage** may serve to undermine the level of accountability that elections are supposed to achieve.

Incumbents tend to have an advantage because:

- They have had the opportunity to establish a track record of experience and achievement that untested opponents may not be able to match.
- They have had the opportunity to raise their public profile through their work that challengers may not be able to match. Politicians

are often invited to high-profile events and are frequently interviewed by the media.

- In the case of members of Congress, incumbents have access to a range of resources that enable them to communicate directly with constituents and keep them informed of their efforts and achievements. These include franking privileges, that enable them to send out mailings at no cost to themselves, websites and, above all, a large staff who can respond to most queries and requests.
- Because of these advantages, and the consequent expectation that incumbents will win their next election, people and groups hoping to be able to influence policy are more likely to provide campaign funds for incumbents than for their opponents.

Some Americans, particularly on the right, argue that these built-in advantages can be dealt with by limiting the number of terms that can be served in Congress (as is already the case with the presidency, which is limited to two terms, and in many state legislatures). A constitutional amendment would be needed and in 1994, the Republican manifesto for the Congressional elections, known as the Contract with America, proposed limiting all members of Congress to serving for a maximum of twelve years (six terms in the House of Representatives and two terms in the Senate). The proposal did not get through Congress, and was therefore never presented to the states to be adopted as a constitutional amendment, although some Republicans elected that year imposed term limits on themselves and left Congress by 2006.

## Redistricting

An additional concern is that the political parties are using the electoral process to add further protections to their incumbents.

After each census, at the start of each decade, the number of Congressional districts in each state may change to reflect population shifts, and the boundaries of each district may also be altered to reflect population changes within the state. This process is known as **redistricting**, but when it is done in such a way as to benefit one party over another it is often referred to as **gerrymandering** (meaning the designing of districts to ensure that the supporters of a party will almost always command a majority). With the development of super-computers that can use data from a range of sources such as market research and income distribution, it has become easier to create districts in which gives one party a significant, but not overwhelming, majority. When repeated multiple times across the state, this can lead to the minority party winning many votes but few seats. In Florida, for example, where George W. Bush beat Al Gore by just 535 votes in the 2000 presidential election, the Republican-controlled legislature produced a map with eighteen Republican-leaning districts and seven Democratic ones. In Michigan, a Republican Congressman won the 8th District by just 160 votes in 2000, but after redistricting his seat became so safe that in 2002 he did not even have a challenger.

Only one state, Iowa, puts the redistricting process in the hands of neutral civil servants. Five others set up commissions made up of members from both the Republican and Democratic parties. In every other state, the party that has a majority in the state legislature controls the redistricting process.

Furthermore, gerrymandering appears to be on the increase. In Texas, redistricting took place after the 2000 census but, in 2003, after the Republican Party had won control of the state legislature in Texas, they embarked on a second round of redistricting that gave their party six extra seats in the House of Representatives.

Following the success of this initiative, other states drew up plans to redraw district boundaries before the next census, raising the possibility that redistricting could take place each time a state legislature changes hands or data becomes available that can be used to its advantage by the majority party.

Some resistance has emerged to these developments. The Texas redistricting plan faced a challenge in the Supreme Court and, in 2005, initiatives were placed on the ballot in California and Ohio to put the redistricting process into the hands of a non-partisan commission. However, neither of these initiatives succeeded and the leading electoral commentator in the USA, Charlie Cook, has warned that there are now fewer than 30 truly competitive districts in the whole country, compared with over 120 in the early 1990s.

# Concerns about the electoral system: voter participation

Although the people of the USA have the opportunity to participate in more elections than in most other countries, there are a range of factors that make this more difficult than in other democracies.

### Voter registration

In contrast to many other countries, where the electoral authorities actively seek out unregistered voters and encourage them to register, in the USA there is a presumption, in most regions, that citizens will take the initiative to locate and complete the necessary forms.

Procedures vary from state to state and, as almost one-fifth of American voters move to a new location every five years, at any given election many voters will not have met their new district's registration requirements or may simply not have got around to registering in their new districts.

The **'motor voter'** Act of 1993 was introduced to allow voters to register when they renew or change their address on their driving licence. Since its introduction, an estimated 9 million additional people have registered to vote, but there is some evidence that many of these people have not used their vote in elections.

In addition, some states limit the participation of adults who have served a prison sentence or suffered mental illness. In thirteen states, a felony conviction results in disenfranchisement for life. In the 2000 presidential election, this meant that more than 200,000 people in Florida alone were excluded from the electoral process despite having 'paid their debt to society'.

Other factors that are seen as hindering participation in elections are:

- *Voter fatigue* Paradoxically, the fact that Americans have the opportunity to participate in so many elections (at local, state and Federal levels, with primaries for many of the posts) means that voters may find the range of choices confusing or simply become jaded with the frequency of elections and choose not to participate.
- *Poverty* The motor voter law was aimed at people who were not sufficiently motivated to make an effort to register to vote, usually the

poorest in society. However, this lack of motivation may stem from a belief that politicians are unable, or unwilling, to effectively address many of the issues that are of greatest concern to the poor and vulnerable, such as racial tension and spiralling healthcare costs.

### Rising participation

Despite the hindrances to voting, turnout has increased in the new millennium, reducing concern about this aspect of the electoral system. In the presidential election of 2000, 105 million people voted, while 131 million voted in 2008, an increase of 25 per cent when the population as a whole increased by just 8 per cent.

## Perspectives on the electoral system

### How accountable are politicians in reality?

At a time when democracy was seen as potentially dangerous, putting power into the hands of a poorly educated population, the Founding Fathers took the risk of using elections to hold politicians to account. Their concerns about giving this authority to 'the mob' were outweighed by their concerns that even people of the highest integrity could be corrupted by power unless they were held to account. As democracy became more widely accepted, this principle was applied to almost everyone with the power to take decisions that could affect the quality of life of Americans, often with representatives serving short terms of office. Under these circumstances, the question of accountability should hardly be worth debating. Yet, concerns that the electoral system is failing to serve its purpose have regularly risen to the top of the political agenda, leading to calls for far-reaching reform.

### The view from the right

For conservatives, the electoral system is often judged by the extent to which it produces a **citizen legislature**. Their concerns that freedom is threatened by remote politicians who make decisions that fail to recognise the particular needs and wishes of local populations in different parts of the USA lead them to advocate reforms that promote the election of ordinary citizens who understand and relate to their peers. This, they believe, is best achieved by regularly rotating those in office by limiting the number of times they can run for election through the passing of a constitutional amendment imposing term limits on Congress. They would also like to see the system of recall elections (see above) applied to members of Congress.

Term limit proposals, however, have met with opposition because:

- They lead to office holders who are performing well being barred from office when they may well have more to contribute to the community they serve.
- They lead to a loss of expertise in the legislature.
- Many ex-politicians already go to work as lobbyists for pressure groups, where they use their contacts and experience to influence their former colleagues (known as the 'revolving door syndrome'). The pool of ex-politicians would increase with term limits while the overall level of expertise in Congress would inevitably fall, thereby boosting the influence of lobbyists. Instead of a legislature reflecting the wishes and interests of citizens, a term-limited Congress could well reflect the wishes and interests of pressure groups – a charge often levelled at state legislatures that have adopted term limits.
- Ultimately, elections, when working well, serve as term limits on politicians who have become remote from their constituents while allowing responsive politicians to continue in office.

The right's political opponents argue that, despite the rhetoric of promoting citizen legislatures, these outcomes (which favour the wealthy interests that tend to support right-wing policies) may be the true reason that conservatives promote these reforms.

### The view from the left
For progressives, the electoral system is often judged by the extent to which it engages the interest of all sections of the population, including those who feel marginalised from mainstream society, and by the extent to which it enables anyone who has a contribution to make to public life to run for office.

For left-wingers, therefore, the progressive extension of the franchise throughout the twentieth century represents meaningful progress. However, they also believe that these gains may not be secure, especially in areas where there has been a long history of discrimination, and that it is imperative that electoral authorities are closely monitored for evidence that they are making it difficult for minorities to vote.

The left's greatest electoral concern, in recent decades, has been to ensure that there is a level playing field for all people wishing to run for high office and guarding against such positions being monopolised by the wealthy. An indication of the extent to which rich people dominate the most important political positions is the situation in the Senate where, in the 111th Congress (2009–11), there was only one Senator who was not a millionaire. Consequently, the left has actively supported campaign finance regulations that limit the advantages enjoyed by those who can use their own wealth or their connections to such large amounts of money that poorer potential rivals choose not to challenge them or, in the race, they heavily outspend their opponents.

Not everyone, however, supports campaign finance regulations. They meet with opposition because:

- Limiting the amount of money people can give is seen as an infringement on their freedom to express their support for a candidate in whichever way, and to what extent, they see fit.
- The ability of candidates to raise funds (if the source of the funds is transparent) tells the electorate a great deal about them. Those who receive large amounts from a few donors, or fund their own campaigns, are likely to be seen as less effective than candidates who build up a broad base of support – even if they raise less money than their wealthier rivals.
- The candidate with the most money does not necessarily win (as advocates of campaign finance regulations tend to assume), as demonstrated by Senator John McCain in the 2008 Republican primaries when he was a distant third in the money race but won the nomination.
- On a purely practical level, having to raise campaign funds in small donations is very time-consuming and has not kept down the overall cost of elections. It could be argued that this time would be better spent promoting policies or (in the case of incumbents running for re-elections) doing their jobs.

Moreover, the left has somewhat undermined its own case for campaign finance reform by its actions. It was left-wing pressure groups that invented 527 groups that reintroduced soft money into election campaigns after it was banned by the **Bi-partisan Campaign Reform Act**. It was also the left-leaning candidate for the presidency in 2008, Barack Obama, who appeared to destroy what was left of the system of public financing for elections by refusing public funds for his general election campaign.

### The view from the centre

Centrists tend to attempt to avoid reforms to the electoral system that appear to be particularly to the benefit of one specific section of the electorate. Moreover, they tend to place greater emphasis on the strengths of the electoral system: the very fact that it has been repeatedly refined to ensure that it effectively fulfils its role of making sure that the powerful are closely monitored by the people, and that it has spawned distinctive public interest groups, such as Common Cause, which actively publicise any flaws which undermine the impact of ordinary voters and lead campaigns for improvements which enhance accountability is taken by centrists as evidence that, although not perfect, the electoral system is valued by the people of the USA as a key instrument to keep those in power in check.

## Conclusion

The people of the USA have a range of opportunities to directly shape public policy, choose representatives to manage public policy on their behalf and can hold their representatives to account on a regular basis. Despite this, concerns about the electoral system have surfaced regularly since the 1970s. Public scandals have been seen as signs that politicians have their own interests at heart, not those of the electorate, and that they have little fear of being held to account at elections. There has been a widespread suspicion that elections do little to stop politicians from losing touch with their voters once they have departed to Washington DC, not least because gerrymandered Congressional districts give them cause to believe that they are highly unlikely to lose their seats. And it remains widely believed that the cost of elections makes politicians more grateful to their donors than to their voters and that their conduct when in office reflects this.

However, there are a range of views on how to address these

concerns, often based on rival ideologies and who stands to benefit from any reforms, and the future of the electoral system will be shaped by the way in which these debates and disputes are resolved.

. . . . . . . . . . . . . . . . . . . . . . . . . . . . . . . . . . . . . . . . . . . . .

## ✔ What you should have learnt from reading this chapter

- At the Constitutional Convention, there were differences among the Founding Fathers about the extent to which the people could be trusted with the power to choose their own representatives, with some fearing that they could be easily led and manipulated by the very politicians they were supposed to hold to account. Advocates of limited democracy prevailed (although, at state level, a wider range of direct and representative democratic mechanisms were adopted). Subsequently, both the number of directly elected politicians at the national level, and the range of people entitled to vote, have increased.

- There are distinctive features to Congressional and presidential elections. How presidential elections work in practice is illustrated by developments through the 2008 campaign.

- The cost of elections, the advantages enjoyed by incumbents and the level of participation in elections have all been matters of concern since the 1970s.

- The best solution to these concerns is a matter of dispute, with different ideological positions having sharply different views on how best to improve the electoral process.

## 🔎 Glossary of key terms

**Anti-Federalists** A term applied to the people who opposed the adoption of the US Constitution because they feared that it gave too much power to the central government.

**Battleground states** (also known as **swing states**) Those states which are not consistently won by either party at presidential elections and are consequently seen as key to the outcome of the elections.

**Bi-partisan Campaign Reform Act (BCRA), 2002** Law that banned candidates and parties from raising soft money, while aiming to encourage a reliance on hard-money donations.

**Blanket primaries** Public contests to choose the most suitable candidate to represent a party in an election, in which voters could cast a vote for both main parties until this type of primary was declared unlawful by the Supreme Court in 2000.

**'Blue' states** Those states consistently won by the Democratic candidate at presidential elections.

**Caucus** A means of choosing someone to represent a political party in an election through meetings in which attendees attempt to persuade each other to support their preferred candidate.

**Citizen legislature** A law-making body composed of people who are not full-time, permanent politicians (and, perhaps, more in tune with the voters).

**Closed primaries** Public contests to choose the most suitable candidate to represent a party in an election, in which only voters who have declared their party affiliation can participate.

**Direct democracy** Forms of democracy in which all qualified citizens can participate in the policy-making process (such as referenda, initiatives and propositions).

**Electoral college** The mechanism used to elect the President, in which each state is allotted a number of votes, based on its population, which are then awarded to the candidate who wins the most votes in each state. Candidates need to win 270 electoral college votes to win the election.

**Exploratory committee** An organisation set up by potential presidential candidates that is legally entitled to raise a limited amount of money (maximum $5,000) that can be used to conduct opinion polls to see if the wider public views them as viable candidates.

**Faithless electors** People who represent their state in the electoral college, but do not cast their votes in line with the popular vote of the state.

**Federal Elections Campaign Acts (FECA)** A series of laws passed in the 1970s to regulate how campaign funds could be raised and spent.

**Federal Elections Commission (FEC)** The organisation established to monitor whether the Federal Elections Campaign Acts (regulating how campaign funds could be raised and spent) were being obeyed and to impose punishments when they were not.

**Federalists** A term applied to the people who supported the adoption of the US Constitution and would, in many cases, have been prepared to increase the power it gave to the central government.

**First Past the Post** The electoral system used in most elections in the USA in which the candidate with the most votes is declared the winner.

**Fiscal conservatives** A term applied to a strand of conservative thought that favours minimal government intervention.

**527s** Organisations set up in response to the Bi-partisan Campaign Reform Act (2002) to raise and spend soft money in elections after candidates and parties were banned from doing so by the Act.

**Front-loading** The practice of states moving the date on which they hold their presidential primaries nearer to the start of the process in January, in order to increase the influence they have on the outcome.

**Gerrymandering** Redrawing the boundaries of Congressional districts in ways designed to give one party an electoral advantage.

**Hard money**  Campaign donations that may be used by candidates or parties to persuade voters to support them at elections.

**Incumbency advantage**  The benefits enjoyed by people holding an official position when facing a challenge from an opponent.

**Incumbents**  People who hold an official position.

**Initiatives**  (also known as **propositions**) A vote providing the public with an opportunity to support or oppose a proposal put forward by their fellow citizens (only used by some states, never the Federal government).

**Invisible primary**  The period between the formal announcement that candidates are running for the presidency, and the start of the official primaries, when contenders aim to become sufficiently well known across the country and to have raised sufficient funds to be able to present themselves as a credible presidential candidates.

**Matching funds**  A system designed to encourage candidates to limit the campaign funds they raise privately in return for funding provided by the taxpayer (to give those with limited ability to raise funds privately a realistic opportunity to compete for high office).

**Mid-term elections**  Congressional elections that take place halfway through a presidential term, with all the House of Representatives and one-third of the Senate standing for election.

**'Motor voter' Act (1993)**  Properly known as the National Voter Registration Act, this law was designed to make registering to vote easier by making registration forms available whenever someone applied for a driving licence or for social services.

**National conventions**  The events, held in the summer of each presidential election year, when the political parties formally adopt their candidates for the general election and set out their main policies.

**Open primaries**  Public contests to choose the most suitable candidate to represent a party in an election, in which all voters, regardless of their party affiliation, can participate.

**Political Action Committee (PAC)**  An organisation established for the specific purpose of raising funds to be spent in election campaigns that must operate within the rules established by the Federal Elections Campaign Acts (FECA) and are subject to monitoring by the Federal Elections Commission (FEC).

**Primary**  The mechanism used to select candidates to represent the main parties at elections, in which the general public can vote for the person they think would make the most suitable candidate.

**Propositions** see **Initiatives**.

**Raiding**  A tactic that may be used in open primaries by supporters of the one party who cross over and vote for a weak candidate to represent the other party.

**Recall elections**  A procedure enabling voters to remove an elected official from office before his/her time has expired.

**'Red' states**  Those states consistently won by the Republican candidate at presidential elections.

**Redistricting**  The process that takes place after each census at the start of each decade to redraw the boundaries of Congressional districts to reflect population shifts.

**Referenda**  Votes providing the public with an opportunity to support or oppose a proposal put forward by the government (only used by some states, never the Federal government).

**Social conservatives**  A term applied to a strand of conservative thought that emphasises the importance of promoting a set of values as central to constructive policy-making.

**Soft money**  Donations given for the purpose of expanding political party activities, political education or promoting political participation (but not supposed to be used to persuade the electorate on which party/candidate to support).

**Superdelegates**  Senior Democrats (such as members of Congress, Democratic governors, ex-Presidents and so on) who are given votes in the selection of a presidential nominee on the basis that the judgement and experience of the party's most important members is given some weight in the nomination process.

**Super Tuesday**  Name given to the day in the presidential primary calendar when the most states hold their primary simultaneously.

**Swing states** see **Battleground states**.

## ❓ Likely examination questions

Issues examiners may expect students to be able to effectively analyse include:

- How the electoral system works

- Whether the electoral system is effective in holding elected representatives to account

- Ways in which the electoral system is deficient in holding elected representatives to account

- The outcome of recent elections and the factors that have shaped the outcome

Thus, examples of the kind of questions which could be asked include:

Explain the significance of mid-term elections.

'Anyone, regardless of background, can become President of the United States.' Discuss.

# Helpful websites

There is a wealth of websites dedicated to the various aspects of the electoral system.

Covering elections as they happen, the leading news organisations in both the USA and Britain provide in-depth coverage of developments. Particularly recommended are:

- The website of the BBC at www.bbc.co.uk.

- The website of the *Guardian* and *Observer* newspapers at www. guardian.co.uk.

- The website of the US 24-hour news service CNN at www.cnn.com.

- The website of the *New York Times* at www.nytimes.com.

All candidates run campaign websites which are easy to find through any search engine.

To view past political advertising visit the Political Communications Lab at Stanford University. Its web address is www.pcl.stanford.edu/campaigns. Another website with a library of campaign advertisements is thelivingroomcandidate.org.

Between elections, useful websites are:

- Politics1, which proclaims itself to be the 'ultimate guide to US politics and elections . . . since 1997'. Its web address is www.politics1.com.

- Charlie Cook, one of the leading commentators on US elections, has his own website, the Cook Political Report. Although some of the material is only available to subscribers, there is a considerable amount of free information, such as the most competitive races in the House and Senate. Its web address is www.cookpolitical.com.

A variety of organisations provide information on campaign finance, either seeking to reform the campaign finance regulations or making information on campaign donations available to the general public:

- Common Cause is 'a nonpartisan nonprofit advocacy organization founded in 1970 as a vehicle for citizens to make their voices heard in the political process and to hold their elected leaders accountable to the public interest'. Its web address is www.commoncause.org.

- Democracy 21 is 'a nonprofit, nonpartisan organization dedicated to making democracy work for all Americans'. Its web address is www. democracy21.org.

- The Election Reform Information Project provides up-to-the-minute

news and analysis on election reform. Its web address is www.
electionline.org.

- The Campaign for Responsive Politics runs a highly accessible website
  which makes no comment on campaign finance, allowing the figures
  on 'who gives' and 'who gets' to speak for themselves. Its web
  address is www.opensecrets.org.

## Suggestions for further reading

For an in-depth account of elections at all levels, consult *US Elections
Today* by Philip John Davies, in the Politics Today series published by
Manchester University Press.

Alternatively, the *Almanac of American Politics* by Michael Barone includes
profiles of every member of Congress and every governor alongside in-
depth and up-to-date narrative profiles of all 50 states and 435 House
districts, covering everything from economics to history to, of course,
politics. Available on Amazon.com and the website of its publisher, the
*National Journal*, it is rather expensive at around $70, but is the 'ultimate
guide for political junkies'.

# CHAPTER 5

# Political Parties

## Contents

## Overview

*Two empty bottles with different labels?*
On 28 April 2009, Senator Arlen Spectre of Pennsylvania announced that he was leaving the Republican Party and joining the Democratic Party because 'the Republican Party has moved too far to the right'.

Many in the party he had just deserted were not sorry to see him go. A leading conservative in the Republican Party, Newt Gingrich, argued that a welcome consequence of fewer moderates in the party would be to 'make clearer the profound difference between the Democratic Party of big government, big bureaucracy, high taxes and big unions and the Republican Party of lower taxes, less bureaucracy and small business, with its emphasis on the work ethic, civil society and local control back home'.

Yet in 1973, just thirty-six years earlier, David Broder won the most prestigious literary prize in the USA for his book *The Party's Over*, in which he argued that political parties in America had become such broad coalitions, with party leaders having such little control over their supporters, that they had little ideological identity and were becoming almost irrelevant in US politics.

This chapter surveys the development of political parties and examines the extent to which they are providing sharply different policy alternatives, as Newt Gingrich claims, or whether they continue to have only a vague ideological identity, as David Broder claimed.

## Key issues to be covered in this chapter

- The role of political parties in a democracy
- How the two main parties developed through the nineteenth and twentieth centuries
- The current ideological stance of the two main parties
- The patterns of support for the two main parties
- The role of minor parties in the US political system
- The extent of, and desirability of, political polarisation of political parties in the early twenty-first century

## The role of political parties

In a democracy, political parties have a range of roles to play. They help engage the interest of people in politics and provide opportunities for political participation. Political leaders also often emerge through political parties. Also, they help educate people on political issues. All of these roles, however, may also be played by other political organisations, most notably pressure groups.

There is one other political role played by parties that is quite distinctive: they provide coherent packages of policies for the population to choose from, and offer teams of people to put those policies into effect. Pressure groups, by contrast, while serving to educate the public on political issues and encourage them to get involved, tend to focus on one policy area and to persuade policy-makers rather than try to implement their preferred policies themselves.

If political parties fail to provide clear alternative packages of policies, as suggested by David Broder in *The Party's Over* (see Overview), they can be criticised for failing to perform their key role, essential to a healthy democracy. However, when there is a clear divide between political parties (as advocated by Newt Gingrich in the introduction) they may also be subject to criticism for promoting sectionalism, setting one part of the population against another and fostering competition and confrontation rather than co-operation and mutual support. It was this possibility that was the main concern of the country's leaders in the USA's earliest years.

## The development of the main political parties

### Federalists v. anti-Federalists

The Founding Fathers were extremely suspicious of political parties, with their writings consistently expressing the view that they would be divisive and used to promote the interests of their members at the expense of the wider community. Even as the Constitution was being written, however, the Founding Fathers themselves divided into two camps on the central issue of how much power an effective national government could have without the risk of it becoming oppressive.

A passionate debate erupted (outlined in greater detail in Chapter 1) between the Federalists and anti-Federalists. The former, led by

Alexander Hamilton, believed that a strong national government was needed to protect the country from foreign threats and deliver the freedoms promised by the Constitution. The latter, led by Thomas Jefferson, believed that a strong central government would itself become a threat to freedom and would undermine the Constitution.

By the time the first President, George Washington, left office in 1797, two parties had clearly emerged, each believing that they were fighting to protect the values embodied in the Constitution. The antagonism between them was so deep that it contributed to an amendment to the Constitution. Originally, the winner of the presidential election became president and the runner-up (invariably from another party) became Vice President. After the 12th Amendment was passed in 1804, the two positions were elected jointly.

### The emergence of the Republicans and Democrats

The issues dividing Americans changed over the following decades, as did the names of the parties. However, the issue that produced the parties that now dominate US politics, the Republicans and Democrats, was slavery.

The Republican Party was founded in 1854, primarily as an anti-slavery party, and rapidly attracted support in the Northern states where slavery no longer existed. However, after the Civil War (1861–5), as the party of the North, it became associated with the interests of the rich industrialists who dominated the region. Thus, the party that enabled slaves to become citizens developed as the party of business and the middle class.

The Democratic Party, which had a much longer history, enjoyed support among poorer people in Northern cities and in the South. These two branches of the party split when the Civil War broke out in 1860, but gradually came together again after it was over. The two groups appeared to have virtually nothing in common. In the South, the party represented the interests of racist Anglo-Saxon Protestants in mainly rural areas. In the North, it represented ethnic groups from parts of Europe often looked down on by Anglo-Saxons, such as Ireland, Italy and Poland. These immigrants were overwhelmingly Catholic and worked in the most heavily industrialised parts of the country. However, compared to the people represented by the Republican Party, both groups felt like outsiders.

## Two 'umbrella' parties

By the twentieth century, therefore, each party represented such a diverse range of people that it was difficult to describe either as standing for something distinctively different to the other.

The Republicans, as the party of business, were conservative, resistant to change and to government intervention in the economy. With a history of abolishing slavery, however, it attracted some **liberals** who believed that government had a moral duty to look after the interests of those genuinely unable to help themselves.

At the same time, the Democrats in the South were even more right-wing than most Republicans. Determined to assert white racial superiority over the freed African Americans who had previously been their slaves, they used every method available to them, including violence, to enforce the 'Jim Crow' laws that segregated the races (outlined in more detail in Chapter 3). Like the Republicans, however, the party had its liberal wing, mainly in Northern cities, which used the resources of local government to provide jobs and homes for poor, newly arrived immigrants.

Further, unlike in other parts of the world, no significant socialist party emerged, committed to capturing political control to redistribute resources from the rich to the poor to ensure not just equality of opportunity but equal outcomes. Periodically, parties representing groups disenchanted with the Democrats and Republicans emerged to threaten their dominance, such as the Populists, who represented small farmers suffering great hardship in the 1890s, and the Progressives, who represented people determined to eradicate political corruption before the First World War. Each time, however, either or both of the main parties adopted many of the policies of the minor party, eliminating the threat and leading to an even wider range of people and policies in each party.

With both parties covering most of the political spectrum, from the extreme right to the moderate left, and no major party offering a clearly socialist alternative, both parties became known as **'umbrella' parties**, covering most people. The main reasons that voters chose one party over the other was often linked to their community's historical ties with the party. Catholic immigrants were grateful to the Democrats for providing for their needs when they first arrived in the country. White Southerners were taught from a young age that it was considered treason to vote for Abraham Lincoln's Republican Party, which had invaded their region and imposed its values upon them. Even a century after the Civil War, the Democrats' slogan in the South was 'Vote as you shot'.

### The 'New Deal Coalition'

In the 1930s, the Democrat umbrella was extended to cover another group, African Americans. Over the previous decade, African Americans had adopted a range of strategies in response to legalised segregation in the South. One of these was simply to leave the region and move to the Northern states, which, at the time, were going through an economic boom and recruiting workers. When, after the Wall Street Crash of 1929, the USA went into a period of prolonged recession, African Americans were particularly hard hit, as employers adopted an attitude of 'last hired, first fired' towards their black workers.

African Americans were, therefore, among those with reason to be grateful to the Democrat President, Franklin D. Roosevelt, when he introduced his 'New Deal' programme, providing benefits for people without work, generating jobs and improving the employment rights for people in work. Before the introduction of this programme, the few African Americans with the right to vote usually gave their support to the Republican Party because of its role in ending slavery. With the wave of migration to the North, the number of African Americans able to vote increased dramatically, and after benefiting from the policies of FDR, their support swung overwhelmingly to the Democrats.

### 'The Party's Over'

By the 1950s, the tensions within the Democratic Party in particular were evident on television screens around the world. African Americans prepared to risk their lives in the Civil Rights movement were loyal supporters of the same party as committed segregationists prepared to kill as they resisted the advance of black Civil Rights. Furthermore, in the 1960s the party saw an influx of anti-Vietnam war protesters, many of them very left-wing, who questioned the role that the USA was playing in the world.

By the early 1970s, it was being argued by political commentators, most notably David Broder in his book *The Party's Over*, that the party system in the USA was failing to fulfil the roles that it should play in a healthy democracy in the following ways:

- *Policy formulation* Political parties *should* play the role of providing the electorate with choices of how the country should be run and visions of its future. The umbrella parties that had developed by the 1960s were seen by commentators as offering no distinct alternatives to the electorate.
- *Recruitment and nomination* Parties *should* be responsible for providing suitable candidates and providing them with the resources to stand at election, with a view to winning office and implementing their vision. The increasing use of primaries, since the 1960s, to nominate candidates for elections (outlined in more detail in Chapter 4) meant that party leaders played a diminishing role in choosing who represented their party. In addition, during primaries competition between candidates of the same party can become so intense, with mutual insults and accusations, that the party's public image is seriously damaged. Moreover, they encourage candidate-centred campaigns that emphasise personal qualities rather than the party's agenda, and provide an opportunity for 'raiding' by supporters of one party who cross over and vote for a weak candidate of the opposing party.
- *Fundraising and campaigning* Once a candidate has been selected, parties *should* provide them with funds and teams of volunteers to fight the general election against the other party. However, to pay for elections, candidates often rely more on their own fundraising resources than financial support from their parties. Candidates may also assemble their own campaign teams. In part, this has been due to the decline in the number of people joining political parties or expressing a strong commitment to either of the main parties. Between the Second World War and 1976, the number of voters defining themselves as independents doubled, peaking at 26 per cent.
- *Voting patterns* In roughly the same period, the proportion of voters who engaged in **split-ticket voting**, supporting candidates from different parties at the same election (for example, voting for the Republican candidate for President at the same time as

voting for the Democratic candidate for Congress) rose from just 12 per cent after the Second World War to a peak of 30 per cent by 1972.

* *Governing* If a party wins an election, it *should* work in a co-ordinated fashion to implement its policies. However, the decline of parties as vehicles for formulating policies; the lack of dependence on parties by many of their members at elections; the growing dependence on independent groups for election funding and campaigning; and the system of separation of powers between the legislature and executive all combined to create a situation whereby political parties struggled to implement a programme that commanded the clear support of most of their active supporters. In 1968, President Lyndon Johnson decided not to seek re-election, in part because he was exhausted after five years of having to bully his fellow Democrats in Congress to pass his legislative proposals and in part because the most severe criticisms of his two main programmes (the Vietnam War and the Great Society policy) were coming from activist within his own party who wanted the war to end and much more money invested in the Great Society programme.

## 'Two empty bottles'

The overlap in policies between the parties and the difficulties they faced in implementing their programmes led to the charge that they were 'like two bottles, with different labels, both empty'. However, as commentators in the early 1970s were explaining why political parties were in steep decline and at risk of becoming almost irrelevant, trends were developing which would transform the party-political landscape.

## Party realignment

In 1964, after signing the Civil Rights Act, President Johnson commented to a young aide, 'I think we delivered the South to the Republican Party for your lifetime and mine.' Events were to prove him right, as the African Americans who had previously supported the Republicans switched their support to the Democrats, and whites in the South began to contemplate the possibility of voting for the party of Abraham Lincoln.

## Conservatives of the heart

The white voters of the South who had fought the abolition of slavery replaced it with legalised racial segregation and then violently resisted the Civil Rights movement, were outraged that the Democratic Party which they had loyally supported for generations passed the laws which gave meaningful political rights to African Americans. They were still more outraged when the Democratic Party gave its support to Affirmative Action programmes designed to ensure that African Americans had the means to take advantage of their newly won rights. Yet, the tradition of 'Vote as you shot' was so deeply engrained that many of them could not bring themselves to vote for the Republican Party. In 1968, they were able to turn to an independent, segregationist Democrat, George Wallace, who won almost 10 million votes and 46 electoral college votes. No similar candidate appeared thereafter and by 1980 the white South was prepared to give a Republican who shared their values a chance.

Other traditional supporters of the Democratic Party began to desert it at the same time. In the North, some of the Catholic ethnic groups that had migrated from Europe in the nineteenth century, and had always voted for the party that had supported their communities when they first arrived in the USA, began drifting towards the Republican Party. In part, this was because many of them had become wealthier and moved to suburban areas in which the Republican Party was seen as the most effective defender of their interests. In part, it was because they resented Affirmative Action programmes that were seen as giving one community opportunities that others, as outsiders also facing discrimination, had fought for.

Furthermore, at a time when many Americans perceived Communism to be a growing threat around the world to the USA's interests and values, the Democrats were widely seen as weak on defence issues. A significant group left the party in the 1980s, in response to the Carter presidency, which was perceived as appeasing America's enemies.

These 'conservatives of the heart' came together to join traditional supporters of the Republican Party to elect Ronald Reagan in 1980. After winning the party nomination, he launched his presidential campaign in Philadelphia, Mississippi, where the local community had refused to co-operate with investigations into the murder of three civil rights workers in 1964 (featured in the film *Mississippi Burning*). Like the Catholic voters he attracted, Reagan was of humble origins and had used his talents and determination to reach the top. Those who felt strongly that the USA needed to strengthen its defences and be more confrontational towards its enemies found, in Ronald Reagan, a man who shared their views with equal passion.

The core of the modern Republican Party had been established. People with conservative views who had previously voted Democrat, because of historical community ties to the party, had switched parties.

Once President Reagan had to leave office in 1988, having served two terms, there was no strong conservative leadership to keep these groups together. His successor, President George Bush Snr, was more moderate and, with Communist regimes around the world collapsing, focused on the USA's role as the world's only superpower.

However, in 1994, the rise of another forceful conservative Republican, Newt Gingrich, helped reunite conservatives of the heart, and towards the end of the decade, the torch was passed to George Bush Jnr, who led this group into the twenty-first century.

## Liberal Democrats

As conservatives who used to vote Democrat have left the party, the remainder of the old 'New Deal Coalition' are, on the whole, relatively liberal.

The industrial white working class, which looks to government to provide a high-quality education for their children, protection from unfair employment practices and support through periods of economic or medical misfortune, remains overwhelmingly loyal to the Democratic Party. African Americans have proved even more loyal since the 1970s, with 90 per cent, or more, consistently voting for the party because of its support during the Civil Rights movement and its commitment to Affirmative Action since.

Other groups who believe that government has an important role to play in protecting the vulnerable are less reliable supporters of the party, including sections of the various Hispanic communities and some of the super-rich, especially those in the entertainment industry, who believe that the more fortunate should share their wealth with the less fortunate.

# The modern Republican Party

Although it is increasingly accurate to describe the Republican Party as conservative and the Democratic Party as liberal, both parties have distinct strands running through them.

The Republican Party is dominated by two strands, both conservative. People who fall outside these strands can still be found in the party, even in important positions, but they are a declining minority.

## Social conservatives

It is a core conservative belief that human beings are essentially selfish. Some conservatives reach this conclusion by observation of the world around them; others refer to religious texts, such as the Bible, which they say teaches that all people are sinful. In order to live and work together, everyone needs clear moral guidance, strong effective leadership and disincentives to giving into selfish desires.

Clear moral guidance, for **social conservatives**, requires a shared understanding, throughout society, of what is right and wrong. Without this, society can crumble under the strain of managing reckless, irresponsible and dangerous behaviour. People learn their values in strong family units in which parents provide both a moral framework and strong role models. Moreover, this moral framework needs to be reinforced outside the home by policy-makers ranging from education, through business to politicians. This kind of positive leadership, for those who overcome their instincts, needs to be balanced by punishment for those who do not, and these penalties must be severe enough to act as a deterrent to wrongdoing.

As an organised political force, social conservatives began to emerge in the 1970s in response to what they saw as the country's downward moral spiral. The previous decade had seen the breaking down of many social taboos. For social conservatives, free sexual expression, rising divorce rates, more single-parent families and increasing crime were all evidence of moral and social decay. Then, in the Supreme Court decision, *Roe* v. *Wade* (1973), women were given the constitutional right to abort a pregnancy, violating what social conservatives saw as one of the must fundamental moral principles – the right of the vulnerable and innocent to live. New political groups sprang up which channelled what many Americans saw as their civic, and in many cases religious, duty to turn the tide and rescue their nation from moral decay.

Unsophisticated and amateurish at first, these groups have developed into a highly organised, well-resourced, network with a clear set of linked goals:

- *Protecting the unborn child* Sanctity of life is the most fundamental moral principle in a society operating on Judeo-Christian values and, consequently, one of the highest priorities of social conservatives is to have *Roe* v. *Wade* overturned. This means working to ensure that one of their allies is in the White House when a Supreme Court vacancy occurs and that there are enough of their supporters in the Senate when a suitable nominee is being confirmed. In the absence of *Roe* v. *Wade*, restrictions on abortion would be made by elected officials at state level, who would be subject to pressure from anti-abortion groups.

- *Protecting the home from immoral influences* As children are being raised in homes promoting traditional, religion-based values, they are subject to a range of influences that undermine those values, including a casual attitude towards relationships and marriage by celebrities; provocative sexual imagery in adverts and music videos; violent computer games or pornography on the internet or at the corner shop. Social conservatives have been pushing to reduce access to inappropriate material, especially that imported into the home via the television. Since 2000, by law, every television sold in the USA must be equipped with a V chip that blocks any programme a householder finds inappropriate. So, when inappropriate material finds its way into mainstream family viewing, such as Janet Jackson baring a breast during the half-time show of the 2004 Superbowl (the programme with the largest audience in the country), it generates a storm of protest. Conversely, social conservatives actively support material that promotes religious, especially Christian, values. When *The Passion of Christ*, which tells the story of the crucifixion of Jesus Christ, was released in 2004 it was actively promoted by social conservatives in order to demonstrate that films with a strong moral theme can be commercially successful.

- *Protecting moral values at school* Social conservatives believe that schools have a responsibility to reinforce society's moral values, based in large measure on biblical principles, and have invested heavily in recent years in campaigns to increase religious influences in schools. With notable exceptions, these campaigns have not been successful, but the battle continues to be fought. Social conservatives would like to see the *Engel* v. *Vitale* (1962) Supreme Court decision overturned, which ruled that school prayers were unconstitutional in publicly funded institutions because the 1st Amendment keeps government out of religious matters. This has been challenged, but upheld, on six occasions, most recently in *Santa Fe Independent School District* v. *Doe* (2000), which ruled that prayers could not be delivered over the public address system before school football games. Social conservatives also tend to be suspicious of sex education in schools, fearing that it has the effect of encouraging teenagers to become sexually active and promiscuous. They have promoted, as an alternative, 'abstinence only' sex education, which encourages teenagers to understand the risks associated with becoming sexually active. These programmes have benefited from millions of dollars of Federal funds since the passage of the Adolescent Family Life Act, passed by Congress in 1981, and have survived a legal challenge, *Bowen* v. *Kendrick* (1988). These principles have also influenced foreign policy: when, in 2003, President George W. Bush announced $15 billion to fight AIDS in Africa, a third of it was for abstinence education and none of it was distributed through organisations that provided abortions. Above all, social conservatives have been at the centre of a battle over the teaching of evolution in science lessons, which, as they see it, undermines the biblical account of creation. This, it is argued, subtly erodes the moral foundations of a society based on biblical principles. They favour putting scientific theories (note that they are called theories, not facts) of how the world was created, and of its development, on the same academic basis as biblical accounts. This approach, known as creationism, was ruled unconstitutional by the Supreme Court in *Edwards* v. *Aguillard* (1987) on the basis that it was a way of promoting a religious viewpoint. The controversy continued, however, with the development of an alternative to creationism, called Intelligent Design, which argues that there is scientific evidence that 'certain features of the Universe and living things are best explained by an intelligent cause, not as part of an undirected process, such as natural selection'. In December 2005, in the case of *Kitzmiller* v. *Dover*, a Federal judge also ruled this Intelligent Design as unconstitutional, as it advances a version of Christianity. Despite these setbacks, two avenues have emerged that can be used by families who feel they cannot get a school education that respects their values. One is a school voucher scheme, offered in a number of states, starting in Milwaukee, Wisconsin, in 1990. This provides families with a voucher equivalent in value to the cost of educating a child in a community school, but which can be used in any school, including private schools. As a significant percentage of private schools are religious, this scheme was seen by critics as another device to introduce the values of social conservatives into the school system. However, this use of taxpayers' money was upheld by the Supreme Court in 2002 in *Zelman* v. *Simmons-Harris*. The other avenue is the development of the homeschool network. Some two million students are taught at home by a parent, free from restrictions on religion. These families are able to offer each other mutual support through the Home School Legal Defense Association, which, in 2000, set up its own university, Patrick Henry College.

• *Protecting the moral values of the community* Social conservatives believe that, even if people come through childhood with their moral values intact, the world is full of pressures that can lead adults astray. This is less likely to happen, however, if positive influences are promoted and negative forces confronted. Among the negative forces to be eliminated from the community are drug use and crime (often linked), and the most effective means of confronting them are well-resourced law enforcement agencies and punishments that will serve as deterrents. The most positive influence is traditional marriage and protecting this institution has become, since 2003, the highest priority on the social conservative political agenda. In the case of *Lawrence* v. *Texas* (2003), the Supreme Court ruled that laws banning homosexual sex were unconstitutional and then went further, proclaiming that 'the state cannot demean their existence or control their destiny by making their private sexual conduct a crime'. This apparent assertion of gay rights, invalidating laws that can be interpreted as 'demeaning' gay people, was seen by many as opening the door to gay marriage. Further, when the Supreme Court in Massachusetts ruled, four months later, that gay marriage was constitutional in that state, the judges mentioned the *Lawrence* case. The campaign to resist this rising tide of gay rights led to ballot initiatives banning same-sex marriage in thirteen states in 2004. These contributed to some 4 million additional social conservative voters coming to the polls, the majority of whom voted for George W. Bush, who went on to win the presidential election by 3.5 million votes. Thus, these 'values voters' have firmly established themselves as a dominant force within the Republican Party.

## Fiscal conservatives

Just as social conservatives are driven by the concern that the selfish nature of human beings can lead to the collapse of order in society unless people are bound by a strong moral code, so the other main branch of American conservatism is driven by the belief that selfishness can be harnessed to produce a dynamic, productive society.

For **fiscal conservatives**, people can be trusted to make sensible, appropriate decisions in their own best interests and, through the free market, those choices will lead to progress and general benefit. In common with social conservatives, they believe that society needs well-resourced law enforcement agencies and punishments that will serve as deterrents for individuals whose selfishness exceeds the bounds of social norms. However, fiscal conservatives are less concerned that people are likely to make choices that will lead to a breakdown of social order. Rather, they believe that market forces will, almost invariably, guide people to make the most profitable use of the resources available to them, leading to economic growth and a shared sense of well-being. Consequently, they are highly suspicious of any form of government intervention beyond maintaining law and order and defence of the nation.

Fiscal conservatism emerged as a force in the 1970s at the same time as social conservatism was coming to public prominence, and together they were referred to as the '**New Right**'. However, fiscal conservatives were motivated by a different set of concerns and developed a different set of policy priorities. During the 1970s, the US economy was barely growing, while inflation was a serious problem. Two highly respected economists at the University of Chicago, Friedrich Hayek and Milton Friedman, argued that this was due to years of government intervention, which had distorted market forces, created a culture of dependency though welfare programmes and undermined incentives for the wealthy to invest through high taxes. Their solution – to cut back the role of government and allow creativity and resourcefulness to flourish – struck a chord with many Americans, especially in the West, who associated such qualities with the expansion and development of their nation.

Small government, meaning lower taxes and fewer rules and regulations, had obvious attractions for businesses, but the idea also attracted other groups. Advocates of gun rights also resent government interference in what they see as their constitutional right to 'keep and bear arms' of their choice. Advocates of property rights resent restrictions on the use and development of their land, often as a result of environmental regulations. Even recreational fishermen and off-road vehicle enthusiasts, both subject to government regulation, are attracted by this political creed.

In order to reduce the scope of government, fiscal conservatives have a range of policy objectives:

- *Promoting tax cuts* When Ronald Reagan became President in 1981, he proclaimed that 'Government is not the solution to our problem; government is the problem.' Fiscal conservatives wholeheartedly agree and see tax cuts as the means of solving the problem. As long as government has the resources to fund an ever-increasing range of programmes, interfering in the daily lives of Americans and distorting the free market, it will do so. Tax cuts are a way of 'starving the beast', leading to a reduction in the size and scope of government. Additionally, allowing citizens to maximise the benefits of their labour and/or investment encourages an atmosphere of self-reliance, reversing the dependency culture that fiscal conservatives view as the source of irresponsible behaviour in society. There would be fewer single-parent families, for example, if mothers could not depend on welfare to support them. Conversely, if they knew that they could keep most of their earnings, they would be encouraged to work, provide for their families and be positive role models to their children. Finally, they argue, tax cuts stimulate the economy, providing more disposable income, which leads to demand for products, which leads to competition to meet the demand, which, in turn, leads to innovation, increased production and more jobs. Since George W. Bush became President, this wing of the party has been delighted to see two massive tax cuts, in 2001 and 2003, with smaller packages in 2002 and 2006. They have been distressed, however, to see that these measures have done nothing to 'starve the beast'. Rather, Federal spending dramatically increased during the presidency of George W. Bush. In part, this was due to the expenditures associated with the aftermath of the 9/11 attacks, on both military action and improving homeland security. This, fiscal conservatives can accept. Yet much of the additional spending has gone on expensive commitments such as expanding Medicare (healthcare for the elderly), increasing Federal financial support for education, paying for the reconstruction of New Orleans after Hurricane Katrina and so on, which fiscal conservatives find much harder to accept, especially as the combination of tax cuts and increased spending resulted in a record deficit of nearly $9 trillion.

- *Eliminating earmarks and promoting a line-item veto* To complement tax cuts, fiscal conservatives want to see wasteful spending curtailed. Congressmen attach projects for their districts, known as earmarks, to bills as they pass through the legislature (see Chapter 8 for more details), which accounts for a significant proportion of Federal spending. The influence of pressure groups tends to inflate this kind of expenditure. Fiscal conservatives would like to see this kind of spending drastically curtailed or even eliminated. As a fallback position, they would like the President to have the power of a line-item veto that would enable him to strike out wasteful spending from bills before signing them. A line-item veto was passed by Congress in 1996 but was struck down as unconstitutional by the Supreme Court in *Clinton v. City of New York* in 1998, on the grounds that if the President modified laws he breached the constitutional requirement that only Congress legislates. Fiscal conservatives would like to pass a modified version of the 1996 law that takes account of the Supreme Court's objections.

- *Social security reform* All working Americans pay a proportion of their wages, matched by their employers, into a fund to cover pensions and disability benefits. This money is used by the Federal government to fund general spending, as well as pensions. Current projections are that there will be insufficient funds in the budget to cover the benefits paid to retired people by 2041, and it is generally agreed that action needs to be taken now to address the projected deficit. In January 2005, immediately after his re-election, President Bush announced a plan to reform social security so that some of the contributions by employees would go into a personal account that they would then control. This approach, long advocated by fiscal conservatives, would remove from Congressional control some of the funds they currently have available; it would make people (not the government) responsible for their future; it would encourage more people to learn about investing money; and it would (if the stock market remained buoyant) result in higher pension benefits. The progress of this initiative in many ways reflected the relationship between the President and his fiscal conservative supporters: they were elated by his decision to adopt one of their ideas as his flagship policy for his second term, but deeply disappointed by his lack of determination to fight for it in the face of fierce opposition from those who believed that the plan would create uncertainty over benefits for retirees.
- *Promoting a balanced budget amendment* Ultimately, fiscal conservatives would like to see these measures become unnecessary because they would like to see the Constitution amended so that the Federal government would not be able to spend more than it raised. If a balanced budget amendment were passed, any tax cuts would inevitably 'starve the beast', but the most recent attempt, in 1997, failed to gain the necessary two-thirds support in the Senate by just one vote.
- *Promoting welfare reform* As well as financial responsibility by the government, fiscal conservatives want to see financial responsibility on the part of citizens. One of their highest priorities was achieved under a Democrat President, Bill Clinton. The welfare programme, Aid to Families with Dependent Children, was seen as a subsidy to unemployed single mothers, discouraging them

from seriously looking for work. By the time it was replaced, it covered 14 million people in 5 million families. The replacement law, Temporary Assistance for Needy Families, required welfare recipients to be in some kind of work-related activity for at least thirty hours a week and, with some exceptions, families could not receive benefits for longer than five years. Since the programme was introduced, the number of welfare recipients has halved, in part because of an expanding economy providing more jobs, and in part because some have exceeded the time they are allowed to remain in the programme.

- *Promoting school vouchers* Fiscal conservatives favour providing families with a voucher equivalent in value to the cost of educating a child in a community school, but to be used in any school, including private schools. This policy is also supported by social conservatives, albeit for different reasons. For fiscal conservatives, vouchers are about giving people control over important areas of their lives by giving them a viable range of options and introducing market forces into education, forcing poor schools to raise their standards in order to retain their students. For social conservatives, vouchers are primarily about providing a religious-based education for those who want one. However, only about 32,000 students across the country benefit from such programmes.

- *Opposing Affirmative Action* Of the range of arguments against Affirmative Action, fiscal conservatives are most likely to adopt the view that it is a form of discrimination that distorts the labour market. While acknowledging that it is a measure to compensate for decades of discrimination against minority groups, especially African Americans, fiscal conservatives argue that all discrimination causes fear and anxiety, and that while African Americans continue to experience the fear of discrimination, Affirmative Action has extended that fear to white Americans, making the overall situation worse rather than better. The most recent challenge to Affirmative Action, the Supreme Court case *Grutter* v. *Bollinger* (2003), left the constitutional position unchanged, to the disappointment of fiscal conservatives.

- *Promoting tort reform* Small-government advocates were, arguably, more successful under the presidency of George W. Bush in non-budgetary matters. In February 2005, the President signed into law the Class-Action Fairness Act, which authorised Federal courts to hear lawsuits involving damages greater than $5 million, and involving persons or companies from different states. Business has long complained that they operate in constant fear of lawyers who can shop around for the state court where they expect to win the most money for clients who may not even have a valid claim, making it cheaper to settle the lawsuits, rather than risk a massive jury award. That threat has been reduced by the Act.

- *Protecting gun manufacturers from lawsuits* In October 2005, the President signed into law a bill that protects the gun industry from lawsuits by victims of crimes in which their weapons have been used. Without this law, manufacturers and dealers would have had to be much more careful about who they sold guns to, a kind of gun-control through the courts.

- *Reductions in environmental regulation* Of all the small-government groups, opponents of environmental regulation appear to have had the most to smile about since the election of George W. Bush. Very publicly, when he came to office in 2001, he withdrew the USA from the Kyoto Protocol on Global Warming because of the costs it would impose on American businesses. Less publicly, in his first term his administration eased controls on coal-fired power plants, expanded logging and oil developments on Federal lands, and encouraged the military to get exemptions from the endangered species act. One of the President's top second-term priorities was to open up the Arctic National Wildlife Reserve to oil drilling.

Conservatives have also developed a distinctive approach to foreign policy. Led by a group known as neo-conservatives, their response to the end of the Cold War and the emergence of the USA as the sole superpower was to develop a set of guiding principles for foreign policy. These are:

- To increase defence spending significantly.
- To strengthen the ties between the USA and its democratic allies, while challenging regimes hostile to its interests and values.
- To promote the cause of political and economic freedom abroad.

These principles have played a major role in guiding policy, especially since the attacks of 9/11, and explain the decision to attack Iraq despite the absence of evidence of involvement in those events.

## Moderate conservatives

Social and fiscal conservatives are sometimes referred to collectively as the New Right, a reflection of their rise to prominence in the relatively recent past, since the 1980s. A more moderate strand of conservatism, often called **Rockefeller conservatism**, has been, until recently, the dominant form of conservatism in the Republican Party.

Rockefeller conservatism is **paternalistic** in character. While, in common with other conservatives, it holds that there will inevitably be inequalities in society (and, therefore, policies should encourage talented people to make the most of their abilities), society has a responsibility to take care of its less fortunate members – just as a father will protect all of his children. Thus, these moderate conservatives would agree with fiscal conservatives that a low tax economy is preferable and that government should not interfere in people's lives any more than necessary. However, they would disagree with fiscal conservatives over the nature of the 'safety net' that governments provide for people who are struggling to support themselves: while fiscal conservatives see most forms of welfare as an incentive to be lazy and irresponsible, moderate conservatives believe that there is a legitimate place for government to intervene in the economy to protect those who are unable to protect themselves. Similarly, while moderate conservatives believe in the importance of traditional social values, they often disagree with the policies of social conservatives that tend to marginalise or exclude all who do not share their specific set of values. For moderate conservatives, traditional values should serve to draw most people together rather than divide them and one of the leading Rockefeller conservatives, John McCain, famously criticised social conservatives as 'agents of intolerance'.

Many of the more famous figures in the Republican Party are moderates, including the former Mayor of New York, Rudy Giuliani, his successor, Michael Bloomberg (who has since become an independent), and former Governor Arnold Schwarzenegger of

California. They are organised in a faction called the Republican Main Street Partnership.

The nomination of one of this group, John McCain, as the Republican Party candidate for the presidency in 2008 was seen as an indication of the continuing influence of this strand of conservatism in the party. However, as explained in Chapter 4 (in the box on the 2008 primaries), his success had more to do with the failings of his rivals than his popularity with the party's activists. Only a minority of the people making phone calls, distributing literature and campaigning on doorsteps were enthusiastic Rockefeller conservatives. Consequently, to engage the support of the **party base** (its most committed supporters), he had little choice but to choose a social conservative as his vice-presidential running mate. Indeed, such is the decline in influence of this strand of the Republican Party that in the 111th Congress, starting in January 2009, there were only four members of the Mainstreet Partnership in the Senate and this was reduced to three when Senator Spectre defected to the Democrats.

**Nativists**

At the opposite extreme, the Republican Party has always had a 'nativist' faction that opposes large-scale immigration. In the nineteenth century, this group was extremely influential in the party and was a significant factor in ethnic groups giving their support to the Democrat Party. For much of the past century, this faction has been small, but noisy, with periodic upsurges of support. In 1994, the Republican Party rode a wave of anti-immigrant feeling in California by campaigning for Proposition 187, which denied social services, healthcare and education to anyone who could not prove that they were legal immigrants. This measure, aimed primarily at Mexicans, passed but gave the party such a reputation for extremism that it ruined its election prospects in the state until Arnold Schwarzenegger's victory in 2003. Another upsurge began in the states bordering Mexico in 2005. Armed anti-immigrant activists, calling themselves 'minutemen' (after the eighteenth-century elite militiamen who defended their communities from foreign invasion), began patrolling the border to illustrate their claim that the authorities were failing to stem a tide of illegal immigration. Condemned as vigilantes by Republican President George W. Bush, they were hailed as 'heroes' by the leader of the nativist tendency in Congress, Tom Tancredo, who chaired the Congressional Immigration Reform Caucus.

### Unity and division in the Republican Party

Splits between factions in political parties occur periodically and at all times there is competition between different strands to influence party policy. The effectiveness of a party depends on how well its leaders reconcile different strands. This can be particularly difficult for the Republican Party, as one of its main strands favours strong leadership, providing moral guidance, while the other favours minimal government intervention. Despite these tensions, since the 1990s and the first few years of the twenty-first century, the party has maintained a high degree of unity. This has been due to two main factors:

- *Willingness to compromise* The two main wings of the party have proved willing to focus on what they have in common rather than what divides them. Sometimes this is straightforward, such as on school vouchers, which both strands support although for different reasons. At other times they have found creative ways of harmonising their policies. When fiscal conservatives have proposed packages of tax cuts, for example, they have made families the main beneficiaries, providing a financial incentive for marriage, which appeals to social conservatives. Co-operation is also helped by regular contact between the leaders of the two wings of the party. In Washington DC there is a regular programme of conservative breakfast meetings, lunches, seminars and dinners attended by supporters of both wings of the party. This kind of overlap is also evident in their grass-roots supporters, with high levels of gun-ownership among Evangelical Christians and nearly half of small-business owners defining themselves as born-again Christians. Above all, conservatives are agreed that they need, at all costs, to keep out of power a Democratic Party that they see as regulatory and secular.
- *Forceful leadership* Since the current generation of conservatives gained control of the House of Representatives in 1994, their leaders organised party affairs in Congress in such a way as to

ensure that they delivered as much of their electoral agenda as possible. Under Newt Gingrich, then under Dennis Hastert and Tom DeLay, the House leadership selected influential committee chairmen on the basis of loyalty to the conservative agenda rather than the traditional basis of seniority; designated 'leadership issues' that required committee leaders to consult with the House leadership before making decisions; placed all of the staff working for Republicans under the direct authority of the Speaker; and completely bypassed committees when drafting legislation, if they felt it necessary. In this way, they were able to make life extremely difficult for the Democrat President, Bill Clinton, while his Republican successor, George W. Bush, was not put in the position of having to veto a single bill while his party was in the majority in Congress for the first six years of his presidency.

Even in the aftermath of electoral setbacks in the 2006 mid-term elections, when the Democrats unexpectedly won control of both houses of Congress, and the 2008 elections, when the Democrats increased their majorities in Congress and decisively won the presidency, there was a high level of unity in the Republican Party.

After electoral defeats, party factions often blame each other for the result and argue for their policies to be adopted in order to revive the party's fortunes. To some extent, this happened after the 2008 presidential election, with moderates claiming that the uncompromising and confrontational approach of the social and fiscal conservatives had alienated key independent voters. Apart from these voices of dissent, however, most Republicans swiftly united in opposition to the new President with every Republican in the House of Representatives voting against Barack Obama's first major measure, to stimulate the economy (despite a similar measure having been passed in the final weeks of George W. Bush's presidency) and were equally solid in their opposition to President Obama's headline policy in his first year in office, healthcare reform.

## The modern Democratic Party

It has been less easy to define what the Democratic Party stands for than the Republicans. As long ago as 1989, a leading pollster wrote,

'Democrats have been struggling to assert an identity, constrained by their narrowing base, bedevilled by Republican mischief, and muted by the party's own caution about Democratic principles.' That analysis has remained, largely, valid through a series of Congressional defeats between 1994 and 2006 and through victories since 2006 when Democratic success was attributed more to the unpopularity of the Republican Party than to enthusiasm for the Democrats. Even the election of Barack Obama as President in 2008 did little to define the Democratic Party, with many commentators and observers finding it difficult to classify his ideology through his primary campaign, the general election campaign and the early months of his presidency.

Republicans, on the whole, measure the health of their political system by the extent to which it interferes in people's lives or promotes moral values, and their policies appeal to people who are dissatisfied with aspects of modern America and want to see traditional values restored. Democrats, on the whole, measure the health of the political system by the extent to which it protects constitutional rights and their policies appeal to people who welcome many of the extensions to rights in the twentieth century to previously excluded groups such as African Americans, women and people with disabilities. This, however, makes the Republicans the party of change (which generates enthusiasm among supporters) while the Democrats have become the party of protecting the status quo (which is far less inspiring), or of extending the rights of minority groups who are often unpopular among the wider population, such as gays and lesbians.

The modern Democratic Party, as a result, is divided between a range of strands of opinion on how to develop a rival agenda for change that will inspire supporters in the way that the Republican Party has done so successfully in recent decades.

## Blue Dog Democrats

The most conservative faction of the Democratic Party is organised as a group under the banner of the **Blue Dog Coalition**, which promotes its views on policy and attempts to influence the overall direction of the party.

Its members have much in common with the moderate conservatives of the Republican Party but believe that its more extreme New

Right groups have become so dominant in the Republican Party that the Democratic Party is a better vehicle for promoting their views.

What unites the Blue Dogs is a 'deep commitment to financial stability', focusing on ensuring that laws can be funded without increasing taxes or adding to the amount borrowed by the Federal budget. On other issues, from abortion to gun control, members of this faction may have distinctly differing views, and in its annual assessment of the ideological position of all members of Congress the highly respected political magazine *The National Journal* has found that, overall, Blue Dogs range from distinctly right of centre to somewhat left of centre.

With fiscal responsibility being their over-riding concern, Blue Dogs have at times been at odds with their Democratic colleagues and willing to work with Republican moderates. Indeed, they are the least likely to vote on party lines of any identifiable group in Congress. This, however, means that they have frequently been the subject of attacks from both the right and the left. Staunch conservatives insist that the Blue Dogs often compromise on their principles for the sake of party unity while other Democratic factions have periodically expressed frustration that Blue Dogs are insufficiently supportive of party policy and even describe them as 'Republican lite'.

The sharp economic downturn of 2008–10 proved particularly challenging for the Blue Dogs. With widespread agreement that concerted government intervention was needed to rescue an economy that appeared at one point to be on the brink of collapse, the national debt soared to record levels, to the distress of many conservatives, and the Blue Dogs found their views being largely ignored by the Democratic Party leadership.

However, in the 111th Congress, starting in January 2009, there were forty-seven Democrats in the Blue Dog Coalition, which has put them in a position to make their voice heard in many policy areas when legislation is being drafted.

### Democratic Leadership Council

Centrist members of the Democratic Party founded this faction in 1985, seeking to establish a political agenda for the Democratic Party that appeals to the conservative heartland of the USA. The group is often identified with Bill Clinton, who became its leader in 1990 and, of course, went on to become President two years later. He argued that the Democrats had not been trusted by middle-class voters to 'defend our national interests abroad, to put their values into social policies at home, or to take their taxes and spend it with discipline'. According to the **Democratic Leadership Council** (DLC), therefore, party policy has to combine 'progressive ideals, mainstream values, and innovative, non bureaucratic, market-based solutions . . . promoting opportunity for all; demanding responsibility from everyone; and fostering a new sense of community'. In sum, the DLC has adopted a position of advancing traditional left-wing goals, such as protecting the interests of the poor, through methods that have traditionally been associated with the right, such as boosting opportunities through economic growth – a combination that was labelled the 'third way' in the late 1980s and early 1990s.

While this message proved to be politically successful in the 1990s, with Bill Clinton winning two presidential elections, it has been subject to mounting criticism within the Democratic Party since President Clinton left office, for failing to inspire potential supporters who look to government for help in their hour of need while also failing to attract the support of conservatives who have committed like-minded alternatives to turn to. Thus, the DLC has come to be seen as embodying all of the weaknesses of the modern Democratic Party: failing to provide an inspiring vision for America and only winning elections when their opponents are unpopular. Thus, although in the 111th Congress, starting in January 2009, there were fifty-eight members of the **New Democrat Coalition**, that serves as a forum for centrist Democrats, their influence in terms of ideas and policy proposals has distinctly declined in the early twenty-first century. In recognition of this, centrists have established some new think-tanks, such as the New America Foundation and the Center for American Progress, to provide new ideas and energy.

### The left

Many Americans associate the Democratic Party with liberal policies which, in the context of US politics, are on the left of the political mainstream. It was Democratic Presidents in the twentieth century who pioneered policies in which government intervened to care for those who cannot help themselves and promoted the inclusion of groups that have been marginalised by society. Thus, the left of the Democratic Party, also referred to as **Progressives**, celebrate the New Deal of the 1930s when government rescued millions of unemployed Americans from poverty and hopelessness with a variety of programmes, the Great Society programme of the 1960s, when government made a concerted effort to eradicate poverty, and the activism of the Supreme Court in the 1960s and 1970s, when Constitutional protections were extended to groups such as racial minorities and women seeking an abortion. Their critics, however, associate these policies with massive, wasteful spending and unnecessary government interference.

In Congress, the left works together to advance its agenda through the **Congressional Progressive Caucus**, which had seventy-one members in the 111th Congress (starting in January 2009), making it the largest organised group in the Democratic Party. Perhaps of greater significance than its numbers was the fact that ten of its members chaired committees in the House of Representatives, including some of the most powerful committees, such as the Ways and Means Committee and the Rules Committee, and the most powerful person in the House of Representatives, Speaker Nancy Pelosi, used to be a member. Outside Congress, it consists of a loose coalition of people and groups who share similar values and broadly support the same policies and often forge links through internet sites such as MoveOn.org and The Daily Kos.

In recent decades, the left has had great difficulty in promoting its policies. From 1968 to 2008, there were only two Democratic presidents (Jimmy Carter, who served only one term, and Bill Clinton, who served two terms) and progressive policies were not at the top of the agenda of either man. Then, Republican control of Congress from 1992 to 2006 further reduced opportunities to shape public policy. For much of this time, the left put most of its efforts into fighting conservative measures that they saw as threatening hard-won rights such as abortion, civil rights for racial minorities, gay rights and so on.

With the success of the Democratic Party in Federal elections since 2006, and especially the substantial impact made by activists on the Obama election campaign through their internet networks, the Progressives have switched their emphasis to pressing for a package of reforms that they hope to see enacted while President Obama is in the White House, including:

- The introduction of Universal Healthcare, ensuring access to treatment for all Americans.
- Improved rights for trade unions and for people who wish to join a union.
- Regular increases in the minimum wage.
- A programme of building affordable homes.
- The reversal of the tax cuts for the wealthiest, initiated by President George W. Bush, and the additional revenues invested in anti-poverty programmes.
- Substantially enhanced regulation of the financial sector (banks, pension funds and so on).
- A shift from military action to diplomacy to resolve global issues.
- A reduction in the USA's greenhouse gas emissions and an expansion of the use of renewable energy sources.

**Unity and division in the Democratic Party**
The range of views within the Democratic Party, from moderate conservative to left-wing, is significantly wider than the range of views in the Republican Party (especially when, as is often the case, the New Right simply ignores the views of moderate Republicans). This makes unity harder to achieve in the Democratic Party, particularly when they are in power. In opposition, they can unite around a joint challenge to Republican policies. In power, however, Democrats have to build a policy agenda they can all accept. This has often meant that each group within the party has been dissatisfied with the end result.

The proposals to reform healthcare in the first months of the 111th Congress illustrated the point. Although almost all Democrats favoured the passage of a law that reduced the number of Americans without healthcare insurance (and most Republicans in Congress put up determined resistance to the proposals), the left pushed hard for the introduction of a government-run healthcare programme that would guarantee universal healthcare coverage while the Blue Dogs supported calls for healthcare to remain in the private sector and prioritised minimising the cost of any reforms. Consequently, a variety of proposals languished in Congress for months, allowing opponents of healthcare reform to gain the initiative and the eventual passage of a bill that was far less ambitious than the original proposals.

## Party supporters

### Identifying the party faithful

In the 2004 presidential election, the Republican electoral strategist kept a card in his pocket showing that the percentage of independent voters had fallen from 15 per cent in 1988 to 7 per cent in 2002. Hence his strategy to almost ignore undecided voters and concentrate on maximising turnout among committed Republicans. The Democrats adopted a similar approach. So who are the committed Republicans and Democrats?

### Race and ethnic identity

One of the clearest indicators of party support in the USA is race or ethnic identity.

African Americans have tended to vote Democrat since the New Deal in the 1930s, and have overwhelmingly given their support to the party since the Civil Rights movement in the 1960s. In the 2008 presidential election, the Democratic Party won 95 per cent of the African American vote and has consistently gained around 90 per cent of the black vote since the 1960s.

Jews have also been reliable supporters of the Democratic Party over the same period because of the party's association with Civil Rights and moving forward the standard of living for minority groups. In the 2008 election, 78 per cent of Jews voted Democrat.

European Catholics, primarily those who came to the USA in the nineteenth century from Italy, Ireland and Poland, have also been traditional supporters of the Democratic Party. This support has been steadily eroding, however, since the 1960s. In part, this is due to income: as an increasing percentage of these ethnic groups have become wealthier they have migrated to the suburbs, away from the communities that have historically voted as a bloc. In part, their change of allegiance is due to the Civil Rights movement, which opened up new competition for jobs in sectors traditionally dominated by white Catholics, especially in services such as the police force and firefighting. They tend to be particularly hostile to Affirmative Action, which they see as giving minority groups an advantage in competition for these jobs. Moreover, in recent years social issues have significantly influenced Catholic voters, adding to defections to the Republican Party. In the 2008 presidential election, 53 per cent of this group voted Democrat, but four years earlier, with the church taking a public stand on abortion, effectively encouraging Catholics to vote for President Bush, 52 per cent of the white Catholic vote went to the Republican Party.

The other large Catholic group of voters in the USA, the Hispanics from Central and South America, is difficult to categorise, as it is made of many nationalities. Based on past experience, recent immigrants with low incomes can be relied on to vote Democrat. This has generally proved to be the case with Mexicans and Puerto Ricans. Other factors, however, seem to play a significant role in Hispanic voting patterns. The periodic upsurges of the 'nativist' faction within the Republican Party, typified by proposition 187 in California, which appeared hostile to Hispanic groups, drives them into the arms of the Democrats. When the 'nativist' faction is quiet, Hispanic voting patterns are more fluid. Politicians who reach out to them, such as the former Governor of Florida, Jeb Bush, who speaks good Spanish, are rewarded with high levels of support. The Republican Party has demonstrated an ability to attract wealthier members of these communities and some of the party's social policies, such as opposition to abortion, accord with Catholic teachings. Additionally, the fiercely anti-Castro Cubans who are unswervingly loyal to the Republican Party, which they see as taking a tougher line with their arch-enemy. Overall, however, the Democrats hold a distinct, but insecure, lead among this diverse group. During the 2008 presidential election campaign, one of the more significant issues in the Republican primary was illegal immigration, and the hostility towards Hispanics evident in this debate alienated this group, which supported the Democratic ticket in the general election by a margin of 66 per cent to 31 per cent.

## Gender

There is a longstanding pattern of women being more likely to vote Democrat than men. Surveys consistently demonstrate that healthcare is the highest priority of women, followed by equal pay and job security. Third is education, providing the best opportunities for their children. The Democrats are seen as the more committed to taking action on each of these issues.

Research indicates that the gender gap grows as education increases. A survey of more than 40,000 women in 2003 indicated that among those with a high school diploma or less, women were 10 per cent more likely than men to vote Democrat. For those who had gone on to university, but failed to complete their degree, the gender gap grew to 15 percentage points. Among those with a degree, it rose to 20 per cent. And for voters who had taken postgraduate courses, it reached 28 percentage points, almost triple the gender difference among the least-educated voters. On the other hand, when women get married their voting patterns change and the gender divide almost disappears.

The result, overall, is a fairly consistent pattern of 54 per cent of women voting Democrat and 53 per cent of men voting Republican.

**Geography**
The political parties, as well as examining how and why specific sections of the electorate vote, also pay close attention to regional patterns of support, which is particularly important when making electoral college calculations.

When evaluating the outcome of recent elections, and their implications for the future, Michael Barone, author of the *Almanac of American Politics*, has divided the country into three parts, each with roughly equal population. One is the East and West coasts, around New York state and California, which has consistently cast around 55 per cent of its votes for the Democratic Party since the mid-1990s. The Democrats consolidated these regions in 2008. Another is the 'heartland' of the Midwest and Rocky Mountain states, which have cast around 53 per cent of its votes for the Republican Party over the same period. However, in 2008, the Democrats made inroads into this area, winning Colorado, New Mexico, Nevada and Indiana. The third is the South, made up mainly of the Confederate states that fought against the Union in the Civil War, which has cast around 55 per cent of its votes for the Republicans. Even here, however, the Democrats made progress in 2008, taking Virginia and North

Carolina as well as the key swing state of Florida that had gone to the Republicans in the previous two presidential elections.

### Religion

Before 1972, there was no difference in the voting patterns of those who regularly attended a place of worship and those who did not. Then, in the 1972 election, a 10 per cent gap emerged as Richard Nixon appealed to the 'silent majority' who favoured a return to traditional values after the social upheavals of the 1960s. This gap widened during the presidency of Bill Clinton amidst rumours, then admissions, of marital infidelity. Since the beginning of the twenty-first century, white evangelical Protestants who consider 'values' to be a primary factor in their voting choices have consistently favoured the Republican Party by a margin of 3:1.

### Lifestyle

Added to the array of indicators that parties can use to identify who is likely to vote for them, experts in voting behaviour can now provide indicators from people's lifestyles to help more precisely target their messages. For example, of the two most popular evening talk shows, Republicans are more likely to watch the one starring Jay Leno, while Democrats are more likely to watch the one starring David Letterman. The overwhelming majority of men who watch NASCAR, stock car racing, vote Republican. Almost everyone who drives a Volvo votes Democrat.

## Minor parties

### Obstacles to success for minor parties

Every President since the Civil War (1861–5) has been either a Democrat or a Republican. Only Vermont has returned an inde-pendent Congressman and an independent Senator to Washington DC in recent years. At the local level, third parties have had some electoral success, such as the Liberal Party in New York, and Jesse 'The Body' Ventura (a former professional wrestler) was elected Governor of Minnesota in 1996. Why is it so difficult for members of minor parties to gain high office?

The most important factor is the lack of ideological 'space'. For most of American history, the political arena has been filled with two 'umbrella' parties large and broad enough to organise and draw support across an extremely large, extremely diverse country. With no room on the political spectrum for more than two umbrella parties, minor parties have tended to be focused on specific issues and highly ideological in character. Consequently, they have had difficulty attracting wide support unless they have promoted an issue which the main parties had ignored and which resonated with many of the voters. Even when this has happened, the main parties have woken up to the issue, absorbing it into their programme.

Furthermore, the evolution of the main parties, in recent years, has not created any vacant political territory space for the minor parties. Both Democrats and Republicans appeal to approximately 50 per cent of the nation and offer two clear ideological choices, encouraging voters to support one of the two main parties in order to keep out of power the party they most dislike, even when the alternative is not very attractive, rather than casting a 'wasted' vote for a minor party.

Third parties also suffer a number of disadvantages arising directly from electoral rules and practices, including:

- The first-past-the-post electoral system, which has a tendency to produce two dominant parties wherever it is used. This is particularly true of US presidential elections, where candidates have to win a majority of the votes cast in each state in order to win electoral college votes. It is so unlikely in most elections that minor parties will achieve this goal that they generally lack credibility.
- Many states have restrictive regulations that make it difficult for candidates to be included on the ballot unless they have already demonstrated (by raising signatures) that they have significant levels of support. This often causes expensive distractions from campaigning by the candidates who may have the fewest resources.
- Many states allow 'straight ticket' voting, which encourages voters to cast their votes for one of the main parties in all posts being contested. This penalises minor parties that may have not have candidates for all posts. Minor candidates receive, on average, twice as many votes in districts that do not allow straight-ticket voting.

- Federal funds are only available to parties that gained more than 5 per cent of the vote in the previous presidential election and full funding is only available to parties that gained over 25 per cent.
- Campaigns are getting steadily more sophisticated and expensive, and minor parties often have limited funds and expertise at their disposal.

## Limited success for minor parties

Despite these obstacles, third-party candidates have also had some impact in recent years:

- In the 1992 presidential campaign, multi-billionaire Ross Perot managed to get his name onto the ballot in all fifty states. He spent more than $65 million on his campaign, much of it on thirty-minute 'infomercials' that outlined his strategies to reduce the budget deficit and criticised the lack of policies on the issue from the two main parties. His support in nationwide opinion polls enabled him to participate in the presidential debates and in the election he won 18.9 per cent of the vote. However he won no electoral college votes.

    The success of his campaign can be measured by the votes drawn away from the Republican Party and the effect it had on the policy platforms of both main parties. Had he not been in the race, election analysts estimate that a majority of the 19 million votes cast for him could have gone to President Bush, who would have been re-elected as a result, instead of Bill Clinton. Also, deficit-reduction measures were a prominent feature of the 'Contract with America', the manifesto that enabled the Republican Party to win control of the House of Representatives in 1994. The bill they passed was then signed into law by President Clinton, who was as keen as his political opponents to claim credit for a policy which had proved so popular, and by the end of the decade the Federal budget was in surplus.

    Perot's less successful campaign in the 1996 presidential election illustrates how difficult it can be for minor parties to maintain momentum. His main policy had, by that time, been adopted by both of the dominant parties and he won just 8 per cent of the vote.

- In the 2000 election campaign, Ralph Nader, a veteran consumer rights activist, represented the Green Party, forcing the issue of the environment to be debated. He won just 2.7 per cent of the vote, but this included more than 97,000 votes in Florida, almost all of which would have gone to the Democratic candidate, Al Gore. George W. Bush won Florida by just 537 votes, which gave him the 25 electoral college votes that determined which of the two men became President.

Even in the 2004 presidential election, when Ralph Nader won only 0.38 per cent of the vote, the possibility of his participation leading to a repeat of the 2000 election result meant that both of the main parties diverted time and funds as the Democrats fought to keep him off the ballot in many states and the Republicans provided assistance to help him.

Overall, however, the minor parties have been characterised as being like a bee: they may sting but the pain they inflict is rarely serious and, afterwards, they die.

## Polarisation

To the extent that political parties have a key role to play in a democracy, providing coherent packages of policies for the population to choose from, how well have they fulfilled this function?

### Party decline

There have been times when US political parties have been seen as failing to provide clear policy alternatives. In the 1950s, when conservatives played a dominant role in both of the two main parties (especially when resisting the extensions of Civil Rights), the American Political Science Association complained that it was difficult for voters to know which party to hold to account when there was so much overlap between them. Then, in the 1970s the prize-winning author and journalist David Broder was equally critical of the failure of the main parties to provide political leadership because of what he saw as a lack of a clear ideology in either party.

The factors that have undermined the ability of parties to

establish, and maintain, clear distinctions continue to be evident in US politics:

- The diversity of US society, which means that political parties tend to be broad enough to accommodate the wishes and needs of different sections of the population.
- The use of primaries to nominate candidates, which means that the senior members of political parties are less able than their counterparts in other countries to control who represents their party in elections.
- The system of separation of powers, which means that members of the same party in different branches of government may have contrasting, even rival, interests.

Thus, even though the criticisms of the 1950s and 1970s appear to have diminished in validity (see below), some political observers claim that there is a limit to the extent to which the main parties in the USA are able to establish a clear ideological divide, presenting the voters with two distinct, rival alternatives.

Moreover, the political scientist Morris Fiorina has argued that the American people neither want nor need two polarised political parties. Opinion poll evidence, he claims, demonstrates that the electorate are moderate and tolerant, sharing largely similar views on the majority of the most important issues of the day. His view is that apparent divisions in party politics have more to do with a relatively small number of political activists who exert influence out of proportion to their numbers. If this analysis is correct, there is a limit to the extent to which political parties can ever provide distinct policy alternatives and it would not be desirable for them to do so. His perspective, however, is strongly disputed by other observers of US politics.

### Party renewal

As long ago as 1949, the social commentator V. O. Key criticised the failure of US political parties to offer clear alternatives. 'Over the long run,' he argued, 'the have-nots lose in a disorganised politics'. When policy is made through deals struck between competing groups, the poor and marginalised who have little to bargain with are poorly placed to secure their interests while the already wealthy and powerful are well placed to reinforce their dominance. Consequently, as parties, especially the Democrats, encompassed an ever wider range of people and policies in the 1960s, political participation declined, especially among the poor. Thus, by the early 1990s, 86 per cent of the wealthiest Americans were regularly voting while barely half of the poorest did so.

This analysis suggests that greater political polarisation is to be welcomed and, in the first decade of the twenty-first century, the evidence suggests that the contrast between an increasingly conservative Republican Party and a Democratic Party that is heavily influenced by its left wing has served to galvanise voters of all races and income brackets in record numbers. Indeed, one of the leaders of the Republican Party has been quoted as asserting that 'partisanship, based on core principles, clarifies our debates and constantly refreshes our politics with new ideas'.

The change in the voting patterns of white voters in the South has clearly transformed both of the main political parties (see the sections on party realignment and conservatives of the heart above) but other factors have also contributed to claims that the main political parties have become increasingly polarised since the 1980s, including:

- The establishment of national headquarters for each party. Historically, the national party only had a significant role to play once every four years, during presidential elections. During the 1980s and 1990s, however, both parties established permanent headquarters in Washington DC, which played an increasingly important role in fundraising, keeping databases on supporters and identifying vulnerable districts which would benefit from help in the form of money or volunteers.
- The introduction of superdelegates by the Democratic Party, in the mid-1980s, to the National Convention, which selects their Presidential nominee. This gives elected office-holders, such as members of Congress and governors, voting rights equivalent to 20 per cent of the total when choosing the nominee.
- Reforms in Congress, made by the Republicans after their 1994 mid-term election victory, strengthened the control of the party's leadership in the legislature, bringing an increase of vote on party lines.

Moreover, these developments have been seen by some political scientists, in contrast to the analysis provided by Morris Fiorina (see the section on party decline above), as reflecting a growing divide between sections of the population who have contrasting visions for the future of their country – a divide that has become known as the '**culture wars**'.

## Conclusion

The concerns of the Founding Fathers that political parties would prove a divisive force in US society have, at times, proved well founded, with the early twenty-first century being seen by many observers of US politics as evidence of how divisive party politics can be.

However, when parties have been broad-based, with little to distinguish them, they have been criticised for excluding the weak and vulnerable from policy-making, thus becoming vehicles for the wealthy and the social elite, which was also a development that the Founding Fathers feared and distrusted.

Whether going through a period of party decline or party renewal, therefore, the US party political system has been subject to considerable criticism.

· · · · · · · · · · · · · · · · · · · · · · · · · · · · · · · · · · · · · · · · · · · · · · · · ·

### ✔ What you should have learnt from reading this chapter

- The Founding Fathers were extremely suspicious of political parties, fearing that they would be divisive and promote the interests of their supporters at the expense of the wider community.

- The emergence of two 'umbrella' parties, each representing a diverse range of people, appeared to ensure that this would not happen.

- However, this led to the main parties failing to provide meaningful alternatives for the electorate to choose from in elections.

- Increase in partisanship, since the early 1990s, has been welcomed by some, partly because of the choices they provide for the American people and partly because 'umbrella parties' have been criticised for largely excluding the less influential sections of society from policy-making.

- Some commentators, however, argue that in a society as diverse as the USA, with decentralised decision-making, it is neither possible nor desirable to have parties with a narrow ideological focus.

- Moreover, the party system has been criticised for limiting the ability of minor parties to play an prominent role in US politics by denying them any ideological 'space' both when the main parties have been broad-based and when they have been ideologically polarised.

## Glossary of key terms

**Blue Dog Coalition** An organised faction of the Democratic Party (the most conservative of its factions) that advocates financial discipline in public policy.

**Congressional Progressive Caucus** An organised faction of the Democratic Party (the most left-wing of its factions) that favours government intervention to extend rights and extend the interests of the poor.

**Culture wars** A term applied to the conflict between those values considered conservative and those considered liberal or progressive.

**Democratic Leadership Council** A centrist faction of the Democratic Party that advocates attempting to advance 'progressive' ideals (such as protecting the interests of the poor) though 'market-based solutions'.

**Fiscal conservative** A view, found mainly in the Republican Party, that government interference in the daily lives of citizens, especially the levying of taxes, should be kept to a minimum.

**Liberal** A view, found mainly in the Democratic Party, that government has a responsibility to actively intervene to protect the interests of vulnerable groups in society (often used interchangeably with 'progressive').

**New Deal Coalition** A term applied to the sections of the electorate whose support for the Democratic Party was cemented by President Roosevelt's policies in the 1930s to combat the effects of the depression.

**New Democrat Coalition** A centrist Congressional faction of the Democratic Party that, like the Democratic Leadership Council, advocates attempting to advance 'progressive' ideals, such as protecting the interests of the poor, though 'market-based solutions'.

**New Right** A collective term for social and fiscal conservatives, which rose to prominence (displacing traditional conservatism) in the 1980s.

**Party base** The most committed supporters of a political party, who almost always support it in elections, usually participate in primaries and form a high proportion of its active campaigners.

**Party decline** A theory that political parties have diminished in importance and have failed to fulfil their roles in the political system, especially in providing a clear ideological choice at elections.

**Party realignment** A change in the patterns of support among the voters for the Democratic and Republican parties.

**Party renewal** A theory that political parties have grown in importance and increasingly represent distinct, contrasting ideological positions.

**Paternalistic** An approach to politics based on the view that the economic and social elites in society have a responsibility to protect and advance the best interests of the less fortunate, just as fathers have a responsibility to protect and look after their children.

**Progressive** see **Liberal**.

**Rockefeller conservatism** A centrist strand of conservatism that resists radical change, but accepts a substantial role for government in helping those unable to help themselves.

**Social conservative** A view, found mainly in the Republican Party, that government has a responsibility to actively intervene to create a moral framework for society that promotes a shared set of values that bind a diverse population.

**Split-ticket voting** Supporting candidates from different parties at the same election (for example, voting for the Republican candidate for President at the same time as voting for the Democratic candidate for Congress).

**Umbrella parties** Political parties with no clear ideological focus, seeking to win support from a wide range of groups with dissimilar interests.

## Likely examination questions

Issues examiners may expect students to be able to effectively analyse include:

- The ideology of the two main parties: what they believe in, and why

- Who supports the two main parties; the evolution of the patterns of support and the significance of these for the ability of each party to win power

- The significance of minor parties

- The extent and desirability of polarisation between the two main parties

Thus, examples of the kind of questions which could be asked include:

What is meant by party renewal, and in what sense has it happened?

Are minor parties doomed to failure?

##  Helpful websites

Republican Party:

- The official website of the party is www.rnc.org.

- To keep up to date with the views of the social conservative wing of the party, go to the website of the Arlington Group at www.renewamerica. us.

- To keep up to date with the views of fiscal conservatives, go to the website of the Republican Study Committee, accessible through the website of its chairman, which at time of publication was Congressman Tom Price at rsc.tomprice.house.gov.

- To keep up to date with the views of Republican moderates, go to the website of the Republican Mainstreet Partnership at www.republicanmainstreet.org.

Democratic Party:

- The official website of the party is www.dnc.org.

- To keep up to date with the views of the conservative wing of the party, go to the website of the Blue Dog Democrats at www.bluedogdems.com.

- To keep up to date with the views of the moderate, centrist wing of the party, go to the website of the Democratic Leadership Council at www.dlc.org.

- To keep up to date with the views of the left of the Democratic Party, visit either of the two websites which are most influential in promoting an aggressive, anti-conservative agenda, www.moveon.org or www.dailykos.com.

Minor Parties:

- www.Politics1.com has a comprehensive list of US political parties, including minor parties in alphabetical order. These include parties that have either put people up for election or endorsed candidates, and some very strange fringe groups which have yet to do either. The views of each party are briefly summarised and there are links to the websites of each group.

Party Support:

- For the latest developments on the patterns of support for each party, go to the website of veteran elections commentator Charlie Cook at www.cookpolitical.com.

## Suggestions for further reading

For an authoritative analysis on the unfolding patterns of political support for the two main parties, the introduction to the *Almanac of American Politics* by Michael Barone is hard to surpass. Available on Amazon.com and the website of its publisher, the *National Journal*, it is rather expensive at around $70, but can also be used for its profiles of every member of Congress and every governor.

CHAPTER 6

# Pressure Groups

## Contents

## Overview

*'Money talks?'*
On 2 March 2004, Senators were seen reading an e-mail message on their BlackBerry pagers from the executive vice president of the National Rifle Association (NRA), Wayne LaPierre. Objecting to an amendment that had been added at the last moment, he was urging them to reject a bill that had been expected to pass by a wide margin. When the votes were counted, the bill was defeated by 90–8. 'They had the power to turn around at least sixty votes,' said Senator Dianne Feinstein, of California, who had proposed the amendment, 'that's amazing to me.'

However, not all Americans would share the Senator's dismay at the NRA's influence. The group was only able to persuade politicians to listen to its views because of its ability to mobilise more than 3 million members. Generating this level of political participation can be seen as a positive contribution to an active, inclusive democracy that helps ensure that the Founding Fathers' goal of avoiding concentration of political power is realised in modern America.

This chapter examines the methods used by pressure groups to achieve their objectives, using the opportunities presented to them by the US political system, and weighs up the arguments that they enhance or undermine democracy.

## Key issues to be covered in this chapter

- Pressure groups and the Constitution
- The aims and objectives of pressure groups
- Access points available to pressure groups: why, and how, they seek to benefit from them
- The extent to which pressure groups have a positive or negative effect on American society and democracy

# Pressure groups and the Constitution

### Creating a favourable climate for pressure groups

When drawing up the Constitution, the Founding Fathers relied on three mechanisms to avoid concentrations of power and, thereby, protect liberty: strict separation of powers in the Federal government; sharing power between the states and Federal government; and making elected officials accountable to the people. This had the effect of providing a political structure that suited those who may wish to influence policy-making, by creating a wide variety of **access points** where important decisions can be made (or resisted) and providing alternatives if one political institution is unsympathetic to a particular group or cause.

Then, in the Bill of Rights, freedom of expression and the right to 'petition the Government for a redress of grievances' were protected by the 1st Amendment. This guaranteed that pressure groups would always have the means to take advantage of the opportunities provided by the political system to influence decisions.

The Founding Fathers recognised that this presented a potential problem. In the public debate that accompanied the ratification process, James Madison, one of the principal authors of the Constitution, expressed concern that some groups, or sections of society, would be able to benefit disproportionately from the opportunities to shape public policy, to the disadvantage of the rest of the population. 'Factions,' he argued, would be 'adverse to the rights of other citizens, or to the permanent and aggregate interests of the community'. However, as the only way to limit the potential power of pressure groups would be to limit freedom of speech, he reached the conclusion that safeguarding the freedoms that the Constitution was designed to protect was the higher priority.

### Exploiting a favourable climate

Almost as soon as the Constitution came into effect, Americans took full advantage of the opportunities it provided to influence the political process. As early as 1835, the French commentator Alexis de Tocqueville wrote, 'In no country in the world has the principle of association been more successfully used, or applied to a greater multitude of objects, than America.'

This pattern continues to the present day, with groups using some, or all, of the political access points available to shape their society.

## The aims and objectives of pressure groups

### The purpose of pressure groups

People form groups in order to advance an interest that they share, or to promote a cause they believe in. They then seek to persuade as many people as possible to share their outlook.

If their views/policies become widely accepted, they may become the social norm and routinely shape public policy. For example, the establishment of a system of racial supremacy in the South after the Civil War began as an organised movement before becoming a part of the social and political fabric of the Southern states where segregation was practised.

More commonly, pressure groups have the support of specific sections of society, or a specific community, and have to actively work to promote the objectives they favour – often facing other pressure groups that wish to thwart their aims. In these cases, they have to devise strategies for success, calculating which sections of society may be most (or least) receptive to their messages, which policy-makers to target and what methods to use, taking into account their membership and resources.

The following sections outline why specific access points are targeted, the strategies used and the effectiveness of pressure groups.

### The controversial nature of pressure groups

The fact that (as de Tocqueville observed) Americans do not simply leave policy-making to their elected representatives, but actively engage in the process through groups, can be seen as a positive feature of the political system in the USA. Rival viewpoints on almost any issue of significance are likely to be aired through public campaigns, often using the media. In 2009, for example, when Congress was addressing the issue of healthcare reform, campaigners for and against the proposals placed advertisements in newspapers, and bought airtime on radio and TV. This, in principle, should lead to the public being well-educated on the issue and legislators having a full understanding of the views of both supporters and opponents of the proposed policy.

However, clearly not all groups have equal resources and (for reasons outlined below) it is often easier to block change than to pass reforms, which means that pressure groups have been seen as reinforcing systems that benefit the privileged at the expense of the marginalised.

The debate on whether pressure groups make a positive or negative contribution to US democracy will be explored in greater detail at the end of the chapter.

## Access points: why, and how, they are exploited

### Individuals

Although it may not appear to be a political strategy, the most effective way for a group to achieve its goals would be to persuade each member of society to behave in a manner consistent with its aims and objectives. Shared values and similar behaviour arguably benefit society as much as the groups that promote them. Historically, groups such as the scouts, Little League baseball and the League of Women Voters were credited for bringing together people of different classes and races in shared community-building activities that provided social bonds for a diverse society. They can also be a practical forum for applying democratic principles. Community groups require people to run meetings, handle membership dues and keep records. Leaders of local groups also had to be responsive to the views of their members. In the 1950s, it was calculated that the twenty largest national associations had 5 per cent of the adult population taking a leadership role in their local communities.

Such face-to-face group activity has diminished substantially since the 1950s. However, encouragement to participate in groups may have risen with increasingly sophisticated marketing by pressure groups, using direct mail and e-mail to target people who may be sympathetic to their views or goals. Following a high-profile campaign in 2005 to save the life of Terri Schiavo, a woman in a prolonged coma whose life-support system was turned off despite the objections of her parents, the list of donors who supported the campaign was sold to 'right to life' groups opposing abortion. Other groups, such as the National Rifle Association, provide services to their members, such as banking facilities, a travel service and a mobile phone service, while encouraging them to meet at events, such as gun shows, and to participate in campaigns to resist gun control.

For some groups, the specific targeting of individual behaviour is part of their wider political strategy. Anti-abortion groups are constantly devising methods to put pressure on women seeking an abortion to change their minds. In 2002, taking advantage of advances in digital photo technology, anti-abortion groups began posting pictures of women attending abortion clinics on their websites, to deter visits, until ordered to remove them by the courts. Then, pregnancy centres operated by anti-abortion groups began installing ultrasound equipment, which shows women the babies they are carrying. Reportedly, 90 per cent of women considering having an abortion change their minds if they attend one of these clinics (which often do not make it clear that they are part of an anti-abortion campaign).

### Communities

A political culture of accountability means that in most US communities any service that has a direct impact on people's lives may be run by elected people who can be held accountable if the service is not of an acceptable standard. This may include sanitation (garbage disposal), education and law and order. Consequently, there are many opportunities for groups to help shape their communities.

Education has been a particularly controversial area. As explained in Chapter 5, social conservatives have sought to gain control of school curriculums to ensure that moral values are a part of children's education, which has brought them into conflict with the courts. It is estimated that more than a quarter of the 15,000 school districts in the USA are dominated by groups with a social conservative agenda.

Law and order policies in the USA are also heavily influenced by local elections. In many areas, the Sheriff (who determines police priorities), the District Attorney (who decides on prosecutions) and the judges (who manage court cases and decide on sentencing) are all elected. This gives organisations such as Mothers Against Drunk Driving (MADD) an opportunity to promote their agenda that the police should put more resources into monitoring driving offences, the DA should push for heavier penalties for drunk drivers and judges should imprison those found guilty as a deterrent to others.

In addition, local councillors and the mayor are all elected, which provides opportunities to shape developments on a large scale. The mayor of New York City, for example, is sometimes described as the second most powerful executive in the nation. Mayor Giuliani's zero-tolerance policing policy, which has proved influential around the world, drew heavily on the 'broken windows' strategy. This was devised by two sociologists working for the Manhattan Institute, a right-wing think-tank, who argued that petty criminals developed over time into serious criminals and that this process could be stemmed by focusing on minor crimes, leading, in due course, to a reduction in major crime.

Political developments in communities can also be shaped through local democracy. In many states, voters are provided with opportunities to influence affairs through amendments to the state constitution, initiatives, propositions or recall elections. How this is done, and the impact this can have, is outlined in Chapter 4.

### States

States have enormous powers, including levying taxes; spending money on the welfare of the population; passing and enforcing laws; regulating trade within the state; administering elections; and protecting the public's health and morals.

All of this has an effect at local level. The money available for education, road-building and so on is largely determined in the state capital by the state legislature and the governor. So too are important policies such as whether or not to adopt the death penalty for certain crimes. In the 1990s, pressure groups were able to change the law in California through propositions (opportunities for citizens to vote on issues of importance) that particularly affected minority groups. In 1994, Proposition 187 withdrew benefits, including education, from the families of illegal immigrants, the majority of whom were from Mexico. In 1996, Proposition 209 banned Affirmative Action to ensure access to higher education for groups who had been historically discriminated against in the state's universities. In 1998, bilingual education, usually English and Spanish, was banned in the state's schools. In 2008, a ruling by the California Supreme Court permitting gay marriage was overturned by Proposition 8.

Policies pioneered at state level can also substantially affect national politics. In the 1990s Wisconsin introduced school vouchers. Instead of paying schools for the cost of educating each student, the money went to families, who could decide which school to spend it in. This would, in principle, increase choice and force schools to improve their performance or close for lack of students. The policy was driven by a right-wing think-tank, the Bradley Foundation, which was close to the Republican Party, and some Democrat African American activists who believed that existing policies were failing their community's children. It was adopted by George W. Bush for his presidential election campaign in 2000.

When George W. Bush became President, he refused to sign international agreements on measures to tackle climate change. Actively lobbied by environmentalist groups, eleven states have introduced (or plan to introduce) air quality regulations that are much more strict than those of the Federal government. Unless the regulations are overruled in the courts, as a result of lawsuits brought by car manufacturers, greenhouse gases from cars will have to be reduced by roughly 30 per cent between 2009 and 2016. With these states, including California and New York, accounting for about one-third of auto sales, they may create a situation in which it becomes uneconomic for car companies to produce two varieties of each of their models and simply build cars with lower emissions.

## Elections

With significant power being wielded at so many levels (including the Federal level, below) by so many people it is clearly beneficial for pressure groups to:

- Help sympathetic people to win elections.
- Make sure that they use their power to advance the agenda of the group(s) that helped them win.

There are a variety of strategies used by groups to accomplish these two goals.

- *Creating voters* Pressure groups can, literally, create voters. Significant sections of society have, historically, been denied the right to vote, including African Americans, Native Americans and women. Each required robust, lengthy campaigns before the franchise was extended to them. Two notable groups are the focus of continuing campaigns to extend their limited voting rights: residents of Washington DC, who cannot vote in Congressional or Senate elections (because the district is not in any of the fifty states), and released convicts who, in thirteen states, lose the right to vote for the rest of their lives.

Pressure groups also play a significant role in helping people to register to vote. At any given time, in a highly mobile society, many voters may not have met the registration requirements to be able to vote in their new districts, or may have not yet registered to vote by the next election. Others, relatively recent immigrants to the country, may be unsure of the registration procedures. Pressure groups often play a prominent part in supporting and advising people in these situations. The leading African American Civil Rights group, the National Association for the Advancement of Colored People (NAACP), led the campaign for the 'motor voter' Act of 1993, which was introduced to allow voters to register when they renew or change their address on their driving licences. Since its introduction, an estimated 9 million additional people have registered to vote.

- *Choosing the right candidate* Registering sympathetic voters is the first step. Persuading the main political parties to adopt candidates who support the group's objectives is the next. Before most elections in the USA, from town council to President, voters are given an opportunity to play a part in selecting which candidate will represent the main parties. Pressure groups donate funds to candidates they support; provide information to their members on why they should vote for the group's preferred candidates in the primaries; encourage their members to volunteer to work on the campaigns of favoured candidates; provide assistance to anyone who wishes to vote in the primaries but may have difficulty getting to a polling station; and may even produce their own election material explaining to the wider electorate why they support particular candidates.
- *Electing the right candidate* After the primary, if the pressure group's preferred candidate has won, the next task is to get the voters out to ensure that the candidate wins the election

against the opposing party. This is done by assisting the candidate's campaign: distributing leaflets, displaying signs in front of homes, telephoning voters to remind them of the election and providing transport to get voters to the polling stations. Pressure groups that are particularly effective may have helped sympathisers to win the primary of both parties, meaning that the group wins whatever the outcome of the election. For example, in the race to represent the 3rd District of Colorado in the 2004 election, the National Rifle Association (NRA) fully endorsed both candidates. Understandably, there has long been concern that pressure groups play too significant a role in elections, potentially making politicians more responsive to their agenda than to the concerns of the voters. Attempts to limit this influence, and the response of pressure groups, are outlined in Chapter 4.

Once a politician has been elected, those pressure groups that have helped him/her to win want to ensure that their policy priorities do not get overlooked. Commonly, this is done by providing all elected officials with a list of their legislative priorities. The list is also distributed to members and put on the group's website. Politicians are aware that the level of support, or opposition, they can expect from pressure groups depends on the extent to which they promote the groups' agendas.

Ahead of the next election, pressure groups will issue 'report cards' on how much support their agendas have received from politicians seeking re-election. As with school reports, politicians are graded on a scale of A–F. Those with highest grades can expect considerable support in their campaign in terms of both funds and volunteers. Those with a grade F can expect to face active opposition throughout their campaigns.

In 2006, Republican Senator Mike DeWine of Ohio, who was facing re-election that year, was given a Grade F by the NRA for opposing the group's top legislative priority the previous year, a bill that prohibited lawsuits against gun manufacturers for unlawful use of their firearms. The bill passed but the group was determined to punish him in the 2006 election for his decision.

## House of Representatives

At the Federal level, the strategy of influencing politicians through electoral support is most effective in the House of Representatives because all of its members have to stand for re-election every two years. A significant proportion of the seats are so safe that the Congressmen are not seriously threatened at elections and therefore do not need to mount expensive campaigns. In competitive seats, however, members are acutely aware of the need to raise a substantial war chest, as much as $10,000 per week between elections.

However, both Congressmen and pressure groups are conscious of the suspicion aroused in the media and among voters of relationships that appear to be based exclusively on money. Both are keen to develop relationships that are seen to be constructive, bringing mutual benefit to the Congressman's constituents as well as to the pressure group. This is done by:

* *Developing a relationship* Relationships between Congressmen are often based on ideology. Republicans are likely to be approached by conservative groups to promote their proposals. For example, when President George W. Bush proposed reforming social security in 2005, the Free Enterprise Fund, which had advocated such reform for years, approached Congressman Paul Ryan (Wisconsin, 1st District) to introduce a bill that reflected their views. At the same time, the Cato Institute, another conservative think-tank, which supported reform, approached Congressman Sam Johnson (Texas, 3rd District) to introduce a rival bill reflecting their proposals for reorganising the system. A similar ideological relationship is commonplace between Democratic Congressmen and liberal pressure groups.

    Pressure groups will also attempt to forge relationships with Congressmen, including their opponents, because of their committee assignments. For example, John Lewis (Georgia, 5th District), a liberal African American Congressman, consistently opposes the interests of the pharmaceutical industry, and because he sits on the Ways and Means Health Subcommittee this opposition has a direct impact on the industry. Over the years, large pharmaceutical firms have provided medical scholarships to African Americans in his district to increase the proportion of black doctors, provided study weekends for his staff in exotic locations and put on events to commemorate Congressman Lewis's contributions to the Civil Rights campaigns in the 1960s. None of these contributions have persuaded the Congressman to vote in their interests but they may have helped reduce the volume of his criticisms.

Relationships between Congressmen and pressure groups may be based on local priorities. For example, the largest employer in Congressman Lewis's district is Coca-Cola. Representatives from the firm are always welcome in his office and his staff are always receptive to their requests. Relationships may also be built on the personal commitments of the Congressman. For years, Congressman Lewis campaigned for a National Museum of African American History and Culture to be added to the Smithsonian complex of museums in Washington DC, and welcomed any support offered. Having submitted a bill to Congress to authorise and fund the project on fifteen occasions, the proposal was signed into law in 2003 and a prestigious location on the Mall allocated in 2006.

- *Professional **lobbyists*** Pressure groups employ people, on a full-time basis, to build these relationships on their behalf. Professional lobbying has been a growth business since the 1930s, when, under the New Deal, the scale of government began to grow rapidly and, with it, the scale of government contracts and regulations that could benefit or harm organisations. Between 2000 and 2009, Federal spending increased from $1.79 trillion to $2.9 trillion, and at the same time the number of registered lobbyists in Washington DC rose from 16,342 to 34,789.

The people best placed to foster relationships with Congressmen, and their staff, are those who already know them, and the legislative procedures that they wish to influence, well. Thus, many lobbyists are former Congressional staff members or former Congressmen. For those with the best contacts in Congress, and the greatest experience of the legislative system, becoming a lobbyist can be extremely lucrative. For example, after twenty-five years representing the 3rd District of Louisiana, Billy Tauzin stepped down to take up the post of president of the Pharmaceutical and Research Manufacturers of America for an estimated $2 million per year. This is known as the **revolving door syndrome**, with people leaving Congressional employment only to reappear almost immediately as lobbyists. It should be noted, however, that periodically the revolving door takes people from lobbying into elected positions, often with a significant drop in pay. The most notable recent example would be Haley Barbour, current Governor of Mississippi, who left the lobbying firm that he had established and built up to be one of the largest, wealthiest firms in Washington DC in order to run for office.

The close relationships that exist between professional lobbyists and members of Congress have given rise to concern that meaningful power has become concentrated in a small, elite group of people who are the only ones who fully grasp the vast array of complex regulations. To address this concern, the Federal Regulation of Lobbying Act was passed in 1946. Limited to setting up a system of registration and financial disclosure of those attempting to influence legislation in Congress, the law did not attempt to regulate the conduct of lobbying. Then, in 1954, the scope of the Act was narrowed by a Supreme Court ruling in *United States* v. *Harriss* that it only applied to the paid efforts of people who spent more than half of their time directly contacting Congressmen (not their staff) on legislative matters. It took a scandal in the 1980s to push Congress into tightening up the law, when it came to light that a large corporation had hired numerous lobbyists to help win government contracts without reporting their work. In 1995, the Lobbying Disclosure Act was passed, which extended disclosure of information to all forms of lobbying, not just legislative, and included disclosing lobbying of Congressional staff. It also addressed concerns about the revolving door syndrome by requiring people who have worked in Congress to wait for a year before lobbying their former colleagues.

For critics of the system, such as Common Cause, Democracy 21 and Public Citizen, the Lobbying Disclosure Act does not go far enough. While there are restrictions on providing gifts and meals for Congressmen and their staff, these can be easily evaded. If a large corporation, for example, provides tickets to its box at a sports stadium, it will value the cost at a rate below the threshold value for gifts from lobbyists. In any event, the authorities in the

House of Representatives and the Senate do not invest significant resources into investigating violations of the law.

In 2006, there was a surge of support for further tightening lobbying regulations as a result of a series of media revelations of lobbying sliding into unethical conduct. In September 2004, an executive for the Boeing Aircraft Corporation, who had formerly worked for the Department of Defense, was convicted of conspiracy over a contract she had negotiated, worth $20 billion, knowing that she would be joining the firm. In November 2005, the Congressman for California's 50th District was forced to resign when it was revealed that he had accepted gifts to the value of $2.6 million dollars from a defence contractor while he was on the Appropriations Defense Subcommittee. Then, in January 2006, top lobbyist Jack Abramoff was convicted of defrauding some of his clients. The investigations revealed that he had strengthened his relationship with politicians through expensive meals and golfing trips to Scotland. Among the proposals to strengthen lobbying regulations are:

– A ban on members of Congress, or their staff, accepting gifts or meals from lobbyists.
– Disclosure of who paid for travel.
– A ban on becoming a lobbyist for two years (instead of one).
– Not allowing former members of Congress to use private areas within the building, such as the gym, which present opportunities for discreet lobbying.
– More detailed disclosure of lobbyist activities, especially expenditure.
– Heavier penalties for breaking the rules.

However, for all the concerns expressed about professional lobbyists, it is generally agreed that they can play a useful role in Congress. The legislative process can be, at times, quite chaotic, with a wide range of diverse interests holding up bills or adding amendments largely unrelated to the purpose of bills (see Chapter 8). Professional lobbyists can be particularly helpful in:

– Negotiating deals between members of Congress to move legislation forward without losing its focus.
– Helping members of Congress to generate support for proposals through their links with important people, contributing

articles to influential newspapers and by mobilising the grass-
roots members of their organisations.

– Helping Congressional staff who may need guidance on
the full implications of legislative proposals so that they can
provide appropriate advice for their busy Congressmen.
Lobbyists are usually experts in their field, making their advice
particularly valuable.

– Helping members of Congress to promote causes that have
not captured the public imagination, such as the campaign for
a National Museum of African American History and Culture
outlined above.

In any meeting between Congressional staff and a professional
lobbyist, each side will ask the other what help they can offer. A
healthy relationship can be of mutual benefit and help the process
of government. An unhealthy relationship can lead to corruption.
The challenge for political leaders, which they have yet to fully
meet, is to find a way to inhibit unhealthy political relationships
without damaging constructive relationships.

## The Senate

Pressure groups that seek to influence the House of Representatives
also seek to influence the Senate, for much the same reasons and
using similar methods. However, the Senate has some procedures
and powers that are not shared by the House, which makes it particularly attractive to some pressure groups:

• *Groups opposed to the dominant party in Congress* Even when one political party has a majority of seats in both houses of Congress, the
Senate provides opportunities for organisations opposed to that
party to make an impact. Each state, regardless of size, has two
members in the Senate, giving the smaller states disproportionate influence. This bias is reflected in the chamber's procedures,
which make it possible for minorities to hold up its work, such as
the **filibuster**, which enables a small group of Senators, or even
a single Senator, to hold up the work of the entire chamber. When
the Republican Party controlled Congress between 2002 and
2005, Democratic Senators, urged on by liberal pressure groups
such as People for the American Way, blocked the appointment

of ten of the President's Federal court nominees who they considered to be so conservative that they were 'outside the mainstream' of US politics. Similarly, with the Democrats in firm control of the Senate after 2008, proposals to reform America's healthcare system had to be substantially diluted with conservative groups pressuring Senators from conservative-leaning states to resist a substantial overhaul of the system.

- *Groups that take a particular interest in foreign-policy issues* The Senate has the exclusive power to ratify treaties. After the President has negotiated and signed a treaty with another country, or a wide-ranging international agreement, it has to win the support of two-thirds of the Senators before it comes into force. This check on presidential power provides an opportunity for pressure groups opposed to the treaty to persuade Senators to obstruct it, knowing that it only takes thirty-four Senators to block ratification. Thus, when President Clinton signed the Kyoto Treaty on Climate Change in 1999, he never presented it to the Senate for ratification as it was clear that the argument presented by business groups that it would damage the competitiveness of US industries had persuaded many Senators to oppose it. Apart from business groups, the sectors that tend to take a particular interest in the Senate's foreign-policy powers are defence specialists; sympathisers of countries seeking to improve or reinforce their diplomatic relationships with the USA; campaign groups seeking US support for poorer nations; and environmentalists.

- *Groups that take a particular interest in the Federal courts* As Presidential appointments can be so significant, especially those to the Federal judiciary, where judges may interpret the Constitution 'during good behaviour' for a quarter of a century or more, pressure groups take a particular interest in the confirmation process. In 1986, a coalition of liberal pressure groups spent over $15 million on a campaign, ultimately successful, to oppose the nomination of Robert Bork to the Supreme Court. On the other side of the political spectrum, in 2005 the nomination of Harriet Miers to the Supreme Court was withdrawn by President Bush in response to attacks from right-leaning activists challenging the depth of her conservative credentials.

## The presidency

There are two distinct parts to the executive branch of government, providing distinctively different opportunities for pressure groups to make an impact.

The President plays a leading role in setting the policy agenda for the country when, each January, he makes his State of the Union speech that outlines his priorities for the rest of the year and follows this up by unveiling his budget. For much of the year, Congress devotes the majority of its time to dealing with bills proposed by the President.

Any pressure group that can gain privileged access to the White House has a chance of having its priorities adopted by the President, which may lead to their inclusion in the State of the Union Address and being turned into law by Congress. Gaining this level of access may require:

- *Funding* Presidential elections are expensive: in 2004, George W. Bush's re-election campaign raised over $367 million. Groups that made substantial contributions to this, coupled with successful campaigns to get their supporters to vote were subsequently well placed to gain access to the White House. This included the National Federation of Independent Business, the National Rifle Association, the American Medical Association and the US Chamber of Commerce.

- *Support for the President's agenda* The President and his senior advisors need a great deal of help if they are to implement their political goals. Many of their objectives depend on Congressional legislation for funding and authorisation. Sympathetic pressure groups can play an important role in persuading Congress to implement the President's agenda. Equally important, pressure groups can provide the White House with feedback on policies. With high levels of security, it is very difficult for the President, or high-profile members of his administration, to mingle with ordinary citizens, getting a feel for their views. Pressure groups can play a valuable role for the President in providing this kind of input.

For groups that are unable to gain this type of access, either because they lack the profile and resources to be considered by the President's team or because they are political opponents, there may still be access to the part of the executive branch that is responsible for implementing laws. The government departments staffed by civil servants are known as the **Federal bureaucracy** and this has long been identified by pressure groups as an access point in the executive branch.

Not all of the 3 million people employed in the Federal bureaucracy will be in sympathy with the priorities of the President and, frequently, different government departments are at odds with each other. The Defense Department, which looks towards military solutions to international disputes, has had rifts with the State Department, responsible for US diplomacy under virtually every President. Similarly, the Commerce Department favours minimal restrictions on business while the Interior Department is responsible for protecting America's forests, wildlife and waterways, which often means placing restrictions on businesses.

Similarly, Congressional committees may be committed to programmes that they have funded for years but are at odds with presidential policy.

Where pressure groups can forge strong ties with departments, or senior civil servants, and with Congressional committees that fund government programmes, in combination they may create a wall of resistance to change that the White House may not be able to breach. When the three groups operate in this way, it is known as an **iron triangle**.

### The judiciary
In practice, the Constitution of the USA means whatever the Supreme Court says it means. Consequently, if a pressure group successfully influences the Court to adopt its views, it can effectively shape the framework within which all public policy operates. Such an outcome is desirable for all pressure groups, but is particularly important to minority groups who do not have sufficient representation in the elected branches of government to effect far-reaching change. There are a variety of strategies a pressure group can adopt to achieve this goal:

- *Influencing appointments to the Federal judiciary* Interest groups will adopt a range of strategies in support of nominees who share their

political outlook, or opposition to nominees who may rule against
their interests, including:

– Compiling detailed dossiers on the judgements (and private
  life) of the nominee.
– Ensuring that their members know the group's views on the
  nominee and encouraging them to write to their representatives in Congress.
– Mounting demonstrations during the confirmation hearings.
– Funding newspaper and TV advertisements explaining why
  the nominee should/should not be confirmed.
– For opponents, briefing their allies in the Senate on the most
  damaging questions to ask the nominee.
– For supporters, coaching the nominee on how to answer difficult questions.

In the case of high-profile appointments, especially to the Supreme
Court, analysis of how much impact the rival campaigns are
having will dominate news programmes between the announcement of the nomination and the completion of the confirmation
process, often several months.

- *Bringing test cases to court* Some pressure groups specialise in providing the highest standard of legal assistance in court cases
  that have the potential to alter the existing interpretation of the
  Constitution. One example is the NAACP Legal Defense Fund,
  which, in 1954, won the case of *Brown* v. *Board of Education,
  Topeka, Kansas.* This case, which outlawed racial segregation,
  may have had a greater impact on US society than any other
  pressure-group initiative in the twentieth century. The organisation has continued to fund Civil Rights cases, including those that
  uphold the constitutional right to implement Affirmative Action
  programmes. Meanwhile, fighting to have Affirmative Action
  declared unconstitutional is the Center for Individual Rights, a
  pressure group dedicated exclusively to 'aggressively litigate and
  publicize a handful of carefully selected cases that advance the
  right of individuals to govern themselves according to the natural
  exercise of their own reason'. The Center provided the funding
  and legal expertise to bring the case of *Grutter* v. *Bollinger* to the
  Supreme Court in 2003, arguing that the Affirmative Action
  programme of the University of Michigan Law School was

unconstitutional. The Court ruled against the Center but the fight will continue.

- *Submitting amicus briefs* Pressure groups may also make contributions to cases in which they do not play a direct role but which impact on issues that concern them. These contributions are called **amicus curiae** briefs, meaning 'friends of the court', and are a formal mechanism for courts to understand the views of people and groups beyond those directly involved in the case. Where a decision may have the effect of reinterpreting the Constitution, wider input is considered appropriate. In the *Grutter* v. *Bollinger* case, more than 350 amicus briefs were submitted and the verdict mentioned their influence on the Court's decision. Other notable recent cases attracting large numbers of amicus briefs include *Laurence* v. *Texas* (2003), which struck down laws that discriminate against gay men and lesbians, and *Hamdi* v. *Rumsfeld* (2004), which ruled that detainees at the Guantanamo Bay detention centre (arrested during the US invasion of Afghanistan) were entitled to legal representation.
- *Influencing the climate of legal opinion* The legal experts working for groups that bring test cases and submit amicus briefs often submit articles to scholarly legal journal arguing in favour of the causes they support. These journals, read by judges as well as other lawyers, play a role in shaping the climate of legal opinion and can be helpful to the legal campaigns mounted by their pressure groups.

## Assessing the impact of pressure groups

### A continuing debate
As with other parts of the US political system, pressure groups are subject to debate on whether they play a positive, constructive role in US politics and society or whether they tend to be divisive and promote the interests of some sections of society at the expense of others.

### The pluralist perspective
One view of politics is that power ought to be dispersed so that no group can dominate political processes and impose their views, or

policy preferences, on others and that pressure groups play a valuable role in ensuring that this continues to be the case. According to this view, as long as there are many groups competing to persuade policy-makers of the merits of their case, no single group or interest will be able to establish political dominance. Consequently, pressure groups are seen as making a meaningful contribution to the Founding Fathers' aspiration that power in America would never be concentrated in relatively few hands.

Some supporters of the pluralist perspective tend to see pressure groups operating in a freewheeling market of ideas and interests. Each works tirelessly to promote its views and win the best possible deal for the group it represents. As in all markets, there will be winners and losers. However, crucially, they argue that no group wins all the time and that even though some are better positioned to take advantage of the access points available in the US political system than others, over time there will be different winners and losers. This may be because of changing circumstances, or evolving social values, or simply the power of ideas, leading to the rise of new interests and the decline of others. Comparisons have frequently been made with commercial competition, such as the computer industry, in which IBM, the overwhelmingly dominant company in the 1970s, was displaced by its more nimble, ambitious, aggressive rival, Microsoft, which, in turn, has found its dominance being challenged by the creative minds of Google in the twenty-first century. This may explain why some of the most significant changes in recent times have been to the benefit of the kind of minority groups that were largely excluded from the corridors of power. For example, *Brown* v. *Board of Education* transformed the South by declaring racial segregation unconstitutional, *Roe* v. *Wade* meant that vulnerable women no longer had to resort to back-street abortions, *Lawrence* v. *Texas* meant that laws that discriminated against gays were declared unconstitutional and, in 2004, gay marriage was permitted in Massachusetts. This parallel between the role of pressure groups and the free market tends to be made by conservatives who then reach the conclusion that competition will be distorted by government interference. Conservatives, therefore, have tended to resist the regulation of pressure groups, whether it be lobbying regulations (see the section on professional lobbyists, under the heading 'House of Representatives', above) or campaign finance reform (see Chapter 4). Regulation, they argue, inevitably infringes on two of the most treasured constitutional freedoms, freedom of speech and freedom of association, because rules require government to determine the way in which pressure groups and/or their representatives interact with policy-makers. Moreover, they claim that regulations have almost always been ineffective because groups looking to advance their interests will always find ways to blunt their impact.

Those who are sceptical of the conservative perspective on pressure groups argue that, despite the claims that all groups have an opportunity to advance their interests, the wealthy and well-connected are by far the greatest beneficiaries of America's access points and have a powerful incentive to resist regulation. Thus, although conservatives may pretend to be defending a system from which everyone benefits they are, in reality, cynically protecting their own best interests.

A variation on this theme, that also suggests that it is neither necessary nor desirable to subject pressure groups to regulations, has been advanced by the political scientist Robert Salisbury. He argues that there has been an explosion in the number of pressure groups since the 1950s and that each of them faces another with competing interests. For example, in the area of farming (often seen as having one shared interest that is ruthlessly pursued in the corridors of power) there are, in fact, many conflicting interests, such as grain farmers wanting higher prices who are challenged by producers of meat who feed grain to their animals and want lower grain prices. Even the long-standing agricultural pressure group the American Farm Bureau Federation, which has had close ties to the Republican Party for decades, has been challenged by the National Farmers Union, which adopts a far more liberal position. The conclusion Robert Salisbury reaches is that all these competing interests effectively battle each other to a standstill, resulting in them having far less real influence than their prominence suggests.

Centrist supporters of the pluralist perspective, who believe that pressure groups enhance US democracy, emphasise their role in proposing innovative policies, providing expertise, mobilising citizens who may not otherwise be aware of decisions which affect them and complementing political parties by driving the political agenda when parties have lacked a coherent set of policies and providing support to an ideological agenda when parties have a clear agenda. However, in contrast to conservatives, they are willing to accept that pressure groups do not operate on a level playing field and that there have been times when it has been appropriate to regulate the competition between groups to ensure equality of opportunity. Hence their support for the passage of the Federal Election Campaigns Acts (FECA) in the 1970s, when questionable relationships between the President and his donors were revealed by the Watergate scandal, and the passage of the Bi-partisan Campaign Reform Act in 2002, when it was clear that FECA was proving ineffective (see Chapter 4 for more details). Similarly, when the Federal Regulation of Lobbying Act (1946) proved ineffective, it was replaced with the Lobbying Disclosure Act in 1995.

### The elitist perspective

Famously, the political scientist E. E. Schattsschneider proclaimed that 'the flaw in the pluralist heaven is that the heavenly chorus sings with a strong upper-class accent'. His point was that the wide range of opportunities to influence people in power can only be effectively exploited by pressure groups that have large memberships, effective lobbyists, effective lawyers and considerable wealth. Those most able to achieve all of these goals tend to be those who already dominate society in terms of group numbers or wealth. The less wealthy and minorities, by contrast, tend to lack the organisation, political connections and voting power to make themselves heard in the corridors of power.

Moreover, the US political system has something of an in-built bias in favour of those seeking to resist change, which tends to be to the advantage of those who have benefited from the system. The checks and balances designed to limit political power can be used by the pressure groups that support the status quo to block measures that could change the balance of power. Thus, as shown above, the Senate is an ideal forum for blocking bills even if the opponents of the bill are in a minority.

The perception that the wealthy have greater organisational power and benefit from a political landscape that makes it difficult to challenge their privileged status is a view that is often held by those on the left wing of the political spectrum. From this viewpoint, pressure groups tend to play a damaging role in the political system and society at large. If the groups advancing the interests of the elite, the wealthiest and most influential sections of society, are able to play a dominant role in the policy-making process, they are likely to use their position to strengthen their advantages at the expense of the rest of the population.

Just as supporters of pluralist theory use metaphors (the market) to illustrate their arguments, the supporters of elite theory draw on sports to illustrate how they see pressure groups operating. In any given game, a sporting minnow may cause an upset by defeating a well-resourced sporting giant such as the New York Yankees (baseball) or Manchester United (soccer). Over a season, however, the resources of the giant almost guarantee greater success and over many seasons that success will generate ever more revenues that will increase the gulf with sporting minnows. Thus, the periodic success of political underdogs, such as *Brown* v. *Board*, *Roe* v. *Wade* and *Lawrence* v. *Texas*, are seen by advocates of elite theory as welcome, but exceptional, examples of the underdog winning and neither typical nor representative of the relationship between society's dominant and marginal groups. It is seen as significant that these victories are both few in number and spread across half a century.

Moreover, each of these successes came about through influencing the judicial branch of government. This suggests that the majority of access points (in most cases controlled by elected representatives) are not, in practice, available to groups that lack numbers and/or financial resources. There have been many academic studies to support this point of view, such as Philip Stern's *The Best Congress Money Can Buy*, which demonstrated that members of Congress who relied heavily on specific industries for campaign funds voted consistently in the interests of those industries when legislation was passing through their chamber.

The left points to the 'K Street Project' as revealing the extent to which the wealthy and well-connected shape the policy agenda. The modern Republican Party has close links with a network of conservative groups, including think-tanks, TV and radio stations, magazines and newspapers, campaign groups and policy strategists who work together to advance their political agenda. In 1995, after the party had taken control of the House of Representatives, the majority whip launched a project (named after the street where the largest lobbying firms have their headquarters) to pressure Washington lobbying firms to hire Republicans in top positions, in return for access to influential officials.

For advocates of elite theory, policy-makers should not idly stand by while the privileged use the political system to extend their advantages over the rest of society, but should establish a framework for both regulating pressure groups and monitoring their operation to ensure transparency so that all can see if they are using their resources to give their members an unfair advantage. Thus, the left has tended to be very supportive of measures such as campaign reform legislation and lobbying regulations and have urged law-makers to tighten the rules further.

## A unifying or divisive force?

The impact of pressure groups on society as a whole has also been scrutinised. They have been credited with helping to bind a diverse and highly mobile society. In the post-war period, for example, when America's suburbs emerged, millions of Americans formed new communities. They came from varied districts and, with people leaving Italian, Irish and Jewish enclaves for the first time, had greater ethnic diversity than older communities. Groups such as the scouts, Little League baseball and the League of Women Voters were credited for bringing people together in shared community-building activities that provided social bonds. Although the USA is not going through such a dramatic transformation today, it remains a highly mobile society with up to one-fifth of Americans moving to a new location every five years, and the process of forging and building new communities remains of great importance.

Pressure groups have also been a practical forum for applying democratic principles. Community groups require people to run meetings, handle membership dues and keep records. Leaders of local groups also had to be responsive to the views of their members. In the 1950s, it is calculated that the twenty largest national associations had 5 per cent of the adult population taking a leadership role in their local communities. Furthermore, operating in the political arena, pressure groups were associated with establishing close ties with incumbents of either or both political parties, without a significant ideological element in their activities.

However, pressure groups have been accused, in recent years, of playing an increasingly divisive role by:

- Promoting issues that serve as a '**wedge**' between Americans. People are, today, as likely to be members of pressure groups that are the focus of intense disagreement, such as abortion and gun control, as they are to be members of groups that have helped to unite Americans.
- Pressure groups focusing on these divisive issues have increasingly aligned themselves with one or other of the main parties and often actively work to have these issues included in the political platform of the party they are close to. This may well have the effect of widening the ideological gulf between the parties and deepening the divisions and hostility between their supporters.
- Reinforcing these divisions, pressure groups provide support in terms of money and staff for any elected official who supports their agenda, including a 'safety net' of a lucrative job for those who lose an election as a result of this support.
- They also fund academic research that lends greater credibility to their campaigns.
- They may even fund, and run, their own separate 'parallel campaigns' during election cycles, to promote their cause, politicians who support it and to target their political opponents.

A third view of the role of pressure groups in society is that, while they increasingly play a divisive role, they are not the cause of the divisions but reflect the growing polarisation of the country. In his influential book, *Bowling Alone*, Robert Putnam argued that although Americans are as likely to join pressure groups as in the past, they are less likely to be community-building organisations. Instead, as lifestyles have changed, with people indulging their preferences in solitary ways (listening to their specific choice of music on iPods or watching their favourite programmes on multi-channel TV while other members of the family are watching another programme in another room) the kind of pressure groups they join have changed in similar ways. Now, they tend to become members of groups made up of people who share their specific interests. If pressure groups play a divisive role in society, according to this view, responsibility rests primarily with their members who actively seek out people like themselves and avoid those with whom they may have little in common or with whom they may disagree.

## Conclusion

The Founding Fathers feared the prospect of society splitting into rival, hostile groups and hoped that the political system they had created would avoid this outcome. However, they also recognised that the fragmented policy-making structure that was designed to limit concentrations of power in order to prevent an over-mighty government was well-suited to pressure group activity and even in their lifetimes active competition between groups emerged.

Whether the contribution made to US society and politics has proved beneficial or detrimental depends on the point of view of the observer. For those who praise their contribution, there is little or no case for regulating the operation of pressure groups, while those who criticise their role actively campaign for tighter rules and full disclosure of pressure group activity.

This debate, on the merits of pressure groups and the extent to which government needs to monitor and regulate them, has been one of the major fault lines in US politics and continues to be so.

. . . . . . . . . . . . . . . . . . . . . . . . . . . . . . . . . . . . . . . .

### What you should have learnt from reading this chapter

- The political system in the USA, with multiple opportunities for pressure groups to influence the decision-making process and guarantees of free speech, provides a favourable climate for pressure groups.

- This includes opportunities to influence policy at local and state level, through elections and in a variety of ways at Federal level, depending on the particular aims and resources of the pressure groups.

- However, since the days of the Founding Fathers, there have been concerns that pressure groups that take advantage of these opportunities can concentrate power and resources in the hands of some sections of society at the expense of others, leading to social division.

- Whether these concerns are justified depends, in large measure, on political viewpoints. Some Americans believe that pressure groups play a largely positive role, providing all sections of society with opportunities to voice their opinions and campaign in support of their members or cause, while also helping to promote political participation and bind a diverse population. Other Americans see pressure groups as a means for the already wealthy and powerful to reinforce their position at the expense of the rest of the population who may be more needy or deserving and, as a result, the source of social tension.

- The debate between those who believe that pressure groups need to be subject to strict regulation and those who fear that restricting pressure groups will have little impact other than to limit the freedoms enshrined in the Constitution has been, and continues to be, one of the greatest sources of division in US politics.

## Glossary of key terms

**Access points** Political institutions, or processes, that decide public policy and how resources should be allocated.
**Amicus curiae** Documents or testimony from individuals or groups who are not directly involved in a case but have an interest in the outcome.
**Federal bureaucracy** The government departments, staffed by civil servants, responsible for implementing Federal laws.
**Filibuster** A device available to Senators enabling them to block a vote on a measure by prolonging a debate.
**Iron triangle** A strong bond between a pressure group, government department and Congressional committee, all with shared political goals.
**Lobbyists** People with extensive political contacts who work full-time on persuading decision-makers to support the interests of the groups for which they work.
**Revolving door syndrome** A tendency for people leaving elected office, or employment with a politician, to then work for a pressure group, using their knowledge and contacts to influence their former colleagues.
**Wedge** A political or social issue that serves to reinforce or emphasise divisions between Americans.

## Likely examination questions

Issues examiners may expect students to be able to effectively analyse include:

- Why, how and with what effectiveness pressure groups access specific points in the political system

- Understanding of methods used by pressure groups, such as professional lobbying

- The impact of pressure groups on the democratic system

- The effectiveness of legislation to limit the influence of pressure groups

Thus, examples of the kind of questions which could be asked include:

How important are professional lobbyists?

To what extent are pressure groups a divisive force in the USA?

## Helpful websites

To learn more about large pressure groups, which aim to influence all access points in the US political system, go to any of the seven websites below. The first three have a liberal agenda, the second three have a conservative agenda and the last is independent.

- The National Association for the Advancement of Colored People is an African American Civil Rights group. Its web address is www.naacp. org.

- The National Organisation of Women campaigns to bring about equality for all women. Its web address is www.now.org.

- The AFL-CIO is the umbrella organisation for trade unions in the USA. Its web address is www.aflcio.org.

- The National Rifle Association campaigns against gun control. Its web address is www.nra.org.

- The Christian Coalition provides a vehicle for people of faith to be actively involved in shaping government policy. Its web address is www.cc.org.

- The National Federation of Independent Businesses represents the interests of small companies. Its web address is www.nfib.com.

- The AARP represents the interests of people over fifty years of age. Its web address is www.aarp.org.

To learn more about pressure groups that have a particular interest in influencing the Senate on foreign policy, go to any of the websites below.

- The American Israel Public Affairs Committee works to strengthen US–Israeli relations. Its web address is www.aipac.org.

- The Sierra Club is an environmental organisation that campaigns for the US government to participate in international initiatives to confront global warming. Its web address is www.sierraclub.org.

To learn more about pressure groups that specialise in influencing policy through the courts, go to either of the websites below.

- The NAACP Legal Defense Fund brings lawsuits against violators of Civil Rights. Its web address is www.naacpldf.org.

- The Center for Individual Rights brings lawsuits which, if successful, reduce the scope of government activity. Its web address is www.cir-usa.org.

## Suggestions for further reading

For a more detailed account of how specific pressure groups have made a significant impact in recent years, read *Faith in the Halls of Power* by Michael Lindsay, which examines the influence of the Christian Right, or *The Politics of Gun Control* by Robert Spitzer.

# PART III

# TESTING THE LIMITS OF FEDERAL POWER – THE JUDICIARY, THE LEGISLATURE AND THE EXECUTIVE

# CHAPTER 7

# The Judiciary

## Contents

## Overview

***'The Constitution is what we say it is'***

On 12 June 2008, in the case of *Boumediene* v. *Bush*, the Supreme Court declared unconstitutional the Military Commissions Act that had been passed two years earlier. The Act, which had been passed in response to an earlier Supreme Court ruling, had allowed the President to set up military tribunals to try suspects who had been arrested or captured in the 'War on Terror' that followed the attacks on US targets on 11 September 2001 and had barred the courts from interfering. The Court's decision, which was supported by five of the judges and opposed by the other four, ruled that the Act failed to guarantee that the suspects would have a fair trial. It also ruled that Congress had no right to exclude the courts from a judicial matter.

Many Americans, especially conservatives, were outraged at the ruling. They objected to a group of unelected judges over-ruling elected politicians on a military matter in which judges have little expertise. Other Americans, especially liberals, applauded this ruling as an example of the core Constitutional principles of liberty being protected even at a time of national insecurity about the threat of terrorism.

This chapter examines the role of the judiciary in interpreting the Constitution and the conflicting views on how judges should use their powers.

## Key issues to be covered in this chapter

- The role of the judiciary
- The Constitution and the judiciary
- Judicial review
- The political character of judicial review
- Judicial philosophies
- Judicial appointments
- The Roberts Court

## The role of the judiciary

In the political theory of separation of powers, the judiciary has a specific role. It is the responsibility of judges to adjudicate. They resolve disputes that cannot be settled without legal action. To do so, they reach conclusions according to a set of rules, such as referring to previous judgements on similar issues to ensure consistency.

The same theory holds that there are certain roles that are reserved for the other two branches of government, the executive and the legislature. It is their responsibility to make policy. It is up to the people to make political choices, expressed through their elected representatives, and if the people are dissatisfied with the laws that their representatives have passed or object to ways in which policies are being implemented, they can convey their displeasure at the next election (or, in some states, even earlier through recall elections – see Chapter 4 for more details).

To use a common sporting metaphor for the separation of powers, politicians are responsible for creating and amending the rules of the game while judges are referees/umpires who see that the game is played fairly according to those rules. Clearly, referees should not participate in the game and should be scrupulously neutral when making decisions.

However, there is another way of looking at the role of the judiciary. Legal processes should lead to justice. If the rules are unfair, and judges do nothing more than apply them in a consistent fashion, the courts will not be an arena for people to seek justice. Thus, there is a long-standing tradition, dating back to before the War of Independence, of laws and government actions being challenged in court and judges declaring that key rights have been infringed. This is called **common law**, also sometimes known as judge-made law. In this sense, especially in respect of protecting the individual's civil liberties from government and asserting Civil Rights, the judiciary has long had a policy-making role and has never been strictly confined to adjudicating.

## The Constitution and the judiciary

Article III of the Constitution, outlining the role and powers of the judiciary, provides few indications of whether the Founding Fathers expected judges to be strictly limited to adjudication or to play a role in limiting the ability of the other branches to threaten rights.

The Article only addresses the arrangements for establishing a national judiciary, arrangements for keeping it independent (free from political interference or pressure from the other branches of government) and certain limitations on their powers. Article III is summarised in table 7.1 overleaf.

Since the eighteenth century, when the Supreme Court was established by the Constitution, its workload has expanded enormously. As a result, Congress has established lower Federal courts, which hear cases involving Federal laws. The Supreme Court is the highest court of appeal for these cases.

Each of the fifty states has its own court system to hear cases arising from state laws. Cases that have reached the highest court of appeal in this system, the State Supreme Court, may then be appealed to the Federal Supreme Court in Washington DC.

Thus, the Constitution shaped the US judicial system without clearly indicating the nature of the role of judges when political disputes arose. Most significantly, the Constitution did not specify whether the Supreme Court should be responsible for interpreting the Constitution. These matters were resolved later and the consequences have dominated US politics to this day.

## Judicial review

Interpreting how the Constitution should be applied to specific circumstances or issues confers immense power on whichever group of people carries out that task. Since all laws and government actions, at both Federal and state level, have to conform to the Constitution, whoever defines exactly what each provision of the Constitution means and how it should operate in practice effectively imposes limits or requirements in every policy-maker in the USA. Did the Founding Fathers not realise this?

## Table 7.1 Article III of the Constitution

| | |
|---|---|
| **Establishing the Federal judiciary** | • There would be a separate, independent judicial branch of the national government<br>• The national judiciary would be 'Supreme'<br>• This 'Supreme Court' should be responsible for hearing certain types of cases. These **original jurisdiction** cases were defined as those involving the states or foreign diplomats<br>• Because it would be the highest court in the land, it would also be the final **court of appeal**<br>• Additionally, Article I of the Constitution gave Congress the power to establish other, lower, Federal courts |
| **Protecting judicial independence** | • To insulate Federal judges from political pressure they would not be elected (as was the case in some states) but appointed<br>• To ensure that the judges had a significant level of independence from the people who appointed them, the appointment process was split. The President would be responsible for nominating Supreme Court judges but the support of a majority of the Senate was required<br>• To ensure that judges' decisions were based entirely on the merits of the case they were hearing, without concern about political pressure, they were provided with the following protections:<br>  – They could not be removed from office for political reasons. Once appointed, they would serve for life or until they retired<br>  – Their income could not be reduced, which would be another way of putting them under pressure<br>  – The only reason they could be removed would be if their personal conduct were inappropriate for a judge |
| **Restrictions on the judiciary** | • Jury trials were to be guaranteed<br>• The crime of treason, and punishment if convicted, was strictly defined |

There are some indications that they did not fully appreciate the full significance of Constitutional interpretation:

- A codified Constitution was novel and somewhat experimental in the eighteenth century. Previously, all Constitutional rules had been seen as political instruments to be developed and refined over time by political processes. It may have been that the Founding Fathers expected the meaning and application of the Constitution to take shape through constitutional amendments.
- There was limited debate on the extent of the powers of the Supreme Court during the Constitutional Convention and the ratification debate that followed it, which suggested that they did not expect it to have substantial power. This impression was reinforced by Alexander Hamilton, who made one of the few notable pronouncements on the courts in this period. He declared that 'the judiciary is beyond comparison the weakest of the three departments of power'.
- When Washington DC was built, there was not even a building constructed for the Supreme Court – it met in a basement committee room in Congress.
- In its earliest days there were few enthusiastic candidates to take up the seats on the Supreme Court and the first Chief Justice gave up his position to become Governor of New York.

Based on these inauspicious beginnings, some Americans have drawn the conclusion that the Founding Fathers never intended the Supreme Court to have the power of **judicial review** and certainly did not expect it to grow to the powerful institution that it has become. However, there are also indications that although the Constitutional Convention did not give the Federal judiciary the role of interpreting the Constitution, they were aware that it would inevitably take on that responsibility:

- A codified Constitution is the highest law in any territory it covers. This is true of the USA, but it was also already true, before the Constitutional Convention, of the thirteen individual states that made up the country. Each of these already had their own codified Constitutions and the issue of how they should be interpreted has already arisen in at least four states.

- *Commonwealth* v. *Caton*, in Virginia in 1782
- *Rutgers* v. *Waddington*, in New York in 1784 (in which Alexander Hamilton was one of the lawyers)
- *Trevett* v. *Weedon*, in Rhode Island in 1786
- *Bayard* v. *Singleton*, in North Carolina in 1787

In the Virginia case, the ruling declared 'the court has power to declare any resolution or act of the legislature, or of either branch of it to be unconstitutional and void'.

- Moreover, although debate about the role and powers of the Supreme Court was limited during the Constitutional Convention and the ratification debate, the issues of judicial review (and its implications) did arise. An anti-Federalist pamphlet warned, 'I question whether the world ever saw . . . a court of justice invested with such immense powers.' Its judges would 'feel themselves independent of Heaven itself'. In response, Alexander Hamilton acknowledged that constitutional protections of liberty 'can be preserved in practice in no other way than through the medium of the courts of justice; whose duty it must be to declare all acts contrary to the manifest tenor or the constitution void. Without this, all the reservations of particular rights or privileges would amount to nothing.'

Based on this evidence, other Americans have drawn the conclusion that the Founding Fathers recognised, and accepted, that the nation's highest judges would take responsibility for interpreting the nation's highest law.

It did not take very long for the judiciary to assert its right of Constitutional interpretation. One of the Court's first decisions had a powerful impact. In *Chisolm* v. *Georgia* (1793), the Court ruled that a citizen had the right to sue a state. The prospect of states being paralysed by the threat of lawsuits against everything they did led to the 11th Amendment, changing Article II, Section 2 of the Constitution on which the decision was based. The fact that it took a constitutional amendment to overturn a decision of the Supreme Court was an early indication of the Court's power.

Then, in 1803, in the case of *Marbury* v. *Madison*, the Supreme Court formally laid claim to the power of judicial review, which means declaring whether or not acts of the legislative and executive branches of government are constitutional. Since then, it has been accepted that this is a legitimate judicial power. The case arose from a 1789 Act of Congress setting up lower Federal courts. In 1801, just before his term of office ended, President Adams appointed forty-two new Justices who shared his political views and they were all confirmed by the Senate. Four of them had not received their letters of appointment and the new President ordered his Secretary of State, Madison, not to deliver them. One of the four, Marbury, applied to the Court to enforce his appointment. The Supreme Court's decision, to declare Section 13 of the Act to be unconstitutional, established that they had the right to decide the precise meaning of the Constitution in relation to specific cases.

In 1819, the Supreme Court made it clear that its power of judicial review applied to the states as well as Federal government. In the case of *McCulloch* v. *Maryland*, it was ruled that the State of Maryland did not have the constitutional right to impose a tax on a bank that had been established by Congress.

## Box 7.1 The judicial process

It is not easy to get a hearing before the Supreme Court. Either a lower court may refer a case to the Supreme Court or it can be petitioned to hear a case involving a serious constitutional issue. It is up to the Supreme Court, however, to decide if they will accept the case.

During the course of the Supreme Court year (also known as a 'term') the Justices hear up to 100 cases, although in recent years this number has declined to around 70 as the current Chief Justice and his predecessor have both sought to prioritise careful deliberation over volume. In the first week of October, the Justices choose between thirty and forty cases which will occupy most of their time for the first half of the year and will leave room to accept others before their year ends around the 4 July Independence Day holiday. All cases are summarised by the law clerks of the Justices, and then considered. It takes four of the Justices to agree for a case to be accepted.

Once the court has accepted a case, the lawyers for each side present a brief, which is a written statement with their legal arguments, any relevant facts and supporting precedents. Other briefs, called **amicus curiae** or 'friends of the court', may also be submitted by other groups with an interest in the case, usually pressure groups or government departments. In a 2003 case deciding whether to allow Affirmative Action to continue, *Grutter* v. *Bollinger*, over 350 amicus briefs were submitted. The Court freely admitted that they were heavily influenced by those from highly respected groups such as major corporations and the armed forces in reaching their decision to uphold Affirmative Action. A date will be set for oral argument, when each side will have thirty minutes to summarise their key points. The judges may interrupt at any time, to ask questions or to challenge a point and, when time is up, the lawyer must stop speaking immediately, even if in mid-sentence.

Having read the papers and heard the arguments, the Justices meet to discuss the case and vote. All votes have equal weight, including that of the Chief Justice. It does not require a unanimous vote to reach a decision. An opinion then has to be written that will explain the decision to the general public and provide a guide to lower courts considering similar cases. If the Justices are split, a **majority decision** will be written, with the minority explaining their points of disagreement in a **dissenting opinion**. Judges on both sides can add points to the two main opinions by writing **concurring opinions**. In *Grutter* v. *Bollinger*, the majority decision was supported by two concurring opinions and the dissenting opinion was supported by three concurring opinions, making seven opinions issued by nine judges.

As with the selection of cases, law clerks play an important role. Often they write the first draft of the opinion to be presented by the Justice for whom they work. Sometimes these drafts are not amended. This is a huge responsibility for people who, although drawn from the most highly regarded law schools in the country, may not have had any previous legal experience. Unsurprisingly, with this start, many clerks go on to have very successful legal careers and, in some cases, have risen to become Supreme Court Justices themselves.

## The political character of judicial review

The power of judicial review has put the Supreme Court at the heart of the USA's most controversial issues. Indeed, as an observer of American society in its earliest days, Alexis de Tocqueville, put it, 'scarcely any political question arises in the United States that is not resolved, sooner or later, into a judicial question'.

It was a Supreme Court judgement, *Dred Scott* v. *Sandford* (1857), ruling that African Americans had no rights under the Constitution, that has been widely seen as triggering the Civil War. In the early twentieth century, the battle between employers and working-class Americans on the extent to which the Constitution entitles workers to minimum conditions and wages was often fought in the courts. In the closing decades of the twentieth century and the start of the twenty-first century, however, the courts have been at the heart of a wide range of issues that divide Americans, thereby heightening their significance in the political processes of the country.

However, while the courts may be drawn into the political arena, a range of factors limit the extent to which they may be seen as purely political in character.

## The political dimension of the judiciary

The forces that may result in Federal courts acting in ways that may be described as 'political' include:

- The Supreme Court's decision to hear certain cases, while turning others away, may itself be 'political', as these decisions reflect the issues considered most important by the Judges. Thus, the decision in the early 1970s to rule on whether a woman has a Constitutional right to an abortion served to make this issue a more significant political matter.
- The Supreme Court's decisions may be described as 'political' if they serve to establish a new policy that affects everyone in the country, such as the case of *Boumediene* v. *Bush* (outlined in the introduction).
- The Supreme Court may also be seen as 'political' if the judges carefully tailor their decisions to the anticipated response from the public: for example, when the Court ruled racial segregation to be unconstitutional, the nine justices agreed that despite substantial disagreements between them they would have to deliver a unanimous decision because any dissent would certainly have been seized upon by segregationists as a rallying point to resist the decision.
- Even when a judgement is not policy-making, the opinions of the judges can have a political impact. This point is illustrated by

the case of *Northwest Austin Municipal Utility District* v. *Holder* (2009). The Voting Rights Act of 1965 was challenged on the grounds that areas of the country with a history of blocking racial minorities from voting should no longer be subject to close monitoring by the Justice Department because so much has changed since the 1960s. The Court upheld the Act but the Chief Justice's explanation of the decision suggested that it would not survive future challenges unless it were reformed. This, in effect, told Congress to alter the law (just three years after Congress had reviewed it) and invited further challenges if Congress took no action.

- Across America there are individuals and groups who seek to use the judiciary to advance their cause or aims. Sometimes by deliberately generating a lawsuit and sometimes by participating in someone else's case by submitting amicus briefs, Americans actively use the courts for their political purposes, which is a reality that all Federal judges have to deal with.

## Factors limiting political pressure on the courts
There are also a range of factors that limit the ability of judges to act in ways that may be characterised as 'political', including:

- *Legal process* Judges can only decide matters that are brought to them in the form of legal cases. While politicians can decide that there is a policy that they disagree with and try to change it, judges cannot. They can only use their power of judicial review when ruling on a case that has been submitted to them. (In practice, almost every issue on which they may have an opinion is likely to be the subject of a lawsuit.) Also, judges will not offer advisory opinions, in which they explain what they are likely to do if a case is brought before them.

- *Court traditions* Judges only consider cases where their decision will make a real difference. So, when the State of Idaho asked the Court to decide if it could withdraw its support for a constitutional amendment, the Court refused to hear the case, as the deadline for the amendment had already passed and their decision, while interesting, would have had no effect. They will also only consider cases in which a considerable number of people are affected and in which it is claimed that considerable harm has been caused.

With the exception of appeals against a death sentence, the Court will not consider cases in which only an individual or a small group are affected, or cases in which people who have not been harmed to any significant degree are claiming unfair treatment.

- Judges make the distinction between their personal views and what the law requires. As they are not elected, they have a particular obligation to use their power responsibly, which may require them to reach a decision which, personally, they would prefer not to reach.

- *Lack of Enforcement Power* It is the judicial branch of government that decides what the laws mean, but the executive branch, meaning the President at the Federal level and governors at state level, that is responsible for ensuring that the law is upheld. Early in the Court's history, when it made a decision that President Jackson disliked, it was reported that the President said, 'John Marshall has made his decision, now let him enforce it.' Since then, there have been many examples of the Court's decisions being ignored or actively resisted, such as the refusal by Southern states to end racial segregation in the 1950s and 1960s, after a Supreme Court ruling to do so.

- *Checks and balances* On two occasions, Supreme Court judgements have been overturned by a constitutional amendment. This was first done in 1793, when the case of *Chisolm* v. *Georgia* was overturned by the 11th Amendment, and again in 1913 when the 16th Amendment was passed. Also, Congress has the power to remove judges who are abusing their power, through a process known as impeachment (explained in Chapter 9). In 1805, there was an attempt to impeach Justice Samuel Chase because his views clashed with the President and his party. The impeachment failed, reinforcing the independence of the Court, and all twelve impeachments that have taken place since have been the result of personal misconduct on the part of the judge. Less dramatically, Congress can modify laws that have been declared unconstitutional so that, despite a Supreme Court ruling, a law continues to apply in an altered form. Finally, Congress has the power to change the number of judges on the Supreme Court. Since 1869, there have been nine Justices on the Supreme Court. However, in 1937 President Roosevelt, frustrated that he was unable to implement his New Deal to tackle the economic recession because the Court kept declaring his laws unconstitutional, proposed to Congress a 'Court-packing' plan. He offered to 'help' all judges over the age of seventy with their workload by appointing another judge to assist them. This would have added six new judges to the Court. The proposal was rejected by Congress but, thereafter, the Court did not reject any of the President's New Deal projects. Clearly the threat to change the number of judges made an impact and, as a judge on the Court put it, 'the President's enemies defeated the court reform bill – the President achieved court reform'.

Thus, there are two aspects to the Court's work: political and legal. Whether by choice or circumstance, judges have to make decisions that are often political in character, but they do so according to legal procedures and traditions. How they balance these two aspects is a matter of great public interest and depends, in large measure, on their judicial philosophies.

## Judicial philosophies

Judges have different views of the role of a judiciary in a democracy and also differ on the intentions of the Founding Fathers in respect of the extent of judicial power. These differences have developed into five distinct schools of thought that are outlined in this section.

The first two emphasise the importance of limiting judges to an adjudicative role and leaving policy decisions to elected politicians in a political system based on checks and balances. They also tend to be based on the belief that the Founding Fathers did not intend the judicial branch to be as powerful as it has become.

The other three all, to a greater or lesser extent, emphasise the importance of the judicial process leading to justice – especially for those who have not been adequately protected by the political system or struggle to get their voices heard through the democratic process. They also tend to be based on the belief that the Constitution, and the Bill of Rights in particular, was designed to protect against the tyranny of the majority and that the courts have a key role to play in guaranteeing that these protections are made meaningful in the day-to-day lives of Americans.

**Majoritarianism (also known as judicial restraint)**
This is the view that, in a democracy, policy decisions should be made by elected representatives of the people. Unless it is very clear that the Constitution has been violated, courts should not interfere with laws passed by democratically elected legislatures, either at federal or state level; nor should judges make decisions about the legitimacy of the actions of executives – the state governors or the President.

This approach to constitutional interpretation was first outlined by Harvard law professor James Bradley Theyer in 1893. He argued that judges should only overrule the elected branches in exceptional circumstances. It is not enough for the judges to have doubts about the merits of or consequences to a decision taken by an elected branch of government: the courts should only step in when there is almost no doubt that the terms of the Constitution have been breached.

Theyer offered two main justifications for this approach. Firstly, he identified the danger of judicial rulings entrenching particular political viewpoints as being 'constitutional', with the consequence that, as society and popular sentiment changes, elected politicians may be unable to implement policies which are appropriate to new circumstances and for which they may have a mandate. This type of situation arose a short time after Theyer outlined his views. In the early 1900s, the Court was dominated by judges who interpreted the 14th Amendment (that protects people against government depriving them of their liberties) to mean that the government could not regulate industry or commerce as to do so would infringe 'liberty of contract', in which employers and employees were free to reach any contractual arrangements they chose. On this basis, they consistently struck down laws designed to ensure minimum standards for employees. The Supreme Court continued to apply this interpretation of the Constitution in the 1930s, when the USA was suffering mass unemployment and President F. D. Roosevelt had a massive electoral mandate for unprecedented economic intervention, and repeatedly struck down the laws passed to implement his New Deal. Throughout this period, the most famous exponent of judicial restraint, Supreme Court Justice Oliver Wendel Holmes, argued that 'a constitution is not intended to embody a particular economic theory', and eventually he was proved right when the Court responded to political and public pressure and stopped striking down the New Deal laws. Majoritarians argue that this principle applies to any creative interpretation of the Constitution.

Secondly, Theyer argued that judicial restraint is an essential requirement for a healthy political system. If the judiciary appears to be political in character, rather than judicial, there is a risk that the prestige of the court system will be diminished. It could also damage the other two branches of government. If the courts regularly overturn their decisions they are likely to stop making policy on the basis of right and wrong, or the best interests of their voters, and think primarily in terms of what judges will allow. All three branches of government, therefore, risk a loss of credibility and authority if the courts are interventionist.

In practice, judges subscribing to judicial restraint have adopted the following approaches to constitutional interpretation:

- They tend to demonstrate a preference for '**stare decisis**', leaving things as they are. This means respecting **precedent**, past decisions made by judges.
- Their respect for the choices of elected politicians is summed up by Justice Oliver Wendell Holmes' observation that, as a judge, it was his duty to enforce 'even laws that I believe to embody mistakes'. However, they tend to be especially deferential when it comes to security and foreign policy matters on the grounds that judges are particularly unqualified to second-guess presidential decisions that have been made on the basis of briefings from top military advisors, senior diplomats and the intelligence services. Thus, in the case of *Korematsu v. United States* (1944), the Supreme Court upheld the Second World War internment of Japanese Americans, ruling that the imprisoning all people of Japanese origin despite scant evidence of collaboration or even sympathy for the enemy was justified by military necessity.
- They attempt to rule only the legal aspects of cases, not addressing wider political implications if they can be avoided. For example, in the case of *Ayotte v. Planned Parenthood* (2006), that dealt with the issue of whether a state legislature could pass a law requiring parental notification if a girl was seeking to have an abortion, it was widely expected that the Supreme Court would review

its previous rulings on the constitutional right to abortions for all women. However, the Court decided, unanimously, to 'limit the solution to the problem' and not to 'revisit our abortion precedents'.

- Where policy-making issues cannot be avoided, majoritarians apply the principles of **strict constructionism**. This means considering the precise meaning of the relevant parts of the Constitution, together with any evidence of the thinking of the people who wrote the relevant sections. The famous case of *Plessy* v. *Ferguson* (1896) that permitted Southern states to pass laws that segregated communities by race, relied heavily on evidence that when the 14th Amendment (granting ex-slaves rights under the Constitution) was being debated in Congress it appeared that there was no expectation that the constitutional amendment would lead to the integration of white and black Americans.

## Criticisms of majoritarianism

Judicial restraint has always faced opposition. If the courts overturn policies that are only in the clearest breach of the Constitution, many laws that can reasonably be interpreted as contrary to the spirit of the Constitution would be left untouched. The very fact that the Supreme Court deferred to the racial hostility of the white majority in *Plessy* v. *Ferguson* (1896) is seen as evidence that judicial restraint can accept considerable infringements of core civil liberties, including freedom of movement and expression, as falling short of its criteria of a clear breach of the Constitution's provisions. Similarly, majoritarians would not have supported the policy-making judgements of *Brown* v. *Board of Education* (1954), which declared racial segregation unconstitutional, and *Roe* v. *Wade* (1973), which ruled that women had a constitutional right to decide whether or not to terminate a pregnancy, on the grounds that there was no majority support for either policy and (in the case of *Brown*) judicial precedent weighed heavily against the Court's verdict. Critics of judicial restraint argue that these judgements illustrate the extent to which majoritarianism would permit tyranny of the majority, leaving in place policies that are an expression of prejudice or bigotry. Indeed, although Justice Oliver Wendell Holmes, the foremost majoritarian, is regarded as one of the greatest figures in US judicial history, he is associated with one of the Supreme Court's more disgraceful decisions, *Buck* v. *Bell* (1927), in which a law providing for the compulsory sterilisation of people of low intelligence was upheld.

They also point out that social change, particularly the inclusion of minorities that have been marginalised by the majority community, would be far harder to achieve if the courts left such developments to elected politicians fearful of a backlash from the electorate.

In short, opponents of judicial restraint argue that majoritarianism is a recipe for judges passively accepting practices that are contrary to constitutional values, on the grounds that they are not flagrant abuses of the Constitution – thus rendering the Constitution meaningless much of the time. They also argue that, although presenting itself as a way of ensuring that judges do not get involved in policy-making, judicial restraint has a distinctly political character as it tends to leave the social order undisturbed and therefore has a particular appeal to conservatives.

### Originalism (also known as textualism)

Advocates of originalism see the Constitution as playing a role similar to that of a ship's anchor: it serves to stop society being tossed around by every new wave of opinion or storm of moral outrage that sweeps the country. Clearly, an anchor has to have sufficient flexibility to allow a ship to move around just enough to adjust to changing tides and weather conditions, and advocates of originalism see their judicial theory as having sufficient flexibility to accommodate changes in society. However, they are strongly opposed to other judicial philosophies that seek to continually update the Constitution, in light of changing circumstances. They compare these ideas (explained below) to sailors who repeatedly pull up the ship's anchor, inspecting it and refining it, while leaving the vessel unstable and vulnerable.

The starting point of originalism is the view that, in a democracy, judges should confine themselves to adjudication. The Constitution, and all of its subsequent amendments, came into being after a process of ratification in which the will of the overwhelming majority of the people was expressed. It is not for nine unelected judges, therefore, to effectively overrule the people through judicial review. They should only provide an explanation of its meaning in respect of whatever issues come before them.

In order to ensure that they do not stray outside of this strictly adjudicative role, they argue, there is only one approach that can be adopted when judges interpret the Constitution. They should endeavour to establish what the relevant part of the Constitution was understood to mean at the time it was ratified and then make a judgement based on this understanding. In this way, they are ensuring that they are not making judgements based on their own opinion or preferences (which a politician is entitled to do, but not a judge) but reaching neutral conclusions.

The Supreme Court's decision in the case of *District of Columbia* v. *Heller* (2008), written by one of the originalists on the Court, Justice Antonin Scalia, provides an illustration of how this judicial philosophy works in practice. The case was about the laws governing the private ownership of guns in Washington DC which had, before the case, some of the most restrictive gun-ownership regulations in the USA, making it extremely difficult to get a licence to own a weapon and requiring that it be kept disassembled in the home. It was argued that, under the 2nd Amendment, such restrictions were unconstitutional. In his lengthy explanation of the judgement, Justice Scalia examined the two key phrases in the 2nd Amendment, which states that 'the right of the people to keep and bear arms shall not be infringed' but appears to make this right conditional on meeting the purpose of maintaining 'a well regulated militia'. Using dictionaries and other documentary evidence from the late eighteenth century, when the 2nd Amendment was ratified, he concluded that everyone was expected to rally to the defence of their community when it was threatened, thus the term 'well regulated militia' meant 'everyone'. He further concluded that the right to 'keep and bear arms' meant the right to have an operating weapon available. Therefore, the Washington DC gun laws (and all similarly restrictive laws in other parts of the country) violated the 2nd Amendment as they made it impossible for everyone to own a gun if they so chose and barred them from keeping it in an operative condition.

The implications of this judicial philosophy are far-reaching:

- Because originalists believe that their reading of the Constitution is not open to alternative views, they are far more ready than majoritarians to overturn legislation. As in the case of *District of*

*Columbia* v. *Heller,* any law or governmental action that contravenes an originalist understanding of the Constitution may be overturned.

- The originalist approach to constitutional interpretation does not allow for the recognition of any rights that are not clearly spelled out in the Constitution. Originalists argue that this does not cause the Constitution to freeze in time as constitutional amendments have extended rights to groups who were not recognised in the eighteenth century: the 13th, 14th and 15th Amendments provided rights to African Americans after slavery was abolished and the 19th Amendment gave women the right to vote. It is not for judges, however, to 'discover' rights that are not clearly specified.
- Moreover, as there have been many court rulings, especially in the 1960s, that have departed from an originalist understanding of the Constitution, originalists are far less willing to respect precedent than majoritarians. This includes landmark decisions that have become widely accepted features of US society, such as *Roe* v. *Wade,* which legalised abortion.
- Originalist judges, committed to recovering a 'lost Constitution' that has been (in their view) distorted out of all recognition by wrongly decided cases, tend to have a distinctively aggressive, confrontational and uncompromising style. On the current Supreme Court, one of the originalist Justices, Antonin Scalia, is noted for his caustic criticisms of other judges and decisions he disagrees with and the other, Justice Clarence Thomas, is noted for dissenting even from judgements that he supports if they do not go far enough.

### Criticisms of originalism

Opponents of originalism contest its starting point that, in a democracy, judges should confine themselves to playing a strictly judicial role. As explained in the section on the role of the judiciary (above), there is a view that judges have a long and honourable tradition of acting as a check on the elected branch's use of their powers, through common law rulings on rights and liberties.

Also, the originalist view that the Constitution should be treated almost as a sacred document, not to be tampered with and faithfully followed at all times, is questioned, even derided, by critics. Amongst its opponents, originalism is referred to as judicial fundamentalism because of its similarity to the ways in which religious fundamentalists treat sacred texts. There is ample evidence that the Founding Fathers would not have expected the Constitution to be treated that way. Thomas Jefferson, principal author of the Declaration of Independence and one of the Founding Fathers, made it clear in many of his writings that he expected the Constitution to be updated by subsequent generations, declaring that the 'laws and institutions must go hand in hand with the progress of the human mind. As that becomes more developed, more enlightened, as new discoveries are made, new truths disclosed, and as manners and opinions change, institutions must change also, and keep pace with the times.' Would the Founding Fathers, if they experienced life in the twenty-first century, expect rights to be limited to those who were seen to be deserving of them in the eighteenth century, as the originalist approach to constitutional interpretation implies? Critics are sure that they would not, and claim that originalism is, ironically, not faithful to the thinking of the Founding Fathers, who they treat with such reverence.

Developing this point, critics point out that the Founding Fathers would have been fully aware that many of the key phrases of the Constitution would change in meaning over time. For example, what was considered 'cruel and unusual punishment' (prohibited in the 8th Amendment) was very different in the eighteenth century to earlier times and could be expected to be understood in different ways by subsequent generations. As one of the greatest Supreme Court judges, Felix Frankfurter, put it, 'Great concepts like "commerce among the several states", "due process of law", "liberty", "property" were purposely left to gather meaning from experience . . . and the statesmen who founded this nation knew too well that only a stagnant society remains unchanged.'

A third, related, point is that those Founding Fathers who initially resisted the inclusion of a Bill of Rights in the Constitution did so from a fear that 'if we list a set of rights, some fools in the future are going to claim that people are entitled only to those rights enumerated, and no others'. The 9th Amendment, that 'the enumeration . . . of certain rights shall not be construed to deny or disparage others' appears to address this concern and to run counter to the originalists' insistence that only specified rights should be recognised.

Leaving aside the question of whether originalism lives up to its own claims of being truly faithful to the words and spirit of the Founding Fathers, opponents of this doctrine are hostile to the objectives of originalist judges who not only reject claims to rights that be made in the future but to reverse earlier rulings that they see as having departed from an accurate interpretation of the Constitution. During the 1986 confirmation hearings for Robert Bork, the first originalist judge of modern times nominated to the Supreme Court, Senator Edward Kennedy characterised Bork's judicial philosophy as one that would lead to 'a land in which women would be forced into back alley abortions, blacks would sit at segregated lunch counters, rogue police could break down citizens' doors in midnight raids, school children could not be taught about evolution, writers and artists could be censored at the whim of the government, and the doors of the federal courts would be shut on the fingers of millions of citizens for whom the judiciary is – and often is the only – protection of the individual rights that are at the heart of our democracy'. Ultimately, Robert Bork was not confirmed but the record of the two who are now on the Supreme Court shows that Senator Kennedy's warnings, although expressed in extravagant language, were not entirely misplaced. Both Justice Scalia and Justice Thomas are committed to reversing *Roe* v. *Wade*, thereby removing the constitutional right of a woman to decide whether to have an abortion on the grounds that no such right can be found in the Constitution; would like to see Affirmative Action declared unconstitutional; have voted to allow improperly obtained police evidence to be used in trials; have voted to strike down provisions in laws to protect women and people with disabilities; and have opposed judicial recognition of gay rights.

However, the aspect of originalism that most infuriates its opponents is its claim to be politically and morally neutral. Its reactionary character, seeking to turn the clock back to an earlier 'golden age', appeals to the most right wing of conservatives. And, when an originalist approach to constitutional interpretation has not produced the outcome that conservatives would prefer, originalist judges seem to have been all too willing to abandon it. In the case of *Bush* v. *Gore* (2000), although the Constitution clearly gives authority over electoral matters to the states, all of the conservative judges on the Supreme

Court (including both of its originalists) voted to order the State of Florida to stop its recount of votes in the presidential election, thereby handing the presidency to the conservative George W. Bush.

## Judicial activism (also known as the doctrine of the 'Living Constitution')

The starting point for judicial activism is a belief that the preamble to the Constitution (which declares a commitment to 'establish justice . . . promote the general Welfare, and secure the Blessings of Liberty') perfectly summarises the essence of the Constitution, but that at the time the document was written, and since, the political reality has not lived up to these noble sentiments.

The history of the USA has been the struggle to make the promises of the Constitution meaningful to all Americans, both those who were initially excluded and those who, lacking political power and influence, have been unable to assert their rights. Sometimes, it has been the democratically elected leaders of the country who have promoted the extension of liberties and rights to those who have been denied them. More often, they have done so only in response to public demands expressed through high-profile campaigns, such as the suffragette movement that led to votes for women. Just as frequently, however, elected politicians, with the support of the majority of the population, have resisted the extension of rights and liberties. Who will make the Constitution meaningful under these circumstances? The answer is, in the view of judicial activists, the courts.

Adopting this role means, of course, that unelected judges will find themselves playing a policy-making role. Both of the two judicial philosophies outlined above, majoritarianism and originalism, emphasise the view that it is highly inappropriate for unelected people to adopt such an approach in a democracy. Both suggest that holding policy-makers to account is such a central principle of the Constitution that policy-making judges are failing to abide by the spirit of the Constitution. Judicial activists, however, make no apology for judicial policy-making (what is sometimes known as '**legislating from the bench**'). It will only happen, they argue, when the elected branches of government are failing in their duty to be faithful to the Constitution values in general and specific provisions in particular.

Moreover, judicial activists point out that the Founding Fathers had deep concerns that politicians, empowered by an electoral majority, could represent a threat to rights and liberties. One of the purposes of the Bill of Rights was to provide protection against the **tyranny of the majority** by making it difficult for politicians to take away the rights of sections of the population that are disliked or feared by the democratic majority who elected them. The Bill of Rights applies to everyone, including minority and marginalised groups; it serves to protect everyone or, at the very least, provide justification for arguing for equal treatment. Thus, the Bill of Rights has a distinctive **counter-majoritarian** character, guarding those who may be adversely affected by decisions taken by the majority, and has served as a platform for excluded groups to campaign for full inclusion in the mainstream of society. However, lacking the numbers or resources to use the electoral process to advance their claims, marginalised groups have often had only the courts to turn to. Activists argue that without judicial intervention, the Constitution's promises would be virtually meaningless for millions of Americans.

In practice, this approach to constitutional interpretation means:

- The Supreme Court placing few restrictions on Congress when it comes to the expansion of rights, but not allowing Congress to restrict rights. For example, in the case of *Katzenbach* v. *Morgan* (1966), that limited the right of Puerto Ricans in New York to vote if they were not literate in English (but were literate in Spanish), the Supreme Court ruled that Congressional power to modify rights does not include the authority to 'restrict, abrogate or dilute' constitutional protections.
- When Congress fails to legislate to provide protection to groups that are not receiving 'justice', or are excluded from the 'General Welfare' or are not enjoying the 'Blessings of Liberty' that are promised by the Constitution, then it is up to the Federal courts to step in. This means applying the principles of the Constitution to contemporary reality – an approach known as **loose constructionism**. The heyday of this brand of **progressive** (left-wing) judicial activism was in the 1950s and 1960s, when Earl Warren was Chief Justice of the Supreme Court and there was a group of committed activists driving the agenda: Justices William Brennan,

Thurgood Marshall (the first African American Supreme Court justice) and William Douglas. Groups that they supported in this period included:

- Racial minorities, especially African Americans, who were subject to racial discrimination. The case of *Brown* v. *Board of Education* (1954), which ruled that segregation marked the separated race as inferior and was therefore unconstitutional, is widely regarded as the start of this era of judicial activism. The courts continued to play an active role during the Civil Rights campaigns. Other notable rulings in this period included *Boynton* v. *Virginia* (1960), which ordered the desegregation of inter-state public transport, and *Baker* v. *Carr* (1962), in which the Court ruled that states could no longer put large numbers of African Americans into a single Congressional district, thereby limiting their political representation. Even in the early 1970s, when the era of judicial activism was on the wane, the Federal courts continued to play a role in maintaining the drive for racial equality. In *Swann* v. *Charlotte-Mecklenburg* (1971), the Supreme Court ruled that continued segregation in the schools of Charlotte, North Carolina, had to end and specified the means to do so – that school buses take white and black children to each other's schools. In 1974, a Federal District Judge, Arthur Garrity, ordered the same remedy for the schools of Boston, Massachusetts. When the local school board refused to obey the order, the Court appointed its own administrators and ran every aspect of the Boston school system for three years, including setting the curriculum and hiring teachers, taking judicial activism to a new level that included enforcing its own decisions.
- Suspects in criminal cases. It was clear in the 1960s that many people who came into contact with the criminal justice authorities were either unaware of their constitutional rights or were in no position to exercise them. In *Mapp* v. *Ohio* (1961), the Supreme Court ruled that, under the 4th Amendment, which prohibits unlawful searches and seizures, any improperly obtained evidence cannot be used in a prosecution. In *Gideon* v. *Wainwright* (1963), the Court ruled that defendants in criminal cases who could not afford a lawyer were entitled to one

provided by the state in order to ensure a fair trial, as required by the 6th Amendment of the Constitution. In *Miranda* v. *Arizona* (1966), the Court ruled that a suspect must be told of the right, guaranteed by the 5th Amendment, not to incriminate themselves and to remain silent during police questioning. All of these decisions were widely criticised as they appeared to be providing criminals with loopholes to escape justice.

Although this type of judicial activism has become far less common since the early 1970s, when Chief Justice Earl Warren and a number of other activist judges retired, the Supreme Court has continued to periodically establish policy in areas where Congress either has been reluctant to legislate or has been seen as actively contributing to limitations on constitutional rights. For example:

* *Abortion* In the landmark judgement of *Roe* v. *Wade* (1973), the Justices ruled that the 9th Amendment, which protects rights other than those mentioned in the Constitution, provided a right of privacy and that any law which made abortion illegal was an 'unjustifiable intrusion by the Government upon the privacy of the individual'.
* *Women's rights* In *Frontiero* v. *Richardson* (1973), the Supreme Court ruled that men and women in the military have to be treated equally. Before the case, wives of soldiers were automatically treated as dependents, and were provided with benefits such as accommodation, while the husbands of women serving in the military had to prove that they were dependents and entitled to similar benefits. In the decision, the Court made it clear that as well as intervening directly to ensure gender equality, it was sympathetic to Congressional measures to enhance gender equality.
* *Employment rights* In *Garcia* v. *San Antonio Metropolitan Transit Authority* (1985), the Supreme Court extended the power of Congress to protect employment rights. They authorised Congress to require state and local governments to provide a minimum wage and overtime pay, reversing earlier rulings that such regulations were a matter (under the 10th Amendment) for local and state governments.
* *Gay rights* In the case of *Lawrence* v. *Texas* (2003), the Supreme Court asserted that gays and lesbians were entitled to respect for their private lives, that political authorities could not act in ways which

'demean their existence' and that moral disapproval of homo-sexuality could not be the basis for infringing their constitutional rights.

- *National security* In the twenty-first century, the Supreme Court appears to have largely abandoned its unwillingness to get involved in foreign and security matters. However, following President George W. Bush's declaration of a 'War on Terror' (following the attacks of 11 September 2001) and the arrest and detention without trial of people classified as 'enemy combatants', the Supreme Court has adopted an aggressively interventionist stance and challenged the policy:
  - In *Rasul* v. *Bush* (2004), the Court ruled that detainees held on a US military base in Guantanamo Bay, Cuba, were entitled to constitutional protections.
  - In *Hamdi* v. *Rumsfeld* (2004), the Court built on the *Rasul* deci-sion to rule that one of the specific constitutional protections to which detainees were entitled was to challenge their deten-tion before an impartial judge.
  - The administration of George W. Bush set up military tribu-nals to provide a judicial mechanism for the detainees. When this was challenged, in *Hamdan* v. *Rumsfeld* (2006), the Court ruled that the detainees could not be subject to military trials without the specific authorisation of Congress.
  - The Republican majority in Congress responded to the *Hamdan* verdict by passing the Military Commissions Act. Then, in *Boumediene* v. *Bush* (2008), the Court ruled that the Military Commissions Act was unconstitutional as it failed to include adequate provisions to guarantee a fair trial.

### Criticisms of judicial activism

Opponents of judicial activism argue that it is both impractical and wrong in principle. In at least three ways, judicial activism is criticised on a purely practical level:

- The Constitution provides a clear, understandable framework for policy-makers to carry out their roles. However, if the Constitution is treated as a 'living' thing, constantly changing, it fails to play this role.

- When highly controversial and potentially divisive issues come to court, all interested parties want to know that the judgement is made on objective grounds. However, judicial activists, who aim to 'perfect' the Constitution, are widely seen as expressing their policy preferences rather than applying the law. This serves to undermine both the Court and the process of constitutional interpretation. As former Chief Justice William Rehnquist, as a critic of judicial activism, put it, 'there is no conceivable way in which I can logically demonstrate to you that the judgements of my conscience are superior to the judgements of your conscience, or vice versa'.

- When judges are seen to be enforcing clear, widely accepted rules, they have the authority to stand up to other branches of government if their actions are threatening liberty. If, however, they appear to be using judicial review to advance their own policy preferences, they risk eroding the standing and authority of the Court and thereby weakening its ability to challenge the legislature and executive.

The criticism that judicial activism is wrong in principle is based on a view that it undermines separation of powers, the constitutional feature that is at the very heart of the Founding Fathers' design. As judicial activism unapologetically promotes policy-making by judges, it intrudes into the responsibilities of the legislature, but without the safeguard of accountability. In fact, during its most activist phase, in the 1960s, the Supreme Court was variously described as **quasi-legislative**, **usurping the powers of the legislature** and an **imperial judiciary**. With separation regarded as the most important protection against tyranny, its erosion, especially by an unaccountable body, is seen as a betrayal of the Constitution.

## Democratic Constitutionalism

Although, in recent years, the Supreme Court has periodically issued rulings that can be characterised as 'activist', welcomed by left-wing (or progressive) Americans, it has been over forty years since a judge who can be described as a wholehearted judicial activist has been appointed to the Court. By the 1970s, a conservative-led backlash had led to a widespread belief that the Warren Court had been imposing the policy preferences of an unrepresentative, left-leaning elite drawn from the law schools of the Ivy League Universities in the North-East of the country who thought that they knew what was best for everyone and treated the rest of the population with contempt. None of the Republican presidents in this period were inclined to appoint a judicial activist and the only Democratic president who had an opportunity to fill Supreme Court vacancies in the latter part of the twentieth century, President Clinton, was reluctant to fuel a stereotype of left-wing elitism by appointing activists. When it comes to constitutional interpretation, therefore, progressives have been largely unable to influence public debate and have been able to make little or no impact on the Supreme Court.

Democratic constitutionalism is a doctrine, driven mainly by law professors at Yale University, that aims to develop a form of judicial activism that can win greater public acceptance and is suited to the political climate of the twenty-first century. It emphasises the ways in which judicial activism is faithful to the text of the Constitution. For example, the Constitution is clear that the President of the USA must be at least thirty-five years old. When the Constitution was written, a thirty-five year old would have been middle-aged and rapidly approaching old age (and therefore considered mature). Today, a thirty-five year old is young, having completed barely a third of an average lifespan. Democratic constitutionalists would not contemplate, however, reinterpreting such a clear constitutional provision. Where the Constitution is ambiguous, however, they argue that the principles and purposes behind the text should be examined to ensure that it is applied in the ways most appropriate to current circumstances.

They argue that each generation (not just the Warren era) has used the text and principles of the Constitution to debate, and update, its meaning. However, the way in which they see the courts contributing to this process represents a significant break from 1960s judicial activism. Whereas the Warren Court saw the Constitution being defined primarily by the judiciary, Democratic constitutional-ists see political movements and democratically elected institutions as leading the process of advancing the continuing process of creating a 'more perfect union'. They point out that the elected branches of government have a responsibility to pass laws and build institutions that carry out the Constitution's purposes (and not just avoid violating the Constitution). Thus, many constitutional developments start at local level then move to the national stage before the Supreme Court gets involved and makes rulings that extend these developments to the nation as a whole. The development of gender equality illustrates the process. There was a time when equal treatment for men and women would have been seen as a strange, unnatural concept. Then, the women's movement led to changing attitudes which, in turn, led to laws addressing sex discrimination, culminating in the courts changing its understanding of the meaning of the Constitution's 'equal protection' clause.

Thus, democratic constitutionalism may operate as follows:

- A movement emerges claiming the recognition of rights that have previously been denied. (In the early twentieth century, the most significant movement has been for the extension of gay rights.)
- In contrast to the Warren era, the Federal courts stand aside as the campaign unfolds, sometimes enjoying success (as the gay right movement has in states across the country from Washington to Iowa to Vermont) and sometimes suffering setbacks in other parts of the country (such as the Proposition 8 campaign in California).
- Once a significant majority of states has recognised civil unions or gay marriage, the Supreme Court can legitimately intervene to add these rights to the others that are recognised as constitutional, and force the resistant minority to follow suit.

Democratic constitutionalism is a relatively new, and still developing, doctrine. However, it is of significance because, on the basis of the limited evidence available, it appears to be in line with the thinking of President Obama who (as of 2009) had appointed one judge to the Supreme Court and was thought likely to have the opportunity to appoint at least two others. In his writings, during his time in the Senate (when he voted against both of President George W. Bush's nominees to the Supreme Court) and in his pronouncements as President, Barack Obama has emphasised both the importance of 'empathy', meaning the ability of judges to understand and identify 'with people's hopes and struggles', and his objections to judges who use their 'formidable skills on behalf of the strong in opposition to the weak'. If, by the end of President Obama's presidency, up to a third of the Supreme Court subscribe to this form of modest judicial activism, then the judicial philosophy of democratic constitutionalism will be influencing the process of constitutional interpretation for at least a generation.

## Criticisms of democratic constitutionalism

As a relatively new set of ideas, democratic constitutionalism has not been the subject of as much debate as the other judicial philosophies outlined above. Nonetheless, the ways in which it is at odds with other judicial philosophies can be determined.

For majoritarians, its willingness to defer to legislatures at state and national level is to be welcomed but because of its emphasis on constitutional changes that appeal to progressives it is likely that this deference will be selective, meaning that democratic constitutionalism can still be criticised as a doctrine that is based on judges indulging their political preferences.

For originalists, democratic constitutionalism has at least two flaws. Firstly, although it has a more democratic dimension than 'old-style' judicial activism, democratic constitutionalism still seeks to 'discover' rights in the Constitution that would not be recognised by the Founding Fathers. Also, in contrast to the clear set of rules that originalism provides for judges to follow, democratic constitutionalism provide only broad outlines and is, by comparison, vague. In particular, it is far from clear at what point a court may legitimately intervene on the basis of a sufficient consensus having built up behind the recognition of a new right. For example, in the case of *Kennedy* v. *Louisiana* (2007), the Supreme Court ruled that it is unconstitutional for convicted child rapists to be executed, arguing that with only six states adopting this kind of punishment for this crime there was therefore a national consensus that capital punishment for child rapists amounted to 'cruel and unusual punishment' (8th Amendment). In a strongly worded dissent, Justice Antonin Scalia pointed out that a number of state legislatures had draft legislation to apply the death penalty to child rapists and that the trend, therefore, was a growing national consensus that execution was an appropriate penalty. Since almost all statistical evidence can be interpreted in different ways, he argued, trends make an unsuitable benchmark of what should or should not be deemed unconstitutional.

For traditional judicial activists, democratic constitutionalism is simply too timid. If judges have a clear sense that there is a compelling case, on the basis of evolving social standards, to extend constitutional recognition of rights that have previously been denied, they should do so and not allow the more intolerant or prejudiced sections of the population to set the pace of change.

## Minimalism

Judicial minimalism, as a distinct set of ideas, is also comparatively recent (although its advocates can point to a long history of judges adopting a 'minimalist' approach to constitutional interpretation). Like democratic constitutionalism, it emerged in response to the growing influence of conservative judicial philosophies and the decline of judicial activism. Its most prominent exponent, law professor Cass Sunstein, argues that it offers a 'third way' between the highly politicised conservative doctrine of originalism and the equally politicised progressive doctrine of judicial activism, because he sees it appealing to both moderate conservatives and moderate liberals.

It aims to do this by not having a grand theory that will attract passionate support or opposition. Instead, it proposes that judges respect precedent whenever possible and, when this is not possible, make narrow (or shallow) rulings rather than broad (or deep) ones, resolving the dispute that is before the court without addressing wider constitutional implications. Minimalists, Sunstein argues, 'have no desire to revolutionise the law . . . they think that the law, and even social peace, are possible only when people are willing to set aside their deepest disagreements, and are able to decide what to do without agreeing on exactly why to do it'.

In some ways, this appears to be quite similar to majoritarianism, that commits judges to upholding precedent and deferring to legislatures in all but the most extreme of cases. (Indeed, Sunstein claims that one of the most celebrated majoritarians, Justice Felix Frankfurter, was a minimalist.) However, majoritarianism places almost no restrictions on democratically elected politicians while minimalists would not permit such latitude.

Despite these claims of political neutrality and commitment to finding common ground, minimalism is seen as a heavily diluted form of judicial activism as its reluctance to address controversial constitutional issues would protect the policy-making rulings of the 1960s. (It should come as no surprise, therefore, that Professor Sunstein took up a position in the administration of President Obama in 2009.) Thus, while minimalists would be far less likely than judicial activists or democratic constitutionalists to declare gay marriage a constitutional right, they would forcefully resist efforts by originalists to reverse earlier judicial extensions of constitutional rights such as a woman's right to decide whether or not to have an abortion. Moreover, although minimalists would not add new, dramatic interpretations to the way in which the Constitution is understood, they are willing to build on those rights that have been previously recognised, in small increments.

## Criticisms of minimalism

For majoritarians, the doctrine of minimalism is far too erratic. While both sets of ideas favour respect for precedent, minimalism is less consistent when it comes to respect for laws passed by democratically elected legislatures. Anything deemed oppressive by a minimalist judge is likely to be struck down but, in the absence of a clear, consistently-applied theory, there will always be uncertainty as to when this line is crossed.

Democratic constitutionalists share the minimalist inclination to protect the extension of the constitutional rights won since the 1960s. However, they would like to see the process of creating a 'more perfect union' to proceed at a faster pace than the incremental progress envisaged by minimalists. For them, therefore, minimalism is too defensive.

Both originalists and judicial activists regard minimalism with a considerable measure of contempt. Originalists object to minimalism presenting itself as politically neutral when it was developed as a doctrine primarily to resist the growing influence of originalism in the 1980s as conservatism grew in strength. Also, originalists strongly believe that one of the most important roles of constitutional interpretation is to provide a well-understood framework within which policy-makers can operate with confidence, while minimalism takes pride in avoiding providing answers to big questions that can let policy-makers know where they stand. Judicial activists, meanwhile, find little to respect in a doctrine that criticises landmark rulings, and appears to believe that there should not be any rulings of this type in the future, while making it a priority to defend those that judicial activists have made in the past.

## Judicial appointments

With judicial review having such far-reaching consequences and there being so many different ways in which judges may approach the interpretation of the Constitution, the process of appointing people to the USA's highest courts has become a matter of intense public interest and political controversy.

### Vacancies

Appointments to the Federal courts are for life. This means that a vacancy only occurs when a judge decides to retire or dies. As the average lifespan lengthens, judges often serve for a quarter of a century or more. Vacancies are therefore becoming increasingly significant as they are becoming less frequent (for example, there were no vacancies on the Supreme Court between 1994 and 2005) and appointees are likely to contribute to the shaping of US society for at least a generation.

### Nominating judges

From the lower Federal courts to the Supreme Court, judges are chosen by the President and then confirmed by the Senate. On the Supreme Court there are nine Justices, led by the Chief Justice.

The most obvious, and most significant, factor in the President's choice of nominee is the judicial philosophy of the people being considered to fill a vacancy. The Supreme Court has been described as a presidential 'echo chamber' because a President's views may still be heard there many years after he has left office (and, in some cases, even years after he has died). However, judges, once appointed, do not always act as expected. Conservatives, especially, have been dismayed that a significant proportion of Supreme Court Justices have proved to be far less conservative than the presidents who nominated them expected. In the 1950s, President Eisenhower described his appointment of Earl Warren to Chief Justice as 'the biggest damn fool mistake I ever made'. Of the Justices currently on the

Supreme Court, the most liberal, Justice Stevens, was appointed by a Republican president, as was Justice Kennedy, whose voting patterns fluctuate considerably.

This tendency of judges becoming less conservative once they are appointed to the Supreme Court led President Reagan to set up a system for vetting potential nominees far more intensively. He set up a committee to analyse all the court judgements, published writings and statements of people being considered and to interview them on their views on politically controversial issues. Subsequent presidents have adopted the same system.

This process is complemented by the intervention of pressure groups. Both allies and opponents of the President keep dossiers on possible nominees and are swift to mount campaigns after the President announces his choice. The response of these groups can provide an early indication of the level of support or opposition that the candidate is likely to receive. In 2005, when there were two vacancies, President George W. Bush nominated the little-known Harriet Miers to fill one of them. The hostile response from his allies in conservative pressure groups, who wanted a judge with a strong conservative track-record, led to the President withdrawing her nomination and replacing her with Justice Samuel Alito.

There is also a range of other, non-ideological, factors that the President will consider when selecting a candidate:

- *The American Bar Association* Since 1952, the Association's Committee on the Federal Judiciary has been consulted concerning almost every Federal judicial appointment, rating each nominee as 'exceptionally well qualified', 'well qualified', 'qualified' or 'not qualified'.
- *Balance* Throughout the history of the judiciary, most judges have been white Anglo-Saxon men but, over time, there has been an increasing expectation that the courts that play such an influential role in US society should both reflect the country's diversity and draw upon its rich range of experiences. On the Supreme Court, the first Jewish Justice, Louis Brandeis, was appointed in 1916; the first African American, Thurgood Marshall, in 1967; the first woman, Sandra Day O'Connor, in 1981; the first Italian American, Antonin Scalia, in 1986; and the first Hispanic, Sonia Sotormayor, in 2009.

- *Geography* Presidents have always done their best to ensure that all regions of the United States have been represented on the Supreme Court. In 1932, the principal objection to the strongest candidate, Justice Cardozo, arose from the fact that he was from New York and there were already two Justices from that state on the bench. One of the other Justices from New York generously offered to resign so that Justice Cardozo could be appointed.
- *Payment of political debts* Although not a common reason, on occasion Justices have chosen to reward them for past service. Chief Justice Earl Warren was promised a position on the Court in return for not running against Eisenhower in the 1952 presidential election.

### Confirming judges

The **confirmation** of Federal judges requires a vote by a majority of the Senate. Historically, this has not proved difficult to achieve. In the early days of the Supreme Court, before it developed the status and authority with which it is now associated, the main challenge was to find suitable candidates who would not resign as soon as a more attractive position became available. Until 1967, most confirmations did not even require a formal vote.

However, since President Reagan's drive, in the 1980s, to fill vacancies with reliable conservatives, which met with determined resistance from progressive political forces, the confirmation process has come to resemble an election campaign, with live television hearings and millions of dollars being spent in support of or opposition to the candidate. These political battles have, at times, been dramatic. In 1987, the controversial (originalist) nominee Robert Bork faced twelve days of public hearings in which liberals set out to discredit his record and, subsequently, the Senate refused to confirm him. Four years later, in 1991, the public was transfixed by live television coverage of the confirmation hearings of Clarence Thomas, who was accused of sexual harassment. Added to the suggestion that he harboured extreme right-wing views and was inadequately qualified to sit on the Supreme Court, he polarised opinion in the Senate and in society at large. Eventually, he was confirmed by a vote of 52–48, the narrowest margin of victory in the twentieth century.

Although no subsequent appointment has generated anything like the level of controversy of these two nominees, activists on both the right and left maintain substantial financial war chests in case such a battle should erupt again, and the average time period between nomination and confirmation has lengthened from just seven days before 1967 to more than sixty-seven days by 2006.

As well as face hearings, nominees have to:

- Meet with Senators of both parties to discuss any issues or concerns they may have.
- Fill out a questionnaire, prepared by the Senate Judiciary Committee, explaining their approach to making judgements and indicating their views on the major issues of the day.

As the Constitution requires a simple majority to confirm a nomination, fifty-one votes should be enough for an appointment to be made. However, the Senate has a procedure that allows a minority to block anything they feel very strongly about. This is called a **filibuster**. This blocking mechanism can only be overcome if sixty Senators vote to end the filibuster. Between 2002 and 2005, ten of President George W. Bush's more controversial nominees to lower Federal courts were filibustered by the minority Democratic Party in the Senate.

It should be noted, however, that despite all the drama accompanying the nomination and confirmation process, most candidates for the Supreme Court over the past quarter of a century have been appointed: only Robert Bork and Harriet Miers have not.

## The Roberts Court (from 2005 to 2009)

This section examines the extent to which the rival judicial philosophies are represented on the Supreme Court, as of 2009, and the significance of the balance of power on the Court for the pivotal issues of the early twenty-first century.

Between 1969 and 2009, the White House was occupied by a Democrat for only three terms (twelve years) and there were no vacancies on the Supreme Court during the term of President Carter (1977–81). Not surprisingly, therefore, a majority of the Justices on the Supreme Court have been appointed by Republican Presidents, each of whom has aimed to make the Court more conservative. However, as shown in the section on nominating judges,

## Table 7.2  Supreme Court Justices

| Supreme Court Justice | Nominating President | Year of Confirmation | Age of Justice (at end of 2009 term) | Judicial Philosophy of the Justice |
|---|---|---|---|---|
| John Paul Stevens | Gerald Ford (Republican) | 1975 | 89 | Moderate judicial activist |
| Antonin Scalia | Ronald Reagan (Republican) | 1986 | 73 | Originalist (describes himself as a 'faint-hearted' originalist, because willing to respect precedents, even if he disagrees with them) |
| Anthony Kennedy | Ronald Reagan (Republican) | 1988 | 72 | The court's 'swing' judge, sometimes joining the group that tends towards activism while, at other times, joining those who tend towards originalism |
| Clarence Thomas | George Bush Snr (Republican) | 1991 | 61 | Staunch originalist |
| Ruth Bader-Ginsburg | Bill Clinton (Democrat) | 1993 | 76 | Minimalist, tending towards activism |
| Steven Breyer | Bill Clinton (Democrat) | 1994 | 71 | Minimalist, tending towards activism |
| John Roberts (Chief Justice) | George W. Bush (Republican) | 2005 | 54 | Describes himself as a minimalist but his opinions repeatedly demonstrate that he is prepared, gradually, to overturn long-standing activist precedents |

| Table 7.2 (continued) | | | | |
|---|---|---|---|---|
| Supreme Court Justice | Nominating President | Year of Confirmation | Age of Justice (at end of 2009 term) | Judicial Philosophy of the Justice |
| Samuel Alito | George W. Bush (Republican) | 2006 | 59 | Since joining the court, has adopted an increasingly originalist position each term |
| Sonia Sotomayor | Barack Obama (Democrat) | 2009 | 55 | Was a judge for seventeen years before joining the Court, but dealt mainly with technical business-related matters and therefore did not have a judicial record that demonstrated her stance on the most controversial political issues relating to protection or extension of rights |

members of the Supreme Court do not always adopt the judicial philosophy that the nominating President expected, as the above table illustrates:

Thus, the ideological balance on the Supreme Court is narrower than might be expected. Justices Scalia, Thomas, Roberts and Alito usually vote together, to form a 'conservative' bloc. Justices Steven, Bader-Ginsburg, Breyer and Sotomayor are generally classified as 'liberals'. Justice Kennedy, usually casting the decisive vote in the most controversial and closely watched cases, is seen as the 'swing vote' on the Court, determining whether conservative or liberal judicial philosophies triumph when contentious issues are being decided.

---

### Box 7.2 The role of the Chief Justice

The Chief Justice has a number of responsibilities in addition to participating in the cases that come before the Supreme Court, including:

- Being responsible for the administrative arrangements for both the Supreme Court and lower Federal courts.
- Presiding over the swearing-in ceremony for the President (and other senior Federal appointees, such as judges).
- Presiding over impeachment proceedings, when holders of high office are accused of misconduct or corruption.

When Supreme Court cases are being decided, the votes of all nine justices have equal weight, including that of the Chief Justice. However, the Chief Justice has one power that, used skilfully, can influence the outcome of the voting: he decides who will write the detailed explanation of the Court's decision in each case (although, if the Chief Justice is in the minority in the initial voting, this power passes to the longest-serving judge in the majority).

Chief Justice Roberts has increasingly used this power to assign this task to whichever conservative has the views that are closest to those of Justice Kennedy, which has often proved to be the decisive factor in drawing Justice Kennedy into the conservative camp. Thus, despite some victories for the liberals, the dominant characteristic of the first four terms of the Roberts Court (2005–9) has been the progressive erosion of long-standing activist precedents and laws promoting government intervention.

---

This makes Justice Kennedy clearly the most influential judge on the Court (and, with the US Supreme Court widely regarded as the most powerful court in the world, he is arguably the most powerful judge on the planet). In the first four terms of the Roberts Court, he has tended to lean towards the conservatives.

A summary of the most controversial issues addressed by the Supreme Court between 2005 and 2009 illustrated the dominance of the conservatives in that period:

- *Abortion* Conservatives tend to be hostile to the right to have an abortion. In *Gonzales* v. *Carhart* (2007), the Court upheld Federal law banning an abortion procedure used late in pregnancy (reversing a decision the Court had made just six years earlier, before Justice Kennedy became the 'swing' judge). This was the greatest restriction on reproductive rights since *Roe* v. *Wade*.

- *Race* Conservatives are almost universally hostile to Affirmative Action. In *Community Schools* v. *Seattle School District* (2007), the Court restricted the ability of schools to use race-conscious measures to achieve or preserve integration. However, Justice Kennedy refused to support arguments advanced by the more conservative members of the Court who wanted to go beyond admissions policies and ban considerations of race in all school policies. In *Northwest Austin Municipal District* v. *Holder* (2009), the Court's conservatives did not accept the opportunity to overturn the Voting Rights Act of 1965, despite it being evident during the hearing that they believed there was no longer any justification for the Federal government closely monitoring districts with a history of obstructing minorities from voting. Instead, to keep Justice Kennedy in their camp, they settled for a narrow ruling while clearly signalling a willingness to overturn the law at a later date. In *Ricci* v. *DeStefano* (2009), the Court ruled that a fire department discriminated against white firefighters when it decided not to proceed with a round of promotions in which no racial minorities had qualified to rise to a higher rank.

- *Campaign finance* Conservatives tend to be hostile to campaign finance regulations, on the grounds that they amount to a limitation on freedom of speech. In *FEC* v. *Wisconsin Right to Life* (2007), the Court struck down some provisions of the 2002 campaign finance law (BCRA). In *Citizens United* v. *Federal Elections Commission* (2010) the Court went further, removing the restriction that companies and trade unions could only use money for political activities that had been specifically raised for those purposes and lifting a ban on them broadcasting campaign adverts shortly before a primary or a general election.

- *Criminal justice* Conservatives have been deeply frustrated by the tendency of judges to protect the interests of suspects and/or criminals and add to the burdens of investigators and prosecutors. In *Rita* v. *United States* (2007), the Court made it more difficult for defendants to challenge a sentence on the grounds of whether or not it was 'reasonable'. In *Uttecht* v. *Brown* (2007), the Court made it easier for prosecutors to have anyone with doubts about the death penalty removed from a jury if a death sentence was a potential verdict (thereby appearing to make a vote for the death penalty more likely). In an example of the Court chipping away at a well-established right without actually overturning a long-standing precedent (which might be more than Justice Kennedy could accept) in successive terms the Court reduced the restrictions on use of evidence that may have been improperly obtained by the police in the cases of *Hudson* v. *Michigan* (2008) and *Herring* v. *United States* (2009). In *District Attorney's Office* v. *Osborne* (2009), the Court ruled that there is no constitutional right for inmates to have access to DNA evidence that might prove their innocence.

- *Access to the Court* Conservatives also object to the judicial system being used by criminals to repeatedly challenge aspects of their trial (thereby denying closure to victims) or for what they see as frivolous suits against employers that make it difficult to manage the workforce and increase employment costs. In *Ledbetter* v. *Goodyear* (2007), the Court reduced the ability of plaintiffs in gender and race discrimination matters to bring a case against an employer; in *Bowles* v. *Russell* (2007), the Court even ruled that an inmate given an incorrect date by a judge for a court hearing could not appeal the verdict handed down in his absence.
- *Gun ownership* Conservatives have long believed that it is both constitutional and desirable for law-abiding citizens to buy and own guns for self-defence, especially in sparsely populated areas where the nearest police officers may be many miles away. In *District of Columbia* v. *Heller* (2008), the Court provided its clearest ever explanation of the 2nd Amendment, protecting private gun ownership and making it far more difficult for states and local authorities to place restrictions on the purchase and possession of weapons.

So frustrated were the liberal minority at the end of the 2006–7 Supreme Court term that they took to reading dissents from the bench, which is traditionally only done when a judge passionately disagrees with the Court's decision. Justice Breyer summed up their feelings when he declared that 'rarely in the history of the law have so few undone so much so quickly'.

However, the liberal bloc has enjoyed some successes in this period and, when they have done so, it has usually been because they have drawn Justice Kennedy into their camp:

- In all of the cases since 2004 in which the Supreme Court challenged the policies of President George W. Bush on Guantanamo Bay detainees, Justice Kennedy sided with the liberals. These were the cases of *Rasul* v. *Bush* (2004), *Hamdi* v. *Rumsfeld* (2004), *Hamdan* v. *Rumsfeld* (2006) *and Boumediene* v. *Bush* (2008).
- Justice Kennedy provided the pivotal vote, and wrote the opinion for the Court, in *Kennedy* v. *Louisiana* (2008), that struck down all state laws providing for the death penalty for child rapists.
- In *Caperton* v. *A. T. Massey Coal Company* (2009), with the conservatives strongly dissenting, Justice Kennedy joined the liberals in ruling that the state judge, who had been elected to his post, could not participate in a case that involved people who had made a substantial donation to his election campaign.

Occasionally, a liberal victory came as a result of the originalists on the Court reaching the conclusion that the text of the Constitution requires a ruling that runs counter to the outcome preferred by conservatives. For example, in the case of *Melendez-Diaz* v. *Massachusetts* (2009), the liberal-originalist alliance decided that crime laboratory analysts have to appear in trials rather than submit written reports (as suggested in Amendment VI of the Constitution, which says anyone standing trial is entitled to 'be confronted with the witnesses against him') even though this adds to the burdens of the prosecuting authorities.

Overall, it is unwise to make definitive judgements about the Roberts era after just four terms. However, on the basis of early indications the main trend has been for the Roberts Court to move in incremental, or minimalist, steps towards an originalist understanding of the Constitution on the country's most controversial issues.

Another way of looking at the early years of the Roberts Court is, as the *New York Times* put it, that the Constitution 'means what Justice Kennedy says it means'.

## Conclusion

The most appropriate role for judges, in a democracy, has been a matter of passionate debate for much of the history of the USA, not least because the Founding Fathers left little by way of guidance when they wrote and ratified the Constitution. Does their lack of accountability make it inappropriate for judges to be active participants in the political process? Or does their insulation from pressure, especially bigoted social attitudes that have periodically dominated public opinion, make judges the only appropriate guardians of the values at the heart of the Constitution?

In recent decades, this debate has become deeply entwined with wider ideological divisions. Liberals have rejoiced each time that judges have interpreted the Constitution in ways that have made them agents of social change, while conservatives have responded with fury to their inability to resist these changes through the democratic system and have mounted a sustained campaign to win control of the courts and limit, or even reverse, key precedents of the Supreme Court's progressive activism of the 1960s and 1970s.

This conflict has developed into a battle of ideas, with the development of rival judicial philosophies, battles over appointments to the courts and sharp divisions between judges on how the Constitution should be applied to specific cases.

Thus, understanding the origins of these disputes, developing a secure grasp of the rival judicial philosophies and recognising how influential each viewpoint has been in recent years are all essential to a full understanding of the significance of the judiciary in contemporary US society and politics.

· · · · · · · · · · · · · · · · · · · · · · · · · · · · · · · · · · · · · · · · · · ·

## ✔ What you should have learnt from reading this chapter

- Historically, the judiciary has played two roles: resolving disputes and protecting the rights of the individual from their political overlords.

- While the Constitution set up a Federal judiciary and outlined its powers, it did not clearly define whether it would continue to play its traditional common law role of protecting rights or whether it would have the power of judicial review.

- Once it was clearly established in 1803, in *Marbury* v. *Madison*, that the Supreme Court would have the final word on the meaning of the Constitution, the Federal judiciary emerged as an immensely powerful institution.

- Ever since, there have been intense debates about how the power of judicial review should be exercised. Conservatives have tended to be drawn to the judicial philosophies of majoritarianism and originalism which, in practice, usually leave the status quo intact or reverse any novel interpretations of the Constitution. Liberals and progressives have tended to be drawn to radical or moderate versions of judicial activism that treat the Constitution as a living document that evolves in tandem with society and its values.

- These rival viewpoints have led to the appointment of judges to the Supreme Court, whenever there is a vacancy, becoming an ideological battleground with the President, Senators, pressure groups and the media all engaging in a struggle to promote their preferred candidate or, at the very least, to block the appointment of the least desirable person.

- Since John Roberts became Chief Justice in 2005, the conservatives on the Supreme Court have been rather more successful than the liberals at enticing the key swing judge, Steven Kennedy, to join them when the most contentious issues have been decided. However, there is no guarantee that this will remain the case in the future.

## Glossary of key terms

**Amicus curiae** Documents or testimony from individuals or groups who are not directly involved in a case but have an interest in the outcome.

**Common law** Law made by judges, usually in defence of individual rights or limiting the powers of government.

**Concurring opinion** A written statement by a judge, supporting the conclusion reached by another judge in the same court but giving different reasons for reaching that conclusion.

**Confirmation** (of appointee) The process by which the Senate gives, or withholds, its support for a judge who has been put forward by the President to fill a vacancy on a Federal court.

**Counter-majoritarian** The principle that the democratic will of the majority may not always be wise or fair and, therefore, precautions need to be taken to protect those who may be adversely affected by decisions taken by the majority.

**Court of appeal** Courts that hear and decide cases that have been before a lower court.

**Dissenting opinion** A written statement by a judge, giving reasons for rejecting the conclusion reached by another judge in the same court.

**Filibuster** A device available to Senators enabling them to block a vote by prolonging a debate.

**Imperial judiciary** Judges or courts acting as if they are taking over the responsibilities of the other branches of government.

**Judicial review** The act of declaring laws and actions of government to be constitutional or unconstitutional.

**Legislating from the bench** Judges acting as policy-makers.

**Loose constructionism** The use, by judges, of the Constitution and precedent as guides but without being tightly restricted by them if other factors are considered more important.

**Majority decision** The official decision of a court, without the support of all the judges.

**Original jurisdiction** The constitutional authority to hear and decide cases that have not been before a lower court.

**Precedent** Previous rulings that judges use as a guide when making rulings.

**Progressive** A term for left-wing Americans, often used interchangeably with 'liberal'.

**Quasi-legislative** Judges or courts acting as policy-makers.

**Stare decisis** Leaving the legal position unchanged.

**Strict constructionism** The use, by judges, of the Constitution and precedent as guides with all other factors given far less weight.

**Tyranny of the majority** The idea that the democratically expressed will of the majority of the people will not always have a positive or constructive outcome: numerical advantage may be used to oppress the minority (or minorities).

**Usurping the powers of the legislature** Judges acting as policy-makers.

## ? Likely examination questions

Issues examiners may expect students to be able to effectively analyse include:

- Factors that enable Federal justices to be 'politicians in disguise', if they so choose

- Factors that encourage Federal justices to avoid entering the 'political thicket'

- The significance of recent appointments to the Supreme Court

- Why the judiciary has become one of the arenas for the 'culture wars' of US politics

- The thinking behind the rival judicial philosophies

Thus, examples of the kind of questions which could be asked include:

'The Supreme Court has too much power for an unelected body.' Discuss.

Explain judicial restraint and its political significance.

# Helpful websites

www.supremecourtus.gov and www.uscourts.gov are the two official websites of the Federal judiciary.

www.pfaw.org. and www.aclj.org. are the websites of two of the organisations at the forefront of the judicial 'culture wars'. The first is a liberal group, People for the American Way, which played a major role in blocking the confirmation of President Reagan's nominee, Robert Bork, in 1987. The second is the American Center for Law and Justice, which provides speakers who regularly appear on US current affairs programmes, promoting conservative legal positions.

# Suggestions for further reading

A wide range of general books about the Supreme Court are available, from bookstores or Amazon.com, ranging from the *Oxford Companion to the Supreme Court of the United States* by Kermit L. Hall to *Supreme Court for Dummies* by Lisa Paddock.

There is also at least one biography of each member of the Supreme Court.

The two dominant judicial philosophies on the Supreme Court are originalism and minimalism. To learn more about them, read *Radicals in Robes* by Cass Sunstein, which explains in detail the thinking behind minimalism, and *A Matter of Interpretation* by Antonin Scalia, which offers an in-depth debate on the merits of originalism.

# Congress

## Contents

## Overview

*The most powerful legislature in the world?*

On 7 January 2009, with both houses of Congress controlled by the Democratic Party and preparations underway for the inauguration of a Democratic president, the Chairman of the Senate Finance Committee, Max Baucus, issued a warning that the President could not expect Congress to simply follow his lead. In relation to the proposed stimulus bill, which was a package of measures to revive the ailing economy, he said, 'I think the committee clearly wants to have its stamp on the stimulus. The committee wants to be cooperative and work together with the new President, but it clearly has its own ideas too as to how to effectively create new jobs.'

It was this kind of tension between the branches of government, even with the same party in control of both Congress and the presidency, with each challenging the others over the limits of their power, that the Founding Fathers envisaged when they designed a system of checks and balances to ensure that no individual or faction became too powerful.

Yet, consistently, opinion polls show that the American people have a very low opinion of the performance of Congress, regardless of which party is in control. It is perceived as inefficient, too tied to special interests and insufficiently responsive to the needs and wishes of ordinary people.

Examining the work of Congress, this chapter considers its constitutional roles and the balance fluctuations between the legislature and the other branches of government, and evaluates how well it serves the modern USA.

## Key issues to be covered in this chapter

- Congress and the Constitution: its role in the system of checks and balances
- Congress and the other branches of the Federal government
- Legislating: the process of passing laws
- Representation: promoting the interests of constituents
- Political parties in Congress
- The effectiveness of Congress

## Congress and the Constitution

### The most important branch of government

Had the Founding Fathers heard the statement of the Senate Finance Committee Chairman, Max Baucus, they may well have endorsed his approach to dealing with the executive branch of government. They may, however, have been disappointed that it was an example of Congress responding to presidential initiatives rather than the other way around.

After the USA gained its independence from Britain, with its King who they saw as largely unaccountable, the Founding Fathers were determined to design a system that would stop one person from holding too much power. One of the ways this was achieved was by taking almost all law-making responsibilities away from the executive branch of government and putting it into the hands of the legislative branch. This was expected to make Congress the most important and powerful branch of government, which is why its powers and responsibilities are outlined in the first article of the Constitution.

### Limiting Congressional power

However, even in the hands of a group of people, rather than one individual, power can be abused and the Constitution included a range of restrictions on the power of Congress, including:

- Dividing power between two chambers (creating a bicameral legislature) that would have to agree on the precise wording of any bills before they could become law.
- Making the members of the lower chamber, the House of Representatives, accountable to 'the people' through elections held every two years. The voters (who did not include women, Native Americans or African Americans) would be able to replace any representative who was abusing his power.
- Giving the power to deal with financial issues to the House of Representatives, who would face electoral defeat within two years if they imposed high taxes or did not use the people's money wisely.
- Giving the states the power to each appoint two members of

the upper chamber, the Senate, so that they could look after the interests of their state on equal terms regardless of their size or population.

- Giving Senators a six-year term of office, with one-third of them replaced every two years. Anticipating an event like 9/11, when a tide of emotion swept the country, the Founding Fathers set up a system that prevented one political group from gaining complete control of Congress.
- Giving Congress specific responsibilities, which were laid out in Article I, Section 8 of the Constitution. These powers, called **enumerated powers** because they are numbered from 1 to 18, can be categorised as five economic powers (raising taxes, borrowing money and so on), seven defence powers (declare war, provide a navy and so on) and six miscellaneous powers (naturalising citizens, establishing post offices and so on). The final enumerated power is known as the '**elastic clause**', which gives Congress the right to make all 'necessary and proper' laws to carry out its responsibilities. It is called the 'elastic clause' because it allows Congress to stretch its powers to respond to situations the Founding Fathers could never have anticipated.
- To ensure that this final power was not abused, the Constitution gave the President the right to veto laws. Congress would be able to **override a veto** with a two-thirds majority, a very difficult hurdle to clear.
- The Constitution also limited the powers of Congress by laying down, in Section 9, specific restrictions on laws that could be passed. For example, no law can be passed that punishes a person without a jury trial, Congress may not pass laws favouring one state or region over another, and they were not allowed to place restrictions on the slave trade until 1808.

## Constitutional amendments affecting Congress

This balance of powers and restraints has remained largely un-changed since the Constitution was ratified in June 1788. Only three significant changes have occurred since, namely:

- The 17th Amendment, passed in 1913, so that Senators were directly elected by the people instead of by state legislatures.

- The number of representatives in the House was set at 435 in 1929.
- The 20th Amendment, passed in 1933, laid down that Congress would start its new session on 3 January, after each Congressional election.

However, the use that Congress has made of its powers, and its relationships with the other branches of government, has changed substantially over the past two hundred years.

# Congress and the presidency

### Division of responsibilities
Considering the weight that the Founding Fathers placed on limiting the power of the executive branch, the role of scrutinising the presidency could be considered the most significant activity undertaken by Congress.

It is not surprising, therefore, that some of the scrutinising mechanisms available to Congress tend to attract nationwide publicity and controversy. This applies particularly to forms of scrutiny that are the constitutional responsibility of the Senate: **confirmation** of presidential appointments and **ratification** of treaties. This also applies to the form of scrutiny that is the constitutional responsibility of the House of Representatives: analysing the budget. However, other forms of day-to-day scrutiny, shared by both chambers, tend to go largely unnoticed.

### Scrutinising presidential appointments
Once the President takes office, after winning an election, one of his first constitutional responsibilities is to appoint people to senior positions. These include the most important positions in the government departments and ambassadors. Over the following four years, until the next election, vacancies may arise in other important areas of government, such as judgeships on the Federal courts and the highest ranks of the armed forces, and the President is also responsible for appointing their replacements.

In each case, the Senate is constitutionally responsible to give 'advice and consent' on each appointment. In practice, this means investigating the record of each person nominated by the President, holding hearings that give Senators an opportunity to question the candidate and anyone else who has a strong view on the appointment, and then taking a vote. If a majority of Senators vote in favour of the nominee, he/she is able to take up the position. If not, the President must choose someone else, who then has to go through the same process.

In the vast majority of cases, this process is completed without any controversy, although there are so many positions to be filled that it may take many months before an incoming President has a full team in place. Indeed, many hearings consist mainly of the Senators expressing their confidence that the nominee is supremely qualified to do an outstanding job (many people entering public service are giving up a better-paid job in the private sector) and congratulating them on their confirmation, even before a vote is taken. In a minority of high-profile cases, however, the confirmation process can be bitter and divisive:

- President Bush Snr had his first nomination for the post of Defense Secretary rejected, in 1989, when Senate investigations revealed evidence of womanising and excessive drinking.
- Similarly, in 1993, President Clinton had his first two nominations for the post of Attorney General rejected by the Senate, when it was controlled by his own party. It emerged in both cases that they had failed to pay social security taxes for domestic staff working for them. Cases like these are embarrassing for the President and unhelpful to his reputation, but it is political battles over appointments that do most to put the confirmation process into the headlines.
- In 1987, the Senate refused to confirm Robert Bork, a judge with extremely right-wing views who had been nominated to the Supreme Court by President Reagan. He failed to convince the Senators that he would protect the rights that vulnerable groups in society had won over the previous thirty years. Liberals across the USA were elated by his defeat while conservatives remain resentful that someone who shares their views was blocked from taking up a highly influential position.
- Four years later, in 1991, the public was transfixed by live television coverage of the confirmation hearings of Clarence Thomas,

who was accused of sexual harassment. Added to the suggestion that he harboured extreme right-wing views and was inadequately qualified to sit on the Supreme Court, he polarised opinion in the Senate and in society at large. Eventually, he was confirmed by a vote of 52–48, the narrowest margin of victory in the twentieth century.

- Between 2002 and 2005, ten of the most controversial nominees put forward by President George W. Bush to Federal courts were blocked by the minority Democratic Party in the Senate. They made use of a procedure, exclusive to the Senate, that allows a minority to stop a vote being called on anything that they feel very strongly about. This is called a **filibuster**. This blocking mechanism can only be overcome if sixty Senators vote to end the filibuster.

- Even when the political climate appears favourable to the President, such as when President Obama came to office amid the national euphoria of being the first African American President, it can be a challenge to get appointees confirmed. Simply the fact that nominees will be subject to scrutiny means that the President's team will closely examine the personal and political record of all candidates for key positions, which slows down the process. Six months after taking office, therefore, fewer than half of the positions that require Senate confirmation had taken office in President Obama's administration and some of his most high-profile nominees had been forced to withdraw because of embarrassing revelations during the confirmation process, such as his first choice as Health Secretary.

Despite these limitations, the President can get around the Senate's refusal to confirm a nominee, through the use of **recess appointments**. Article II, Section 2 of the US Constitution says, 'The President shall have Power to fill up all Vacancies that may happen during the Recess of the Senate, by granting Commissions which shall expire at the End of their next Session.' This clause, written before the invention of modern transport systems, addressed the difficulties faced by Presidents in filling vacancies when the next meeting of the Senate could be weeks away. In the modern era it is used simply as a loophole.

After winning re-election in 2004, President George W. Bush failed to get his nominee for the post of US Ambassador to the United Nations (UN), John Bolton, confirmed. Partly this was due to reports that he had a record of bullying staff he was responsible for, but mainly it was due to his reported hostility to the UN, which, it was argued, would undermine his effectiveness.

Recess appointees must be approved by the Senate by the end of the next session, or the position becomes vacant again. John Bolton's recess appointment enabled him to represent his country at the UN until January 2007 without having to complete the nomination process. The appointment was made knowing that there would have been elections in November 2006, with one-third of Senators having to defend their seats. The presidential calculation may have been that John Bolton would face a less hostile Senate in his 2007 hearings. Equally, President Bush will have been aware that confirmations are often even harder to achieve after a recess appointment as Senators of both parties resent the President evading their scrutiny. In the end, with the Democratic Party gaining control of the Senate in the 2006 Congressional elections, it became clear that there was no chance of John Bolton being confirmed and he resigned before the hearings could take place.

## Organisation of the executive branch

In addition to facing scrutiny over who can be appointed to key positions, Presidents are restricted in how they organise the government departments they control. It is Congress that sets up the Executive Departments (such as the Department of Defense), which have primary responsibility for running the government; the Executive Agencies (such as the Federal Reserve Board), which have a greater degree of independence from the President and are also responsible for managing crucial areas of policy; and Independent Regulatory Commissions (such as the Federal Election Commission), which have an even greater degree of independence.

The organisation of these bodies can only be altered by an Act of Congress, giving the President extremely limited flexibility. When President Carter, for example, tried to transfer education programmes for ex-servicemen from the Veterans Administration to the Education Department, he was unable to gain sufficient support in Congress to make the change.

Presidents have more control over the Executive Office of the President (EOP), which they can reorganise whenever they choose. It was no surprise, therefore, that when it was proposed to set up an agency for Homeland Security after the attacks of 9/11, the President wanted it to be established as a part of the EOP. However, Congress insisted on establishing a new Executive Department, accountable to itself.

## Scrutinising treaties

As each presidency unfolds, agreements will be concluded with other nations. The President is responsible for diplomatic negotiations but once a formal agreement (or treaty) is reached, it must receive the support of two-thirds – sixty-seven votes – of the Senate. If the treaty receives the necessary level of support, sometimes with amendments, the President ratifies it and it becomes law. If the Senate and President cannot agree, however, the treaty does not come into effect.

When the Versailles Treaty, formally ending the First World War, was negotiated in 1919, it was largely based on proposals from President Wilson. Yet, when it was considered by the Senate it did not have the level of support it needed and the USA never ratified it. Since then, most treaties negotiated by US Presidents have gained the support of the Senate. A significant minority, however, have not:

- In 1979, President Carter negotiated the second Strategic Arms Limitation Treaty (SALT II) with the Soviet Union, which limited the manufacture of large nuclear missiles. Six months after the treaty was signed, but before the Senate had completed its consideration of the agreement, the Soviet Union invaded Afghanistan, relations between the two countries rapidly deteriorated and the treaty was never ratified. Despite this, both sides honoured the terms of the agreement.
- In 1996, President Clinton negotiated the Comprehensive Test Ban Treaty (CTBT), which banned testing of nuclear weapons as a way of stopping countries that did not already have such devices from being able to acquire them and test their effectiveness. The Senate did not vote on the treaty until 1999, as the President sought to build support for it, but when they did vote it fell far short of the two-thirds majority needed. Its opponents argued that it

risked eroding the USA's lead in nuclear weapons technology and would be impossible to monitor.

- In 1998, the Clinton administration signed the Kyoto Protocol, an international treaty to reduce greenhouse gas emissions and thereby reduce global warming. Even before the Kyoto Protocol was negotiated, however, the US Senate unanimously passed by a 95–0 vote the Byrd-Hagel Resolution, which made clear that the Senate did not believe that such a treaty would be in the best interests of the USA. Consequently, the treaty was never put to the Senate for its agreement.

As with presidential appointments, however, there is a loophole for Presidents who realise at an early stage that there is insufficient support in the Senate for a treaty being negotiated. An **executive agreement** can be signed between the President and a foreign head of state. These do not require the approval of two-thirds of the Senate, but the Supreme Court ruled in 1937, in *United States* v. *Belmont*, that such agreements have the same status in international law as a treaty. The United States is currently a party to nearly 900 treaties and more than 5,000 executive agreements.

Congress attempted to close this loophole in 1972 with the passage of the Case-Zablocki Act, which required the President to report on executive agreements within sixty days of negotiating them. The ability of Congress to do anything about them, however, was limited by a 1983 Supreme Court decision in *INS* v. *Chadha*, which ruled that the Act breached separation of powers.

### Scrutinising presidential use of the armed forces

As well as negotiating with other nations, most Presidents since the Second World War have deployed US armed forces. Among the countries in which US troops have seen action over the past sixty years are Afghanistan, Bosnia-Herzegovina, Grenada, Haiti, Iraq (twice), Korea, Kosovo, Lebanon, Libya, Panama, Somalia and Vietnam.

Under the Constitution, only Congress can declare war. In none of these cases, however, was war declared. The President deployed America's armed forces in his capacity as Commander-in-Chief. That this could be done in Vietnam, in a conflict lasting over ten years, demonstrated that this was another area in which the President appeared able to avoid constitutional checks and balances. In 1973, at the end of the Vietnam War, the **War Powers Resolution** was passed to reassert Congressional control over armed conflict. It required the President to consult Congress whenever possible before using the armed forces and, in every case, to report to Congress within forty-eight hours of introducing troops to an area of conflict. Thereafter, if Congress does not declare war within sixty days, the troops have to be withdrawn.

In practice, Congress has proved reluctant to exercise this right to challenge the President's actions for fear that it may undermine morale among the armed forces or signal division to an enemy.

### Scrutinising presidential legislative proposals

These kinds of loopholes are not as evident in domestic policy. Each January, usually around the 20th, the President makes his State of the Union Address, outlining the challenges facing the country and his policy proposals for dealing with them. Over the following months, he will put forward legislative proposals to change Federal laws to meet his objectives. The President cannot, however, introduce bills into Congress. He requires sympathetic members of the House of Representatives and of the Senate to introduce his bills into the two chambers.

The process that the bills then go through are outlined in detail below. It is a convention that the President's proposals will not be blocked as they make their way through Congress. In common with other bills, however, they may be amended during their passage. Indeed, presidential proposals are more likely than most to be amended *because* they are virtually guaranteed to clear the many hurdles all bills face and therefore represent a prime opportunity to attach amendments that will benefit districts of individual Congressmen and Senators.[1]

By the time the President's proposals return to him, to be signed into law, they will certainly have been substantially changed and may have been transformed so dramatically that he finds himself forced to

---

[1] Members of the House of Representatives are known (confusingly) as Congressmen/Congresswomen; members of the Senate are known as Senators.

veto them. This situation can arise even when the two chambers of Congress are controlled by the same political party as the President.

### Overriding vetoes

A bill does not become law unless it is signed by the President. If he finds a bill unacceptable, there are a number of responses at his disposal (see below). One option is to veto it, which is done by refusing to sign the bill and returning it to Congress with an explanation of his objections.

The bill will become law, however, if two-thirds of both chambers vote to override the veto. This is a very challenging hurdle to clear. During his two terms as President, Bill Clinton vetoed thirty-six bills and had his **veto** overridden just twice.

### Scrutinising presidential budgetary proposals

On the first Monday in February, the President follows up his State of the Union Address by sending up a detailed budget to Congress, outlining the costs of his proposals and precisely how he would like to see the Federal taxes for that year spent.

Article I, Section 7 of the Constitution makes the House of Representatives responsible for scrutinising 'all bills for raising revenue' first, although the Senate may do so later. The House and Senate both have budget committees that spend the next couple of months developing their own budget proposals, and amendments can be offered at each stage of the budget's passage through Congress. The result is that most budgets become 'Christmas Tree' bills, covered with presents for the voters of the 435 districts of the USA.

Congress does not only add to the President's proposals. Where there is strong disagreement, Congress may also cut proposals. Thus, in 2003, when President George W. Bush proposed tax cuts of $550 billion, members of his own party who were concerned about the growing budget deficit managed to reduce the amount in the final package to $350 billion.

### Congressional investigations

When a major issue arises that suggests that the executive branch has been corrupt or incompetent, any Congressional committee may mount an investigation. Often, if the issue has attracted a great deal of media attention, a number of committees may mount simultaneous investigations.

The most famous example of Congress investigating corruption in the executive branch in modern times was the Watergate hearings, looking into a complex web of political scandals between 1972 and 1974 that ultimately led to the resignation of President Richard Nixon. Other similar investigations, such as the Iran-Contra hearings in 1987, which examined illegal sales of arms to Iran to raise funds for anti-government forces in Nicaragua, made much less impact.

In 1994, Congress added to its armoury, passing the **Independent Counsel** Law, which gives the House or Senate judiciary committees the right to require the Justice Department to investigate claims of criminal behaviour by senior members of the executive. This law has proved controversial because, although it is designed to effectively investigate abuse of power, there are no limits to the Independent Counsel's powers of investigation. In 1994, Kenneth Starr was appointed Independent Counsel to investigate investments made by President Clinton some years earlier. By 1998, Starr had widened his investigations to include allegations of sexual misconduct by the President, leading to **impeachment** proceedings.

After Hurricane Katrina devastated the city of New Orleans, with heavy loss of life, in 2005, both the House of Representatives and the Senate investigated why the authorities failed to effectively protect the city's mainly African American residents. No fewer than nine committees investigated the disaster and produced reports and recommendations:

- Senate Homeland Security and Government Affairs Committee
- Senate Environment and Public Works Committee
- Senate Commerce, Science, and Transportation Committee
- House **Select Committee** on Hurricane Katrina
- House Transportation and Infrastructure Committee
- House Energy and Commerce Committee
- House Science Committee
- House Government Reform Committee
- Government Accountability Office

Note that among these committees was one set up specifically for the purpose of investigating the consequences of the hurricane (highlighted). These are known as select committees. They study one specific issue and report their findings to the House of Representatives or the Senate.

### Impeachment

In the event of there being evidence of wrongdoing by a senior member of the executive branch, or judicial branch, impeachment proceedings may begin.

If it is presented with evidence of 'Treason, Bribery or other High crimes and Misdemeanours' (Article II, Section 4 of the Constitution), it is the exclusive responsibility of the House of Representative to bring articles of impeachment (charges) against the accused person. These charges must have the support of a majority of Congressmen.

If a vote passes in the House, a trial takes place in the Senate. If the proceedings involve the President, then the Chief Justice of the Supreme Court acts as the judge. The House of Representatives, having brought the charges, acts as the prosecution. The accused person will have a team of defence lawyers. The Senate acts as the jury. If two-thirds (sixty-seven) of the Senate votes against the defendant, a guilty verdict is delivered and the person is removed from office.

As a result of the investigations carried out by Independent Counsel Kenneth Starr in December 1998, the House of Representatives charged (impeached) President Clinton with two counts of lying under oath (perjury) and obstructing justice. At the end of the trial, the Senate voted 55–45 in the President's favour on the perjury charge and 50–50 on the obstruction of justice charge, leading to his acquittal.

Two other Presidents have had impeachment proceedings brought against them. In 1868, President Andrew Johnson was acquitted by just one vote and in 1974 President Richard Nixon resigned before the trial could take place.

This form of scrutiny is, arguably, the most dramatic action that Congress can take against a President. It is also, however, the least frequently used and when considering its importance this should be taken into account. Its significance is greater in relation to the judiciary, as a number of judges have been successfully impeached.

## Congress and the judiciary

### Limited range of checks

As the Constitution provided the judicial branch with few constitu-tional powers, it faces few constitutional checks. However, it subse-quently acquired the power of judicial review, enabling it to declare laws unconstitutional. Congress has developed two responses to the use of this power.

### Modifying laws

When the Supreme Court declares a law unconstitutional, it gives detailed reasons for its decisions. Congress, often with the help of constitutional experts, may closely examine the Justices' opinions and then make minor, technical adjustments to their legislation to address the objections of the Court without significantly altering the purpose of the law.

In 2000, for example, in the case of *Stenberg* v. *Carhart*, the Supreme Court struck down a Nebraska law banning a particular type of abortion, 'partial birth abortion', on the grounds that the law did not make an exception for the procedure to take place if the mother's health was at risk. In 2003, Congress passed a partial birth abortion law that was almost identical to the Nebraska law. However, taking note of the Supreme Court's earlier ruling, it included a clause stating that this type of abortion was never medically essential and therefore a health exception was not needed. In 2007, in *Gonzales* v. *Carhart*, the Supreme Court upheld this slightly modified Federal law banning 'partial birth' abortion.

### Initiating constitutional amendments

Supreme Court decisions can be overruled by a constitutional amendment. This has happened on two occasions.

In 1795, the 11th Amendment was passed in response to the Supreme Court's ruling in *Chisholm* v. *Georgia* that citizens could bring lawsuits against a state. There was a widespread view at the time that this could result in the states losing authority.

In 1913, the 16th Amendment was passed in response to a ruling that the Federal government did not have the constitutional right to levy income tax.

## Impeachment

As with the executive branch, Congress has the right to remove judges from office for wrongdoing. Constitutionally, this power may not be used because a majority in Congress disagree with judicial decisions but there have been attempts to use it in this way. There were repeated calls, especially from the South, for Chief Justice Earl Warren to be impeached for exceeding his constitutional powers after the ruling banning racial segregation. The only Supreme Court Justice to face an impeachment trial was Samuel Chase, who was acquitted in 1805. The unsuccessful proceedings were a blatant attempt by the President's party to intimidate their political opponents.

Eleven other Federal judges have been impeached, of whom seven have been found guilty and removed from office. The most recent was Walter Nixon of the US District Court for Mississippi, who was removed from office in 1989 for a range of offences including lying to a grand jury.

# Legislating

## Limited government

The process for passing laws in Congress makes it much easier for initiatives to be blocked than for them to pass. Each year, as many as 10,000 bills may be introduced but often fewer than 500 become law.

Such a low rate of success could be seen as a sign of ineffectiveness. It could also be seen, however, as consistent with the constitutional values of limited government. The great fear of the Founding Fathers was that the national government would grow in power and, ultimately, become oppressive. Each law passed has the potential to add to the powers of those who pass and administer them, eventually realising the Founding Fathers' worst nightmares. Fewer laws ought to limit the growth and scope of government, reducing the risk of intrusion into people's lives. Furthermore, if only a few, essential, laws are passed, then the quality of the legislation ought to be high.

Critics of Congress, however, argue that the legislative process often has the opposite effect, with legislation that enhances the likelihood of being re-elected being prioritised over laws that would be of greatest value to the nation.

## Types of laws

Legislative proposals introduced into Congress fall into one of five categories. The first two are proposed without any expectation that they will become law:

- Those that demonstrate the commitment of a member of Congress (usually to the voters) to a policy that has no realistic chance of being adopted. Often this serves to put on record the member's hard work for his/her district.
- Those that serve to educate the public on an important area of public policy. Often these are sponsored by pressure groups, seeking to influence the public agenda. For example, the 'End Racial Profiling Bill', strongly supported by African American Civil Rights organisations, has been repeatedly introduced to highlight the view that police officers continue to stop and search people on the basis of their race despite earlier legislation to end the practice.

Other laws have a higher likelihood of passing:

- Private bills that are used by Congressmen to highlight a specific concern of one of their constituents or remedy an injustice on the part of the executive branch. Once commonplace, the number of these bills has declined significantly.
- Joint resolutions, which go through the same processes as a bill but are often used to amend or correct errors in earlier bills.
- Public bills, which cover major issues, usually with national significance.

Some public bills have a higher probability of becoming law than others:

- Presidential proposals, introduced on his behalf by Congressmen, are by no means guaranteed to survive their passage through the legislature. However, they tend to receive more publicity than most other bills and the President is able to use his high, nationwide-profile campaign for his proposals and to argue that members of Congress are failing to put the interests of the country ahead of their own local concerns.
- Reauthorisation bills provide funds for important public projects, such as maintaining the nation's transport systems, for a number

of years before being reviewed. These bills are almost certain to pass, although they may encounter difficulties as they do so.

## The Congressional timetable

Apart from the series of hurdles a bill has to clear before it becomes a law, the amount of time available to consider the annual avalanche of proposals is extremely limited.

- *January* A session begins at noon on 3 January. The first few weeks may be spent working on any major bills left over from the previous session. Work on new proposals tends to wait until after the President's State of the Union Address, usually around 20 January, which largely shapes the political agenda for the year.
- *February* Congress receives the President's budget on the first Monday of the month. Most of the month is spent reviewing this and rival budgetary proposals, except for the third week of February when Congress recesses for a week for President's Day. (During recesses, members of Congress have an opportunity to spend time in their districts.)
- *March* Congress, ideally, completes work on the budget so that it is known how much money will be raised in taxes to fund any bills that become law that year. Other bills start to make their way through Congress.
- *April* Work on the bills continues but there will be a week-long recess for Easter. Most years the budget is still being debated by this time and work on other bills is held up as a result.
- *May* Bills should be nearing completion, but often the work that should have been done in April takes place this month. Congress recesses for the last week of the month for Memorial Day. In an election year, Congressmen may have to face a primary election in their district around this time.
- *June* Appropriations committees, which decide how much money each proposed project may have, start work.
- *July* There will be a week-long recess for the 4 July Independence Day holiday. Outstanding work on bills and by the appropriations committees should be completed by the end of the month, although most years very few bills are as advanced as scheduled.
- *August* Summer recess.

- *September* The House and Senate should have each passed their versions of appropriations bills and will need to reconcile them, although it is almost unknown for the process to be completed this early. In election years, those who have survived their primaries are conscious that the first week of November is fast looming.
- *October* Work to complete bills continues, except in election years when all Congressmen and a third of the Senators return home to campaign.
- *November–December* This should be time for members of Congress to spend a prolonged period in their districts. Most years, there is still a substantial amount of work to be done and work may continue up to Christmas Eve, with a recess for Thanksgiving in the third week of November.

### The legislative process: first reading

Two magic numbers are required for a legislative proposal to become law: 218 and 60. These are the votes a bill must receive in the House of Representatives and the Senate for it to pass through both chambers of Congress, in identical form, to become law. The following six sections will consider the various ways the magic numbers are reached and why, much of the time, they are not.

The first two stages of its passage are known as the first reading and only a small proportion of bills successfully survive this part of the process.

*Stage 1: Introducing a bill* Each bill is drafted by a member of Congress, with the support of his/her own staff, perhaps a pressure group, perhaps a White House staff member or perhaps a lawyer from one of the Congressional committees. The member will attempt to attract co-sponsors to show that the bill has wide support. The member will also need to find a sympathetic member of the other chamber to introduce the bill.

In the House of Representatives, the bill has to be placed in a wooden box, known as the Hopper. In the Senate, it is given to the presiding officer's clerk. In each case the bill will be given a number and name. Acronyms are popular, such as the Provide Tools Required to Intercept and Obstruct Terrorism (PATRIOT) Act of 2001.

*Stage 2: Committee action* All bills are sent to a committee for detailed consideration. In the House, the Speaker decides which committee to refer it to. The Speaker can make a range of choices about the future of a bill, and this decision is highly political. The speaker can:

- **Refer** it to a single committee that deals with its subject matter for consideration.
- Send it to two or more committees for **concurrent referral**, in which they work on the bill at the same time.
- Send it to two or more committees for **sequential referral**, in which first one, then the others, consider the bill.
- Split the bill into several portions that are then sent to as many committees as appropriate in a **split referral**.
- Put a limit on the time the bill has to complete its passage.

The choices the Speaker makes significantly influence the likelihood of a bill passing. Referral to a single committee with no time limit reduces the number of hurdles a bill has to clear. It also indicates the Speaker's support for the proposal. As everyone in the House with key decision-making powers owes their position to the Speaker, Congressmen are careful not to alienate him/her and so bills with his/her support have a greater likelihood of negotiating obstacles in their way.

The equivalent stage in the Senate is much more straightforward. Bills are referred to committee by the staff of the presiding officer, with none of the political implications that accompany such decisions in the House.

When a bill reaches its designated committee, one of three things can happen.

- If it does not enjoy the support of the committee chairman, it can be simply ignored. This is known as **pigeonholing**, and a majority of bills get no further than this point.
- Alternatively, the chairman can bring the bill before the whole committee, or a subcommittee, for consideration. If a majority of the committee do not support the proposals, and vote against them, the bill will be killed.
- The third possibility is that the bill will be given careful, sympathetic consideration. If this happens, then:
  - **Hearings** will be held, in which experts and pressure groups will testify on the advantages and disadvantages of the bill.

- At the end of this process, the committee will **mark up** the bill, including any amendments they decide are appropriate.
- The committee will then **report out** the bill to the whole chamber. Ideally, from the point of view of its sponsors, it will leave with a positive recommendation, but it can be reported out without a recommendation.

### Committee chairmen: legislative czars

With so much power residing in the hands of this small group of people, the position of committee chairman has always been controversial. One political scientist compared them to a 'toll bridge attendant who argues and bargains with each prospective customer; who lets his friend go free, who will not let his enemies pass at any price'.

Traditionally, chairmen were appointed on the basis of seniority. This had the advantage of rewarding experience and the consequent expertise that developed over time. It was challenged, however, because it was perceived to reward longevity over merit and, because chairmen were almost guaranteed re-election, was thought to lead to political complacency and abuse of power.

Two waves of Congressmen have challenged the seniority principle. In the 1974 mid-term elections, at the height of the Watergate scandal, the new young Democrats who swept the election on a promise to clean up government were not prepared to wait until they attained seniority before they made an impact and challenged the existing chairmen. The seniority system gradually re-established itself until, in the 1994 mid-terms, Republicans captured the House with their Contract with America campaign, which included a raft of proposals to reform Congress.

The then Speaker, Newt Gingrich, selected the Congressmen who he believed to be most committed to the Contract as committee chairmen, in consultation with the House Republican Steering Committee, which contained the other leading members of the party such as the majority leader. His decision required the ratification of all the other Republicans in the House, organised into the Republican Conference.

In many cases, he found the most senior Republican on each committee to be acceptable, but anyone who had been too accommodating to Democrats was passed over and the chairmanship given to a more committed conservative, including the chairmanship of the powerful Appropriations Committee. The Speaker also has the power to reorganise the committees, which may include eliminating or adding some.

This wave of Republicans also imposed a rule on themselves (which did not apply to Democrats when they regained control of the House) that committee chairmen can serve no longer than six years. The only exception to this rule was the House Rules Committee, whose chairman 'serves at the pleasure' of the Speaker.

The term limits imposed in 1994 took effect after the 2000 election. Retirements, followed by replacements, meant that some of the chairmen had not yet served six years at that point, but fourteen out of twenty House chairmen were forced to step down. As before, the Speaker (by then Dennis Hastert) allowed the most senior Republican on each committee to become the next chairman in most instances, but in some cases, such as the powerful Ways and Means Committee, installed a Congressman who did not have seniority.

This arrangement highlighted three advantages of the old seniority system that were not widely recognised at the time. Firstly, since chairmanships are usually the pinnacle of a Congressman's career, they often leave the House once they lose their position. Of the fourteen who were term-limited in 2000, nine left the House within two years. Opponents of the system argue that it leads to the unnecessary loss of talent. Secondly, because of the possibility of leap-frogging more senior members, ambitious Congressmen mount behind-the-scenes campaigns for chairmanships that can last for up to two years before a term limit comes into effect, which is a distraction from their primary commitments and divisive within the party. Thirdly, since 1994 the senior House Republicans, who choose the chairmen, have all been committed conservative on the right of their party. This power of patronage has tended to shift the centre of gravity within the Republican Conference.

### Pork-barrel politics and logrolling
Clearly, it is advantageous to a bill if the Speaker and other key members of Congress support its aims and objectives. They may also find a bill attractive, however, if it provides Federal funds for projects in their districts.

Many bills, therefore, have such proposals added to them to aid their passage. This is known in political circles as **pork-barrel politics**. An example of how this works can be illustrated by the experience of Congressman Bill Young, who represented the 10th District of Florida. He had been bypassed in 1994 as committee chairman for not having a sufficiently conservative voting record. He was somewhat less moderate in the following years and was rewarded with the chairmanship of the Appropriations Committee in 1998. In the 108th Congress, between 2002 and 2004, he saw $80 million allocated to his district for military projects and another $30 million allocated to his state, Florida, to rebuild eroded beaches. In the subsequent Congress, he secured $116 million for Florida projects.

Sponsors of bills also have to be sensitive to the needs of less influential members of Congress. This may involve agreeing to support bills brought forward by other members in return for votes. This is known as **logrolling**.

### The legislative process: second reading

*Stage 3: Floor action* This stage, like the first, sees a significant difference in procedure between the House and the Senate. In the House, the powerful Rules Committee makes two decisions that have a critical impact on a bill:

- When to schedule a bill for debate. The later in the year that a bill is scheduled, the less likely it is to complete its passage before running out of time.
- Which rule a bill should be debated under. The three options are:
  - **open rule**, which permits amendments to a bill. Under this rule, a bill may be amended out of all recognition.
  - **modified open rule**, which permits amendments to specified parts of a bill.
  - **closed rule**, which allows no amendments.

In the Senate, there is a tradition of unlimited debate. The Senate Rules Committee therefore plays a much more minor role than in the House. However, a bill may be subject to a filibuster on the floor of the Senate, a blocking mechanism in which a single

Senator, or a group working together, can stop a vote from being called. If this process continues for long enough, with all other work being held up, supporters of a bill may withdraw it, in which case it dies.

A filibuster can only be ended by a **cloture motion**. Until 1975, it took a two-thirds majority, or sixty-seven votes, to win a cloture motion. After a rule change, the number needed was reduced to three-fifths, or sixty votes (one of the magic numbers), but even this figure is hard to attain.

Once a debate has taken place in both chambers, all members of Congress have an opportunity to vote on the House and Senate versions of the bill, which may be, by this time, quite different. In both cases, a simple majority is required, which is 218 in the House (the other magic number) and 51 in the Senate. If this threshold is not met in one of the chambers, the bill dies. If it clears this hurdle, however, it still faces the challenge of reconciling the two versions.

### The legislative process: reconciling two versions of a bill

*Stage 4: Conference Committee* Both the House and the Senate appoint representatives to negotiate an agreed version of a bill. Usually these are the people who have played the pivotal role of shepherding the bill through their respective committees and much of the negotiating is carried out by phone and e-mail between the specialist staff they employ.

Periodically, the two sides become deadlocked, in which case the bill will die. Usually, however, a bill that has reached this stage has enough support for the conferees to find a way to compromise with each other.

The agreed version is then sent back to the two chambers for their approval. Sometimes one of the chambers finds the compromises made on their behalf unacceptable and votes against it. In this case, further negotiations take place in the Conference Committee, but it is possible that even at this late stage one of the chambers will kill the bill. If, as is usual, both chambers vote for it, the bill will have been approved by Congress.

### Presidential signature

A bill cannot become law until it has been signed by the President. At this stage, any delay in the bill's passage through Congress becomes crucial.

If the bill is sent to the President shortly before the end of the Congressional year, when Congress is about to adjourn, it will die if the President fails to sign it within ten days. The President does not need to publicly reject the bill, he can ignore it and allow it to quietly expire. This is known as the **pocket veto**.

If, on the other hand, a bill is sent to the President while Congress is in session, and he fails to sign it within ten days, it becomes law.

Most bills, however, culminate in a much more public fashion. If the President strongly objects to a bill he will veto it, in which case he will return it to Congress with an explanation of why he has refused to sign it. If the bill has enough support in Congress they can over-ride a veto with a two-thirds majority in both chambers, at which point it becomes law.

If the President signs a bill, he usually does so in a public ceremony that gives him an opportunity to take a significant share of the credit for the benefits the new law will bring. In a rare case, in 2002 the Bi-partisan Campaign Reform Bill was signed behind closed doors, indicating the President's dissatisfaction with a law he described as 'far from perfect'. More typically, in 2001 the No Child Left Behind Act was signed in a classroom in Ohio, with the President surrounded by the Act's most senior Congressional supporters, students and teachers, to demonstrate how many groups had faith in its ability to transform America's education system.

## Representation: promoting the interests of constituents

### Visibility in the district

There is almost 5,000 miles between Washington DC and the most distant state of Hawaii. There may be as much as 3,600 miles between the capital and the district of many other Congressmen. For constituents, the work of their Congressman and Senators is very distant in a geographical sense. With all the technicalities and procedures required to get legislation through Congress, their work may appear distant in a practical sense as well.

Members of Congress, therefore, face a constant challenge to ensure that they are seen to be in touch with the people, issues and needs of their district. This is done in a variety of ways (see below), but none is more important than being seen in the district, sharing in the daily activities of their constituents as well as being available to listen to their concerns in person.

The Congressional year is organised to help Congressmen meet this challenge. Most Congressmen return to their districts most week-ends. For those in distant states, such as California, this will usually mean flying home late on Thursday, fulfilling commitments in their district on Friday and Saturday, having a little family time on Sunday and taking the 3,000-mile flight back to Washington DC on Monday morning. The week-long recesses give Congressmen an opportunity to also spend time in their districts during the working week with reasonable frequency, giving them an opportunity to engage with a different range of people and activities, perhaps in schools and local businesses.

### Accessibility to constituents

Apart from appearances in the district, members of Congress have a variety of methods of making themselves accessible to their constituents:

- *District Office* All members of Congress have at least one office in their district that constituents can contact or visit with enquiries or concerns. In larger districts, such as that of Congressman Earl Pomeroy, which covers the whole of sparsely populated North Dakota, more than one office may be required. He has one in the state capital, Bismarck, and another 188 miles away in Fargo. Similarly, Senator John Cornyn, who represents the whole of the massive state of Texas, has seven offices in different parts of the state. All of the staff in these offices are likely to have requests for his time and attention when he returns home.
- *Washington DC Office* All members also have an office in, or near, the Capitol building, which serves as a base for the specialist policy staff they use to support their work in committee or on

the floor of the chamber. Up to a dozen people work in these offices, of which three or more devote their time exclusively to dealing with constituent affairs. This includes giving tours of the building to constituents visiting Washington, often without prior arrangement.

- *Post* The need to keep constituents informed of their work in Washington DC has meant that members of Congress have long been entitled to free postage. These **franking privileges** may only be used for keeping constituents informed on issues or Congressional business and may not be used for anything relating to election campaigns. Despite this, members use them a great deal more in election years than in other years.
- *Websites* Traditional communications have been supplemented by modern information technology. All members have their own websites, which can be accessed directly or through the House and Senate websites. Generally, member sites cover where they stand on key issues, speeches they have made, how they have voted, photos of events they have attended and how they can be contacted. Overall, member sites seek to convey an understanding of how hard they work in their constituents' interests.
- *E-mail* Members' offices can also be contacted by e-mail. Any member of staff may receive up to 300 e-mails each day from constituents, lobbyists, Congressional staff and others, but those from constituents are almost always given priority.
- *C-Span* The work of Congress, in committee and on the floor, as well as major speeches and press conferences, are carried live on Congress's dedicated broadcasting service, which has three television channels and a radio station. Much of the daily work of Congress makes dull viewing but Congressional staff report that whenever a speech is made or a vote taken, at least two or three phone calls will be received from constituents with an enquiry or an opinion on the member's actions, demonstrating that a significant minority of constituents are keeping an eye on their representatives' work. It is estimated that whatever impression the constituent takes away from their phone call to the office will be shared with, on average, twenty friends, relatives, neighbours or work colleagues, so these frequent contacts are significant.

## Bringing home the bacon

For all the efforts made by members to ensure their visibility and accessibility to constituents, they know that at election time they will mainly be judged by the number of projects, funded by the Federal government, that are authorised by Congress.

Congressmen know they will be judged by voters every two years and are particularly prone to indulge in pork-barrel politics. Senators, facing re-election every six years, are widely perceived to be more thoughtful representatives but also recognise the value of being seen to provide for their states.

# Importance of political parties in Congress

## Ideological commitment

The legislative and representative roles of members of Congress may create the impression that local affairs and winning re-election are the only factors that influence Congressional behaviour. This would be misleading. A majority of politicians first stood for election because they had a view of how their society should be run and, in many cases, were strongly opposed to the policies of the other main party. This kind of ideological conflict has always been played out in the corridors of Congress but has grown in intensity since the Republican Party seized control of the legislature in 1994 with a conservative agenda.

## Concentration of power in the hands of the House leaders

Important legislative proposals make little progress unless they are acceptable to the House leadership. In 2003, key details of the $400 billion Medicare Bill (providing healthcare for the elderly) were decided in private meetings between Speaker Hastert and leaders of the main pressure group representing people over fifty-five years of age, the AARP. The House and Senate Committees were completely bypassed. Then, when the bill completed its passage through the House, the Speaker held open the voting period for an unprecedented three hours, until the leadership had rounded up the Republican votes they needed.

## Partisanship

Under both Republican (1994–2006) and Democratic leadership (since 2006), the minority party has complained about being almost completely excluded from key legislative decisions in Congressional committees. In July 2003, relations between the two sides on the House Ways and Means Committee reached such a low point that the Democrats staged a protest in the committee room at the lack of consultation on major bills, and the chairman called the police to have them removed.

Although this incident was an extreme example of non-cooperation, an atmosphere of partisanship has dominated Congress and deeply affected its day-to-day work since the mid-1990s.

Similarly, in the House of Representatives, there has been far greater use of the closed rule (see above), which does not allow amendments to be proposed during floor debates. Just 15 per cent of bills were passed under the closed rule in the late 1970s; by 2003, the figure had risen to 76 per cent.

In the Senate, the minority party has made increasing use of the mechanisms that enable them to block bills which they are unable to influence. One method is to propose multiple amendments in the Senate, which has a tradition of unrestricted floor debate, thereby slowing down the progress of a bill. In the early 1990s, around 1,500 amendments were proposed per year; a decade later the number had risen to over 2,600. The other method is to filibuster a bill. In the same period, filibusters have risen from twenty-four per year to fifty-eight per year.

These deep divisions between parties has led to an increase in the number of votes that are cast purely on party lines. In the first year of President Obama's presidency, not a single Republican in the House of Representatives voted in favour of his two most important initiatives, the Stimulus Package to revive the economy and the bill to extend healthcare coverage in the USA.

## Evaluating Congress

The Founding Fathers intended the legislature to be the most important branch of the national government with responsibility for:

- Initiating policy
- Passing, or blocking, legislation
- Overseeing how legislation is implemented by the executive branch
- Having primary responsibility for voicing the wishes of the public
- Giving the electorate opportunities to hold policy-makers to account on a regular basis

To what extent has this happened?

## Initiating policy

Congress is clearly a policy-making legislature. It has the ability to formulate its own policies and pass them into law. However, it has not developed into the primary policy-making institution.

The political agenda is largely set by President in the annual State of the Union Address, and most major legislation that takes up the majority of Congress's time is proposed by the President. In practice, responding rapidly to events, as well as formulating a coherent programme of policies, is done more effectively by a small group of people with an identifiable leader.

Moreover, the judiciary has gone through periods of playing a prominent policy-making role. Using the power of judicial review, the Supreme Court led the policy agenda in a range of areas, such as the rights of suspects/prisoners, abortion rights and gay rights.

## Legislating

Once a policy proposal, in the form of a bill, starts to make its way through Congress, the legislature is able to be more assertive. It is able to block or amend (often substantially) proposed laws. Thus, even though Congress has, in large measure, surrendered its role of initiating policy to the presidency, it is still able to place its stamp on important measures and it is relatively rare for the President to get proposals through Congress without them being altered.

Similarly, while Congress is unable to stop the Supreme Court from 'legislating from the bench', it is able to limit judicial power through technical amendments to laws that have been declared unconstitutional, as demonstrated in the case of *Gonzales* v. *Carhart* (2007).

Overall, this may be seen as a negative use of power, with Congress stopping other branches from advancing policies rather than promoting a constructive agenda. This tendency is most evident when the President is from one party and Congress is controlled by the other party. Congress is often blamed by commentators and the public for the consequent **gridlock**, when few laws are passed. During the 110th Congress, starting in 2007, when a Democrat-controlled Congress was frequently at odds with the Republican President, George W. Bush, it was labelled the 'do nothing Congress'.

This negative role, however, may meet with approval from some sections of society. One of the reasons for setting up a system of separation of powers was to make it difficult to find agreement on policy and, thereby, limit the involvement of the national government in the lives of ordinary Americans. For people on the right of the political spectrum, the national government has become far too large and is far too interfering, which, in their view, serves to infringe personal freedoms. Whenever Congress limits the ability of the national government to extend its reach it serves the goal of limited government, which, they point out, was one of the principal objectives of the Founding Fathers.

The left, by contrast, tends to favour minimum standards being applied to all people across the country and often has little confidence in the willingness or ability of states to adequately meet the needs of all their residents, especially the more vulnerable sections of the community, who may be dependent on official support or protection. When Congress goes through a period of inactivity, therefore, it is often a cause for concern for the left.

### Scrutiny and oversight

It is the executive branch of government that is responsible for implementing laws that Congress has passed. The presidency also has primary responsibility for foreign policy and national security. These roles potentially give the executive branch great power and it is the responsibility of Congress to ensure that this power is used responsibly and does not result in the emergence of a monarch-like figure that was so feared by the Founding Fathers.

In this respect, Congress has a wide range of weapons in its armoury, some of which it uses frequently and aggressively:

- It uses its power to organise the executive branch of government to ensure that, as far as possible, each department is answerable to the legislature, as demonstrated when, in 2003, (Republican-controlled) Congress insisted that Homeland Security was managed by an executive department and not, as proposed by the (Republican) President, that it be incorporated into the Executive Office of the Presidency, where it would be subject to less scrutiny.
- It carefully scrutinises proposed presidential appointments.
- It monitors the work of executive departments and agencies, and has the resources and expertise to do so effectively.
- It mounts investigations into any revelations of incompetence or misconduct that has caused public concern (such as the government's response to Hurricane Katrina in 2005).

Each of these checks on executive power, however, relates to domestic policy. In foreign affairs, the loopholes available to the President, to sign executive agreements rather than treaties and to go to war without requesting a formal declaration of war from Congress (using his powers as Commander-in-Chief) have led to a perception that Congress is less effective in this area.

Again, there is some disagreement among Americans, based on ideology, on whether the relative ineffectiveness of Congress in foreign affairs is a cause for concern. For people on the right, who tend to believe that security and protecting the national interest is an important and legitimate responsibility of the national government, it is important for the President to have as much flexibility as he needs in foreign affairs. If he were to have to wait for Congressional approval (which may be preceded by public debates that reveal a lack of national unity) it could weaken his position, which, in turn, could weaken the country's negotiating position in international affairs or even threaten national security. For people on the left, who tend to highlight the extent to which it is people from the poorer sections of society, as well as racial minorities, who make up a disproportionate share of those who are sent to fight and die each time the President sends the military into action, it is important that Congress should play the role intended for it by the Founding Fathers, so that such decisions are not made too swiftly or lightly.

## Representation and accountability

A substantial proportion of both houses of Congress have served for many years (in some cases, decades). This may suggest that they are not being effectively held to account. However, it may also be an indication that members of Congress tend to be responsive to the needs and wishes of their constituents. Certainly, the variety of ways in which they make themselves available to their constituents and the resources and expertise available to them when they need to respond to requests for information suggests that this is the case. If there is a criticism of the way in which members of Congress represent their voters, it is that they give this role too high a priority, putting local interests above the national interest and driving up government expenditure by their determination to include Federally funded projects in bills that are likely to become law, which often makes such legislation unwieldy.

Furthermore, there have also been attempts to ensure that Congress is somewhat reflective of the population of the USA. Since the 1970s, when district boundaries for the House of Representatives have been drawn up, there have been conscious attempts to do so in ways that maximise the representation of racial and ethnic minorities. As state boundaries remain static and there are very few states where distinct racial or ethnic minorities can outvote white communities, minority representation in the Senate remains low.

## Conclusion

Overall, Congress is not held in high regard by most Americans. It is often viewed as inefficient, especially when passing legislation. The Highways Bill, for example, which should have been completed by September 2003, was not completed until August 2005. It is also often viewed as irresponsible. The apparent lack of concern for the Federal deficit and the determination to secure lucrative contracts for their districts result in spending decisions that are widely seen as wasteful. And much of its work, when scrutinising the executive, is dull and routine, not attracting much attention from the media and therefore gaining little credit from the general public. Additionally, in some respects, especially initiating policy, it has clearly fallen short of the hopes and expectations of the Founding Fathers.

However, members of Congress are viewed as effective represent-atives of their constituents. Between elections, they invariably secure projects that produce both jobs and improved services for their con-stituents. As a result, most Americans believe that their representa-tive is doing an excellent job and with so much Federal money being brought into the district, it is rare for members of Congress to be defeated at elections unless they have become embroiled in scandal.

The public perception that Congress is inefficient and often irresponsible has a subtle, but highly significant, impact on its place in the system of checks and balances. Despite the range of restric-tions that Congress actively imposes on the executive branch, there has long been a sense that power has tended to drift away from the Capitol towards the White House, a trend that intensifies at times of crisis. In part, this is due to the executive having taken over respon-sibility for deciding national political priorities. In part, this is due to a widespread belief that Presidents are more likely than Congress to act in the national interest and take decisive action. It is striking that public esteem for Congress has risen, and that it has been particularly effective in imposing its will, whenever respect for the presidency has fallen, such as during the Watergate crisis in the 1970s and when it was revealed that President Clinton had become involved with an intern in the 1990s. Conversely, in the aftermath of the 9/11 attacks in 2001, the standing of the President rose dramatically and Congress adopted a highly deferential role.

Overall, therefore, weighing up the effectiveness of Congress requires an assessment of both its performance in all three of its roles, which are perceived to be of greatest importance, and its responses to the main issues of the day.

· · · · · · · · · · · · · · · · · · · · · · · · · · · · · · · · · · · · · · · · · · · · · · ·

### ✓ What you should have learnt from reading this chapter

- Congress was expected by the Founding Fathers to be the most important and powerful branch of the national government and, in large measure, the Constitution was designed to ensure that this would be the case.

- In order to judge the extent to which the Founding Fathers' expectations have been realised, it is essential to have a firm grasp of the relationship between Congress and the other branches of government and of how legislation is passed. The bulk of the chapter is devoted to providing this information.

- An understanding of the work of Congress is then rounded out with an explanation of the representative role of members of Congress and the impact of political parties.

- All of this information provides a platform for assessing the effectiveness of Congress. There are, however, a variety of ways in which Congress can be assessed. Each of its three main roles (legislating, scrutiny and representation) may be judged separately. Such assessments tend to highlight contrasting ideological perspectives on its work. Alternatively, an attempt can be made to provide an overall assessment of its work, considering all of its roles. To do this, however, requires a judgment both of performance and of the relative importance of each role, as well as an understanding of how changing circumstances can affect an overall conclusion.

## Glossary of key terms

**Closed rule**  A rule that allows no amendments to a bill as it is being debated on the floor of the House of Representatives.
**Cloture motion**  A vote to end a filibuster, requiring three-fifths of the Senate (sixty votes).
**Concurrent referral**  Sending a bill to two or more committees, for consideration at the same time.
**Confirmation**  A process, culminating in a majority vote, agreeing (or refusing) to appoint a person nominated by the President to an executive or judicial post.
**Elastic clause**  The constitutional clause providing Congress with the right to take any 'necessary and proper' steps to meet its constitutional responsibilities.
**Enumerated powers**  Specific powers granted to Congress by the Constitution.
**Executive agreement**  An international agreement, signed between the President and a foreign head of state, that does not require the approval of two-thirds of the Senate in order to come into effect but has the same status in international law as a treaty.
**Filibuster**  A device available to Senators enabling them to block a vote on a measure by prolonging a debate.
**Franking privileges**  Free postage available for members of Congress for official business.
**Gridlock**  A term applied to a situation when Congress and the President cannot agree on policy and, over an extended period, few laws are passed.

**Hearing** A session of a Congressional committee, usually in public, to explore details of a matter the committee is considering, with experts or people with an interest in the issue.

**Impeachment** A term applied to the process of investigating, accusing, trying and convicting a high-ranking government official, although properly it applies to the formal accusation made by the House of Representatives.

**Independent Counsel** A special prosecutor appointed to investigate allegations of misconduct by high-ranking government officials.

**Logrolling** The trading of votes between members of Congress, in which some agree to support a measure, usually benefiting a colleague's district, in return for reciprocal support for measures benefiting their own district.

**Mark up** The process by which a Congressional committee amends and/ or approves a bill before releasing it to be voted on by the whole chamber.

**Modified open rule** A rule that permits amendments to specified parts of a bill when it is being debated on the floor of the House of Representatives.

**Open rule** A rule that allows unlimited amendments to a bill when legislation is being debated on the floor of the House of Representatives.

**Overriding a veto** The process of passing a bill into law, after it has been vetoed by the President, with a vote in favour of the measure by a two-thirds majority in both chambers of Congress.

**Pigeonholing** A decision by a committee chairman not to consider a bill, thereby killing it.

**Pocket veto** The refusal by a President to sign a bill into law within ten days of the end of the Congressional year, thereby causing it to expire.

**Pork-barrel politics** A term applied to members of Congress agreeing to amendments added to appropriations (spending) bills that benefit each other's districts.

**Ratification** A process, culminating in a two-thirds majority vote, agreeing (or refusing) to confirm a treaty entered into by the President.

**Recess appointments** The constitutional power of Presidents to make an appointment when Congress is not sitting, often used to evade the requirement for Senate confirmation.

**Refer (a bill)** To transfer a bill to a committee for consideration.

**Report out** When a Congressional committee has given its approval to a bill, it will report its reasons for supporting it to the whole chamber.

**Select committee** A committee established to consider a specific issue (such as the impact of Hurricane Katrina) and report to its chamber, after which it is usually dissolved.

**Sequential referral** Sending a bill to two or more committees for one to consider it with the other(s) starting work on it only when the first committee has finished considering it.

**Split referral** Splitting a bill into several portions which are then sent to a variety of committees for consideration.

**Veto** The refusal by a President to sign a bill into law, returning it to Congress with his objections.

**War Powers Resolution** A law passed in 1973, requiring the President to consult Congress before using the armed forces whenever possible and, in every case, to report to Congress within forty-eight hours of introducing troops to an area of conflict. Thereafter, if Congress does not declare war within sixty days, the troops have to be withdrawn.

## Likely examination questions

Issues examiners may expect students to be able to effectively analyse include:

- The powers of Congress and each of its two chambers

- The role of Congress in the system of checks and balances

- The operation of Congress (legislative, scrutiny and representation) and its power centres

- The effectiveness of Congress in fulfilling its roles

Thus, examples of the kind of questions which could be asked include:

To what extent are the House of Representatives and the Senate equal in power and influence?

How effective is Congress at holding the President to account?

## Helpful websites

- The official websites of the House of Representatives and the Senate contain information about the legislatives proposals being considered and provide links to the websites of all of the Congressmen and Senators. Their websites are, respectively, www.house.gov and www.senate.gov.

- The website of the respected political journal *Congressional Quarterly* provides a free subscription to its Midday Update, which is sent to subscribers' e-mail inboxes each day that Congress is sitting. It provides concise comments on the latest developments in Congress as well as news and gossip about forthcoming electoral contests. Its address is www.cq.com.

- The two daily newspapers that serve Congress are also available online. They are *The Hill* and *Roll Call*. Their websites are www.hillnews.com and www.rollcall.com.

**Suggestions for further reading**

For an accessible, but detailed, account of the workings of Congress, including advice to Americans on how to make use of Congressional services, read *Congress for Dummies* by David Silverberg. The book, written by a former managing editor of *The Hill*, does not live down to its title.

# CHAPTER 9

# The Domestic Presidency

## Contents

## Overview

### Negotiator in Chief?

On 16 December 2005, the *New York Times* revealed that President George W. Bush had secretly authorised the intelligence service, the National Security Agency, to monitor telephone calls of Americans without a court-approved warrant. This appeared to be a violation of the Foreign Intelligence Surveillance Act of 1948, which requires search warrants from a special court before conducting electronic surveillance of people, inside the borders of the USA, suspected of being terrorists or spies.

The White House, however, was unapologetic. 'After 9/11 the President felt it was incumbent on him to use every ounce of authority available to him to protect the American people,' argued one advisor. The decision to bypass the process for obtaining warrants was justified by the constitutional responsibility of the President, as Commander-in-Chief, to act swiftly to defend the country against all threats.

Others interpreted the Constitution differently. Amidst a tide of outrage at the revelations, one Senator accused the President of assuming 'unchecked power, reserved only for Kings and potentates'. They argued that so much unsupervised power in the hands of a small team of people was precisely what the Founding Fathers sought to avoid when they wrote the Constitution. This chapter considers the extent to which, in relation to domestic affairs, this fear of unchecked executive power is justified.

## Key issues to be covered in this chapter

- The Presidency and the Constitution: its roles in domestic affairs
- The President as head of government
- The President as chief legislator
- The President as head of state
- The President as party leader
- The Vice President

## The presidency and the Constitution

### Giving the executive a secondary role

Keeping the executive branch in check was, for the Founding Fathers, central to their constitutional design. After the War of Independence, there was such a determination to avoid a tyrannical leader emerging that the central government had no executive branch at all. The need for more effective co-ordination of national affairs led to the setting up in 1787 of the Constitutional Convention which drafted the current Constitution.

While the need for a stronger government was evident, the Founders remained fearful of giving too much power to its leader. Thus, they gave primacy to the legislature, with a range of specified powers in the symbolically significant Article I of the document. The executive, reduced to secondary consideration in Article II, would be responsible for carrying out the wishes of Congress and representing the nation in foreign affairs. Considering these concerns, it is surprising that the Constitution is quite vague about the precise powers of the President, especially in domestic affairs.

### Qualifications for the presidency

The first and most detailed part of Article II of the Constitution covers who may become President (and Vice President) and the process of election. The key qualifications are that a candidate must:

- Have been born in the USA.
- Be at least 35 years old.
- Have been resident in the USA for the previous fourteen years at the time of standing for the position.
- Have not served as President for more than one term. This qualification was added in the 22nd Amendment in 1951.

### Powers of the President

Section 2 of Article II outlines the few presidential powers, in both domestic and foreign affairs, specifically identified in the Constitution. In domestic affairs, these are:

- Authorisation (but not the requirement) to form a **cabinet** of the heads of departments of state.
- Pardoning people convicted of crimes, except in cases of impeachment.
- Temporarily filling vacancies in the Federal government when the Senate, whose responsibility it is to confirm nominees, is not in session.

### Duties of the President

Section 3 of the Article outlines the duties of the President. In domestic terms, these are, again, extremely limited. They are:

- Delivering the annual **State of the Union Address**.
- Proposing legislation.

### Executive power

With such a limited range of defined powers and duties, the key constitutional sentence is found in the beginning of Article II: 'The Executive Power shall be invested in a President of the United States of America.'

This vague wording has always been open to a wide range of interpretations and, in the event of the checks on presidential power proving inadequate, created the potential for the development of a powerful executive.

From this, a range of presidential roles have emerged. The sections below outline how they operate in the modern USA and evaluate whether, in practice, the President is the most powerful man in the world or whether he wields limited, highly restricted powers, as envisaged by the Founding Fathers.

## The President as head of government

### The benchmark of presidential success

Unless the USA is at war, Presidents take office knowing that they have been elected on the basis of their policies to strengthen the economy and the nation's social fabric. Central to the success of a presidency, therefore, is the effective management of the executive branch of government, which means:

- Implementation of existing Federal laws.
- Initiation of new laws and programmes to address the needs and development of the nation.
- Management of the economy.

In order to manage the executive branch effectively, however, each President faces a number of challenges, including:

- Assembling a suitable team to lead the departments that administer government policy.
- Exerting effective political control over the civil servants who implement policy.
- Maintaining effective political focus on his political agenda when the next presidential election is looming.

Furthermore, Presidents have a limited period in which to establish their reputations as effective chief executives. Since F. D. Roosevelt became President in 1933, rapidly implementing a range of measures to address the effects of the economic depression, it has become customary for commentators to evaluate the effectiveness of the President after one hundred days in office.

### Choosing the Cabinet

On the day that a President takes office, his team has to ensure the smooth operation of government, even before taking any steps to implement his political agenda. Thus, between winning an election in the first week of November and inauguration in the third week of the following January, a top priority is selecting people to run the fifteen government departments. This means appointing people who can ensure that the President's political priorities are implemented within their departments, work together with other departmental heads whenever co-ordination of policy is necessary and support the President with policy proposals that support his goals.

In this crucial task, however, the President has less freedom of choice than the head of government in many other countries. The restrictions include the following:

- The President cannot adjust the number of departments, or their responsibilities, to help promote his policy priorities. This can only be done by Congress.

- By convention, the head of each department has a background that is compatible with the responsibilities of the department.
- By convention, powerful pressure groups that have an interest in the affairs of a department are consulted in the appointment of its head.
- By convention, the heads of department (who make up the Cabinet) are expected to be broadly representative of the population of the country. Presidents may use the 'egg formula' as one of the factors when considering candidates, to ensure that each ethnic group, both genders and all geographical regions are represented in the Cabinet. This is particularly important when a state governor becomes President, as was the case with both Bill Clinton (Arkansas) and George W. Bush (Texas). It would be inappropriate for the national government to be run almost exclusively by the President's close associates from his home state.

Once the President has found potential appointees to his Cabinet, he still faces a number of obstacles:

- Persuading candidates to move to Washington DC. A President will be in office for a maximum of eight years, which may mean a candidate leaving a well-established career and uprooting a family for a limited period.
- Persuading candidates to take a pay cut. In 2006, the pay of a head of department was $175,700, considerably less than the earnings of senior managers in the private sector.
- The Senate has to confirm the appointees before they can take office. In most cases, this is routine but, as outlined in Chapter 8, confirmation is certainly not guaranteed.

President Obama's first Cabinet, of twenty-two people, illustrates the kind of diversity that has come to be expected (overleaf).

## Working with the Cabinet

The President is able to find people of the highest calibre to head departments despite all the restrictions he faces. When bringing department heads together to form an advisory body, however, Presidents have not found Cabinets helpful on the whole. There has been a general pattern of Cabinet meetings diminishing in frequency

## Table 9.1 President Obama's first Cabinet

| | East Coast | Midwest | Rocky Mountain States and South-West | West Coast and Hawaii | South |
|---|---|---|---|---|---|
| **White (Anglo-Saxon)** | Joe Biden (Delaware) – Vice President | Robert Gates* (Kansas) –Defense | | | |
| | *Hillary Clinton* (New York) – Secretary of State | Tom Vilsack (Iowa) –Agriculture | | | |
| | Timothy Geithner (New York) – Treasury Secretary | *Kathleen Sebelius* (Kansas) – Health and Human Services | | | |
| | Shaun Donovan (New York) – Housing and Urban Development | Arne Duncan (Chicago, Illinois) – Education | | | |
| | | *Christina Romer* (Illinois) – Council of Economic Advisors | | | |
| **White (non Anglo-Saxon)** | Peter Orszag (Massachusetts) – Office of Management and Budget | Rahm Emanuel (Chicago, Illinois) – White House Chief of Staff | *Janet Nepolitano* (Arizona) – Homeland Security | | |

| African American | Eric Holder# (New York) – Justice | | | *Lisa Jackson* (Louisiana) – Environment Protection Agency |
|---|---|---|---|---|
| | *Susan Rice* (Washington DC) – Ambassador to the United Nations | | | Ron Kirk (Texas) – US Trade Representative |
| Hispanic | | Ken Salazar (Colorado) – Interior Department | *Hilda Solis#* (California) – Labour | |
| Asian | | Steven Chu (Missouri) – Energy | Gary Locke (Washington) – Commerce | |
| | | | Eric Shinseki (Hawaii) – Veterans Affairs | |
| Arab-American | | Ray LaHood* (Illinois) – Transportation | | |

Key:
Bold and Italic: women in the Cabinet (7)
*Politically to the right of the President (2)
#Politically to the left of the President (2)

the longer a President remains in office. Both President Carter and President Reagan held thirty-six Cabinet meetings in their first year but just six and twelve respectively four years later.

A range of factors limit the usefulness of Cabinets:

- The fact that heads of department, the Cabinet secretaries, are usually policy specialists means that they may have little to contribute to discussions on unrelated policy areas. The result can be meetings in which little meaningful discussion, which aids the President's decision-making, takes place.
- Some of the heads of department may not be close colleagues of the President. They are even less likely to have a close relationship with each other. As a result, there may not be a deep level of trust within the group. Presidents tend to be wary of discussing sensitive or confidential issues with a group that does not have close bonds.
- Once appointed to head a department, there is an understandable tendency for each member of the Cabinet to develop strong ties to the career officials within their department, as well as other people they work with most closely, such as Congressional committees and pressure groups. In part, this is due to the dynamics of the working environment, which can forge strong bonds and make the White House (and its political priorities) seem remote. Further, this is due to the long-term planning that takes place in departments appearing to be at odds with the short-term needs of a President who will be in office for two terms at most. Additionally, Cabinet members often adopt longstanding rivalries between departments, such as that between the Department of State (which tends to seek diplomatic solutions to international disputes) and the Department of Defense (which tends towards military solutions to disputes), as seen in the first term of President George W. Bush when the Secretary of State, Colin Powell, was frequently at loggerheads with the Defense Secretary, Donald Rumsfeld. Consequently, over time there is a growing tendency for the Cabinet to become divided, as each member becomes increasingly committed to their own departmental priorities rather than a shared agenda.
- Friction between departments also arises due to competition for funds for their programmes.

- Cabinet secretaries are accountable not only to the President but also to Congress. For example, in response to more than one hundred traffic deaths caused by failures in tyres in the late 1990s, Congress passed a law requiring the Department of Transport to issue new rules that would lead to early detection of safety hazards in tyres and vehicles. With each department having to respond to such instructions and to account for its performance to different Congressional committees, their distinctive, separate priorities tend to be emphasised.

A consequence of these shortcomings is that policy-making is often the result of bi-lateral meetings between the President and the most influential 'top tier' Cabinet members: Defense, State, Treasury and Justice.

Notwithstanding these limitations, since George Washington instituted regular meetings with his four Cabinet secretaries, all Presidents have found it beneficial to bring the Cabinet together periodically. The benefits to the administration include:

- Embodying the Presidential platform: for Clinton the Cabinet represented his campaign theme of inclusivity; for George W. Bush, it represented his campaign theme of compassionate conservatism.
- Presenting an image of being 'in touch': having representatives from all sectors of American society creates an image of a government that understands all sectors of American society.
- Presenting an image of open, collective government: Cabinet meetings are always accompanied by a photo opportunity, which counters the sense that most key decisions are taken by a small group of advisors who have never been subject to Senate ratification.
- Although Cabinets have a reputation for limited debate on government policy, there are points in the calendar when the President will usually call the secretaries together to discuss major initiatives that affect all departments, such as when the annual budget is being submitted to Congress.
- At other times, even in the absence of useful policy-making discussions, Cabinet meetings provide an opportunity for information exchange, a check on the progress of legislation, an opportunity for secretaries to meet each other and an opportunity for the

'second tier' secretaries to meet the President. All this can help build team spirit, which can be significant if the administration goes through a period of political turbulence.

Overall, therefore, while Cabinet secretaries, collectively and individually, make some contribution to Presidents, they tend to be a less useful source of support for the head of government in the USA than in many other countries. This can have a significant impact on a presidency.

Of particular concern to Presidents is the difficulty that Cabinet secretaries may have in advancing his political agenda. With about 1.9 million civilian employees, working in offices spread throughout the land, the departments are notoriously difficult to control. Former House speaker Newt Gingrich described the dynamics of government departments in these terms: 'The leader comes into the room and says, "We are going to march North" and the bureaucracy all applaud. Then the leader leaves the room and the bureaucracy says, "Yeah, well, this 'march north' thing is terrific, but this year, to be practical, we have to keep marching south. But what we'll do is, we'll hire a consultant to study marching north, so that next year we can begin to think about whether or not we can do it."' Even more of a concern is the tendency of some members in each Cabinet to be persuaded to support the existing priorities of their departments, which may not be compatible with the President's priorities.

Considering that the work of the government departments touches the daily lives of every American, from regulations on airbags in cars to how much water should be allowed for a clean flush of a toilet, a presidency can be substantially undermined if there is a lack of effective political control exerted over each department, or a lack of co-ordination and co-operation between departments. In short, ineffective leadership of departments and poor co-operation between departments can prove to be one of the greatest 'checks' on a presidency. Finding ways to exert control over the departments, therefore, has been one of the greatest challenges that Presidents face.

## Regulatory commissions, independent agencies and government corporations

This challenge is made even greater by other parts of the Federal government that have, by law, a significant measure of independence from the White House or have the effect of complicating the organisational pattern of government.

The executive branch of government includes **independent regulatory commissions**. These are agencies, established by Congress and independent of the President, with responsibility for regulating important aspects of society. They are empowered to establish rules for the policy area they regulate, which have the force of law, and to enforce their rules. All are run by boards of commissioners, consisting of five or seven members, who are appointed by the President. Their independence from the President is established by long terms of office that end at different times. Thus, at any one time, some of them will not owe their allegiance to the current President. In addition, a maximum of four members of a seven-person board of commissioners, or three members of a five-person board, may be of the same party, so that even if one political party controls the White House over an extended period (for example, when President Reagan was succeeded by George Bush Snr), the views of the opposition party must be considered by the commission. Finally, they cannot be removed by the President if they become a political irritant. In the case of *Rathbun* v. *United States* (1935), the Supreme Court ruled that commissioners could only be removed from office for failing to fulfil their obligations or for abusing their powers. The most visible commissions are the Federal Reserve, the Central Bank of the USA, which oversees the financial sector and sets interest rates, and the Federal Elections Commission, which administers and enforces campaign finance legislation.

The Federal Reserve illustrates how difficult it can be for Presidents to effectively control their administrations. Whenever there is an economic slowdown the President is invariably held responsible, yet the main tool for manipulating economic growth is controlled by the independent Federal Reserve, which does not consider presidential political fortunes when setting interest rates. Conversely, one of the reasons that Al Gore did not win the presidency in 2000, despite having been a leading member of the Clinton administration that had presided over eight unbroken years of economic growth, was that many Americans credited their increasing prosperity to the Federal Reserve.

The executive branch of government also includes **independent**

**agencies**. These are responsible for specific areas of policy and are, in most respects, organised like the fifteen main government departments, headed by people responsible to the President. As such, the President has more control over these bodies than he does over the independent regulatory commissions, but they tend to complicate the organisation of government and lines of responsibility. For example, the Environmental Protection Agency has responsibilities which overlap with, and sometimes clash with, the Department of the Interior, which is responsible for managing inland waterways, forests and national parks, and the Department of Agriculture, which describes itself as 'the nation's largest conservation agency'.

The Environmental Protection Agency (EPA) illustrates how such bodies come into being. In response to the growing public demand for cleaner water, air and land, it was agreed by Congress and the White House that the Federal government was not structured to make a co-ordinated attack on the pollutants that harm human health and degrade the environment. The EPA was thus established to repair the damage already done to the natural environment and to provide guidance on making a cleaner environment a reality.

The executive branch also includes **government corporations**, which are public services administered as business enterprises, such as the United States Postal Service and the national passenger rail service, Amtrak. Inevitably, the President plays a minimal role in the daily functions of these organisations but public perception of the effectiveness of his administration may be significantly affected by the late delivery of the mail or the late arrival of a train.

### Exerting control over the Federal bureaucracy: the spoils system

Considering the importance of effective political control of the executive branch, it is unsurprising that, since George Washington, Presidents have appointed political sympathisers to jobs in the government. The third President, Thomas Jefferson, fired hundreds of Federal employees who supported his predecessor's party and replaced them with his own supporters. By the time that the seventh President, Andrew Jackson, took office the size of the Federal government had grown substantially and he replaced more than a thousand Federal employees. The practice was defended at the time on the grounds that 'to the victor goes the spoils', since when appointment of political supporters has been known as the **spoils system**.

In 1881, President Garfield was assassinated by a man who had been passed over when the 'spoils' were handed out. This led to a reorganisation of government, with most positions held by permanent civil servants, appointed on merit, although about 3 per cent of positions continue to be filled on the basis of political affiliation, rather than merit. Each presidential election year, Congress publishes a list of these jobs in a book referred to by Washington insiders as the 'plum book'.

There are three categories of political appointees put in place to try to ensure that the President's agenda is implemented:

- At the top level, the most senior people who run the departments and agencies that comprise the executive branch – appointees are nominated by the President but have to be confirmed by the Senate.
- 'Schedule C' appointees, who work alongside permanent senior managers, formulating and implementing specific areas of policy.
- 'Buddy system' appointees, who are offered mid-level posts by people in more senior political positions.

### Directing and co-ordinating the Federal bureaucracy: the Executive Office of the President

Even with political appointees in place to monitor the implementation of presidential priorities, there is a need for providing coordination and direction to an executive branch that has become larger and more complex each decade.

This was apparent by the mid-1930s, with President F. D. Roosevelt and his advisors struggling to manage all of the new agencies created to overcome the effects of the economic depression. He set up a committee, generally known as the Brownlow Committee, which reported that 'the president needs help' and recommended that a new team of advisors be 'installed in the White House itself, directly accessible to the president' to co-ordinate day-to-day matters. In response, Congress passed the Reorganization Act of 1939, creating the **Executive Office of the President (EOP)**.

As the size of government increased, and society became more complex, the EOP grew. Its most important elements are:

- *The White House staff* The TV drama *The West Wing* was based on this group of people who form the President's closest and most trusted advisors. Often these ties have been forged well before the President even considered running for the position. For example, Karl Rove, who is credited with masterminding the 2000 and 2004 election victories, first met George W. Bush in 1973. These advisors have the task of:
  - Providing information and analysis of the key issues facing the administration.
  - Providing guidance in specialist policy areas.
  - Evaluating the political and legal significance of presidential decisions.
  - Writing speeches and presenting the President's views to the outside world.
  - Liaising with Congress to gain support for the President's programmes.
  - Filtering who, and what, gets access to the President.
  - Above all, monitoring the work of executive departments and agencies to ensure that they are carrying out the President's political agenda.

  This arrangement has both advantages and disadvantages for the President. It is, of course, beneficial for the head of government to have complete confidence in his closest advisors and to be certain that they are doing everything in their power to ensure that the administration's political agenda is being implemented. Furthermore, because power in Washington DC is often measured by access to the President, the White House Staff can use their privileged positions to exert considerable pressure on his behalf. However, such is the reverence attached to the position of President that even longstanding close friends can find it difficult to present unpleasant news or voice criticism. This can lead to presidential isolation, a problem exacerbated if only a very small group of advisers have direct access to the President, as was the case with President Nixon and President Reagan.

- *The Office of Management and Budget (OMB)* This is the largest agency within the EOP and, after the White House Staff, the most important. It prepares the budget the President proposes to Congress each year, with the amount allocated to each policy area reflecting the President's priorities. In the same way, it reviews all policy proposals produced by the executive departments and agencies to ensure that they are consistent with the President's goals. The OMB is of such importance that the post of director is subject to Senate confirmation.

- *The Council of Economic Advisors* While the OMB tends to focus on short-term economic policy, the Council of Economic Advisors concentrates on long-term economic planning and aids the executive departments and agencies with their long-term plans.

- *The National Security Council (NSC)* The NSC is responsible for co-ordinating foreign and military policy. Given the longstanding rivalry between the State Department and the Department of Defense, as well as traditional mutual suspicion between the two main intelligence services, the CIA and the FBI, some Presidents have found themselves heavily dependent on the advice from their National Security Advisors, notably George W. Bush in the aftermath of the attacks of 9/11.

Each President has added or abolished other agencies within the EOP in accordance with his priorities. President Johnson, for example, set up an Office of Economic Opportunity to support his Great Society programme, but it was abolished by his successor, President Nixon, who wanted to chart a different course in domestic affairs. President George W. Bush set up the Office of Faith-Based and Community Initiatives because he wished to see religious groups play a greater role in resolving the nation's social problems.

It is a measure of the value that Presidents place on the support provided by the EOP that when the government was reorganised to improve domestic security in the aftermath of 9/11, George W. Bush tried to persuade Congress that the new agency should be part of the EOP, rather than a separate department, and only changed his mind when it became evident that his appeal would not be heeded.

## Box 9.1  Policy czars

The kind of policy co-ordination conducted by the OMB, the Council of Economic Advisors and the NSC, making sure that government departments pull in the same direction, has been steadily extended into other areas in recent times. Known in Washington DC as **czars**, co-ordinators have been used to oversee policies as diverse as drug policy, AIDS policy and the smooth transition of technology from the twentieth to twenty-first centuries (when many computers were expected to reset themselves to the year 1900). President Obama took office intending to appoint a number of czars to oversee policies such as healthcare reform and energy/climate change. These policy leaders have been subject to criticism because they are, in some ways, more important than Cabinet members but are not subject to Congressional confirmation or scrutiny, which could be seen as contrary to the constitutional principle of holding those in power to account.

Policy czars have also been criticised for being ineffective. Because they are based in the White House, some czars have lacked the level of detailed knowledge and understanding found in the departments they are supposed to be overseeing. Some czars have adopted a high-handed style that has alienated the departments with which they are supposed to be working, while others have simply been ignored as departments have relentlessly pursued their traditional feuds, as happened with the Departments of Defense and State during the presidency of George W. Bush with National Security Advisor Condoleezza Rice largely sidelined.

However, there have also been times when policy czars have been extremely effective. Departments recognise the risk that policies to which they have devoted a lot of time and resources may be undermined by the work of other departments, making them well-disposed to co-ordination. It can also be advantageous for departments to have a policy advocate in the White House. So, provided the policy czars are seen as being honest brokers who have the President's ear, they can prove very effective co-ordinators.

## Directing the Federal bureaucracy: executive orders and proclamations

The President may issue orders to those working for the government. These **executive orders** often deal with relatively trivial managerial issues. Indeed, until the early 1900s they were rarely announced or recorded. However, they have the force of law and have been the way in which some of America's most important policies have been introduced, including:

- The internment of Japanese Americans in the Second World War (executive order 9066).
- The desegregation of the US armed services (executive order 9981).
- The first Affirmative Action policy (executive order 11246).
- The establishment of special military tribunals, in November 2001 (after the 9/11 attacks), to try suspects accused of plotting or carrying out terrorist acts, together with a number of other executive orders in the same period, such as lifting restrictions on the intelligence agencies' ability to carry out political assassinations.

The President can also issue **presidential proclamations**, which relate to the country as a whole. The most significant, and famous, was the **Emancipation Proclamation** that abolished slavery in 1863.

These presidential actions may be overturned by Congress or the courts. For example, in the immediate aftermath of the 9/11 attacks, President George W. Bush issued an executive order creating a new body in the Executive Office of the Presidency, to oversee the co-ordination of forty-five Federal agencies which had responsibilities that related to the prevention of terrorism. However, Congress passed a law making this body an executive department (the Department for Homeland Security) that they could scrutinise. Also, the executive order setting up military tribunals outside of the Federal judicial system was challenged in *Rasul* v. *Bush* (2004) and rejected by the Supreme Court.

However, either because of a lack of time, a lack of political will or because there is little public pressure to overturn executive orders, many of them remain in place, giving the President more power over policy than is often recognised.

### Making the Federal bureaucracy accountable

Despite having the spoils system and the Executive Office of the President at their disposal, Presidents have continued to feel that the **Federal bureaucracy** has failed to implement their policies as they wished. Consequently, they have tried a number of strategies to make civil servants more responsive and more accountable for their actions.

- President Nixon introduced Management by Objectives, which attempted to identify the goals of Federal programmes and thereby evaluate which were successful.
- President Carter introduced Zero-based Budgeting, which attempted to force departments and agencies to justify the value of their programmes each year.
- President Clinton introduced Reinventing Government, which aimed to reduce the number of government regulations, cut the size and cost of government and improve the quality of government services.

While each of these initiatives have been credited as going some way towards helping Presidents implement their political agenda, all are regarded as having had far less impact than intended.

The progress of President George W. Bush's Management Agenda illustrates why it is so difficult to hold the Federal bureaucracy to account. Proposals to increase accountability included:

- Grading Federal departments and agencies on the results they achieved, with the White House defining 'success'.
- Increased White House oversight of regulations issued, to ensure that they were consistent with the President's aims.
- The introduction of performance-related pay to make it easier to reward or fire employees according to the administration's goals.
- 'Competitive sourcing', which would force Federal workers to compete against private contractors to run programmes.
- Creating a 'sunset' process, which would require Federal programmes to justify their existence every ten years.

They were immediately criticised by civil servants and independent commentators, who argued that:

- It is not realistic to change the entire focus of government every time a new President is elected.

- It is the responsibility of the civil service to execute the laws already in place, not only those passed by the latest administration, and an evaluation system that fails to recognise this is inevitably flawed.
- A framework to make it easier for political appointees to overrule, marginalise or fire career employees who are perceived not to be fully behind the President's agenda undermines the independence and effectiveness of the civil service.
- The overall result is a Federal bureaucracy that loses the ability to raise concerns about waste, fraud and abuse of power for fear of being victimised by political appointees (critics pointed, in particular, to reductions in protection for employees who publicise adverse consequences of the administration's programmes) and too many decisions being taken by people lacking in technical expertise.

All administrations are sensitive to the charge that their reforms of the bureaucracy are leading to its politicisation and undermining its independence and effectiveness. While this does not stop the reforms, inevitably it blunts their impact.

**Conclusion**

Overall, therefore, the President faces a range of challenges that limit how effectively he can impose his will on the branch of government that he leads, including:

- An inability to reorganise the executive branch to meet the needs of his agenda.
- A lack of control over key instruments for implementing policy, such as the Federal Reserve.
- Term limits that cause all political forces to concentrate their attention on the next President once the mid-terms are over.
- The sheer size of the Federal bureaucracy, combined with the complexity of a highly developed economy, which makes it difficult to control.

Despite the spoils system and the Executive Office of the President, which should help him exert control over the executive branch, the

Federal bureaucracy has emerged as a check on presidential power to supplement those which the Founding Fathers designed.

Countering these limitations, however, is the President's use of policy co-ordinators to advance their agendas which, when working well, can help ensure that the Presidents' policies are implemented, and the use of executive orders that enable Presidents to directly implement laws.

Whether these conflicting factors lead to Presidents playing a limited or extensive role in domestic policy will be further examined at the end of the next chapter.

## The President as chief legislator

### The State of the Union Address

It is expected that the legislative agenda for the Federal government will be set by the President. As the only person elected by the whole nation, the President is expected to present a programme for government that meets the nation's needs, and when Congress assembles in January, little meaningful business is done until the President has outlined his priorities for the year.

This is done in the State of the Union Address, a speech to both houses of Congress, which takes place around 20 January. The President identifies the key issues the administration believes need to be addressed and outlines the bills the White House will send to Congress to resolve the issues.

On the first Monday in February, the President's budget is delivered to the House of Representatives, which, constitutionally, is responsible for scrutinising all revenue bills first. This will contain the President's judgements of the cost of his legislative proposals and of the level of taxation needed to fund them.

The State of the Union Address may serve to set the national political agenda for the year, especially in the President's first term. Thus President Obama's first address established that economic stabilisation and healthcare reform were to be the main issues of 2009. George W. Bush's first address established that tax cuts and education reform were to be the main issues in the first year of his presidency.

However, there are circumstances in which the State of the Union Address has limited impact, including:

- Election years, when the priorities of legislators are heavily influenced by re-election.
- A divided Congress, when the opposition party may attempt to promote its own rival agenda, as was the case in 1995 and 2007.
- Events that are beyond the control of politicians, such as the attacks of 9/11 in 2001 and Hurricane Katrina in 2005.
- A misjudged State of the Union that does not strike a chord with the public, such as the attempt by President Bush Jnr to put social security reform at the top of the agenda in 2005.
- A 'lame duck' President, who will soon be leaving office. This may lead to public attention being focused mainly on the candidates to take over the presidency, as happened in 2008.

### Negotiating with Congress

There is an old saying that 'The President proposes; Congress disposes'. By convention, bills drafted by the executive branch will be allowed to clear all of the hurdles that Congress puts in the way of legislative proposals. However, both houses of Congress can, and will, amend bills written by the executive branch, sometimes to the extent that they are no longer acceptable to the President.

Unacceptable modifications come in two forms. Congress may delete key provisions that weaken the bill to such an extent that it will not be able to fulfil its purpose even if it passes. Members of Congress may add provisions to the bill, known as 'riders' or 'earmarks', which benefit their districts. This can lead to presidential initiatives becoming 'Christmas tree' bills, covered with presents for the constituents of the most influential members of Congress at huge expense to the taxpayer.

In order to avoid either of these outcomes, the White House needs to actively engage with key members of Congress. This may mean:

- Working closely with Congressional leaders and committee chairmen on which proposed amendments may be acceptable.
- Invitations to the White House (a rare occurrence for less senior members of Congress) or an offer for the President to visit a Congressman's district.
- When the concern is that a key provision may be stripped from a bill, to offer Federal investment in the district of an undecided member.

## The power of veto

Part of the negotiation process is the threat that the President will use his constitutional power to **veto** an entire bill if it no longer meets his key requirements. This means the President returning a bill to Congress with the reasons for not signing it. This veto can then be overridden by a two-thirds majority vote in both houses of Congress. This is quite a powerful weapon, as Congress will be reluctant to force a veto if there is a perception that the electorate feels they are jeopardising the national interest for their local interests. The fact that the President has a national platform on which to put forward his viewpoint, such as his weekly radio address, while members of Congress have no similar mouthpiece, gives the President a distinct advantage in such a situation. Furthermore, the two-thirds majority required in both houses of Congress to override a Congressional veto is only rarely achieved. Thus, the threat of a veto may be sufficient to wring compromises from Congress. Moreover, the President can use the **pocket veto**: if Congress adjourns within ten days of submitting a bill to the President for signature, and the bill is not signed, it falls. As Congress frequently rushes to complete bills towards the end of the year, either to clear the legislative agenda ahead of the next State of the Union Address or because of the approach of the end of the two-year session of Congress when all remaining bills are lost, many bills are vulnerable to this form of veto which cannot be overridden, which provides a powerful incentive for Congress to find a compromise with the White House.

However, the veto is a blunt weapon, eliminating the benefits of a bill as well as its disadvantages. In the past, Presidents have had the means of ignoring those parts of bills of which they disapproved. It used to be possible for Presidents to **impound** (not spend) money for any programme Congress had funded but which the President did not support. President Nixon impounded as much as $13 billion for social programmes that he did not favour in a single year. This power was removed by the Congressional Budget and Impoundment Control Act (1974). It also became possible for the President to veto only those parts of a bill with which he disagreed, a **line-item veto**, as a result of an act passed in 1997. Just one year later, however, the power to veto only parts of a bill was declared unconstitutional by the Supreme Court on the grounds that it effectively gave the President the power to draft legislation, which breaches the constitutional principle of separation of powers. Also, Presidents may judge that it would not be a good idea to veto a bill, even though they find it objectionable, because of:

- The strength of support for the measure in Congress and the possibility of the veto being overridden, with the associated weakening of presidential authority.
- The popularity of the measure among the electorate and the political consequences for the President and the party of blocking it.
- The frequent use of the veto in the recent past, leading to a sense that the President is inflexible and unprepared to compromise with political opponents.

Thus, making effective use of this blunt weapon requires political skill and judgement. If threats are made too often, there is a risk of the President appearing to bully Congress, rather than engage in constructive negotiation. Alternatively, it could come to be seen as an empty threat, undermining the President's standing. The actual use of the veto also carries risks. The public perception that nothing is being achieved in Washington DC can affect the President's reputation as well as that of Congress.

### Signing statements

In the absence of a mechanism for modifying a bill through impound-ment or the line-item veto, Presidents have increasingly made use of **signing statements**, in which presidential authority is invoked to challenge the provisions of legislation as it is being signed into law.

Although signing statements often consist of uncontroversial com-ments, they have risen to prominence since George W. Bush became President, as he argued that any law that affected his ability to protect the country infringed upon his constitutional role as Commander-in-Chief or his role as head of the Federal bureaucracy. Therefore, he claimed, he was entitled to ignore any law, or part of a law, that had this effect.

In his capacity as Commander-in-Chief, he challenged a law banning the use of torture and another requiring disclosure of infor-mation on how the anti-terrorism law, the Patriot Act, is enforced.

In his capacity as head of government, he questioned the right of Congress to insist on specific measures that affected the running of various departments, such as how border checkpoints in Arizona are managed.

Subsequently, President Obama has continued to make use of signing statements (although less frequently than his predecessor), for example rejecting a Congressional instruction on how to negotiate with international organisations such as the International Monetary Fund and the World Bank.

## Conclusion

Clearly, one of the higher priorities of the Founding Fathers was to limit the President's involvement in law-making beyond offering proposals and the acceptance or rejection of whatever Congress produced. Negotiating with Congress as bills are making their way through the legislature would appear to be mainly a pragmatic strategy for ensuring that legislation is not needlessly vetoed, rather than presidential interference in the process, as members of the executive branch are limited to behind-the-scenes discussions and play no direct role in the legislating.

However, Presidents have repeatedly attempted to do more than just accept or reject the end-product of the deliberations of Congress. The judiciary has had to strike down the practice of impoundment and the line-item veto as unconstitutional. The presidency has, in turn, responded by making greater use of signing statements. And, as outlined in the previous section, Presidents can make extensive and dramatic use of executive orders to shape the law.

Thus, while strict separation of powers in legislation has been largely maintained, the other branches of government have had to be vigilant against the extension of presidential power in this area and the use of executive orders has been, and continues to be, a grey area.

# The President as head of state

### Pomp and ceremony

The President has a range of ceremonial duties that, in most countries, are not carried out by the most senior politician. As head of state, he hosts visiting dignitaries such as kings and queens, as well as presiding over a range of formal events, such as giving awards and medals, lighting the national Christmas tree and throwing out the first ball of the Major League baseball season.

Some of these traditions may seem quirky, especially to foreigners. Every Thanksgiving, the President pardons a turkey that is then guaranteed to live the remainder of its natural life without facing the possibility of becoming the centrepiece of a Thanksgiving meal.

## A political instrument

The President's duties as a head of state make him much more than just a politician. He is a living symbol of the nation, representing the collective image of the USA. The aura that develops around the head of state is enhanced by the lifestyle of the President. The White House is designed to serve the needs and desires of the President: his personal aircraft, Air Force One, is the most expensive, sophisticated, best-protected civilian aircraft in the world, and the people around him treat him with reverence.

When a President has to wrestle with the bureaucracy in order to implement a programme, or has to negotiate with Congress in order to pass legislation, the immense authority and influence that comes with being head of state can be a major asset, especially if it is clear that the President reflects the hopes, fears and mood of the nation. Congress can become more receptive to the President's proposals, aware that they may be seen as putting local interests before that of the nation. The Federal bureaucracy may also be more responsive to his leadership, aware that policies that clearly have the support of the nation have a greater likelihood of remaining in place over many years, beyond the term of office of the incumbent President.

## Using the prestige of head of state as a political weapon

If used with delicacy and skill, the President's standing as the symbol of the nation and its interests can be used as a powerful political weapon.

At the low point in his presidency, in 1995, Bill Clinton faced a hostile Congress with a Republican majority and the two sides could not agree on a budget. Eventually, the government had to be closed down for lack of money, resulting in millions of Americans being unable to use public services on which they were dependent. Inevitably, both sides blamed each other but, by arguing that he was defending the interests of the most vulnerable in society and that he was willing to accept electoral unpopularity by doing what was in the best interests of the nation, President Clinton was able to deflect blame onto his opponents, who were seen as putting their narrow political views ahead of the needs of the nation.

Similarly, at the low point in the presidency of George W. Bush's first term, in the summer of 2001, he faced widespread criticism as a President who spent far too much time on his ranch in Texas or playing golf, and not enough time leading the nation. After the events of 9/11, however, his standing as the leader of the nation's interests soared and for two years he was able to implement his political agenda almost with opposition.

However, if a President fails to recognise how much of his authority comes from his status as head of state, or lacks the political judgement on how best to use it to his political advantage, his entire political progamme and even the powers of the office can be damaged.

When it became apparent, during the Watergate scandal, that President Nixon had been party to breaking the law while in office, he resigned rather than face impeachment. In addition, Congress looked more closely at the powers of the presidency and how they had been used, which led to the passage of a number of laws limiting those powers, including the Case-Zablocki Act of 1972, the War Powers Act of 1973 (see Chapter 10) and the Congressional Budget and Impoundment Control Act of 1974 (see above).

Similarly, when President Clinton's affair with a White House intern was revealed, the impeachment proceedings that followed harmed the international standing of the USA, damaged the reputation of the whole administration, contributed to the defeat of Al Gore in the 2000 presidential election and, politically, paralysed the domestic policy agenda of the President for the remainder of his second term.

The dangers of misusing the status of head of state are illustrated by the transformation of President George W. Bush from leader of a wholly united nation in the autumn of 2001 to being the focus of the bitter, divisive presidential election campaign of 2004. In

2002, President Bush actively campaigned for Republican candidates during the Congressional elections, repeatedly questioning the patriotism of Democrats and arguing that a Republican majority in Congress was essential to prevailing in the 'War on Terror'. Democrats, who had voted for the President's measures over the previous year and prided themselves on their patriotism, were outraged at the President using his prestige in this way.

### Conclusion
In combining the positions of head of government and head of state in one person, the Founding Fathers created a position with the potential to develop in political power by skilfully appearing to rise above politics and present a policy agenda as being in the national interest. This, in turn, can undermine the effectiveness of the system of checks and balances.

However, not all Presidents have had the political skill to effectively exploit this potential loophole in the constitutional design, and others have discovered that if the position is not treated with proper respect then substantial damage can be inflicted on their administration.

## The President as party leader

### Striking a difficult balance
As the most prominent member of his party, the President is effectively (although not officially) the leader of his party. He is, as a result, under pressure to use his position to help the party's political prospects and to reward his supporters for helping him to win office. For the head of state, however, to behave in a partisan way is generally considered inappropriate and (as illustrated above in the section on the head of state) can be highly divisive.

### Building political support
In the exercise of political power, a President is able to accomplish a great deal more if he has supporters in a majority in the other branches of government. In his first six years in office, with a supportive Republican majority in the House of Representatives, President George W. Bush did not have to use his veto on a single occasion and succeeded in passing a majority of his main policies

through Congress. It was not surprising, therefore, that he campaigned as hard as he did for Republican candidates during the 2002 mid-term elections.

The President can also encourage active support for the party by rewarding those who help the party, especially during elections, with appointment to political office.

The President also has an unmatched ability to raise campaign funds. Ahead of the 2006 mid-term elections, with the prominent Pennsylvania Senator Rick Santorum facing a strong challenge, President George W. Bush attended a fundraising event that raised $1.7 million, followed by another nine months later that raised $700,000.

Above all, if the President's policies are popular, the whole party can be relied upon to rally round to provide support to turn proposals into policies that are implemented. These, in turn, can have a coat-tails effect that leads to electoral success for the party around the country.

### Conclusion
The role of party leader is an awkward one for Presidents. Used effectively, it can add to the likelihood of the successful implementation of the President's agenda. Against this, however, Presidents have to be aware that if they appear to be using their position for party advantage, there is a risk of squandering the political advantages that come with the prestige of being head of state.

## The Vice President

### 'Not worth a bucket of warm spit'
Jack Garner, who served as Vice President to F. D. Roosevelt between 1933 and 1941, is credited with saying that the position was 'not worth a bucket of warm piss', although the quote was adjusted a little by reporters. He was not the first Vice President to dismiss the importance of the office. John Adams, the first Vice President, said, 'My country has in its wisdom contrived for me the most insignificant office that ever the invention of man contrived or his imagination conceived.'

These complaints arise from the fact that the Vice President has only two roles outlined in the Constitution, one of which has little practical importance much of the time. The Vice President is officially the presiding officer of the Senate, although on most occasions this role is carried out by a Senator and the Vice President breaks a tied vote in the Senate. The other role is to take over the presidency if the President dies in office or is unable to carry out his duties.

This second role is very important, as both John Adams and Jack Garner would have recognised. Indeed, had an attempt on the life of President F. D. Roosevelt been successful in Miami in 1933 been successful, Jack Garner would have become President. Furthermore, because all Vice Presidents are 'a heartbeat away from the presidency', the position is quite a strong launch pad for a presidential election campaign.

However, for those who were never elevated to the top office, their role and importance in the White House has depended entirely on the discretion of the President, hence the complaints.

## A position of growing importance
Despite the limitations of the vice presidency, it has grown in stature since the Second World War for a variety of reasons:

- The Vice President has played a significant role in winning elections by 'balancing the ticket' and compensating for perceived weaknesses in the presidential candidate.
- As the role of the Federal government has grown, the Vice President has been given increasingly high-profile roles to support the President in running the executive branch.
- Some Vice Presidents have played important advisory roles to the President, such as Al Gore on environmental policy in relation to President Clinton.
- Some Vice Presidents have played an important role in liaising with the party and colleagues in Congress, such as Dick Cheney in relation to George W. Bush.
- Under President Obama, the Vice President has effectively become one of the administration's policy czars, with responsibility for policies that can have a significant impact on middle-class working families.

- Of the eleven most recent Vice Presidents, four have gone on to be President and three more were chosen as their party's presidential candidates.

Overall, therefore, while the importance of the position remains at the discretion of the President, it is increasingly recognised as a post that can be used to assist in the execution of domestic policy.

## Conclusion

With a range of roles, each subject to different checks and balances of varying effectiveness, contrasting views have emerged on how powerful the presidency has become and the extent to which the Founding Fathers' aims of a strictly limited executive branch have been realised. However, a final conclusion cannot be reached until the President's role in foreign affairs has been considered, which is covered in the next chapter, so the debate on the power of the President is addressed at the end of Chapter 10. (**Additional information on the presidency – likely examination questions, helpful websites and suggestions for further reading – will also be found at the end of Chapter 10.**)

. . . . . . . . . . . . . . . . . . . . . . . . . . . . . . . . . . . . . . . . . . . . . . .

### ✔ What you should have learnt from reading this chapter

- It was the intention of the Founding Fathers that the executive branch would not be allowed to develop into a powerful leader, reminiscent of a monarch, but would play a secondary role of implementing the wishes of Congress.

- A range of constitutional checks and balances were put in place to ensure that the powers of the President were restricted.

- In addition, as the USA grew in size and the government grew in scope, a cumbersome bureaucracy emerged that all Presidents have found difficult to control, further limiting their ability to impose their will on the nation.

- However, by giving the President the role of head of state, the Founding Fathers provided the executive branch with a powerful political tool, the immense authority of being the living symbol of the nation, which means that the presidential political agenda can be presented as being in the national interest.

- Whether, on balance, this has resulted in a strong or a weak executive has been, and continues to be, a matter of debate. Several theories have been advanced, but reaching a conclusion on which is the most convincing cannot be done until foreign policy issues are considered, which are covered in the next chapter.

## Glossary of key terms

**Cabinet** An advisory group that may be called upon to aid presidential decision-making, consisting of the heads of the executive departments and some members of the Executive Office of the Presidency.

**Czars** An informal term given to people appointed by the President to co-ordinate specific policies that are dealt with by a range of government departments, such as narcotic drugs.

**Emancipation Proclamation** The declaration, by President Lincoln in 1862, that slaves would be freed when the South was defeated in the Civil War.

**Executive Office of the President (EOP)** A cluster of agencies to provide the President with advice and help in the running of the executive branch.

**Executive order** A rule or regulation issued by the President to those working for the government, that has the same effect as a law.

**Federal bureaucracy** The civil service with responsibility for implementing Federal laws.

**Government corporations** Businesses, such as the Postal Service, that are government-owned.

**Impound** (Congressional funds) To not spend money that Congress had authorised but the President did not support.

**Independent agencies** Similar to the fifteen executive departments, with responsibility for devising and implementing specific areas of policy, but on a smaller scale.

**Independent regulatory commissions** Agencies, established by Congress and independent of the President, with responsibility for regulating important aspects of society.

**Line-item veto** A veto that enables a President to block only those parts of a bill with which he disagrees.

**Pocket veto** A veto that can only be used at the end of a session of Congress, when the legislature is no longer sitting. Any bill presented to the President just before the session ends will not become law if he does not sign it within ten days.

**Presidential proclamation** An announcement made by the President to the general public that has the same effect as a law.

***Rasul* v. *Bush* (2004)** A ruling that asserted that the courts had the right to decide whether the detention of 'enemy combatants' was lawful.

(Previously, the President had claimed that the Constitution gave him the right to make such decisions.)

**Signing statement**  A written statement, presented by the President, commenting on a bill as it is being signed.

**Spoils system**  The award of government jobs to political supporters.

**State of the Union Address**  An annual speech to Congress, in which the President sets out his political and legislative priorities for the year ahead.

**Veto**  The constitutional power of a President to block a bill that has passed through Congress by refusing to sign it into law.

# CHAPTER 10

# The Presidency – Foreign Affairs

## Contents

## Overview

*The most powerful person in the world?*
On 26 March 2003, US forces were attacked by the Iraqi army during an intense sandstorm. The Iraqis, believing that the storm had rendered them invisible, sought to use their experience of local conditions to compensate for the technological superiority of the Americans. However, using satellites and thermal imaging, the US troops were able to track them as easily as on a clear day and within hours the Iraqi forces were destroyed.

This one-sided engagement is the result of decades of defence spending at a level dwarfing other countries. By some estimates, the USA spends more on defence than every other country in the world combined and expenditure is projected to keep rising. The USA is also immensely powerful economically, with a Gross National Product (GNP) on a par with the whole European Union. The US economy is so large that California's GNP alone is estimated to be the equivalent to that of the world's fifth-largest economy.

Yet the Constitution of the USA was written for a nation that was many weeks' travel from the major powers of Europe and Asia, and the Founding Fathers anticipated that their country would have minimal involvement with the affairs of other countries. This is reflected in limited checks and balances being placed on the President in foreign affairs.

This chapter examines whether the emergence of the USA as the world's sole superpower put too much unfettered power in the hands of one man, contrary to the spirit of the Constitution, and, if so, what effect this has had on the overall political design of the Founding Fathers.

## Key issues to be covered in this chapter

- The presidency and the Constitution: its roles in foreign affairs
- The instruments of US foreign policy
- The goals of US foreign policy
- Foreign policy in the twenty-first century
- The impact of foreign policy on domestic affairs
- Evaluating the powers of the President

# The Constitution and foreign policy

### Giving the executive freedom of manoeuvre

For the Founding Fathers, keeping the executive branch in check, so that it could not threaten the freedoms of the American people, was the highest priority. They did not appear to place as high a priority on keeping the executive branch in check in foreign affairs.

When the Constitution was being written, the newly created nation was surrounded by territory controlled by the powerful imperial countries of Europe. The British controlled Canada to the North. The Spanish controlled the land to the South, in what is now Florida. The French claimed sovereignty over all the land to the West of the Mississippi River, from Canada to the Mexican border. All of these European powers had a record of constantly seeking to add to their territorial possessions and posed a genuine threat to the fledgling USA, if it appeared unable to effectively defend itself. When negotiating with them on behalf of nation, therefore, the President was provided with the diplomatic and military powers to respond to whatever situation arose.

Coupled with these concerns was a certain level of complacency that, provided local threats could be neutralised, there was little likelihood of the USA becoming entangled in world affairs. In an age of sail ships, the Atlantic Ocean provided a 3,000-mile-wide buffer between the USA and Europe, which could take weeks to cross. To the West, the USA did not even have access to the Pacific Ocean, and then there was another 4,000 miles or more to the Far East.

Thus, the Constitution gave the President the powers of being chief diplomat, responsible for the conduct of relations with other countries, and Commander-in-Chief of the armed forces.

The Constitution placed a number of congressional checks on how the President used these powers:

- All treaties require ratification by two-thirds of the Senate.
- Senior diplomats and senior appointees to the armed forces have to be confirmed, by a simple majority, by the Senate before they can take up their positions.
- While the President has the power to deploy and use the armed

forces in minor engagements, the Constitution made Congress alone responsible for declaring war.

However, while in domestic affairs, the constitutional emphasis was on giving primary responsibility for policy to Congress, in foreign affairs the balance of powers emphasises responsibility of the executive branch for policy, providing a freedom of manoeuvre that has had far-reaching implications for the power of the President in both foreign *and* domestic affairs.

## Making full use of freedom of manoeuvre

The executive was given greater freedom in foreign affairs despite the expectation of the Founding Fathers that even people of the highest integrity could be tempted to expand the power at their disposal, justifying it on the basis that they could govern more effectively in the public interest.

Just fourteen years after the adoption of the Constitution, events illustrated the importance of effective checks on executive power. In 1803, President Jefferson bought the land claimed by France in an arrangement known as the **Louisiana Purchase**. For $15 million, the USA acquired land that doubled the size of its territory and was eventually made into thirteen new states. The President knew that the transaction tested the boundaries of his constitutional powers. He wrote, 'The Constitution has made no provision for our holding foreign territory, still less for incorporating foreign nations into our Union. The Executive . . . have done an act beyond the Constitution.' However, the fact that Congress failed to challenge him and went on to ratify and pay for the arrangement meant that the expansion of presidential powers in foreign affairs had begun.

The Supreme Court demonstrated a similar unwillingness to challenge the President in his capacity as Commander-in-Chief. When the Civil War broke out in 1861, President Lincoln assumed emergency powers, including the suppression of publications (violating the 1st Amendment) and detentions without trials (violating the 6th Amendment). He argued that the only concern was whether the government would be 'not *too* strong for the liberties of its people [but] strong *enough* to maintain its own existence, in great emergencies'. The Supreme Court made one attempt to challenge these powers, in the case of *ex parte Merryman* (1861), which ruled that detention without trial was unconstitutional, but the army ignored the decision and followed the orders of the President instead. The Chief Justice was forced to recognise that while he had 'exercised all the power which the constitution and laws confer on me' at a time of national emergency, the President's use of his military powers represents 'a force too strong for me to overcome'.

Indeed, faced with the reality that they could not impose their will on the Commander-in-Chief, the judiciary went further and effectively gave its blessing to the expansion of presidential powers. In the Prize Cases of 1863, the owners of four ships that had been captured and sold as prizes of war took the President to court, arguing that such actions were only allowed at wartime and since Congress had not formally declared war the government's actions were unconstitutional. The Supreme Court ruled that if the USA finds itself defending its national interests by force, it is effectively at war even if there has been no official declaration by Congress. Thus, the most significant constitutional check on the President's use of the military was substantially diluted.

US Presidents have also used a device for evading the principal check on their powers as chief diplomat. **Executive agreements** are formal agreements between the USA and the leaders of another country that have the same status in international law as a treaty. However, unlike treaties, which require ratification by two-thirds of the Senate, Executive agreements can be negotiated and implemented without Congressional scrutiny.

Should a President wish to have Congressional support for an international agreement that is unlikely to receive two-thirds support in the Senate, there is the option of negotiating a Congressional-Executive agreement, which is ratified by a simple majority in both houses of Congress. Again, it has been open to question whether this device is constitutional but the Supreme Court upheld its validity in *Missouri* v. *Holland* in 1820.

## Manifest destiny

The Founding Fathers were well aware of the risks of giving the executive too much unchecked power in diplomatic and military affairs. Throughout history, national leaders had bolstered their standing among their people or enhanced their powers by precipitating international crises during which any challenge could be portrayed as unpatriotic and from which they could emerge as national heroes. During the national debate on whether or not to ratify the Constitution, its principal author warned, in *The Federalist* No. 41, that 'the liberties of Rome proved the final victim to her military triumphs, and that the liberties of Europe, as far as they ever existed, have with few exceptions been the price of her military establishments'. Why, then, did they provide so few effective checks on the President in foreign affairs?

A significant factor was a widespread belief in the USA that it was their nation's destiny, ordained by God, to eventually expand to control the whole of North and Central America, and possibly even South America as well. This belief, known as **manifest destiny**, was compatible with giving the President the means to respond rapidly to any situation that provided an opportunity to fulfil the nation's territorial destiny, including military conquest.

## The instruments of foreign policy

### Formulating policy

The development of US foreign policy is the product of the political priorities of the President and the advice/guidance/pressure of three key institutions that have responsibility for implementing decisions.

### The State Department

Originally known as the Department of Foreign Affairs, the **State Department** is responsible for 'the conduct of foreign relations, to promote the long-range security and well-being of the United States'. It fulfils its functions by:

- Keeping the President informed about international developments.
- Maintaining diplomatic relations with foreign governments.
- Negotiating treaties.
- Protecting the interests of Americans abroad.

As an organisation that often spends years carefully cultivating relationships with foreign governments, which it is loath to abandon, the

State Department is often perceived by Presidents as one of the parts of the Federal bureaucracy least responsive to an incoming administration's goals (see Chapter 9). This is particularly true of decisions to resolve diplomatic disputes by use of armed force. In the planning stage of the invasion of Iraq, for example, although the Department was led by a former general, it strongly advised delaying military action until all diplomatic avenues had been exhausted and support for American intervention had been built up around the world.

### The Department of Defense

The largest of all the departments that make up the executive branch of government, with about 800,000 civilian employees and more than a million military personnel, the Department of Defense is often referred to as the **Pentagon**, after the shape of its Headquarters in Arlington, Virginia. Its primary role is to assist the President in carrying out his duties as Commander-in-Chief.

This gives it a very different relationship with the White House, as a military culture tends to be highly responsive to orders issued by their Commander-in-Chief, which, in turn, often results in the Secretary of Defense having disproportionate influence on the President and intruding into the responsibilities of the Department of State. Certainly, during the first term of President George W. Bush, when these two Departments offered conflicting advice the Pentagon usually prevailed.

### Intelligence agencies

When weighing up the most appropriate course of action in relation to foreign nations, the President will need to take into account assessments of the intentions and likely actions of both allies and enemies. For this, he depends on the intelligence services. The most famous of these is the Central Intelligence Agency (CIA) but this is not the only, nor even the largest, intelligence service.

Fifteen Federal agencies belong to the 'intelligence community'. Eight of these, representing more than 80 per cent of the annual budget of $40 billion, fall under the responsibility of the Department of Defense. The work of the different agencies has frequently either overlapped, creating rivalry, or left gaps, leading to mutual blame. Most notably, the CIA failed to recognise the imminent collapse of

Communist regimes in Eastern Europe in the late 1980s and, despite having a significant amount of information, none of the agencies were able to anticipate and intercept the attacks of 9/11.

To prevent further attacks and to make accurate judgements on interventions to promote the goal of spreading democracy, there was widespread agreement in political circles that the intelligence community's command structure needed to be reformed. In 2004, Congress passed the Intelligence Reform and Terrorism Prevention Act, which created the post of Director of National Intelligence with responsibility to co-ordinate the work of all intelligence agencies. Whether the new arrangement will be an improvement will not become clear for many years.

# The goals of foreign policy

### Conflicting objectives
The influence of manifest destiny in US attitudes towards its neighbours would suggest that aggressive expansionism would dominate its foreign policy.

Similarly, one of the legacies of having been ruled from London was that the USA's main commercial links were with the UK. Future prosperity would mean building new markets for American exports. However, with the fierce commercial rivalries between the major European powers, and their control over much of the New World, advancing American commercial interests had the potential to spark conflict.

However, in the USA there was another highly influential view of the country's role in the world which ran counter to the views that were likely to cause American involvement in complex international engagements. For those who believed that US foreign policy should be consistent with the ideals of the first settlers who came to North America, Christian refugees, the primary objective should be to demonstrate their nation's moral superiority by conducting foreign affairs in a way that distinguished America from the greedy self-interest of the European countries their forebears had escaped from. Rather, insofar as the USA engaged with far-flung places, policy should be driven by the promotion of freedom and democracy around the world.

Thus, from the outset, there was a potential for US foreign policy to veer between aggressive self-interest, a reluctance to engage with the rest of the world and a highly moralistic approach to relationships with other nations.

### National interest

In the nineteenth century, US policy was dominated by a determination to expand its territory and assert its influence over the rest of the continent. The expansion of its territory was accomplished through wars, treaties and purchases, including:

- Fighting a war against Britain in 1812, in an unsuccessful attempt to end restrictions on the ports its trading ships could use and to capture territory in Canada.
- Forcing Spain, in 1819, to relinquish control over Florida by threatening to invade the area.
- Starting wars, in the 1830s, with the Native American nations, leading to their expulsion from what is now Oklahoma.
- Gaining control over the North-West of the country, by a treaty with Britain, again after a threat of war, in 1846.
- Acquiring a huge sweep of land, from Texas to California, following the defeat of Mexico in a war between 1846 and 1848, and a purchase of land by the USA in 1853.
- Purchasing Alaska from Russia, for $7.2 million, in 1867.

The process of asserting its influence over the parts of the continent it did not control began with the announcement of the **Monroe Doctrine** in 1823. President Monroe warned the major European powers not to interfere in the American continent. Any unwelcome interventions, in which the USA perceived its 'rights are invaded or seriously menaced', would lead to 'preparations for our defence'.

In the name of protecting small nations in the region from European powers, the USA took control of Cuba, the Philippines, Puerto Rico and Hawaii. When, in 1903, Columbia refused permission for the United States to build a canal linking the Atlantic and Pacific oceans, a local revolution was sponsored that led to the creation of the nation of Panama. This new country then allowed the canal to be constructed and controlled by the USA.

This kind of direct intervention in the affairs of other countries clearly went further than the terms of the Monroe Doctrine and was justified, in retrospect, by the **Roosevelt Corollary** in 1904. President Theodore Roosevelt asserted the right of the USA to ensure that the continent remained 'stable, orderly and prosperous' in the event of 'wrongdoing or impotence' among its neighbours, which required the USA to exercise 'international police powers'.

In the period before the start of the First World War, Presidents tended to use the growing economic power of the USA to shape its relations with other countries, starting with President Taft, who introduced the idea of **dollar diplomacy**, promoting American investments to help ensure economic and political stability while strengthening diplomatic ties. Military intervention became a strategy of last resort.

With the eruption of war in Europe, however, and attacks on US ships, mainly by the German navy, avoiding military intervention became impossible and the USA entered the war on 6 April 1917.

## Promoting freedom and democracy

The immense loss of life during the First World War caused people all around the world to review how international relations were managed. President Woodrow Wilson's peace proposals reflected this mood and, arguably, ushered in a shift in emphasis towards a more moralistic foreign policy. He wanted a new approach to international relations based on:

- Open, honest diplomatic relationships between countries, rather than the secret negotiations that had led to the hostility and insecurity that had sparked the war.
- Free trade, which forged links between countries, rather than the rival economic fortresses that the imperial powers had tried to build at the end of the nineteenth century.
- Restoring land to countries that had lost territory as a result of war, thereby reducing resentment that could, in time, lead to further conflict.
- Self-determination, in which people would be able to live in the same country as others of the same culture and language, and be able to have sovereignty over their own affairs. This would mean the dismantling of empires, first within Europe and later around the world.

- A 'general association of nations' with the power to arbitrate between nations during an international dispute and the means to protect nations threatened by more powerful, aggressive, countries.

Some, but not all, of these proposals were included in the Versailles Treaty, which formally brought the First World War to an end, and even those that were incorporated were often diluted.

The response of the Senate, which had to ratify the treaty before the USA could participate in the new international arrangements it introduced (such as the League of Nations), was to reject the shift towards a moralistic approach to foreign policy and shift towards isolating their nation from future disastrous international entanglements. By a margin of 53–38, the Senate voted against ratification.

This tension between Presidents seeking to build greater stability in international affairs and promote American values, and Congress, inclined to isolationism, continued in the inter-war years.

The USA played a leading role in defusing escalating tension between France and Germany in 1923, over the payment of reparations. The Dawes Plan, named after the US Vice President who led the negotiations, helped stabilise the German economy with US loans, which allowed reparations payments to be made. Six years later, the USA persuaded the other victors of the First World War to accept a longer-term plan for ensuring that Germany could cope with the economic impact of reparations. The Young Plan, again named after the American who led the negotiations, came into effect in 1930. Meanwhile, Presidents kept a close eye on the emergence of totalitarian dictators in the Soviet Union, Germany and Italy. All three were regarded as regimes committed to the destruction of democratic liberties, and through the 1930s US foreign policy was increasingly aligned with European democracies, culminating in the Lend-Lease Act of 1941, in which military resources were provided to countries at war with Nazi Germany. Congress, on the other hand, passed three Neutrality Acts between 1935 and 1937, in an attempt to ensure that the USA would not once again be drawn into any war that erupted in Europe.

The attack on Pearl Harbor, on 7 December 1941, demonstrated how unrealistic a policy of isolationism was in an age of long-range weapons, and when the Second World War was over, the influence of isolationists receded. Between 1945 and 1989, when the regimes of Eastern Europe collapsed, foreign policy was dominated by a global battle of supremacy between the values of liberty and democracy, underpinned by a capitalist economy, and the values of economic and social equality, underpinned by a centrally controlled economy. Led by the USA and the Soviet Union, the struggle to promote each ideology and undermine the other led to levels of hostility that fell just short of war between the two superpowers and often led to proxy wars between their allies around the world.

The US approach to the post-war world was based on the **Truman Doctrine**. In 1947, the President committed the USA to supporting through economic or military assistance all nations around the world who were resisting the advance of Communism. This led to the Marshall Plan, a huge economic aid programme for Western Europe in the aftermath of the Second World War to promote economic and political stability, military intervention in Korea in the 1950s, Vietnam in the 1960s and support for resistance fighters in Afghanistan after an invasion by the Soviet Union in 1979. This was accompanied by an arms race in which weapons became ever more sophisticated and potent in case the rivalry between the two sides ever erupted into direct conflict.

The intensity of this **Cold War** fluctuated. In 1963, the deployment by the Soviet Union of ballistic missiles in Cuba, just ninety miles from the mainland of the USA, almost sparked a nuclear conflict. In the 1970s, however, there was a period of détente when the two sides engaged in diplomacy to reduce tensions and slow the pace of the arms race. The Cold War only came to an end, however, with the collapse of Communist governments in Eastern Europe and the Soviet Union being dissolved in 1991.

What was seen as the triumph of American values shaped US foreign policy in the years immediately following the Cold War. In 1991, President Bush Snr proclaimed a **new world order** based on the principles of liberal democracy, free trade and the renunciation of military aggression to further foreign policy objectives. His speech followed the success of a coalition of thirty-four countries, under US leadership, in ejecting the Iraqi army from Kuwait, which had been invaded the previous year. The prospect of the world coming together ensure stability by protecting the weak from the powerful appeared a realistic prospect, and in the 1990s the USA intervened in a number of countries to bring an end to military aggression, including Somalia (1992), Haiti (1994), Bosnia (1995) and Kosovo (1999).

### Conflicting historical perspectives on twentieth-century foreign policy

Some historians strongly dispute any suggestion that US foreign policy since the First World War was motivated by idealism. They argue that the support offered by the USA, from loans to Germany in the 1920s to the Marshall Plan of the 1950s, required countries that benefited from economic aid to open themselves up to free trade with the USA, thus providing markets for American products.

It is also argued that military assistance to resist the advance of Communism was not a defensive measure, as suggested by President Truman, but part of an aggressive strategy to ensure US global dominance that started with the dropping of atomic bombs on Hiroshima and Nagasaki to demonstrate America's military superiority. Even the war that restored independence to Kuwait in 1991 is seen by critics as a thin veil for US control of Middle East oil fields, on which its economy depends.

Other historians argue that US policy has never been driven exclusively by either self-interest or idealism, but a fusion of both with one element carrying more weight than the other at different times.

## Foreign policy in the twenty-first century

Has foreign policy, since the turn of the century, fallen into the category of self-interest, idealism or a fusion of both?

As candidate for the Presidency, George W. Bush was quite clear about his priorities: he would put America first, engaging only in foreign-policy initiatives he believed to be in the national interest. That would mean not seeking Senate ratification of the Kyoto Protocol on climate change, which, he believed, would damage the US economy while offering only questionable benefits to the environment; withdrawal of support for the International Criminal Court, as it had the potential to infringe the sovereignty of the US judicial system (this policy was implemented in May 2002); withdrawal from the Anti-Ballistic Missile Treaty, which limited the ability of the USA to build a missile defence system (this policy was implemented in June 2002); and an intention to avoid brokering peace deals around the world, such as the Israeli–Palestinian conflict, unless it was clearly in the interests of the USA to do so. To some observers, this appeared reminiscent of the isolationism that dominated Congressional policy in the 1930s.

This policy was transformed into interventionism on 11 September 2001, when airliners were flown into the World Trade Center in New York City and the Pentagon in Washington DC, with the loss of more than 3,000 lives. The initial response was to launch an attack on the group that had organised the attacks, Al-Qaeda (a loose coalition of fundamentalist Muslims who are willing to use violence against any group or country that they identify as hostile to their beliefs), and the government of Afghanistan that had provided protection and facilities to Al-Qaeda.

Thereafter, the administration of President George W. Bush developed a foreign policy designed to address the new type of threat posed by a different type of enemy which was not a traditional nation state and did not fight with a conventional army. The strategy, outlined in a speech given by the President at the military academy West Point in 2002 and in the National Security Strategy for 2002, has become known as the **Bush doctrine**. The key elements of the strategy, which has attracted the support of some policy-makers and sections of the population ever since, are:

- To recognise that the greatest threat to the USA and its allies is a combination of radical groups hostile to liberal democracies and **rogue states** (countries not abiding by the widely accepted norms of international relations) that may be willing to provide them with weapons of mass destruction.
- To recognise that these groups cannot be dealt with in the same way as traditional enemies who wish to protect their territory and people, as fundamentalists do not have a country or citizens to defend and may even welcome death as martyrs.
- Thus the USA, together with any other country that wishes to join it, will seek out and destroy fundamentalist groups that aim

to mount further attacks on US citizens, its commercial interests or its territory.

- The USA will also work with countries that wish to address the circumstances in which fundamentalism tends to thrive, to alleviate poverty and promote rights, justice and tolerance.
- However, the USA will not tolerate countries that support, encourage or provide protection to fundamentalist groups and if it requires military action to neutralise the threat posed by such countries, the USA should be prepared to act, unilaterally (on its own) if necessary.
- Where the USA feels compelled to intervene in this way, it will not attempt to permanently occupy the country but to create the conditions for a new generation of leaders committed to the economic improvement of the country, justice and tolerance, freely chosen by the country's population.

Thus, the Bush doctrine originally consisted of a combination of what is often called 'hard power', the use of military force to achieve objectives, and 'soft power', using diplomacy and aid to accomplish aims.

In his State of the Union Address, on 29 January 2002, President George W. Bush identified North Korea, Iran and Iraq as the three nations most willing to support terrorist groups and implacably opposed to the USA and its interests, describing them as 'an axis of evil'. Although there was no evidence of a direct link between these nations and the group that attacked the USA on 9/11, the logic of the relationship between tyranny and terrorism made them legitimate targets in the eyes of the President. Just over a year later, a US-led coalition invaded Iraq and deposed its dictator, Saddam Hussein.

The policy of 'American internationalism' has the potential to involve the USA in a number of simultaneous conflicts around the world. This, in turn, has led to a thorough review of the armed forces and intelligence services. The military has been expected to adapt its tactics to rely on agile, smaller forces, rapid deployment and precisions strikes. In 2003, the successful invasion of Iraq used less than half as many troops as were needed to expel Iraqi forces from Kuwait in 1991. The intelligence services have been under pressure to detect further terrorist attacks while in their planning stage, which has meant a return to infiltrating small, tightly-knit units, a form of spying that had been largely neglected during the Cold War, when the most useful information was provided by satellites and sophisticated monitoring equipment.

The effectiveness of these policies has been a matter of fierce worldwide debate since the President's 'axis of evil' speech. Critics of the Bush doctrine have argued that:

- If the methods used to combat fundamentalist groups are not seen as legitimate, they may lead to an increase in fundamentalism rather than defeat it.
- The emphasis on unilateral hard power (and corresponding lack of emphasis on the soft-power elements of the original explanations of the doctrine) inevitably causes widespread destruction and loss of civilian life, undermining the legitimacy of the doctrine.
- Some of the methods used against suspected enemies, countenanced by the Bush administration, appeared to run counter to the core values associated with the USA as well as to the political conduct that the doctrine aimed to promote. These included secretly sending terrorist suspects to countries that use methods for extracting information that Americans are banned from using (a process known as **secret rendition**), the detention of prisoners without trial and the use of **enhanced interrogation** techniques that could be described as torture.
- The continued association with regimes that have a poor record in terms of rights, justice, tolerance and democratic legitimacy has also been seen as undermining the legitimacy of the doctrine, especially as the USA has refused to engage with hard-line groups that have done well in elections, such as Hamas in Palestine and Hezbollah in Lebanon.
- In the case of the Iraq war, the limited evidence of links between the government of Saddam Hussein and Al-Qaeda, together with the failure to find any weapons of mass destruction, also led to the legitimacy of the Bush doctrine being called into question.
- To demonstrate that the USA is sincere about not occupying the countries where it has intervened, but handing power to leaders with public support, there have been attempts to hold early elections. However, in countries with no tradition of liberal

democracy, these have often led to violence, the intensification of divisions in society and unsatisfactory leaders. This, in turn, may have set back the cause of liberal political reform in countries around Afghanistan and Iraq.

- These policies associated with the Bush doctrine have the potential to spark further conflict. The logic of a successful operation to replace a dictatorship with a democracy is that it is worth repeating and for countries labelled as an 'axis of evil' there is an obvious incentive to build up their defences with the most powerful weapons at their disposal to ward off a potential US attack.
- In sum, the Bush doctrine has been criticised as having the opposite results to those it was intended to have.

Supporters of the policy, however, argue that although it takes time for the seeds of democratic reform to grow and flourish (especially in parts of the world that have not been fertile territory for democracy in the past), there have already been signs of an 'Arab spring'. They argue that the Middle East has witnessed, on Arab news networks, Afghans participating in free elections for the first time in their history and Iraqis voting despite the threat of car bombs, and that tentative steps towards peace and democracy have been seen in other parts of the region. Libya, in 2004, gave up its weapons of mass destruction; in 2005, Egypt and Saudi Arabia held elections that were more free than any that had preceded them; and Syria was forced by a mass movement to withdraw its army from Lebanon. One of Lebanon's prominent leaders who made no secret of his initial opposition to the US invasion of Iraq said, 'But when I saw the Iraqi people voting, eight million of them, it was the start of a new Arab world. The Berlin Wall has fallen. We can see it.'

Additionally, it is argued, the policy has been more pragmatic and flexible than some critics have recognised. The USA has always made it clear that it does not intend to use military force against North Korea, and in June 2006 the Secretary of State announced that the USA would be prepared to engage Iran in negotiations in return for a suspension of a programme that could lead to the building of a nuclear bomb.

In the early months of the presidency of Barack Obama, there was a marked shift in policy, leading commentators to debate whether a new strategy was being adopted or simply a version of the Bush doctrine with much greater emphasis on its 'soft-power' elements.

In his inaugural address, President Obama stressed the importance of making sure that the USA used its military power in a 'prudent' manner, reached out to the Muslim world to build a relationship 'based on mutual interest and mutual respect', offered to work with hostile nations (principally Iran) if they were willing to engage in a constructive manner, saying 'We will extend a hand if you are willing to unclench your fist', and promising aid to countries experiencing extreme poverty.

A few months later, in a speech in Cairo, Egypt, he developed the theme of finding ways to engage rather than confront. There will be times when the USA has little choice to use force, he asserted, as it had legitimately done in Afghanistan in response to the attacks of 9/11 in coalition with forty-six other countries. However, America was not at war with Islam, it was pouring billions of dollars into Afghanistan and neighbouring Pakistan in development aid and was willingly working to promote democracy, freedom, tolerance, rights and justice throughout the Muslim world.

Then, later in the year, speaking at the United Nations, he stressed America's readiness to open a new chapter of international co-operation, but also argued that other countries had to be willing to work with the USA and not wait for America to solve all of the world's problems.

## The impact of foreign policy on domestic affairs

### Is the system of checks and balances working?
James Madison, the principal architect of the US Constitution, observed that since the days of the Roman Empire, countries that became world powers have suffered a loss of domestic liberty as a direct result of the concentrated power at the disposal of national leaders, combined with the immense stature of bringing greater glory to their countries.

With the USA having emerged as the world's sole superpower by the end of the twentieth century, and its policies being central to global politics in the new millennium, has the President become such a dominant figure, bolstering his position in domestic as well as foreign affairs, that the constitutional checks on him have become largely ineffective, thereby exposing a major flaw in the constitutional design?

## Disregarding the Constitution at times of national crisis

There is certainly substantial evidence that when defence of the nation has been at the top of the political agenda, Presidents have been able and willing to evade the restriction imposed by the Constitution, including:

- President Lincoln, during the Civil War, blockaded Southern ports despite no declaration of war having been made, suspended habeas corpus, spent money without Congressional authorisation and imprisoned 18,000 suspected Confederate sympathisers without trial.
- President F. D. Roosevelt, during the Second World War, issued Executive Order 9066, which resulted in 120,000 Japanese Americans being held in internment camps for up to three years. The policy was upheld by the Supreme Court in *Korematsu* v. *United States* (1944), which ruled that the detentions were justified by military necessity. (Subsequently, in 1988, Congress issued a formal apology and authorised the payment of reparations for the infringements of their rights.)
- President Truman, during the Korean War, seized control of the steel industry to secure the necessary raw materials for the armaments industry. The decision was challenged and overturned by the Supreme Court in *Youngstown Sheet and Tube Co.* v. *Sawyer* (1952), which ruled that even in a national emergency the President could only use exceptional powers if authorised by Congress.
- President Johnson was able to escalate US involvement in the Vietnam War from 16,000 men in 1963, when he took office, to 500,000 in 1968 when he left office, without war being declared.
- President Nixon, during the Vietnam War, authorised secret military operations into Cambodia and Laos, run directly from the White House, after Congress had expressly rejected his plans. Some commentators link the ability of the administration to circumvent the law with its decision to take a similar approach to domestic politics and authorise a break-in at Democratic

headquarters in the Watergate Building in Washington, to steal documents and install wiretaps on phones.

* The administration of Ronald Reagan, in the 1980s, secretly sold weapons to Iran in violation of international sanctions, in an attempt to increase its influence with a hostile regime. The proceeds of the sales were then secretly channelled to anti-Communist forces in Nicaragua seeking to overthrow the government, again in violation of international law.

### Strengthening constitutional safeguards in foreign affairs

The combination of the executive branch fighting a full-scale war in Vietnam, without a formal declaration of war, and President Nixon's flagrant disregard of the constitutional constraints in both foreign and domestic affairs, led Congress in the mid-1970s to strengthen its checks on the President. New laws included:

* The **Case-Zablocki Act (1972)**, which required the President to report on executive agreements within sixty days of negotiating them. However, as a result of a 1983 Supreme Court decision, *INS* v. *Chadha*, Congress cannot simply overrule an executive agreement it does not support but must negotiate with the President on any amendments it wishes to make.
* The **War Powers Resolution (1973)** requires the President to consult with Congress prior to the start of any hostilities, inform Congress of developments until US armed forces are withdrawn and to remove US armed forces within sixty days if Congress has not declared war or passed a resolution authorising the use of force. In practice, Congress has been reluctant to invoke the resolution and force a withdrawal, as to do so may be seen as undermining the armed forces.

Both laws were intended to 'fulfill the intent of the framers of the Constitution of the United States' in ensuring that Congress should be fully consulted on foreign policy in order to properly carry out its duties as a check on executive power. Neither was very effective and they were resented by all Presidents, of both parties, as undermining their ability to act decisively in an international crisis.

### The impact of foreign policy on domestic affairs in the twenty-first century

When George W. Bush became President, he was convinced that there had been an erosion of executive powers, with Congress having overstepped its constitutional boundaries, and that it was a priority to restore the balance. In the aftermath of the attacks of 9/11, it appeared that he had the opportunity to enhance presidential power at home as well as abroad.

A month after the attacks, Congress overwhelmingly passed a resolution giving the President its support in whatever military and diplomatic measures he thought necessary to defend the country. The President, bolstered by record levels of public support, took full advantage of the opportunity by:

- Taking the nation to war in Afghanistan and Iraq.
- Pushing through the PATRIOT Act, which extended the powers of law enforcement agencies.
- Imprisoning 'enemy combatants', including US citizens, without charge or legal representation.
- Removing or withholding government information from official websites.
- Authorising electronic surveillance on US citizens without a warrant, disregarding the Foreign Intelligence Surveillance Act (1978), which outlines procedures for such measures.
- Secret 'rendition' of people suspected of involvement in terrorism, transferring suspects to countries where torture is permitted during interrogations.
- Attempting to obstruct a bill (introduced when the practice of secret rendition was revealed) banning 'cruel, inhuman and degrading treatment' of detainees and, when this was unsuccessful, making it clear that 'the executive branch shall construe it in a manner consistent with the constitutional authority of the commander in chief'.

As the consequences of some of these actions became clear, however, such as the steady loss of US forces in Iraq, the President's assertions of executive power began to be challenged. Congress questioned the cost of the operation in Iraq and whether it was appropriate for the Department of Defense to be in charge of reconstruction after the war. Then, in large measure due to the unpopularity of President Bush's foreign policy, the Republicans lost control of Congress in the 2006 mid-term elections. The Democratic majority then sought to press the President for an early withdrawal from Iraq by attaching a timetable for the withdrawal of troops from Iraq to a bill providing funds for the war. However, when the President announced that he would veto the bill unless the timetable was deleted and that the Democrats would be responsible for the death of any soldier killed as a result of a lack of funds, they withdrew their demands. This suggests that even when there is clear evidence of a lack of support for the President's foreign policy, the ability of Congress to make him change course is extremely limited.

Since the adoption of the Bush doctrine, however, the President has faced a new type of challenge. Historically, the judiciary has avoided involvement in foreign and security matters, on the grounds that the Constitution clearly gives the President responsibility for these areas. However, one specific aspect of the Bush doctrine, the arrest and detention without trial of people classified as 'enemy combatants', has been challenged by the judiciary on four occasions:

- In *Rasul* v. *Bush* (2004), the Court ruled that detainees held on a US military base in Guantanamo Bay, Cuba, were entitled to the protection of the Constitution of the USA.
- In *Hamdi* v. *Rumsfeld* (2004), the Court ruled that a man held without charge as an enemy combatant was entitled to challenge his detention and declared that 'a state of war is not a blank cheque for the president when it comes to the rights of the nation's citizens'.
- In *Hamdan* v. *Rumsfeld* (2006), the Court ruled that the detainees could not be subject to military trials without the specific authorisation of Congress.
- The Republican majority in Congress responded to the *Hamdan* verdict by passing the Military Commissions Act. Then, in *Boumediene* v. *Bush* (2008), the Court ruled that the Military Commissions Act was unconstitutional as it did not guarantee a fair trial.

Strikingly, however, a change of policy on the detention of terrorist suspects did not come about as a direct result of these rulings but because of a new President taking office. President Obama, who had been a critic of detention without trial, ordered the closure of the prison at Guantanamo Bay on his first day in office.

## Evaluating the powers of the President

### Negotiator-in-Chief?

President Harry Truman described his role in the following terms: 'I sit here all day trying to persuade people to do the things they ought to have sense enough to do without my persuading them. That's all the powers of the President amount to.'

It is this frustration at the limitations on presidential power that has led the position to be described, at various times, as 'persuader-in-chief', 'bargainer-in-chief' or 'negotiator-in-chief'.

Yet President Truman sent troops into action (in the Korean War, one of the major conflicts of the twentieth century) without Congressional permission and was willing to put the entire steel industry (one of the biggest industries in the USA at the time) under the control of the Federal government to ensure supplies to the military.

How powerful, then, is the presidency overall?

### Neustadt: the power to persuade

Richard Neustadt, an influential scholar who both studied the presidency and served under several Presidents, argued that with all the constraints faced by Presidents it is difficult for them to achieve anything unless they are skilled in the art of persuasion. Presidential power, in short, is limited to the power to persuade.

Congress has the ability, in principle, to simply disregard the President's political agenda while the Federal bureaucracy (sometimes in concert with Congressional committees and pressure groups) can limit the effectiveness of presidential policies through slow or selective implementation. Even the President's hand-picked Cabinet is prone to pull in several contradictory directions and Cabinet secretaries may become more attached to their departments' priorities than those of the President.

Under these circumstances, Neustadt argued, the President is in a weak position – at least as weak as the Founding Fathers intended – as he can only enjoy success if he is able to persuade all of the other players in the policy-making process that it is in their interests, or the nation's interest, to work with him. Thus, for Neustadt, the power of the presidency is limited to the administration's ability to make deals and pushing or charming legislators and bureaucrats to do those things that Presidents cannot do on their own. Successful Presidents, therefore, will be those who are either great communicators, such as Ronald Reagan, or who build a powerful personal reputation, such as F. D. Roosevelt.

This analysis, however, has the obvious weakness of largely focusing on domestic affairs. Not only does the Neustadt analysis largely ignore the foreign-policy dimension of the presidency, it fails to consider the extent to which the President's foreign-policy powers enhance his status and prestige, thereby strengthening his hand when he seeks to persuade others to advance his agenda.

### Schlesinger: imperial (and imperilled) presidency

Another influential contributor to the debate on presidential power was Arthur Schlesinger, who, like Neustadt, both worked with Presidents and studied them. Writing in the early 1970s, towards the end of the Vietnam War when successive Presidents had committed forces to a protracted conflict (in which over 50,000 Americans died) without seeking Congressional permission, Schlesinger concluded that Presidents were easily able to exceed their constitutional powers and were subject to few effective constraints. He coined the term 'imperial presidency' to describe this situation.

Subsequently, however, with the resignation of President Nixon and the perceived ineffectiveness of Presidents Ford and Carter, it was argued that the presidency had gone into sharp decline, thereby creating an 'imperilled' presidency.

Schlesinger, therefore, initiated a school of thought which argues that presidential power may fluctuate (as Neustadt suggests) but does so not on the basis of the persuasive powers of the President but because of wider political factors that tend to strengthen or weaken the position of the President.

### Wildavsky: the dual presidency

A theory put forward by the political scientist Aaron Wildavsky can be seen as adding a clearer structure to the imperial/imperilled analysis (although it was not developed for this purpose). Wildavsky argues that Presidents have two distinct roles that operate in two distinctively different ways: one in domestic politics that is subject to strict checks and balances, and one in foreign affairs, in which there are fewer and less effective checks and balances. When foreign affairs are dominant, as in the aftermath of 9/11, the President can control the policy agenda, facing few meaningful challenges even on domestic issues (creating an imperial presidency). When domestic affairs are dominant, the checks and balances are so strong that the President looks weak, both at home and abroad (creating an imperilled presidency).

### Howell: power without persuasion

A fourth view is that presidential power has grown steadily throughout the history of the USA in *both* domestic and foreign affairs, and continues to do so. This argument has been developed by many American scholars but is particularly associated with William Howell, whose book *Power without Persuasion* has been very influential.

Howell argues that scholars have tended to concentrate too heavily on the President's ability to get major legislative initiatives through Congress. Those who have succeeded have been seen to be 'strong', while those whose proposals have failed to make it through Congress or have had them amended out of all recognition have been seen to be 'weak'. Scholars have tended, he claims, to overlook the extent to which the use of executive orders, executive proclamations and executive agreements has soared and the extent to which they relate to increasingly important and contentious policy areas. George W. Bush, for example, used an executive order to set new limits on the Federal funding of stem cell research while Bill Clinton put millions of acres of land in the West and Rocky Mountain states under the control of the Interior Department. While, in principle, these are simply directives to government departments, they have consequences far beyond the Federal government, affecting (in the case of stem cell research) university science departments, pro- and anti-abortion organisations and campaign groups for hereditary diseases, while the redesignation of land affected loggers, holiday-makers and environmentalists.

Each initiative of this kind, Howell points out, changes the balance between the presidency and the other branches of government, especially Congress. Instead of putting forward proposals and waiting for a supportive majority to take shape in the legislature, the President can simply implement a policy (for which there may not be a majority outside of the White House) and Congress has to accept it unless it is able to pass a law that overrules the executive order/proclamation.

Presidential initiatives may well meet with resistance. Congress did, eventually, pass a law authorising more far-reaching stem cell research and some of the most controversial anti-terrorism measures, introduced after 9/11, were challenged by the Supreme Court. Even the Federal bureaucracy may effectively resist unilateral presidential action, as President Clinton discovered shortly after coming to power when he announced his intention to overturn the ban on gay men and lesbians serving in the military and was met with strong objections from senior military officers. However, at the core of Howell's argument is the point that it is far easier to derail a presidential initiative as it makes its way through Congress than it is to build a coalition to overturn an initiative after it has been implemented, and that Presidents have increasingly taken advantage of this fact. If there appears to be fluctuations of presidential power, therefore, it is because not all Presidents have made full or effective use of the growing powers available to them, which has served to disguise the presidency's growing power.

## Conclusion

Central to the Founding Fathers' constitutional design was the aim of ensuring that Presidents could never acquire the kind of unconstrained power enjoyed by the leader of the UK. Some influential observers argue that the Founding Fathers' goal has been met and that Presidents have little more than the power to persuade. Others argue that the opposite is true, with the presidency having become steadily more powerful in both domestic and foreign affairs. There are also other views falling between these two extremes which suggest that political circumstances determine how much power a President has and that it rises and falls, depending on factors largely outside his control. In the final analysis, whichever argument is the most convincing shapes views on the nature and functioning not only of the executive branch, but of the entire US political system.

. . . . . . . . . . . . . . . . . . . . . . . . . . . . . . . . . . . . . . . . . . .

## ✔ What you should have learnt from reading this chapter

- In foreign affairs, the Founding Fathers placed fewer, and weaker, constraints on the President than in domestic affairs.

- Foreign policy is conducted through the State Department, the Department of Defense and the Intelligence Agencies.

- There are conflicting views on the purpose of US foreign policy: it could be seen as being motivated by national interest or idealism, or a combination of the two.

- In the twenty-first century, the Bush doctrine and responses to it have been the main focus of foreign policy.

- The President's foreign-policy powers, with their limited constraints, have a substantial impact on his domestic-policy powers.

- Overall, whether this means that the presidency has become a more powerful position than the Founding Fathers intended is a matter of debate.

- At one extreme, the President is seen to be a weak figure with few effective powers.

- Other views of the presidency emphasise the fluid nature of presidential power, arguing that political circumstances shape the amount of power at his disposal.

- At the other extreme, the presidency is seen to have grown substantially in power in both domestic matters and foreign affairs, creating a position that is reminiscent of the monarchy that the USA broke away from and which the Constitution is supposed to guard against.

## 🔎 Glossary of key terms

**Bush doctrine** A term given to the foreign policy and military strategy developed by the administration of President George W. Bush in response to the attacks of 9/11.

**Case-Zablocki Act (1972)** A law requiring the President to report on executive agreements within sixty days of negotiating them (later invalidated by the Supreme Court ruling in *INS* v. *Chadha*).

**Cold War** A term describing the tension between capitalist nations, led by the USA, and Communist nations, led by the Soviet Union, which never erupted into direct conflict.

**Dollar diplomacy** A strategy, introduced by President Taft, to promote American interests through economic and political stability abroad, making military intervention a strategy of last resort.

**Enhanced interrogation** Techniques for obtaining information from suspects (that have been seen by some as forms of torture).

**Executive agreement** An agreement with another head of government, which has the same standing in international law as a treaty but does not require ratification by the Senate.

**Louisiana Purchase** Land claimed by France, bought by President Jefferson in 1803, for $15 million, that was eventually made into thirteen new states.

**Manifest destiny** The belief that it was God's will that the USA would eventually expand to control the whole of North and Central America, and possibly even South America as well.

**Monroe Doctrine** A declaration by President Monroe in 1823 that interference by the major European powers in the American continent would not be tolerated.

**New world order** The idea that, after the ending of the Cold War, international relations could be based on the principles of liberal democracy, free trade and the renunciation of military aggression to further foreign-policy objectives.

**Pentagon** A term applied to the Department of Defense, after the shape of its headquarters, which is responsible for the armed forces of the USA.

**Rogue states** A term applied to countries not abiding by the widely accepted norms of international relations that represent a threat to peace.

**Roosevelt Corollary** An assertion by President Theodore Roosevelt in 1904 that the USA had the right and responsibility to ensure that the American continent remained 'stable, orderly and prosperous'.

**Secret rendition** Secretly sending terrorist suspects to countries that use methods for extracting information that Americans are banned from using.

**State Department** The department responsible for diplomatic relations between the USA and other countries.

**Truman Doctrine** The commitment, in 1947, by President Truman, that the USA would support all nations around the world resisting the advance of Communism, through economic or military assistance.

**War Powers Resolution (1973)** A law requiring the President to consult with Congress prior to the start of any hostilities, inform Congress of developments until US armed forces are withdrawn and to remove US armed forces within sixty days if Congress has not declared war or passed a resolution authorising the use of force.

## ? Likely examination questions

Issues examiners may expect students to be able to effectively analyse include:

* The powers of the President and the effectiveness of the checks on his actions in each of his capacities

* The role of the Federal bureaucracy in aiding or hindering the President's agenda

* The importance of the Cabinet and/or Executive Office of the President

* The importance of the Vice President

* Whether the President's foreign policy powers are effectively checked

* An overall assessment of presidential power

Thus, examples of the kind of questions which could be asked include:

How important is the Executive Office of the President?

'Presidents have only the power to persuade.' Discuss

## Helpful websites

The official website of the President, www.whitehouse.gov, provides some useful information.

Otherwise, to keep up with the latest political developments view the websites of any of the most influential news organisations in the USA or UK. In the USA this could include the *New York Times*, www.nytimes.com, the *Washington Post*, www.washingtonpost.com, or CNN, www.cnn.com. In the UK this could include the BBC, www.bbc.co.uk, or *The Guardian*, www.guardian.co.uk.

##  Suggestions for further reading

The greatest insights into the challenges faced by Presidents, and their responses to them, are found in their autobiographies, such as *My Life* by Bill Clinton and *An American Life* by Ronald Reagan.

## CONCLUSION

# True to its Founding Ideals?

Have the aims and objectives of the Founding Fathers, to construct a political system based on a set of ideas and values, been realised in practice?

The answer, in short, is that Americans have sharply contrasting views both on how they interpret central constitutional values, such as 'freedom', and on the best ways of putting those ideas into practice. They disagreed with each other at the Constitutional Convention, although they made compromises that most found acceptable. They have continued to disagree ever since, at times being unable to compromise, with the result that they have had a civil war and other political upheavals such as the Civil Rights movement.

This book has covered the key issues, political systems and governing institutions at the heart of these disagreements, outlining the thinking behind the main points of view in each case. Having examined all of them it is now for you, the reader, to decide which viewpoint is the most persuasive.

# Index

Bold indicates that the term is defined